Palgrave Studies in Excellence and Equity
in Global Education

Series Editors
Roger Openshaw
College of Humanities & Social Sciences
Massey University
Palmerston North, Auckland, New Zealand

Margaret Walshaw
Massey University
Massey, New Zealand

This series aims to compile a rich collection of research-based contributions that critically examine the tensions and challenges involved in implementing both excellence and equity within public education systems around the globe. In bringing together eminent international scholars to explore the various ways education systems around the world have responded to issues associated with excellence and equity, this series will make a major contribution to the field and act as a state-of-the-art resource on what we know about this topic today.

More information about this series at
http://www.palgrave.com/gp/series/14628

Mahsood Shah • Jade McKay
Editors

Achieving Equity and Quality in Higher Education

Global Perspectives in an Era of Widening Participation

palgrave
macmillan

Editors
Mahsood Shah
Central Queensland University
Rockhampton, QLD, Australia

Jade McKay
Deakin University
Burwood, VIC, Australia

Palgrave Studies in Excellence and Equity in Global Education
ISBN 978-3-319-78315-4   ISBN 978-3-319-78316-1 (eBook)
https://doi.org/10.1007/978-3-319-78316-1

Library of Congress Control Number: 2018940450

© The Editor(s) (if applicable) and The Author(s) 2018
This work is subject to copyright. All rights are solely and exclusively licensed by the Publisher, whether the whole or part of the material is concerned, specifically the rights of translation, reprinting, reuse of illustrations, recitation, broadcasting, reproduction on microfilms or in any other physical way, and transmission or information storage and retrieval, electronic adaptation, computer software, or by similar or dissimilar methodology now known or hereafter developed.
The use of general descriptive names, registered names, trademarks, service marks, etc. in this publication does not imply, even in the absence of a specific statement, that such names are exempt from the relevant protective laws and regulations and therefore free for general use.
The publisher, the authors, and the editors are safe to assume that the advice and information in this book are believed to be true and accurate at the date of publication. Neither the publisher nor the authors or the editors give a warranty, express or implied, with respect to the material contained herein or for any errors or omissions that may have been made. The publisher remains neutral with regard to jurisdictional claims in published maps and institutional affiliations.

Printed on acid-free paper

This Palgrave Macmillan imprint is published by the registered company Springer Nature Switzerland AG
The registered company address is: Gewerbestrasse 11, 6330 Cham, Switzerland

Series Foreword

The series *Palgrave Studies in Excellence and Equity in Global Education* is a bold new initiative for the transnational study of education. The linking of excellence and equity in this timely series is intentional. It is only at a first and indeed, a cursory glance that the two concepts will appear in any way disparate. A more perceptive view will acknowledge the potentiality in considering excellence and equity in dynamic relation to one another. There are two significant reasons why this latter understanding ought to prevail. First, in the view of many researchers, teachers, policy makers and parents, excellence and equity, very far from being incompatible remain dual, even inseparable themes in education today. Second, there is a pressing need for scholars to extend and broaden the various debates and issues that surround excellence and equity in a way that clearly focuses on the various ways education systems around the globe have conceived and responded to them. This being the case it is unfortunate that, as yet, there have been few sustained attempts within a single series to critically examine the way in which excellence and equity both complement and also conflict with one another.

This series is, therefore, designed to serve an important educative function. Specifically, it has a crucial role to play in enabling students, lecturers, researchers and policy makers to develop crucial and critical knowledge regarding the concepts of excellence and equity, and to learn how these play out within a range of different contexts. Thus it is intended that this multinational series will make a major contribution to the broader international and national debates surrounding excellence and equity. A particular feature of the series is that the authors/editors of each volume will illustrate in their various ways how excellence and equity are broadly conceived within their specific region or nation, through fields of inquiry and methodologies as diverse as history, sociology, critical pedagogy, critical theory, feminist studies, ethnicity studies, policy studies and/or political studies, to name but a few of the approaches currently being explored around the globe in the twenty-first century. In turn, this inclusive approach will challenge readers to confront the issue of what the future may hold for the particular site or location of inquiry selected by each volume in the series.

Moreover, the above approaches will enable rigorous reinterpretations of diverse educational contexts such as curriculum, pedagogy, leadership and policy as well as extending across various contested sites such as early childhood education, elementary–primary schooling, secondary schooling, or the tertiary sector. For instance, authors, editors and contributors to the series might choose to analyse in some depth the various ways in which the concepts of excellence and equity have been conceived in the past, conceptualised in the present and how they might be addressed in the future.

Regardless of the method or approach adopted by the scholars involved in writing for the series, however, there is general agreement that the series should seek to clarify for both specialist *and* general readers, the development and rationale behind current policy pronouncements in a manner that is both scholarly and accessible. Readers will thus be able to appreciate the tensions and challenges involved in implementing both excellence and equity within public education systems. They will also be able to identify broad links between their own specific national context and other national contexts. In seeking to achieve and sustain logical coherence, the series will be giving a specific educational expression to the approaches pioneered by a number of transnational studies that have attempted with considerable success in recent years to explore the ways in which past, present and future events and debates have been shaped by processes and relationships that transcend national borders (Curthoys and Lake 2005).

This fourth volume in the series is edited by Jade McKay, Deakin University, Australia, and Mahsood Shah, Central Queensland University, Australia. The volume makes a timely contribution to the synergies between excellence and equity in global education. It includes contributors from Canada, England, Scotland, the United States, New Zealand, Chile, Brazil, Turkey as well as Australia. A central theme is higher education, particularly in the context of the emerging rhetoric of widening participation and access for non-traditional students. Linking the papers is the desire to critically examine the various ways in which higher institutions around the world are developing strategies aimed at facilitating inclusion. In so doing the book as a whole raises fundamental and important questions regarding the nature of the relationship between excellence and equity; quality and participation; structures and aspirations.

Globally, far-reaching changes to higher education policy in relation to teaching and learning, and the development of new funding models and support schemes, together with the increasing diversity within the student body, have resulted in an on-going transformation of higher education at various levels in an unprecedented way. This phenomenon has not been without its tensions. Alongside the shift towards a widening participation agenda has come the suggestion that academic standards are under threat. In response to this claim the contributors to this volume argue that 'quality' and 'excellence' need not be incompatible with 'access' and 'equity'. While there are challenges and barriers in implementing change in the interests of enabling wider participation and access, the contributors argue that all universities need to participate equally to improve not only employment and other desirable social and economic outcomes, but also to enhance the life-chances of typically under-represented students.

A particularly pleasing aspect of this volume is the way readers are introduced to social justice issues in various contexts. There is a particularly useful focus on national strategies for student access to, and success within, higher education. Such strategies seek to embrace a range of tertiary education providers both nationally and internationally. Across nations, however, these strategies will need to be customised to the specific needs of the diverse groups that aspire to become part of the student population and succeed within it. To this end, the nature of the complex student–teacher relationship is explored in depth, including the various ways in which current models have, and are, being modified to better address the needs of indigenous students, learners from lower socioeconomic backgrounds, different student cultural aspirations and ways of thinking.

Taken as a whole, this volume clearly and cogently illustrates how, across the globe, tertiary institutions, together with their administrators, staff and students, have faced common issues and problems intimately related to diversity and participation. The specific national contexts highlighted in the book's individual chapters amplify and extent the analysis whilst emphasising the need for a collaborative effort between government, policy makers, tertiary education leaders, educators and students. Moreover, readers will learn from the various case studies of success across national boundaries, that much has been done, complex issues surrounding participation notwithstanding. Equally, however, they will discover that much more will need to be achieved in the future in order to ensure social justice for all higher education students.

Massey University	Roger Openshaw
Palmerston North, Auckland, New Zealand	
Massey University	Margaret Walshaw
Massey, New Zealand	

Preface: The Quest to Achieve Equity and Excellence

Higher education institutions around the globe are increasingly instituting widening participation agendas to facilitate the access and participation of 'non-traditional' students. While the term 'widening participation' varies across countries also known as social inclusion, fair access and student equity—these terms collectively refer to efforts to foremost improve the participation of students from a range of equity groups; those who have not traditionally entered the hallowed grounds of higher education institutions. While Western countries are more advanced in widening access, other countries in Asia, Africa, South America, the Middle East and Oceania are also experiencing a growing population of students from various underrepresented backgrounds. Recent years have also seen these efforts broaden to extend beyond mere participation and further focus on the improvement of student success.

The widening participation agenda has brought about significant changes in relation to policy, teaching and learning, support schemes and the overall diversification of the student body. Given the growing number of students who often bring with them diverse levels of academic preparedness, questions have arisen as to whether this growth compromises quality. Indeed, some view the entry of non-traditional students as threatening to standards, academic rigour and overall quality. Coinciding with this shift towards widening participation is the suggestion that it poses a threat to academic standards and quality, and the term 'quality' itself is often viewed as mutually exclusive with terms like 'equity', 'access' and 'success'. Many critics associate the entry of larger proportions of non-traditional students with low-entrance scores, academic struggle and an overall decrease in standards. Leathwood and O'Connell (2003, p. 599) explain that the widening participation agenda is premised on a 'discourse of "dumbing down" and lowering standards'. This view is certainly apparent in the work of various theorists (Furedi 2004; Hayes 2003). Gidley et al. (2010) suggest that, 'The UK provides a good case study of the tension between the elite notion of quality in higher education and the social justice ethic towards greater access to higher education'. Lunt (2008, p. 5) refers to this as 'the trade-off between excellence and equity'.

Gidley, Hampson, Wheeler and Bereded-Samuel (2010) posit that these concepts are complex and multi-perspectival—namely, access, success and quality—and can be regarded as conceptual peers rather than being incongruent with each other, and this depends on the underlying ideology of the discourse. Gidley et al. (2010, p. 2) explain that

> …the terms equitable access and success are intimately linked with the notion of social inclusion in higher education. While access is commonly thought of as being synonymous with social inclusion we suggest that it is only the first step. We propose that with the addition of a third concept, participation, the terms access, participation and success can be seen to reflect 'degrees of social inclusion.' In this view access, participation and success are ordered according to a spectrum of ideologies—neoliberalism, social justice and human potential respectively—by way of a nested structure with human potential ideology offering the most embracing perspective.

Instead of quality being in competition with social inclusion, Gidley et al. (2010) strive to bring them into cooperation with each other. Other theorists have made similar endeavours. Indeed, advocates of widening access have argued that higher education institutions must accept the reality that the underrepresented student population will grow; therefore, new strategies, funding models, structures, and reforms are needed to cater to the needs of these particular students.

Preface: The Quest to Achieve Equity and Excellence

This book has drawn on the work of 15 scholars recognized as experts in the field from nine countries to explore the complex issues surrounding the achievement of both equity and academic excellence. These scholars derive from Canada, Australia, USA, New Zealand, Chile, Brazil, South Africa, Turkey and the UK.

The book provides insight into how higher education institutions in nine countries are maintaining academic standards while increasing the access and participation of students from historically underrepresented backgrounds. The book provides varied perspectives from different institutions and disciplines on whether increasing widening access positively affects quality. The chapters traverse a broad spectrum of topics and issues including: equity and excellence; tensions and synergies; whether academic quality is at risk in the emergence of widening participation; leadership of equity and widening participation; whether all universities participate equally in widening participation practices and, if not, why not; case studies of how higher education institutions have raised both equity aspirations and maintained standards; whether student diversity is an ingredient of quality or a reputational risk in the emergence of ranking; measures of success in achieving equity aspirations; course design, assessments, teaching and support of equity and quality; strategies and initiatives deployed in institutions to attract underrepresented students in elite courses.

Focusing on leadership of equity and widening participation, Liz Thomas discusses efforts in the UK to widen participation through the National Strategy for Access and Student Success, and the newly introduced Teaching Excellence Framework (TEF). This chapter draws on two research projects focusing on widening participation and student success, which involved 21 higher education providers, to explore the role of leadership in institutional change to promote diversity and success.

Lesley Andres and Ashley Pullman discuss the British Columbia *Paths on Life's Way* project to explore how education and employment outcomes differ for those who embark on 'traditional' and 'non-traditional' higher education pathways. They argue that ascriptive characteristics in mid-adulthood have had both dissipating and lingering effects on educational and occupational outcomes.

In Chap. 3, 'Supporting Students' Learning: The Power of the Student–Teacher Relationship', Debra Cureton and Phil Gravestock foreground the learning relationship between students and teachers as intrinsic to student success. This chapter explores the complex factors of the student and teacher learning relationship that best facilitate student success.

Marcia Devlin and Jade McKay explore widening participation in the Australian higher education context and specifically focus on efforts made to improve the participation of students from low socioeconomic status (SES) backgrounds and those from regional and remote areas. They suggest that these efforts have necessitated a rethink of current models and strategies and the development of more inclusive curricula, assessment, and teaching to better facilitate the success of students from low SES backgrounds at regional universities, while maintaining academic standards.

In the US context, Michelle Hodara, Di Xu and Julie Petrokubi provide a case study into using developmental education to both raise equity and maintain standards. They describe the most commonly used strategy at community colleges in the US—developmental education programs—which are intended to prepare students for college-level gateway courses. They view these programs as essential in supporting the progress of underprepared community college students but argue that they do have their limitations.

Discussing widening participation in relation to indigenous students in New Zealand, in 'Vision 20:20 and Indigenous Health Workforce Development: Institutional Strategies and Initiatives to Attract Underrepresented Students into Elite Courses', Elana Curtis explores how widening access to competitive programmes of study such as medicine, pharmacy and optometry remains a challenge for many tertiary institutions. This chapter proposes 12 effective practices for tertiary institutional action including: recruitment; admission; bridging/foundation education; and, retention. Curtis stresses the need for tertiary institutions to support indigenous health workforce development through tertiary interventions that are aligned with a widening participation and social justice agenda.

In 'Social Inclusion or Social Engineering? The Politics and Reality of Widening Access to Medicine in the UK', Kirsty Alexander and Jennifer

Cleland explore the complex reasons why the resources invested in widening participation activities have not increased the representation of applicants from lower socioeconomic students within medical schools. They discuss the different discourses of widening access/increasing diversity in the UK context—including those of 'social mobility' and 'increasing diversity to improve workforce efficiency'—and examine the synergies and tensions between widening access and maintaining quality, and the gap between political directives and policy enactment within medical schools.

Oscar Espinoza, Noel McGinn and Luis Eduardo González in Chap. 8 'University Strategies to Improve the Academic Success of Disadvantaged Students: Three Experiences in Chile' explore the widening participation agenda in Chile and find that expansion of access to higher education has thus far had no impact on Chile's high levels of income inequality, which remains one of the highest amongst developed nations. The chapter discusses the literature surrounding types and causes of dropouts, and the key factors which relate to student success and the potential strategies to change a student's likelihood of success.

Paul Garrud and Clare Owen discuss the socioeconomic profile of medical students in the UK and particularly the fact that it has remained heavily skewed towards those from advantaged backgrounds over decades. They draw on the findings from a national project—'Selecting for Excellence'—to explore wide-ranging changes in attraction and selection of entrants to medical schools. The chapter reviews the overall progress and challenges of a 6-year programme to widen participation in medicine to those from disadvantaged backgrounds.

Looking at affirmative action in Brazil, Rubens Becak and Luis Felipe Cirino explore one of the key manifestations of affirmative actions: the quota policy which is widely adopted in various universities in the country. They contend that the quota policy has shown significant results in improving access to higher education, making the university environment more heterogeneous and, above all, enabling the social rise of those historically excluded from higher education.

Sadhana Manik and Labby Ramrathan discuss higher education (HE) in the South African context, and the increasing importance of widening access since South Africa became a democratic state in 1994. More than

20 years later, they suggest there is agreement that the quantitative aspect of widening access for non-whites (also referred to as Blacks) into HE has tremendously improved. However, the literature reveals that the transformational agenda on widening access is constrained by ever-increasing student numbers coupled with infrastructural incapacity, curriculum reform and institutional supportive elements. This chapter explores the achievements, shortfalls and challenges in terms of specifically focusing on issues of institutional support and curriculum reform and the implications these have for the quality of higher education. The authors undertake this through a case study of three public higher education institutions in South Africa, demonstrating the current HE terrain in widening access within a transformational HE plan.

In 'Fees Regimes and Widening Access in the Four UK Nations: Are No-Fees Regimes Necessarily More Socially Inclusive?', Sheila Riddell and Elisabet Weedon provide an overview of the funding and support regimes in the different UK jurisdictions. They explore the range of policy interventions which have been implemented to facilitate widening access to pupils from disadvantaged backgrounds. Drawing on statistical data, they examine the success of the different regimes in attracting students from less advantaged backgrounds into higher education, questioning whether the Scottish no-fees system is more successful than those in other parts of the UK.

Erica Southgate, Susan Grimes and Jarrad Cox discuss how non-traditional students remain underrepresented in elite universities and in high status degrees. In Chap. 13, 'High Status Professions, Their Related Degrees and the Social Construction of "Quality"' they examine the idea of 'quality' as it relates to elite professions and their related university degrees. They present original research on first-in-family medical students and how they understand and experience ideas about 'quality', arguing that there is much critical work to be done to de-naturalize notions of 'quality' in relation to elite contexts.

Stephen Gorard, Vikki Boliver and Nadia Siddiqui draw on a large review of the prior research and student statistics in England from 2006 onwards to discuss how universities in the UK are making decisions about undergraduate admissions with reference to contextual indicators which identify whether or not an applicant comes from a disadvantaged background. However, the authors argue that these indicators used are often chosen because they are readily available, without consideration for possible alternatives. They propose which of the contextual indicators they consider to be worth pursuing and which are not of high enough quality or have the potential to lead to greater injustice.

In 'Governmental Supports for Students in Turkey: Beneficiary Perspective on the Use of Financial and Social Support in Higher Education', Yasar Kondakci, Yusuf İkbal Oldac, Hanife Hilal Senay and Kadir Beycioglu discuss their study which aimed to explore the effectiveness of the support provided by various public institutions (central governments, municipalities and their own universities) relating to access to higher education, facilitating positive learning experiences, and in contributing to their employability after their study. They point to a significant gap between what is intended by the public support system and what is realized in the lives of individual students in Turkey.

Collectively, the chapters in this book provide insight into a range of issues pertaining to the widening participation efforts in nine countries, with topics covering government, policy, leadership, teaching and learning. These chapters show that widening participation is a targeted focus in many countries and that with the right strategies, programmes, support and approaches instituted, so called 'non-traditional' students are enabled and empowered to participate, succeed *and* attain high standards. Maintaining the appropriate standards and overall quality is viewed by all as essential in higher education, but it does need to be premised on a cooperative effort between government, leadership, policy-makers, educators and students alike.

The book provides case studies of success in various countries where institutions have implemented strategies to support students in learning. Various kinds of academic and non-academic support structures are implemented to achieve outcomes. The case studies provide evidence that students from various equity groups are successfully completing elite courses with various support structures. The widening participation agenda has enabled social mobility with students from underrepresented backgrounds completing university study and improving employment and other social and economic outcomes.

The widening participation initiative therefore is ethically and morally right for higher education policy. Such policies provide social justice for all groups of students to participate in higher education and thus changing the life of future generations. Government and universities need to work collaboratively to achieve the best outcome for its citizens.

Deakin University Jade McKay
Burwood, VIC, Australia
Central Queensland University Mahsood Shah
Rockhampton, QLD, Australia

References

Furedi, F. (2004). *Where Have All the Intellectuals Gone? Confronting Twenty-First Century Philistinism*. London: Continuum.

Gidley, J. M., Hampson, G. P., Wheeler, L., & Bereded-Samuel, E. (2010). From access to success: An integrated approach to quality higher education informed by social inclusion theory and practice. *Higher Education Policy*, 23(1), 123–147.

Hayes, D. (2003). New labour, new professionalism. In J. Satterthwaite, E. Atkinson & K. Gale (Eds.), *Discourse, power, resistance: Challenging the rhetoric of contemporary education* Stoke on Trent: Trentham.

Leathwood, C., & O'Connell, P. (2003). 'It's a struggle': The construction of the 'new student' in higher education. *Journal of Education Policy*, 18(6), 597–615.

Lunt, I. (2008). Beyond tuition fees? The legacy of Blair's government to higher education. *Oxford Review of Education*, 34(6), 741–752.

Contents

1 Leadership for Institutional Change to Promote Diversity and Success   1
Liz Thomas

2 Vertically Segregated Higher Education and the Life Course: Comparing Patterns Over 28 Years   25
Lesley Andres and Ashley Pullman

3 Supporting Students' Learning: The Power of the Student–Teacher Relationship   51
Debra Cureton and Phil Gravestock

4 Facilitating the Success of Students from Low SES Backgrounds at Regional Universities Through Course Design, Teaching, and Staff Attributes   73
Marcia Devlin and Jade McKay

5 A Case Study Using Developmental Education to Raise Equity and Maintain Standards   97
Michelle Hodara, Di Xu, and Julie Petrokubi

6 *Vision 20:20* and Indigenous Health Workforce Development: Institutional Strategies and Initiatives to Attract Underrepresented Students into Elite Courses   119
Elana Taipapaki Curtis

7 Social Inclusion or Social Engineering? The Politics and Reality of Widening Access to Medicine in the UK   143
Kirsty Alexander and Jennifer Cleland

8 University Strategies to Improve the Academic Success of Disadvantaged Students: Three Experiences in Chile   173
Oscar Espinoza, Noel McGinn, and Luis Eduardo González

9 Widening Participation in Medicine in the UK   199
Paul Garrud and Clare Owen

10 Affirmative Actions as an Instrument to Balance Access to Superior Education in Brazil: The Quotas Policy   219
Rubens Becak and Luis Felipe Cirino

11 The Conundrum of Achieving Quality Higher Education in South Africa   235
Sadhana Manik and Labby Ramrathan

12 Fees Regimes and Widening Access in the Four UK Nations: Are No-Fees Regimes Necessarily More Socially Inclusive?   261
Sheila Riddell and Elisabet Weedon

13 High Status Professions, Their Related Degrees and the Social Construction of 'Quality'   287
Erica Southgate, Susan Grimes, and Jarrad Cox

14 How Can Contextualised Admissions Widen
   Participation? 307
   Stephen Gorard, Vikki Boliver, and Nadia Siddiqui

15 Governmental Supports for Students in Turkey:
   Beneficiary Perspective on the Use of Financial and Social
   Support in Higher Education 327
   *Yasar Kondakci, Kadir Beycioglu, Yusuf İkbal Oldac, and
   Hanife Hilal Senay*

Index 349

Notes on Contributors

Kirsty Alexander is a doctoral candidate at the Centre for Healthcare Education Research and Innovation (CHERI), University of Aberdeen, Scotland.

Kirsty's PhD research investigates how the medical school admissions process is understood and negotiated by those within it – by medical schools, secondary school teachers and potential applicants. She is particularly interested in the influence these perceptions may have on initiatives to widen access to medicine, an important and current issue within the area. The research is qualitative, and primarily uses thematic and discourse analysis approaches. The first article from her work appears in Medical Education and was runner-up in the ASME Best Original Research Paper Award 2017.

Before starting the PhD Kirsty completed an MA at the University of St Andrews in International Relations and German. After graduating she worked in a widening access role at two different UK universities, which sparked her interest in this fascinating area.

Lesley Andres is a Professor in the Department of Educational Studies at the University of British Columbia. She is the principal investigator of the *Paths on Life's Way* Project, a unique Canadian longitudinal study that has combined extensive qualitative and quantitative data over a 28 year time frame to examine the lives, actions, experiences and perspectives of individuals within a life course framework. This research focuses on educational, occupational and other life course outcomes in relation to various forms of inequality. Her most recent books are *Designing and Doing Survey Research* (2012) and *The Making of a Generation: Children of the 1970s in Adulthood* (2010, co-authored with Johanna Wyn).

Rubens Becak is a Full Professor of the University of Sao Paulo (USP). PhD in Constitutional Law and in Theory of State. Secretary-General of USP from 2010 to 2014. Visiting professor at the University of Salamanca linked to the Brazilian Studies Center and co-Editor of the Journal of Brazilian Studies. Coordinator of the Nucleus of Rights of USP since 2014.

Kadir Beycioglu is an Associate Professor in Educational Administration and Planning at Dokuz Eylul University in the Department of Educational Science. His research focuses on theory and practice in educational administration, teacher leadership, school development, educational change and leaders.

Vikki Boliver is Professor of Sociology at Durham University. Her work focuses on social inequalities of access to higher status universities, and on patterns and processes of social mobility across multiple generations. She currently holds several grants relevant to widening participation and has been advising governmental and near-governmental bodies in Scotland on contextualized admissions.

Luis Felipe Cirino is a Professor of undergraduate studies and of graduate studies at Escola Superior de Direito (ESD). He holds a Master's in Constitutional Law from the University of Sao Paulo and is currently a PhD student in the same University.

Jennifer Cleland is John Simpson Chair of Medical Education Research, and Director of the Centre for Healthcare Education Research and Innovation (CHERI), University of Aberdeen, Scotland; Chair of the Association for the Study of Medical Education (ASME); Director of the Scottish Medical Education Research Consortium (SMERC); Lead for the Association for Medical Education Europe (AMEE) Research Committee; Chair of the Board of Management for Medical Education; Associate Editor for Perspectives in Medical Education; an Invited Member of the Wilson Centre, Toronto; and Adjunct Professor of Medicine at the Uniformed Services University of the Health Sciences, USA.

With nearly 200 peer-reviewed journal articles and book chapters, she has published widely in a broad range of journals including the BMJ and Medical Education.

Jennifer's particular research interests are selection, assessment and performance, and medical careers decision making. Her research spans the continuum of undergraduate, postgraduate and continuing medical education and training.

Jarrad Cox is a secondary English teacher who works in a public school in NSW, Australia. He is interested in social justice and aims to produce research that provides positive and practical solutions to complex equity issues. Jarrad is passionate about qualitative methodologies and providing an authentic voice for individuals that face inequality within the current educational climate.

Debra Cureton is a Research Development Manager and Learning and Teaching Fellow at the University of Wolverhampton, and was awarded a Senior Fellowship of the Higher Education Academy in 2014.

Debra's research interest is in undergraduate retention and success, with a particular focus on differential degree outcomes. Along with Professor Glynis Cousin, Debra co-led a Higher Education Academy-funded research programme into 'Disparities in Student Attainment' and led the University of Wolverhampton's contribution to the *What Works: Retention and Success Programme* (funded by the Paul Hamlyn Foundation and the Higher Education Academy). She co-edited '*Student Attainment in Higher Education: Issues, controversies and debates*' with Graham Stevenson and Lynn Clouder.

Elana Taipapaki Curtis is a Public Health Physician at Te Kupenga Hauora Maori (Department of Māori Health), Faculty of Medical and Health Sciences, University of Auckland. As Director, of Vision 20:20, she has academic leadership of Māori student recruitment, Māori and Pacific bridging/foundation education and the Māori and Pacific Admission Scheme (MAPAS). Her Doctorate of Medicine (MD) focused on indigenous health workforce development and the role of tertiary recruitment, admission, bridging/foundation education and retention. She has received multiple awards for this work including the Māori Television, Te Tupu-ā-Rangi Matariki Award for Health and Science and the Leaders in Indigenous Medical Education (LIME) LIMElight Award for Excellence in Indigenous Health Education Research in 2017.

Marcia Devlin is a Professor and Deputy Vice-Chancellor and Senior Vice-President at Victoria University in Melbourne. Previously she was Associate Deputy Vice-Chancellor Education at RMIT University and Deputy Vice-Chancellor (Learning and Quality) at Federation University Australia. As an elected Lifelong Fellow of the Society for Research in Higher Education, Devlin is internationally recognized for her research in tertiary education policy and practice. With colleagues, she has won just under $6 million in research and other funds and has more than 300 academic, professional, and media publications to her name.

Oscar Espinoza is associate researcher at the Center of Advanced Studies at Universidad de Playa Ancha. He is also researcher at the Center of Comparative Educational Policies at University Diego Portales and in the Interdisciplinary Program of Educational Research (PIIE). He also works as consultant for some

Chilean universities. In the past, he has worked on many research projects funded by international agencies (e.g., USAID, UNESCO, World Bank, UNDP, Ford Foundation and the Organization of Iberoamerican States) and national agencies (Ministry of Education, National Commission of Science and Technological Research, and the National Council for the Innovation and Competitiveness) in issues associated with access, equity, quality assurance, academic performance, accreditation, management and higher education policies.

Paul Garrud works as a principal research fellow in the School of Medicine at Nottingham University. He leads a regional widening participation project in the East Midlands and chairs the Medical Schools Council Selection Alliance. He is passionate about equitable selection and making sure admission to medical school is evidence-based. In his spare time he sings and practises agility with his dog.

Luis Eduardo González has been senior researcher at the Interdisciplinary Educational Research Center (PIIE) since 1973. He has worked in the field of educational policies, social mobility, technical and vocational education, youth and development. In addition, he was Executive Director of PIIE, President and member of the institutional board. As a member of PIIE he has written or edited more than 50 books and 400 articles. He also works as an external consultant in various international organizations such as UNESCO, ECLAC, Organization of American States, Inter-American Development Bank, and World Bank. He is former Director of the University Policy and Administration Area at the International Center of University Development (CINDA) (a network of 40 universities from Latin-America and Europe). Since 1980 he has worked as consultant and project coordinator in fields such as quality assurance, institutional evaluation and accreditation, university teaching methods, curriculum planning, professional skills analysis, national policies for higher education, information systems and student mobility. He has coordinated more than 50 international projects, worked with more than 80 universities and governments in 20 different countries. He holds an Ed.D. in Educational Administration and Planning from Harvard University (USA).

Stephen Gorard is Professor of Education and Public Policy at Durham University. He is a member of the UK DfE Associate Pool, member of the British Academy grants panel, and a Fellow of the Academy of Social Sciences. His work concerns the robust evaluation of education as a lifelong process, focused on issues of effectiveness and equity. He regularly gives advice to policymakers, and is a widely read methodologist, involved in international and capacity-building activities, and used as an adviser on the design of rigorous evaluations by central and local governments, NGOs and charities. He is author of around 30 books and over 1000 other publications. He is currently funded by the ESRC to investigate how measures of educational disadvantage can be used for school improvement, by the ESRC and Scottish Funding Council to determine which indicators of disadvantage are most suitable in contextualized admissions to higher education.

Phil Gravestock is Dean of the College of Learning & Teaching at the University of Wolverhampton, and was awarded a National Teaching Fellowship in 2005. Phil has an interest in inclusion and flexible learning, which arose primarily from his experiences of working with disabled students on geological fieldwork. He was director of the HEFCE-funded *'DisabilityCPD'* project, which resulted in a national online learning course for academic staff in higher education and he was also involved with the Geography Discipline Network's *'Learning Support for Disabled Students Undertaking Fieldwork and Related Activities'* project and the *'Inclusive Curriculum Project'*. He co-wrote *'Inclusion and Diversity: meeting the needs of all students'* with Sue Grace, which is part of the Routledge Key Guides for Effective Teaching in Higher Education series.

Susan Grimes is a PhD candidate at the University of Newcastle. Her doctoral research is on students in higher education whose learning is challenged by mental health issues and/or ongoing medical conditions and disabilities. Susan's research aims to provide evidence to support positive change in learning environments at university. She has a background in primary school teaching, systems analysis and design and in both teacher and higher education.

Michelle Hodara is a researcher at Education Northwest, a non-profit organization in Portland, Oregon, where she leads research and evaluation projects. Dr Hodara uses quantitative and mixed methods to study postsecondary readiness and success with a focus on community colleges and historically underrepresented students. Dr Hodara holds a doctorate in economics and education from Teachers College, Columbia University.

Yasar Kondakci is an Associate Professor in Educational Administration and Planning at the Middle East Technical University, Ankara, Turkey. His research focuses on educational change, social justice in education and higher education.

Sadhana Manik is a senior lecturer in the School of Education at the University of KwaZulu-Natal (UKZN). She is located in the discipline of Geography Education and her interests and publications lie in mobility and migration within education and student access, success and drop out discourses in the context of

South Africa. She serves in various leadership positions: as a UKZN senator and representative on the School Higher Degrees and Research Committee.

Noel McGinn received his PhD in Social Psychology from the University of Michigan. He is Professor Emeritus of the Harvard University Graduate School of Education and Fellow Emeritus of the Harvard Institute for International Development. He is Past President of the Comparative and International Education Society. In 1998 he received the Andres Bello Award of the Organization of American States for Outstanding Contribution to Education in Latin America.

Jade McKay is a leading inter-disciplinary Research Fellow at Deakin University. Dr McKay has extensive experience in both nationally and internationally funded competitive research projects. She played an integral role in the government-funded national studies into facilitating the success of students from low SES backgrounds, exploring enabling pathways for equity students, and facilitating the success of students from low SES backgrounds at regional universities. She is widely published in inclusive teaching and learning approaches which facilitate the success of non-traditional students, particularly those from low SES backgrounds. Dr McKay's research is guided by a focus on minority and disadvantaged groups in both higher education and western culture in general.

Yusuf İkbal Oldac candidate at the Department of Education at the University of Oxford, UK. He is a fully-funded scholar at Oxford Centre for Islamic Studies and a member of the Comparative and International Education research group at the University of Oxford. His research focuses on internationalization of higher education, social justice in education, and school effectiveness and improvement.

Clare Owen is a Policy Adviser at the Medical Schools Council (MSC) in the UK. Before taking up this post she was a Policy Manager at the GMC focusing on student fitness to practise and support. Clare led the Selecting for Excellence project looking at selection and widening participation in UK medical schools. She now leads the MSC's work on selection and widening participation.

Julie Petrokubi is Senior Advisor for Youth Development and Evaluation at Education Northwest. She provides evaluation and technical assistance for a diverse set of initiatives, with an emphasis on deeper learning and systems-level change. She recently completed a multi-year formative evaluation of the Road Map Project, a cradle-to-career collective impact initiative in South King County Washington. This evaluation investigated the interim outcomes of efforts to promote educational innovation and collaboration across seven school districts and their partners.

Other recent projects include: a state-wide implementation study of professional learning communities in schools; evaluation of research-practice partnerships in education; and data capacity building for expanded learning and STEM networks. Petrokubi earned a PhD from the University of Wisconsin-Madison where she studied the institutional conditions, practices, and outcomes of efforts to integrate real-world civic learning into governmental and non-profit organizations.

Ashley Pullman is a SSHRC postdoctoral scholar in The Education Policy Research Initiative at the University of Ottawa. Her research focuses on the relationship between education, skills and employment and life course outcomes. Currently, she is undertaking longitudinal study on income instability, education and skill that utilizes data from Statistics Canada's Longitudinal and International Study of Adults.

Labby Ramrathan is a professor in the School of Education at UKZN and a NRF rated C2 researcher. He has been in leadership positions within the School in various capacities including Head of School, Acting Deputy Dean and Acting Dean. He also currently serves as Secretary for the South African Education Research Association (SAERA).

Sheila Riddell worked as a teacher of English in the south west of England for seven years before doing a PhD at Bristol University in gender and education. She moved to Scotland in 1988 and since then has researched and written extensively on additional support needs, school inclusion and equality. She previously worked as Director of the Strathclyde Centre for Disability Research, University of Glasgow, and for the past six years has worked as the Director of the Centre for Research in Education Inclusion and Diversity at the University of Edinburgh.

Hanife Hilal Senay is a graduate student at the Department of Educational Sciences, Educational Administration and Planning program at the Middle East Technical University. At the same time, she is a research assistant at the Graduate School of Social Sciences of the Middle East Technical University. Her research interest focuses on school climate, school effectiveness and social justice.

Mahsood Shah is an Associate Professor and Deputy Dean (Learning and Teaching) with the School of Business and Law at CQUniversity, Australia. In this role Mahsood is responsible for enhancing the academic quality and standard of courses. Mahsood is also responsible for learning and teaching strategy, governance, effective implementation of policies, and enhancement of learning and teaching outcomes across all campuses. In providing leadership for learning and teaching, Mahsood works with key academic leaders across all campuses to improve learning and teaching outcomes of courses delivered in various modes including face-to-face and online. At CQUniversity, he provides leadership in national and international accreditation of courses. Mahsood is also an active researcher. His areas of research include quality in higher education, measurement and enhancement of student experience, student retention and attrition, student engagement in quality assurance, international higher education, widening participation and private higher education. Before joining CQUniversity, Mahsood led research at the school level at the University of Newcastle, Australia.

Nadia Siddiqui is Assistant Professor at Durham University, leading on evaluation of the impact of student bursaries on widening participation initiatives. She has worked on a number of research projects on overcoming the challenges of poverty that lead to gaps in attainment. She has published research articles and reports on evaluations of teaching approaches that are widely practised in schools. She is also interested in understanding the patterns of poverty through large data sets. She has published several research papers based on the analyses of administrative data sets such as National Pupil Data in England and survey-based data sets in Pakistan.

Erica Southgate is Associate Professor of Education at the University of Newcastle, Australia. She has published widely on equity and education and social marginalization in health. In 2016, Erica was appointed as a National Equity Fellow to investigate increasing fair access to high status professions for young people experiencing disadvantage. A key component of the Fellowship was her report, Immersed in the Future: A Roadmap of Existing and Emerging Technology for Career Exploration, which explored how virtual and augmented reality could be effectively used for career education in low income school communities. Erica is the first in her family to go university and is proud of her working class background.

Liz Thomas is an independent researcher and consultant for higher education and Professor of Higher Education at Edge Hill University, with approximately 20 years' experience of undertaking and managing research about widening participation, student retention and success and institutional approaches to improving the student experience and outcomes. She is committed to using research to inform national and institutional policy, practice and evaluation, and has developed and led change programmes to facilitate this. Liz is an expert member of the Teaching Excellence Framework panel, recognizing her expertise in student retention and success and learning and teaching.

Liz researches and writes about widening participation, student retention and success and learning and teaching. She is the author and editor of over ten books, and many journal articles, reports, briefings and practice guides. She regularly delivers keynote addresses and staff development workshops and programmes at higher education institutions in the UK and abroad.

Elisabet Weedon was deputy director and senior research fellow in the Centre for Research in Education Inclusion and Diversity (CREID) until 2017. She is now an Honorary Research Fellow in the School of Education, University of Edinburgh. Her main research interests are in lifelong learning and higher education, with a focus on widening access to higher education for disadvantaged groups in the UK and in Sweden.

Di Xu is an assistant professor of educational policy and social context at the University of California Irvine and a research fellow with the Community College Research Center at Teachers College, Columbia University, and a visiting scholar with the American Enterprise Institute. Her research uses experimental and quasi-experimental designs to examine policies and educational interventions aimed at improving college students' educational outcomes, with a particular focus on students from low-income and underrepresented groups. Dr Xu's work has been published in several top-ranked education policy journals; the findings from her studies on distance learning and developmental education have also been widely cited in various news outlets including the *New York Times*, *ABC News*, the *Chronicle of Higher Education*, *Inside Higher Ed* and *Diverse Issues in Higher Education*. Dr Xu holds a doctorate in economics and education from Teachers College, Columbia University.

List of Figures

Fig. 1.1	Student retention, success and excellence maturity model	9
Fig. 2.1	Postsecondary institutional sequences of high school graduates over 28 years	34
Fig. 2.2	Postsecondary institutional sequence clusters over 28 years	37
Fig. 6.1	Vision 20:20 pipeline	124
Fig. 9.1	Extract from outreach scoping study (MSC 2016)—showing the distribution of outreach from medical schools by secondary school and college in UK	204
Fig. 12.1	Percentage of school leavers by highest qualification achieved at SCQF levels 5, 6 and 7, by SIMD 2012 quintiles and gender, 2014–15. (Source: Scottish Government data, Authors' own calculations)	275
Fig. 12.2	January deadline application rates for 18 year olds by country, 2006–2016. (Source: UCAS 2016a)	278
Fig. 12.3	Proportion of 18 year olds accepted for entry by UK country of domicile 2006–2016. (Source: UCAS 2016b)	279
Fig. 12.4	Proportion of 18 year olds entering university by cycle and country of domicile, 2006–16. (Source: UCAS 2016b)	280
Fig. 12.5	18 year old entry rates for disadvantaged areas (POLAR3 Q1) by country of domicile, 2006–2016. (Source: UCAS 2016b)	281
Fig. 12.6	18 year old entry rates for advantaged areas (POLAR3 Q5) by country of domicile, 2006–2016. (Source: UCAS 2016b)	282

List of Tables

Table 2.1	Descriptive overview of clusters	36
Table 2.2	Multinomial logistic regression comparing Cluster 1 to all other clusters	42
Table 5.1	Common developmental education reforms	106
Table 5.2	Student-level and institution-level outcomes and measures to consider tracking	113
Table 8.1	Total number of students and first-generation students admitted to the USACH through the Propedeutic Program (2014–2016)	181
Table 8.2	Number of students entering USACH through the Propedeutic who continued the following year (Retention rate for Years 2014–2016)	181
Table 8.3	PENTA students completing the program by school origin (2003–2014)	184
Table 8.4	PENTA graduates entering higher education institutions between 2003 and 2014	185
Table 8.5	SIPEE admission process (2012–2016)	188
Table 8.6	Retention and completion rates of SIPEE students (2014–2016)	189
Table 9.1	POLAR data on current and proposed proportions entering medical school	201
Table 11.1	Enrolments in South African Universities from 2009 to 2015 (CHET 2017)	242

xxxiv   List of Tables

Table 12.1	Undergraduate student support in the United Kingdom before and after devolution	263
Table 12.2	Indicators of educational attainment in the home nations	276
Table 13.1	2015 domestic undergraduate student enrolment in FoE by equity group	290
Table 13.2	2015 domestic undergraduate enrolment by equity group as a proportion of FoE cohort at Go8 and Other universities	291
Table 14.1	Percentage of students with specified characteristics with and without IDACI scores, England 2015	311
Table 14.2	Percentages of students continuing with post-16 education, by ethnicity, England 2008	315
Table 14.3	Mean attainment scores of students by SEN category, England 2015	317
Table 14.4	Percentages of students continuing with post-16 education, by SEN, England 2008	318
Table 14.5	Mean scores of students by FSM, England 2015	319
Table 14.6	Percentages of students continuing with post-16 education, by FSM, England 2008	320
Table 14.7	Mean attainment scores of students by age in months (January 2015), England 2015	321
Table 14.8	Percentages of students continuing with post-16 education, by sex, England 2008	322
Table 15.1	The distribution of participants according to their study areas	339
Table 15.2	Mean and standard deviation regarding participant perceptions on the role of governmental supports in access to and quality life experience during higher education	341
Table 15.3	Frequency distribution of participant perceptions on the role of governmental support in access to and quality of life experience during higher education	342
Table 15.4	Mean and standard deviation values regarding participant perceptions on the role of governmental supports in their access to higher education and their contribution for employability after graduation	343
Table 15.5	Frequency distribution of participant perceptions on the role of governmental supports in their access to higher education and their contribution to employability after graduation	343

1

Leadership for Institutional Change to Promote Diversity and Success

Liz Thomas

Introduction

This chapter explores the contribution of leadership to a whole institution approach (WIA) to WP and student success using empirical evidence from two research studies involving 21 HEPs in the UK. This chapter is based on two key principles. First, increasing student diversity and ensuring that these students are successful in HE and beyond, which equates to a high quality learning experience; and second, ensuring the success of all students, including those from diverse and under-served groups, which requires a WIA. This chapter is structured as follows: an overview of the UK HE context and the relationship between widening access, student success and academic quality; summary details about the two empirical studies; consideration of a WIA and why it is necessary; the introduction of the theoretical framework; a discussion of the evidence

---

L. Thomas (✉)
Edge Hill University, Lanchashire, UK
e-mail: Thomase@edgehill.ac.uk

© The Author(s) 2018
M. Shah, J. McKay (eds.), *Achieving Equity and Quality in Higher Education*, Palgrave Studies in Excellence and Equity in Global Education, https://doi.org/10.1007/978-3-319-78316-1_1

about the role of leadership drawing on the framework and the empirical evidence; and concluding points about the practice of leadership for institutional change to promote diversity and success.

The UK Context

The UK has had a longstanding and comparatively successful approach to expanding participation in HE by students from groups who have been traditionally underrepresented. Each of the four nations—England, Scotland, Wales and Northern Ireland—has over the past 20 years used policies and institutional funding as levers to encourage, incentivise and require HEPs to 'widen access'. This focus on entry quickly extended to embrace the retention, completion and longer-term success of these students, with a strong current emphasis on employment outcomes, all of which can be viewed as indicators of the quality of a higher education system. For example, in England the National Strategy makes explicit the lifecycle approach to WP, and all institutions that charge fees above a minimum threshold are required to allocate a proportion of additional fee income to widening access, student retention and success and progression into employment or further study. Annual Access Agreements set out each institution's commitments (including spending) and outcome targets, and these must be approved by the Director of Fair Access and subsequently published; progress is monitored annually.

The UK HE System

Higher education in the UK is a responsibility controlled at the level of each of the four nations: England, Scotland, Wales and Northern Ireland.

In England alone there are more than 100 universities, and approximately 350 HEPs in receipt of public sector funding. This is in addition to more than 600 private providers, most of which are comparatively small. In 2012–13 there were 2,340,275 HE students at HE institutions, plus 186,455 HE students at further education colleges in England. The majority of students in the UK are registered for full-time study (79%);

and 67% are under 21 when they commence HE study. The young participation rate in England is 38% and in Scotland it is 45%. Participation rates however vary between groups, and in England 51% of young people in the most advantaged quintile participate in HE, while only 20% participate from the most disadvantaged quintile. 43% of students are male, but there are significant differences between subjects. 71% of students identify themselves as 'white' (compared to other ethnic categories) and 82% have no known disability. The student population has been increasing since the system expanded in the early 1990s, and while this has slowed it has not stopped, despite the introduction of student tuition fees (2006) and significantly increased fees (2012/13). The population of part-time students declined significantly in 2012/13 however, and has not yet recovered, but overall student numbers remain intact at the system level. From 2015/16 the recruitment caps were lifted in England, enabling institutions to recruit as many students as they choose, thus reducing some of the challenges for widening participation; while in Scotland student numbers are fixed, with additional places allocated for widening access students from specific areas of disadvantage based on their home postcode (address). In England the non-continuation rate from first to second year of study for young students is around 7% and around 13% for mature students, and the overall completion rate for the sector is 82%.

Diversity and Quality: The Teaching Excellence Framework

Over the past two decades the UK HE system has not only expanded its student numbers and diversity, it has also maintained many of its indicators of quality, including selective admission to HE and high rates of completion. In 2017 the Teaching Excellence Framework (TEF) was introduced as a method of assessing the quality of learning and teaching, making both the outcomes and the evidence publicly available; although this was not its primary purpose, the TEF demonstrates the UK's commitment to diversity and quality.

The TEF assesses HEPs in three broad areas: teaching quality, learning environment plus student outcomes and learning gain. Teaching quality takes into account: contact, stimulation, challenge, student engagement; course design, assessment and feedback; developing students' knowledge, skills and understanding; and recognition and reward of excellent teaching. Learning environment includes: libraries, laboratories and studios; work experience, peer interaction and extra-curricular activities; support for learning and independent study; a personalised academic experience to maximise retention, progression and attainment; and links between teaching and learning, and scholarship, research or professional practice. Student outcomes and learning gain looks for positive outcomes such as lifelong learning skills and contribution to society, economy and the environment; progression to further study; and knowledge, skills and attributes to compete for graduate level jobs.

The TEF utilises common metrics available for all providers and combines this with a narrative prepared by each HEP; the first three standardised metrics are derived from the National Student Survey (an annual survey of final year undergraduate students' satisfaction that all HEPs participate in), and relate to teaching on the course, assessment and feedback and academic support. The other metrics are non-continuation data provided by the Higher Education Statistics Agency (HESA) based on institutions' annual returns, and two employment outcomes—in employment or further study and in highly skilled (graduate) employment or further study—from the Destination of Leavers of HE, a survey conducted with graduates six months after completion. The TEF is concerned with these metrics overall, but also in relation to students from non-traditional and disadvantaged groups, and data are provided in relation to specific groups (socio-economically) disadvantaged, disabled, BME and mature students. Contextual data are also supplied about each provider, such as entry tariffs (the proportion of students entering with low, medium and high entry qualifications), numbers and proportions of students from each of the specific groups named above and additional information, such as the number of local students (based on travel to work areas). The holistic assessment takes into account the differential outcomes as well as the overall outcomes, and indeed the TEF panel includes WP and diversity experts. This all implies that an excellent experience and outcome for all students—including those from diverse and non-traditional backgrounds—contributes to overall assessment of excellence within HE in the UK. This is reflected in the comment from the Director of Fair Access to Higher Education:

> *I welcome the publication of these results. I have always argued that, designed well, the TEF had the potential to improve outcomes for all students. So I am pleased that the metrics have taken students' backgrounds into account, as this will help universities and colleges see where progress is being made for students from disadvantaged backgrounds, and where there are still unexplained gaps in attainment between the most and least advantaged. I look forward to continuing to work with those across the sector to ensure that teaching excellence means excellence for students from all backgrounds.* (OFFA 2017)

Empirical Evidence

This chapter is informed by two studies (each led by author): one focusing on improving student retention and success in HE which concluded that a WIA is required, and the second which was commissioned to better understand a WIA to WP (including student success). These are briefly described now.

Study 1: What Works? Student Retention and Success

In 2008 the *What Works? Student Retention and Success Programme* (WW?1) was launched by the Higher Education Funding Council for England (HEFCE) and the Paul Hamlyn Foundation with the aim of generating better evidence to support institutions to improve student retention to fill a gap identified by the National Audit Office (NAO 2007). The emerging learning, synthesised in Thomas 2012, was then used within an extended 'Change Programme' (WW?2), which recruited 13 universities to implement changes informed by the first phase of the study; the change programme was accompanied by an evaluation of both the outcomes and the process of change (Thomas et al. 2017).

WW?1 found that at the heart of student retention and success is students' engagement and the development of a strong sense of belonging. This is most effectively nurtured through students' participation in mainstream activities that all students participate in, rather than through additional activities designed to support specific groups or address specific challenges and which rely on voluntary participation. This finding shifts the focus to the academic sphere as the most important site for nurturing engagement which creates a sense of belonging, and this puts inclusive learning and teaching at the heart of effective student retention and success.

In WW?2 discipline teams were therefore central to the process of improving retention and success, and each of the participating institutions identified at least three subject areas in which interventions would be located, and 43 discipline teams participated. Each university however was required to have a cross-institutional team, including a project manager, a data expert, an academic, a senior manager and a student and these teams worked with the discipline teams, and changes were implemented locally and centrally. The Change Programme consisted of events, institutional visits, residential meetings, reporting, feedback and other support. The evaluation utilised a mixed methodology and operated at different levels and with different purposes. The process evaluation was undertaken through interviews and surveys with institutional team members, review of project documentation, and observation of and reflection on meetings, visits and events.

Study 2: Understanding a Whole Institution Approach to Widening Participation

The Office for Fair Access (OFFA) commissioned this study to provide evidence and guidance to assist HEPs to further develop and evaluate their WIA. It was designed to answer three key questions: what is involved in a 'whole institution' approach to WP and fair access? How is thematic work, such as WP, managed across a whole institution? What strategies and tools are or can be used to evidence impact when thematic work such as WP is implemented across an institution or organisation? (Thomas 2017). This was undertaken as a more conventional research study, combining a literature review, five diverse institutional case studies, based on a three-hour participatory workshop, using an Appreciative Inquiry approach, and a participatory event for the sector to discuss the interpretation of the evidence and to provide examples from their own institutions and organisations. It was however undertaken over a short time period (and with a comparatively small budget).

Each of the projects has strengths and weaknesses, and advantages and disadvantages. The former involved a significant number of institutions and discipline teams, and it took place over an extended timeframe. The focus of the work was broader, as the programme combined action with research, and research had multiple objectives; thus the methodology was, in some ways less formal. The latter was designed to address specific research questions, and used more conventional and focused research methods; however, the number of institutions involved was small, and the tight timescale and limited budget did not allow for the observation but it relied upon individual and institutional reporting of the issues.

Whole Institution Approach

Across the WP field in both policy and practice there is an emerging consensus of the need for a WIA to deliver the changes in access and student success that are required. For example, the National Strategy for Access and Student Success (BIS 2014), states:

> *We see a strategic, long-term "whole institution" approach as crucial and HEFCE and OFFA will adopt a coherent approach when requesting information from institutions, within which publicly funded higher education providers can set out their strategies and targets for access and student success.* (BIS 2014, paragraph 26)

And it is recognised throughout the Social Mobility Action Group (2016) report *Working in Partnership: enabling social mobility in higher education* that a whole-institutional approach is necessary (see for example recommendation 14). In the guidance to higher education institutions regarding the preparation of their Access Agreement for 2018/19, OFFA said:

> *We encourage you to ensure that the development of your access agreement, and your longer-term access, student success and progression plans, is a whole-institution process, with your core priorities for access, student success and progression embedded at all levels across your institution.*

The policy is therefore clear that a WIA is to be pursued, but what this is, why it is important and how it can be pursued is not clear. In the OFFA glossary a WIA is defined as:

> *An approach to widening participation and fair access that is embedded at all levels of an institution, not limited to a particular unit or department, engaging across all areas of its institutions' work and inclusive of senior management.* (OFFA Glossary)

Earlier research has argued that the purpose of a WIA is to move WP from being a marginal activity within an institution, which is the responsibility of a few, to being a mainstream activity which transforms HEPs into more inclusive learning environments:

> *There is always a risk that single item approaches become marginalised within a university as being the responsibility of a particular interest group. This development [widening participation strategies] has been in response to government direction, [and] has the potential to shape and change institutions so that they become more inclusive.* (Layer 2002)

An inclusive approach can be understood as:

> *… a shift away from supporting specific student groups through a discrete set of policies or time-bound interventions, towards equity considerations being embedded within all functions of the institution and treated as an ongoing process of quality enhancement. Making a shift of such magnitude requires cultural and systemic change at both the policy and practice levels.* (May and Bridger 2010, p. 6)

Improving the quality of the higher education experience and outcomes for a diverse student population requires the development of inclusive learning (Thomas 2016). The *What works? Student Retention and Success Change Programme* (WW?2) goes further. It found that despite a focus on the academic domain and the involvement of discipline teams to create an inclusive learning environment a whole institution approach is required to deliver excellence. The report (Thomas et al. 2017) concluded that:

> *The What Works? programmes have moved understanding, policy and practice about retention and success in the UK to a state of increased maturity … First generation retention and success focused on 'fixing up' the needs of specific groups of students through additional support services to improve retention (pre-What Works?). Second generation retention and success focused on student engagement and belonging in their academic learning contexts to improve success (What Works?1). Third generation retention and success focuses on the whole institution working together and using evidence to understand the issues and implement contextually relevant changes across the whole student lifecycle and the entire institution. (What Works?2)*

This is shown here visually in the Student retention, success and excellence maturity model (Fig. 1.1).

While the WW?2 established the need for a WIA, it only went a limited way in defining what this involved. It requires:

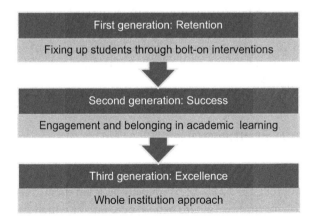

Fig. 1.1 Student retention, success and excellence maturity model

- Leadership at all levels, and the involvement of staff in all roles across the institution;
- A culture that values and prioritises success;
- Policies that prioritise and foster success;
- Systems and processes that enable everyone to work towards success;
- Student involvement in the process of change;
- Data and evidence that inform success; and
- Academic support and regulatory practices that nurture success.

The current OFFA study seeks to go further, and to begin plugging the gaps to understand what a WIA is and how it can be implemented. Broadly, it can be seen to connect with the concept of 'alignment' as it is used by Felten et al. (2016); they draw on the work of other US scholars and define alignment as:

> … *matching resources, policies, and practices with the institution's educational purposes and student characteristics through forging educational partnerships within and among traditional organisational boundaries, especially faculty, academic affairs, and student affairs units.* (Kuh et al. 2010, cited in Felten et al. 2016, p. 92)

Given this alignment between the findings in the UK context and the work of Felten et al. (2016) in the US, it seems appropriate to use their action principles in relation to leadership, to discuss the issue of leadership for institutional change to promote diversity and success. The leadership action principles framework from Felten et al. (pp. 135–162) is presented below, before it is discussed in relation to the empirical evidence from the UK.

Leadership Framework

In their work about the undergraduate experience 'focusing on what matters most' Felten et al. (2016, p. 5) identify six core themes that contribute to an effective undergraduate experience, one of which is leadership. In summary, they write:

In strong institutions, leaders at all levels share a sense of vision and purpose. Those at the top of the organisation chart are crucial actors, but colleges and universities cannot thrive over the long term when a single person or a small group carries a disproportionate share of the load. Instead, people throughout the organisation need to see themselves as part of the leadership team. This requires everyone to work together to nurture an institutional culture of inclusion intentionality, and purpose. (Felten et al. 2016, p. 7)

They identify six 'action principles' in relation to leadership (pp. 137–138):

i. Lead through collaborative practices.
ii. Articulate clear, aspirational goals, linked to institutional mission and values.
iii. Cultivate a culture that keeps students and learning at the centre of decision making.
iv. Foster shared responsibility and leadership at all levels of the institution.
v. Make strategic choices and take informed risks.
vi. Focus on dynamic, improvement-oriented planning, executing and communicating.

These principles form the basis of the discussion about the role and approach to leadership for institutional change to promote diversity and success, drawing on the framework developed by Felten et al. (2016) and discussed in relation to the empirical evidence from the two UK studies described earlier. For each principle, a brief overview of the key issues discussed by Felten et al. (2016) is presented, followed by illustrative examples from the UK studies; there are however some common themes that cut across these principles, and so these are exemplified through the empirical evidence at the most relevant point to avoid duplication and repetition.

Lead Through Collaborative Practices

Higher education institutions are large and complex, and improving the student experience and outcomes requires leadership based on collaboration and empowerment at all levels of the institution, rather than relying on a strong individual leader at the top. In particular the institution needs to work together and reject 'us and them' thinking, and develop and promote a culture of engagement and learning together and from each other to achieve institutional development and change. Collaboration is however easier said than done, as there are cultural divides or different perspectives between groups within institutions; overcoming these different views involves nurturing trust and helping everyone to contribute to both the vision and its implementation. This can be understood as leading by enabling, or having power with, rather than power over others (Johnson and Mayoux 1998).

Both UK studies showed the importance of leadership at different levels within the same institution, and of working together towards a common goal. For example, the University of Wolverhampton noted that working collaboratively led to wider acceptance and engagement by staff:

> *The layered implementation approach, which was discipline led and driven but supported by faculty management and institutional leadership, led to the initiative not being viewed as a wholly top-down process and being more readily accepted by teaching staff.* (Thomas et al. 2017, p. 91)

While the focus of the WW2? was on changes to the curriculum within the disciplinary context, which required leadership and collaboration within course teams and academic schools, implementation was facilitated by changes at the institutional level, for example, in order for disciplinary teams to utilise course and student-level data this needed to be made available in an accessible format. The University of Glasgow undertook an extensive consultation to investigate the data available, the optimal management information report format, the types and granularity of the data required in different areas of the university, and structures for the dissemination of data, requiring collaborative leadership.

Through the WIA study it was discovered that while collaboration and engagement at all levels are important, the work needs to be coordinated or managed, otherwise it can become fragmented, to avoid duplication, and even conflict, as well as gaps in provision. In one institution where staff take responsibility for and lead interventions to improve retention and success, some felt that their work was compromised by other 'competitive' initiatives. Other institutions discussed how opportunities for sharing practice and learning together were important to try to avoid these challenges. Kingston University has an institution-wide Access Planning Group where people share their plans and interventions, while the University of Sheffield publishes an annual report which draws together information about outreach activities across the institution organized by central teams and academic departments.

Articulate Clear, Aspirational Goals, Linked to Institutional Mission and Values

Institutions need an explicit commitment to student success, and these values and goals need to be written into the mission statement and institutional policies. But they also need to be articulated and affirmed through action by institutional leaders at all levels, to ensure that everyone is convinced of the veracity of the institutional commitment.

While WP and student success are espoused goals of many UK institutions, sometimes this commitment is not felt and owned by staff across these institutions. WW2? teams felt that they had senior management support, but this was not fully reflected in wider staff engagement, but the impact was greater when a stated commitment was backed up by action. At the University of South Wales there was some resistance, but senior management action demonstrated commitment to the change and the challenges were overcome.

> … *Buy-in to improved data on belonging, engagement and self-confidence by a senior member of the executive (the DVC) provided a mandate to the data expert to overcome some of the resistance to change identified in pockets of the institution. Without senior management buy-in it would not have been possible to develop the quality and availability of the data in a timely manner.* (USW)

All of the institutions involved in the WIA study felt that WP is an explicit part of their institutional values and missions, but that this needs to be reinforced in other institutional priorities and policies; so valuing learning and teaching was given as an example of this. This could then have implications in other policies, such as staff recruitment, reward and recognition. Aston University make efforts to recruit staff who share the institutional values; as part of the process of recruiting a new vice chancellor the staff consultation drew attention to the need to recruit someone who shared the institutional values, and for academic staff WP is included in the job description. The postgraduate certificate for new staff addresses WP in learning, teaching and assessment, and academic promotion is on the basis of citizenship, teaching, external engagement and research. Within WW2? there were examples of unintentionally conflicting policies: such as the policy which prohibited external catering and so pizzas could not be bought in as part of a co-curricular activity, and the policy that only allowed registered students access to the virtual learning environment so pre-entry tasks could not be given to students.

Cultivate a Culture that Keeps Students and Learning at the Centre of Decision Making

US research has demonstrated that the culture of an institution is key to understanding differential graduation rates between similar institutions (Mehaffy 2015) and, in particular, that all staff believe that their role is to help students become successful. This can be demonstrated and enacted in many different ways, including for example, staff recruitment and the review process, and development and training, as in the Aston example. But also keeping students and learning—or student success—at the heart of all decision making can help to ensure that the institution does not unintentionally undermine its commitment to students. This helps to encourage critical questioning and intellectual debate about the implications of all decisions on student success. Institutional culture is dynamic, and it needs to be continually nurtured to ensure that the institution remains student-centred.

One of the core features of a WIA to WP that emerged from our study was that staff from departments, services and units from across the institution are involved in WP, and not just 'professional WP' staff. (Professional WP staff are those who are employed primarily to deliver WP activities or outcomes, often having WP – or similar in their job title, and who may be funded by WP resources.) But for this to be successful it does necessitate all staff acknowledging, understanding and acting upon their responsibilities—and being accountable. For example, Kingston University rolled out a programme to engage all academic staff in the delivery of an inclusive curriculum and introduced Key Performance Indicators to measure progress in relation to attainment differentials.

Part of the role of the WW2? team at the University of Salford was to situate student success at the heart of the institution's work, and once this was achieved a range of other changes occurred.

> *The project team's aim to raise the profile of student retention and success across the institution has been realised. The profile of retention as an institutional focus has been embedded within strategic documents, language and key performance indicators for the university. Similarly, a wider notion of student success, as espoused by the project literature, has been embraced in the institution's longer-term education vision and strategy. Following reviews of executive and senate structures there is clear, coordinated oversight of the student experience – including both student retention and attainment – across the university's management and governance functions. This will ensure appropriate accountability is maintained and the impact of improvement activities closely monitored.*

Institutional policies were aligned to support and facilitate improving student retention and success. The student engagement, participation and attendance policy sets out the university's approach to supporting the development of students to become confident HE learners who successfully complete their chosen programme of study. The policy foregrounds engagement through supportive structures and the interplay of engagement, participation and attendance in creating student success. The student voice policy was replaced by a new document, 'Always listening: connecting with our students', which emphasizes the importance of regular engagement between students and staff to create agile and effective channels of communication, which in turn help to improve the student experience. The revised 'Student Interruptions and Withdrawals Policy and Procedure' standardises the requirement for students to seek advice and support before making an application to interrupt or withdraw; contact is maintained and students have access to enhanced learning resources during the period spent away from the university.

Foster Shared Responsibility and Leadership at All Levels of the Institution

Effective leadership to enhance student success requires shared responsibility between staff—and students and alumni—across the institutions. This involves a well-communicated shared vision (as discussed), and a concerted effort to develop leaders across the institution, to enable people to step up to working across the institution, rather than relying on external appointments. It should be noted however that shared responsibility also requires access to sufficient resources for staff and students to develop and implement their own approaches. Students and alumni can work in partnership with staff to become agents for change. This approach to nurturing a shared commitment and responsibility helps to develop the institutional culture over time to a single vision, and avoids 'zigzagging from one vision and strategic plan to another in just a few short years' (p. 151).

Within the WW2? programme cross institutional teams worked together, but one of the unintended consequences of the WW2? programme was the development of the capacity of the team members, developing their knowledge of student retention and success and of change management. This has enabled staff to continue developing the student experience in their academic areas, and to be a reference point and resource for others in their academic area, the wider institution and other HEPs. But furthermore, staff have developed new skills, networks and knowledge which enable them to play pivotal roles in their discipline communities and institutions. Capacity has been developed in relation to working across the institution: taking a more strategic perspective; interdisciplinary working; conducting pedagogical research and evaluation; leading and managing change; and inspiring staff and students to engage in the process. Expertise has been developed in a diversity of areas, and productive relationships have developed within and between institutions and disciplinary communities. Birmingham City University (BCU) reported that:

> …*it is interesting to note that every member of the original 'What Works?' steering group has been promoted during their time on the programme. Clearly, participation in the programme and the impact of being seen to drive change have benefited the participants.*

The institution has benefited directly too, and the WW2? team at BCU is now leading the development of the institution's new employability initiative, drawing on lessons and approaches developed through participation in the WW2? programme, thus it has developed the future leaders of the institution.

The WW2? programme required institutions to include students in their cross-institutional teams; however some struggled with the recruitment of students or knowing how to employ them effectively—while others reported on the advantages. Across the programme students were involved in the process of change in a variety of ways, including:

- redesigning the curriculum;
- mentoring and coaching first year students;
- organising academically relevant extra-curricular activities;
- delivering outreach, recruitment and induction activities;
- data collection and evaluation;
- raising awareness of student retention and success issues with other students and ensuring that students have a voice in the development of policy and practice;
- staff development.

For example, the University of South Wales told us in an interview about how students had designed and delivered a staff development activity to raise awareness of the issues from a student perspective:

We've got this little programme going of student-led staff development ... they put a panel together of five students who had considered dropping out of uni. Each student went through ... why they were thinking of dropping out, and then they turned to the audience and said, 'Can you just debate for five minutes, in little groups, what would you have done if you'd heard this from a student? What do you think the university should have done?' ... It was incredibly powerful. (Team leader interview)

As part of the WIA study institutions told us about how not just students were involved—often as ambassadors and mentors—but the University of Sheffield has involved alumni in both financial support, and volunteering in a range of ways to contribute to WP, both pre-entry, and supporting students from non-traditional backgrounds to be successful in HE and beyond. Their Students' Union leads student-led WP work including academic societies that engage with secondary schools, and data sharing allows them to track the participation of WP students in union activities and use of the advice services.

But to foster shared responsibility and local leadership resources of both staff time and money are required. For example, Glasgow Caledonian University used the work allocation model to provide staff with time to contribute to the implementation of the new academic advising process. Within the WIA study transparency of WP funding and resources was identified as contributing to enabling staff to contribute to and take ownership of the agenda. At the University of Worcester staff feel empowered to develop their own initiatives, and they connect with relevant colleagues across the institution—and have access to funding. Kingston University uses the Access Planning Group to provide access to and transparency about WP funding.

Make Strategic Choices and Take Informed Risks

To have a genuine focus on the student experience requires a sharply focused mission and carefully set priorities, which are supported by resources (otherwise they are not institutional priorities) but this may mean letting go of other potential priorities. Decisions however need to be evidence informed, and there must be recognition and acceptance that not everything will be successful. But this process must have measurable standards for accountability and success, which are transparent to everyone in the institution and beyond.

In the current context in the UK all institutions are required to embrace widening access and student retention and success to be eligible to charge tuition fees above a certain level, and this is monitored through annual Access Agreements. However, Aston University—which has a strong track record in this area—explained as part of the WIA study that the institution is highly student-centred and is committed to being successful in this area, but this is in part achieved by not overcommitting itself to some other agendas. One of their unique features is encouraging and supporting students to have a placement year, which improves the achievement outcomes of minority students (Moores et al. 2017), but this requires a huge institutional commitment, and is underpinned by research and evidence.

Within the WW2? programme making informed choices was central, and the programme employed tenets of action research, using emerging findings to refine or reject interventions. For example, the University of Brighton developed an evaluation strategy informed by Appreciative Inquiry, and used the findings to revise interventions.

The project team reviewed the outcomes of the first phase and a number of amendments and improvements based on the findings of the evaluations to the 'retention interventions' were then introduced for the 2014/15 entry cohort.

Across the programme data and evidence was employed to understand the local context, to select or develop appropriate interventions, to evaluate their impact and make changes—or ditch them—and to provide evidence of impact which led to wider engagement and adoption. Evidence was used to:

- Identify disciplines, courses and modules with lower than expected rates of success (e.g. continuation, progression, completion, attainment).
- Identify and understand student characteristics associated with poorer study success outcomes.
- Understand the specific success challenges in each discipline, programme or module in relation to students participating.
- Select interventions that effectively address the issues of concern.
- Tailor interventions to the local disciplinary and student context, as one size does not fit all.
- Monitor and follow up on individual students' engagement and success.
- Formatively evaluate and revise interventions and approaches.
- Assess the impact of interventions on specific groups of students who have lower rates of engagement, belonging, retention or success.
- Promote wider staff engagement, and cross-institutional adoption of effective practice.

Interventions and approaches were evaluated throughout, and each institution used a logic model to develop indicators and to report annually on success, learning and changes. This promoted an ongoing dialogue and culture of inquiry in relation to expectations, there were however important unintended consequences that were also identified through the evaluation process.

Focus on Dynamic, Improvement-Oriented Planning, Executing and Communicating

Developing an institution that is focused on student success is not a one-off activity, but rather it is an ongoing process. It requires a strategic plan, and budgetary and resource allocation processes which are aligned with the plan's major goals, and it requires measurable outcomes to ensure that the question can be answered: 'How will we know specifically when we have achieved these goals?', and a named individual to take responsibility for these outcomes.

As noted, the WW2? programme was evidence informed and dynamic, but this continued beyond the end of the formal programme, demonstrating the need for ongoing development. For example, the University of Ulster synthesized the learning from across its core and disciplinary teams, used this to develop a framework to inform curriculum and engagement development across the institution:

> *The university ... has developed Student Learning Experience Principles aimed at staff and it is planned that these will be implemented from summer 2016. The evidence base from this project has been used to inform this initiative. The six principles are: the learning model; employability; internationalisation; digital fluency; the research teaching nexus; and ethics and sustainability. These have been identified to: define what we mean by the student learning experience at Ulster; provide a shared understanding across disciplines; bring together a range of current learning and teaching strategies; and realise the university's graduate qualities in all students.*

The University of Salford developed an inclusive curriculum pilot project drawing on the principles from WW?2, to be rolled out across the institution, and Glasgow Caledonian University introduced a student engagement project. In all of these examples the institutions have embraced a commitment to student engagement, belonging, retention and success, and have used the evidence and learning from the WW2? programme to align institutional policies and processes, and encourage others to adopt and develop effective practice. The whole process has been underpinned by evidence, communication and ongoing revision and development.

Conclusions

Drawing on this discussion of the role of leadership in institutional change to promote diversity and success in the context of academic quality, a number of key points can be discerned.

- Senior management is necessary, but it is not sufficient, rather staff—and students and alumni—need to engage and lead change in their own spheres of influence.
- Change cannot be mandated or implemented, but rather colleagues have to shape and own the vision, and be empowered to implement change.
- The process of change has to be managed and coordinated, through structures for sharing and learning, to avoid fragmentation, duplication and gaps in the student experience.
- Leaders need to move beyond stating their commitment to a priority, and back it up by action, so that others believe in the change and follow suit.
- Institutional commitments to student success must be reinforced through other policies and processes, especially to avoid undermining the stated priority.
- All staff must be responsible for student success, they need to be made aware of their responsibilities and have the capacity to act, but they also need to be held accountable for the outcomes.
- Fostering responsibility for student success can also develop staff capacity as both experts in retention and success, and as agents of change, and this contributes to the longevity of the vision.

- Students, alumni and Students' Unions can usefully contribute to improving the institution's approach to retention and success.
- For wider engagement in student success there has to be sufficient allocation of resources of both staff time and finance to support the engagement.
- Making student success a priority may mean de-prioritising other potential objectives within the institution.
- Data and evidence must be used throughout the process to ensure the actions are likely to be successful, measured against explicit goals, but failing must also be an option.
- Leading for institutional change to promote diversity and success must be viewed as an ongoing and dynamic process, rather than a one-off activity.

References

BIS (Department for Business, Innovation and Skills). (2014). *National strategy for access and student success*. London: BIS.

Felten, P., Gardner, J., Schroeder, C., Lambert, L., & Barefoot, B. (2016). *The undergraduate experience. Focusing institutions on what matters most*. San Francisco: Jossey-Bass.

Johnson, H., & Mayoux, L. (1998). Investigation as empowerment: Using participatory methods. In A. Thomas, J. Chataway, & M. Wuyts (Eds.), *Finding out fast. Investigative skills for policy and development*. London: Sage Publications Ltd.

Kuh, G., Kinzie, J., Schuh, J., Whitt, E., & Associates. (2010). *Student success in college: Creating conditions that matter*. San Francisco: Jossey-Bass.

Layer, G. (2002). Developing inclusivity. *International Journal of Lifelong Learning, 21*(1), 3–12.

May, H., & Bridger, K. (2010). *Developing and embedding inclusive policy and practice in higher education*. York: Higher Education Academy.

Mehaffy, G. (2015, February 7–10). Re-imagining the first year of college. In *Conference on the First Year Experience*, Dallas, TX.

Moores, E., Birdi, G., & Higson, H. (2017). Placement work experience may mitigate lower achievement levels of Black and Asian vs. White students university. *Frontiers in Psychology, 8*, 1518.

National Audit Office (NAO). (2007). *Staying the course: The retention of students in higher education*. London: National Audit Office.
Office for Fair Access (OFFA). (2017). *OFFA comment on teaching excellence framework year two results*. Bristol: OFFA. https://www.offa.org.uk/press-releases/tef-results-press-release/.
Office for Fair Access (OFFA). *Guidance for institutions on access agreements*. https://www.offa.org.uk/universities-and-colleges/guidance/setting-access-agreement-strategy/
Social Mobility Action Group. (2016). *Working in partnership: Enabling social mobility in higher education – The final report of the Social Mobility Advisory Group*. London: Universities UK. http://www.universitiesuk.ac.uk/policy-and-analysis/reports/Pages/working-in-partnership-enabling-social-mobility-in-higher-education.aspx.
Thomas, L. (2012). *Building student engagement and belonging in higher education at a time of change: Final report from the What Works? Student Retention & Success Programme*. London: Paul Hamlyn Foundation.
Thomas, L. (2016). Developing inclusive learning to improve the engagement, belonging, retention and success of students from diverse groups. In M. Shah, A. Bennett, & E. Southgate (Eds.), *Widening higher education participation. A global perspective*. Kidlington: Elsevier.
Thomas, L. (2017). *Understanding a whole institution approach to widening participation: Final report*. Bristol: Office for Fair Access.
Thomas, L., Hill, M., O' Mahony, J., & Yorke, M. (2017). *Supporting student success: Strategies for institutional change. Findings and recommendations from the What works? Student retention and success programme*. London: Paul Hamlyn Foundation.

2

Vertically Segregated Higher Education and the Life Course: Comparing Patterns Over 28 Years

Lesley Andres and Ashley Pullman

In North America, educational systems generally adhere to what Ralph Turner (1960) coined as a "contest mobility" framework. The central goals of contest mobility are to enhance educational participation for the greatest number of individuals, to minimize tracking within the educational system, and to keep the "contest"—that is, participation in education—open as long as possible. This is in contrast to "sponsored mobility" which is characterized by strict tracking, selection and extraction of a small elite from the mass population, and a limited number of places at the university level.

We thank the British Columbia Council on Admission and Transfer and the Social Sciences and Humanities Research Council of Canada for their financial support of this research.

L. Andres (✉)
University of British Columbia, Vancouver, BC, Canada
e-mail: lesley.andres@ubc.ca

A. Pullman
University of Ottawa, Ottawa, ON, Canada

© The Author(s) 2018
M. Shah, J. McKay (eds.), *Achieving Equity and Quality in Higher Education*, Palgrave Studies in Excellence and Equity in Global Education, https://doi.org/10.1007/978-3-319-78316-1_2

However, contest mobility can take many forms. In Canada, because responsibility for all levels of education rests within each province and territory, distinct differences have emerged over time. For example, in the 1960s, Ontario embraced a binary model of higher education that did not, and for the most part still does not, permit transfer between the non-university and university sectors. The educational system in Quebec is unique in that after completing secondary school at the end of the 11th year all students enrol in the Cégep (*Collège d'enseignement général et professionnel* or *General and Vocational College*). The Cégep system offers either terminal diploma programmes or academic programmes that, upon completion, lead to university study (Andres 2015).

British Columbia and Alberta are considered vertically segregated articulated models—sometimes referred to only as "articulated" or "seamless" systems—of higher education. In principle, at one extreme a student without a high school diploma can enter an adult basic education programme in a non-university institution and wind her or his way through the system with the possibility of eventually earning a PhD. At the other extreme, a student with the requisite high school credentials can enter directly into a university programme. This student, too, may eventually earn a PhD.

How does a vertically segregated articulated system of higher education have an impact on the educational, occupational, and other life course outcomes of individuals from young adulthood through to middle age? The purpose of this chapter is to document the educational and occupational trajectories of the high school graduating Class of 1988 in British Columbia, Canada. Although this study is located in one Canadian province, it can be considered a specific example of the general case of vertically segregated articulated systems of higher education. Following a description of the historical development of the British Columbia higher education system and an overview of theories of social inequality in relation to vertical stratification, we pose the following research questions: *What are the postsecondary enrolment, transfer, and completion patterns of the Class of 1988? What are the long term occupational outcomes of this cohort? Do outcomes differ for those who embarked initially on "traditional" (i.e., direct university attendance from high school) or "non-traditional" (i.e., indirect attendance from high school via the college sector) pathways? And finally, to what extent do ascriptive characteristics have "dissipating" or "lingering" effects on these outcomes?* We employ longitudinal survey data spanning 28 years (1988–2016) from the Canadian *Paths on Life's Way* study (Andres 2002) and the analytical techniques of sequence analysis, cluster analysis, and multinomial regression to consider how education and employment outcomes differ depending on the higher education pathway undertaken.

The Higher Education System in British Columbia: A Short History

The evolution of the higher education system in British Columbia was the result of a vision portrayed in a 1962 report, entitled *Higher Education in British Columbia,* by the President of the University of British Columbia, John Macdonald (Macdonald 1962). By noting advances in computer technology and the potential for scientific and technological knowledge to address the problems facing humanity, and by pointing out that "the cliché that learning should be a life-long process is now becoming a cold fact of economic survival" (pp. 48–49), Macdonald posed the following question: "What kinds of higher education should be made available, in which institutions, and how should students be selected for the various kinds of institutions which may be proposed?" (p. 48).

Informed by the California Master plan, Macdonald's 1962 report provided a detailed blueprint that would launch a completely new system of higher education. One key requirement to achieve excellence and equity in the expanded and extended higher education system that he proposed was *diversification* in terms of the *kinds* and the *geographic locations* of available educational opportunities. Macdonald argued, from a functional perspective, that the need for alternative educational programmes that did not duplicate those offered at the university were "obvious" in that individuals may be suited intellectually and by aptitude and attitude for very many different kinds of vocation …. Clearly many different kinds of education are required for citizens whose talents and interests are so different and whose vocations or careers are so dissimilar. It is inconceivable that any one educational institution can serve successfully the wide range of educational objectives needed for the modern world. (p. 20)

In other words, the new system was to be vertically segregated by design.

Macdonald recommended the establishment of new four-year colleges that would focus on university level education in the liberal arts, sciences, the professions, and graduate studies in major urban centres. In addition, he proposed that several two-year community colleges be created in various locations across the province. The objectives of community colleges would include one or more of the following: (1) two-year academic programmes that would either be terminal in nature or would lead to transfer to degree granting institutions; (2) technical and vocational courses that would not be transferable to degree granting institutions; and (3) continuing adult professional education to provide a lifelong learning dimension.

As part of the first criterion, an articulation component—that is transfer—was added to the vertically segregated structure. Two additional measures would enhance equality of opportunity. First, a comprehensive set of educational opportunities would be available to individuals throughout the province and not only in large urban centres. Second, to enhance student transfer among institutions, programmatic offerings would be parallel rather than identical.

Within 15 years of this publication, the landscape of the British Columbia higher education system had changed dramatically with the establishment of a vertically differentiated system of higher education. In addition to the existing University of British Columbia, two additional universities and 14 community colleges were created which greatly enhanced access to postsecondary education. Over the next 15 years, some identified weaknesses—low participation rates in general, low transition rates of high school graduates to the postsecondary system, and low transfer rates within the system—were addressed (Andres and Dawson 1998; Cowin 2017).

Students in many other Canadian provinces were forced to choose between community college or university attendance, with no possibility for those choosing the former to be able to transfer to the latter. In British Columbia, by the late 1980s high school graduates faced a system that allowed for considerable articulation from sending (e.g., non-university) to receiving (e.g., university) institutions. The British Columbia system was designed to achieve equity and academic excellence by creating multiple pathways through the system. However, it is well documented in the sociology of education literature that the structure of the system is only one factor in determining educational and occupational outcomes.

Vertical Stratification of Higher Education

Davies and Guppy (1997) define two axes that segregate systems of higher education. The first axis refers to hierarchical institutional arrangements according to prestige and selectivity, with two-year community and vocational colleges on the lowest tier and elite universities at the pinnacle. The second axis refers to the intra-institutional stratification of fields of study. Charles and Bradley (2002) labelled the first axis *tertiary level* representing vertical stratification and the second axis, *field of study* representing horizontal stratification. In this chapter we focus on vertical stratification (for a related analysis focussing on horizontal stratification, see Pullman and Andres 2015). We adopt an inclusive social stratification perspective to consider the extent to which educational and occupational outcomes are independent of an array of ascriptive characteristics. Ascriptive characteristics, or structural inequalities, include but are not limited to socioeconomic status (e.g., parental education, occupation, and income), gender, ethnicity, race, and geographic location (Bidwell and Friedkin 1988; Clark 1973). These factors together define one's position along the disadvantage/advantage continuum.

The British Columbia system was designed to increase educational opportunities during a period of higher education massification. In particular, the diversified nature of a vertically stratified system was intended to be a democratising strategy. From a functional perspective, such systems contribute to society by providing the technical skills needed in an increasingly complex economy. However, conflict theorists argue that hierarchical institutional arrangements create an intentional "diversion effect" with the goal of excluding disadvantaged youth from attending universities (Brint and Karabel 1989). Expansion of the number of places at non-elite institutions, according to Charles and Bradley (2002), may indeed increase, rather than reduce, vertical stratification for disadvantaged groups, and in particular, women.

Numerous studies have demonstrated the relationship between origin, in terms of ascriptive characteristics, and educational and occupational outcomes (Andres and Krahn 1999; Krahn et al. 2015; Triventi 2013). Often, however, short time frames (e.g., five years) are used to delineate school-to-work transitions. In this chapter, we embrace a life course perspective to determine the educational and occupational outcomes of a cohort of individuals from late adolescence to middle adulthood. In doing so, we examine not only initial postsecondary educational participation but the sequences of participation by *Paths* respondents over 28 years. Also, we can determine the extent to which ascriptive characteristics have truly "dissipating" or "lingering" effects (Davies and Guppy 1997) as the dataset we employ follows individuals to around age 46. Dissipating effects can be explained through a life course hypothesis (Müller and Karle 1993); as individuals become increasingly independent from their parents and have more autonomy in terms of educational opportunities, the relationship between social background and educational outcomes is reduced. Or, as Mare (1980) claims, due to continuous selectivity, social class effects decline at each level within the educational system. The lingering effects dimension can be seen as an extension of the diversion argument; that is, those from disadvantaged backgrounds may opt to begin their studies at non-elite institutions only to have their intentions to transfer up the vertical hierarchy thwarted due to the "cooling out" (Clark 1960) of their educational aspirations. Also, because the postsecondary system serves as a filter that sorts individuals into different occupations (Arrow 1973), the effects of ascriptive characteristics on various trajectories through the educational system may indeed linger to the point of being permanent fixtures in the lives of individuals and their families.

Research Design

We employ data from the *Paths on Life's Way* project. The *Paths* project began in 1989 as a collaborative governmental and postsecondary institutional endeavour to collect baseline data on the postsecondary attendance patterns of a cohort of high school graduates one year following high school graduation. In 1993, Lesley Andres extended the study and today it is the only longitudinal database of its kind in British Columbia and one of the few remaining longitudinal studies of the transition from youth to adulthood in Canada that combines extensive quantitative and qualitative analyses to examine the lives, actions, and social and cultural contexts of individuals. This database spans 28 years and contains detailed education, work, and life course related information collected at six points in time: 1989, 1993, 1998, 2003, 2010, and 2016. In total, 516 individuals have completed mail out surveys for all waves of data collection. The *Paths* database includes detailed information on postsecondary education, employment, unemployment, and "other" activities, affective variables such as happiness and occupational satisfaction, and personal background information. Hence, the *Paths* dataset is ideal for portraying the nature of transitions and trajectories over a long period of time.

Variables

In this chapter, we use data from the respondents who participated in all phases of the survey mail out data collection and present analyses of the entire 28 years. In total, after accounting for missing data, 485 valid cases are used in the analyses. The foundational data are the institutions that *Paths* respondents attended over 28 years. These institutions are as follows: community college, university college, technical or vocational training institute, university, private institute, a combination of several institutes, and other. Over the years, some of these institutional types have been transformed in terms of the credentials offered and, in some cases, were renamed to reflect these changes. In our analysis, we label the institutional type according to its official definition within a given five-year period (1988–93, 1993–98, 1998–2003, 2003–10; 2010–16) (For more detail, see Andres and Offerhaus 2012).

To interpret sequence and cluster analyses, we use several independent variables. These include dummy variables for gender, if at least one parent had earned a baccalaureate degree or higher, metropolitan location of high school graduation, and eligibility for university admission. We also incorporate a continuous variable of respondents' Grade 12 grade point averages (GPA) and a dummy variable indicating if the respondent graduated high school with the requirements necessary for direct university entry. In addition, continuous variables denote the number of years in full- and part-time postsecondary education and work and dummy indicators represent the proportion of respondents who earned baccalaureate degrees or higher by 2016 and—among them—the proportion with spouses who had earned bachelor's degrees or higher. To examine socioeconomic outcomes, we also provide a continuous measure of respondents' 2016 total household income adjusted for family size, a dummy variable of the proportion who held management duties in their current or most recent 2016 job, and a continuous occupational prestige score of current or most recent job in 2010 (i.e., Blishen score).

Methods and Analysis

Our research utilises three methods: sequence analysis, cluster analysis, and multinomial logistic regression. First, we use sequence analysis (SA) to compare pathways through postsecondary institutions over the complete 28 year period. Sequence analysis is used in the social sciences as a holistic approach to longitudinal research (Abbott 1990). SA portrays change over time by constructing sequences of activities at the individual level. It allows for an examination of enrolment, transfer among different types of institutions, and even postsecondary re-entry later in adulthood through 28 discrete yearly measures that form a complete sequence for each respondent. Next, we conduct optimal matching based cluster analysis to generate sequence groupings. Cluster analysis is based on a pairwise distance matrix that defines differences among each 28 year sequence.

Given that our intent is to illustrate transfer among postsecondary institutions, we use a theory driven substitution matrix for cluster analysis.[1]

Descriptive tabulations and multinomial logistic regression determine the extent to which different background factors and life course experiences characterise each cluster. We transform cluster membership into a nominal categorical variable that indicates to which cluster each respondent belongs. We then use this variable as the dependent variable of a multinomial logistic regression model—also known as a discrete choice model—to examine the relationship between our independent variables and the likelihood of belonging to each cluster (Hosmer et al. 2013). Like logistic regression, multinomial regression is based on a likelihood function which generates conditional probabilities for each outcome category in comparison to a single reference category. The logit coefficients can be transformed to generate the odds of belonging to a cluster compared to the reference group. However, in multinomial logistic regression, the odds are termed the "relative risk ratio" given that cluster membership is independent (Hilbe 2009). We used Stata version 14 (StataCorp 2015) and Stata's Sequence Analysis Distance (SADI) package (Halpin 2014) for the analyses.

Findings

Figure 2.1 illustrates institutional sequences of all respondents over the complete 28 year period, from high school graduation to mid-adulthood. Each line is an individual enrolment trajectory and each colour indicates what type of postsecondary institution she or he reported attending. Figure 2.1 demonstrates that postsecondary enrolment sequences differed widely among individuals—there are 406 unique sequences among the 485 respondents. The mean number of transitions among postsec-

---

[1] To ensure that non-attendance did not drive the formation of clusters, the matrix is comprised of a substitution cost of one for non-attendance, a substitution cost of two for universities, a substitution cost of three for all other institutional types, and an insertion/deletion cost of four. We use discrepancy measures to guide our choice in the number of clusters (Studer et al. 2011).

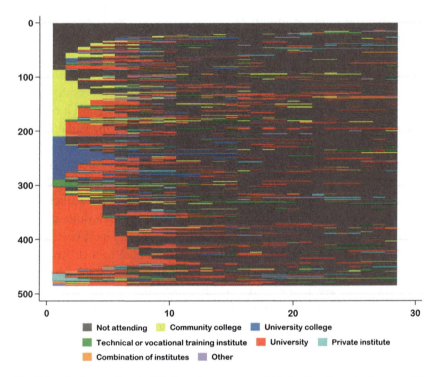

Fig. 2.1 Postsecondary institutional sequences of high school graduates over 28 years

ondary institutions and between attendance and non-attendance is 5.12 (s.d. = 2.85, range 1–15). The educational trajectories through the postsecondary system by *Paths* respondents are clearly heterogeneous, with many participants enrolling in different types of institutions over the course of their lives.

Figure 2.1 also provides evidence of commonality among respondents. Upon high school graduation, most enrolled directly into postsecondary institutions, mainly universities (red), university-colleges (blue), and community colleges (yellow). At the top of the graph a small number of individuals did not make the transition directly from high school to postsecondary study. Over 28 years, only a small number (4.5%) never attended a postsecondary institution. Some individuals who initially attended community colleges and university colleges transferred to universities after one or more years. Trajectories become more diverse over time. Ten years after high school graduation, most respondents were no longer attending postsecondary institutions. Nevertheless, life-long participation is still visible, with many re-enrolling in later adulthood. Finally, over the entire period covered in this analysis, there is comparably less participation in technical or vocational training (green), private (light blue), and other (light purple) institutions.

Next, we use cluster analysis to identify trajectories within the diversity of institutional attendance patterns in Fig. 2.1. Table 2.1 provides a summary of related descriptive statistics. In Fig. 2.2, we identify five postsecondary attendance clusters. Each is described below. The first two clusters are characterised by direct entry into university from high school; however, distinct differences are evident. In contrast, Clusters 3, 4, and 5 entered the college sector primarily after high school graduation and are characterised by varying levels of transfer to university.

Cluster 1. University Only

The first cluster represents 18.1% (n = 88) of all *Paths* respondents. Overwhelmingly, members of Cluster 1 enrolled in university directly after high school graduation and had almost no exposure with other types of postsecondary institutions. Most individuals in this cluster stayed enrolled in university for most of their 20s and a small number continued to attend university into their 30s to gain graduate level and professional credentials. Remarkably, this cluster is overrepresented by males. That is, in the total sample, 61% are female. In this cluster, only 57% are female, which must be viewed in light of provincial university completion rates. In 2017, 26% of women and 20% of men aged 35–44 in British Columbia had earned bachelor's degrees or higher (Statistics Canada 2016). Given that the *Paths* dataset is comprised of 61% women, we would expect a larger proportion of women to belong to this cluster. Also, this cluster has the highest proportion of one or more parents who had earned baccalaureate degrees or greater. Almost 55% completed high school in a metropolitan area.

Table 2.1 Descriptive overview of clusters

	Cluster 1	Cluster 2	Cluster 3	Cluster 4	Cluster 5	Total
Cluster description						
Number of participants	88	78	79	141	99	485
Proportion of *Paths* sample	18.1%	16.1%	16.3%	29.1%	20.4%	–
Demographic characteristics						
Proportion of women	56.8%	52.6%	67.1%	63.8%	64.6%	61.4%
Proportion who have one or more parent with a baccalaureate degree or higher	52.3%	47.4%	35.4%	16.3%	27.3%	33.2%
Proportion who graduated from a high school in a metropolitan area	54.5%	44.9%	22.8%	19.2%	37.4%	34.0%
High school outcomes						
Proportion who graduated with the requirements for university entrance	87.5%	91.0%	80.8%	53.2%	61.6%	71.8%
Median GPA[a]	5.7	5.3	4.7	4.3	4.3	4.7
Postsecondary education outcomes						
Median years of part-time or full-time postsecondary education[b]	5.2	3.5	4.0	1.8	3.8	3.9
Proportion with a baccalaureate degree or higher by 2016	93.2%	74.4%	77.2%	29.1%	45.4%	59.2%
Proportion with baccalaureate degree or higher in a partnership with a baccalaureate degree holder by 2016	62.5%	43.6%	31.6%	14.9%	21.2%	32.2%
Work and income outcomes						
Median years of full-time employment	18.5	20.0	16.9	20.0	18.2	18.8
Median years of part-time employment	2.7	2.0	4.7	3.5	4.4	3.5
Median 2016 household income[c]	$100,000	$80,000	$70,000	$63,805	$65,000	$75,000
Proportion with management responsibilities (current/most recent 2016 job)	50.0%	34.6%	40.2%	48.2%	44.4%	44.3%
Median Blishen score (current or most recent 2010 job)[d]	61	55	57	45	52	52

[a]Range 1–6
[b]Full-time = 1 month, part-time = 0.5 month
[c]Self-reported estimation of total household income before taxes and deductions adjusted by the square root of household size (OECD 2011)
[d]Range 23–102

Vertically Segregated Higher Education and the Life Course...

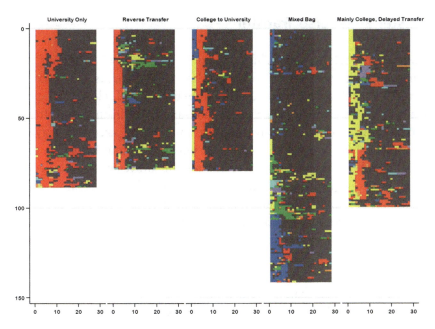

Fig. 2.2 Postsecondary institutional sequence clusters over 28 years

In terms of high school outcomes, members of Cluster 1 were high achievers, with 88% possessing the coursework required for university entrance and a median GPA of 5.7. They were enrolled in postsecondary institutions for a median 5.2 years—a full 1.3 years longer than the total median. By 2016, 93% had earned bachelor's degrees or greater, which is 33% higher than the total average. Also, Cluster 1 members with earned university degrees or higher were far more likely (63%) than any other cluster (32% for the entire sample) to have spouses with the same level of credentials in 2016. Members of Cluster 1 worked full-time for a median of 18.5 years which is not inconsistent with the other clusters. However, a median of 2.7 years spent in part-time work is low. The median 2016 household income was $20,000 higher than any other cluster, as was the proportion holding management responsibilities (50%). Also, the median occupational prestige score for this cluster is highest at 61.

Cluster 2. Reverse Transfer

Respondents belonging to Cluster 2 depicts 16.1% ($n = 78$) of the *Paths* sample. Unlike the "university only" cluster, participants in Cluster 2 tended to enrol in universities directly from high school. However, unlike Cluster 1, they either transferred to non-university institutions after a variable period of time at university; left university to attend other types of postsecondary institutions and then returned to university immediately; or, following four or more years attending university, re-enrolled in non-university institutions later in adulthood. This is the most male dominant cluster (53% female) and is similar to Cluster 1 in terms of parental educational background, possession of the requirements to entry directly into university (the highest of all clusters at 91%), and a high median GPA (5.3). They were about 10% less likely than Cluster 1 to have graduated from metropolitan high schools but this proportion is around 11% higher than the total sample.

Education and employment and outcome patterns were unique to members of Cluster 2. Only 74% earned baccalaureate level credentials or higher by 2016, which is almost 20% lower than Cluster 1. They had spent a median 3.5 years enrolled in postsecondary institutions, 1.7 years less than those in Cluster 1. The proportion of university degree holders in Cluster 2 is 19% lower than Cluster 1, but considerably higher than in the total sample. Among degree holders, a higher proportion have spouses with bachelor's degrees or greater compared to all participants; again, however, this proportion is lower than in Cluster 1. They spent 18.5 and 2.0 years in full- and part-time work, respectively, which is similar to Cluster 1. However, median household income in 2016 was $80,000 which is $5000 higher than the overall average.

The next three clusters present pathways of individuals who did not enrol in university directly after high school.

Cluster 3. College to University Transfer

Cluster 3 highlights traditional "college to university" transfer and represents 16.3% ($n = 79$) of the total *Paths* sample. Upon graduation, most individuals in this cluster enrolled in either community colleges or university colleges for one to two years and then transferred to a university. Most Cluster 3 members did not attend any postsecondary institution after several years, although a small amount of re-enrolment over the life course is evident. Cluster 3 is female dominated (67.1%). Its members are much less likely than members of Clusters 1 and 2 to have one or more parents to have university level credentials; however, this figure is slightly higher than the total *Paths* sample. Cluster 3 members were less likely to graduate from high schools in metropolitan areas: 22.8% compared to 34% of the overall sample. A slightly higher proportion graduated with the requirements for university entrance, but their GPA does not differ from the overall median.

In terms of outcomes, members of Cluster 3 spent slightly longer enrolled in postsecondary education compared to Cluster 2 (4 years) and a slightly higher proportion had earned baccalaureate degrees by 2016 (77.2%) than did those in Cluster 2. The proportion of Cluster 3 members with earned baccalaureate degrees who had spouses with university level credentials by 2016 is comparable to the entire *Paths* sample, but much lower than those in the first two clusters. Over the 28 year period, individuals in this cluster had the lowest level of full-time employment (a median 16.9 years compared to an overall average of 18.8 years) and higher levels of part-time employment (a median 4.7 years; total average 3.5 years). This does not appear to be due to extended periods of time spent in postsecondary study. Their median 2016 household income was also lower than Clusters 1 and 2 and $5000 lower than the median of all *Paths* respondents at $70,000. Members of Cluster 3 had slightly lower rates of management duties in 2016 (40.2%) than the total sample, although they have a higher median occupational prestige (57) score.

Cluster 4. Mixed Bag

Cluster 4 is a "mixed bag" of postsecondary institutional attendance with notably little university participation. It is the largest among the five clusters, portraying 29.1% (*n* = 141) of the sample. Institutional pathways are eclectic, with attendance in community colleges, university colleges, and technical and vocational training institutions. A sizable proportion entered directly into university colleges and either stayed for a short period of time or completed several years of study at this type of institution. Also, a large proportion of Cluster 4 members did not enter the postsecondary system directly from high school, and over 28 years spent very little time in formal postsecondary study. The gender distribution is comparable to the overall sample. Only a small proportion had one or more parent with a baccalaureate degree or higher—just 16.3% compared to 33.2% of the entire sample. Like Cluster 3, only a small proportion of individuals (19.2%) in Cluster 4 graduated from high schools in metropolitan areas. Unlike Cluster 3, a much lower proportion in Cluster 4 graduated with the requirements for university entrance (16%) which is approximately half of the total sample (33%). The median GPA of Cluster 4 members was comparably low, 4.3 compared to an overall median of 4.7.

In examining outcomes, Cluster 4 spent a short time in postsecondary education—a median 1.8 years—notably lower than any other cluster. Only one third of Cluster 4 members had earned baccalaureate degrees or higher by 2016, a rate that is almost one third less than the entire *Paths* sample. Among degree holders, a much lower proportion was in partnerships with baccalaureate degree holders by 2016—the lowest level among all clusters. Although Cluster 4 had comparably lower levels of educational attainment and postsecondary experience, members are tied with Cluster 2 for the highest median years spent in full-time employment (20 years compared to 18.8 for the entire *Paths* sample). Median years in part-time employment are the same as the total sample. However, median 2016 household income is the lowest of all groups and considerably lower than average at $63,805. Although a slightly higher than average proportion of individuals in Cluster 4 hold jobs with management responsibilities (48.2%), their jobs are among the lowest in occupational prestige (Blishen score = 45).

Cluster 5. Mainly College, Delayed Transfer

Finally, Cluster 5 is characterised by "mainly college with delayed transfer" and captures 20.1% (*n* = 99) of all respondents. The presence of later transfer to university is more pronounced than in Cluster 4, although community college attendance dominates Cluster 5. Compared to the entire sample, a slightly higher proportion of individuals in Cluster 5 are women (64.6%) and were high school graduates from metropolitan areas (37.4%). Compared to the total sample, a slightly lower proportion of Cluster 5 members have one or more parents with baccalaureate degrees or higher (27.3%). Like Cluster 4, individuals in Cluster 5 graduated from high school with comparably lower GPAs, although slightly more graduated with the requirements for university entrance—a rate that is still lower than the overall *Paths* sample.

Although Cluster 5 members spent the same median number of years in postsecondary as the overall sample, a lower proportion held baccalaureate degrees or higher by 2016 (45.4%). Like Cluster 4, only a small proportion of degree holders were in partnerships with baccalaureate degree holders by 2016. Transfer to other institutions was predominantly to universities and often with a delay of several years. In many ways, the employment outcomes of Cluster 5 members are comparable to the entire *Paths* sample: members have almost identical median Blishen scores (52), proportion of management responsibilities (44%), and median years of full-time employment (18%). Nevertheless, individuals in Cluster 5 have slightly higher median years of part-time employment (4.4) and lower median 2016 household incomes ($65,000). The median household income is only slightly higher than Cluster 4 even though individuals in Cluster 5 tended to spend more time in postsecondary education and were more likely to earn baccalaureate degrees.

Multinomial Logistic Regression Results

We next conduct multinomial logistic regression to predict cluster membership from the demographic, education, and employment indicators discussed above. The log likelihood ratio tests for the fitted model, shown in Table 2.2, are statistically significant and provide evidence that the inclusion of independent variables improves the overall model fit in predicting the likelihood of respondents being in any cluster other than the reference category (i.e., Cluster 1, university only). The parameter estimates and corresponding relative risk ratios compare each cluster to Cluster 1. A relative risk ratio is interpreted as the change in the odds for each one unit change

Table 2.2 Multinomial logistic regression comparing Cluster 1 to all other clusters

	Cluster 2 Coef. (std. err)	Cluster 2 Relative risk	Cluster 3 Coef. (std. err)	Cluster 3 Relative risk	Cluster 4 Coef. (std. err)	Cluster 4 Relative risk	Cluster 5 Coef. (std. err)	Cluster 5 Relative risk
Demographic characteristics								
Gender (women = 1)	−0.428 (0.418)		−0.247 (0.442)		0.412 (0.452)		0.333 (0.446)	
Parental education (have baccalaureate degree or higher = 1)	0.114 (0.386)		0.103 (0.400)		−0.703 (0.434)		−0.513 (0.422)	
Location of high school graduation (metropolitan area = 1)	−0.234 (0.396)		−1.881*** (0.442)	0.152	−1.946*** (0.450)	0.142	−1.126** (0.426)	0.324
High school outcomes								
Graduated HS with the requirements for university entrance (yes = 1)	0.807 (0.694)		−0.119 (0.624)		−0.09 (0.603)		−0.388 (0.591)	
GPA[a]	−0.273 (0.305)		−1.387*** (0.295)	0.249	−1.526*** (0.300)	0.217	−1.817*** (0.298)	0.163
Postsecondary education outcomes								
Years of part-time or full-time postsecondary education[b]	−0.526*** (0.114)	0.591	−0.306** (0.098)	0.737	−0.627*** (0.117)	0.534	−0.183 (0.098)	
Baccalaureate degree or higher by 2016 (yes = 1)	−0.281 (0.644)		0.183 (0.645)		−1.323* (0.655)	0.266	−1.591* (0.639)	0.204
Participant with degree or higher in a partnership with a degree holder by 2016 (yes = 1)	−0.250 (0.418)		−0.756 (0.437)		0.098 (0.504)		−0.312 (0.486)	

Work and income outcomes

Years of full-time employment	0.016		−0.026		0.035
	(0.051)		(0.050)		(0.052)
Years of part-time employment	0.065		0.119		0.126
	(0.064)		(0.064)		(0.067)
2016 household income in thousands of dollars[c]	−0.001		−0.001		−0.004
	(0.002)		(0.003)		(0.004)
Current/most recent 2016 job has management responsibilities (yes = 1)	−0.574		−0.010		0.009
	(0.375)		(0.385)		(0.391)
Blishen score for current or most recent 2010 job[d]	−0.014		0.018		0.010
	(0.015)		(0.015)		(0.016)
				1.170	
					0.038
					(0.052)
					0.157*
					(0.065)
					−0.002
					(0.004)
					0.304
					(0.393)
					−0.001
					(0.016)
Intercept	4.408*		8.991***		11.309***	10.680***
	(2.204)		(2.116)		(2.163)	(2.147)

*$p < 0.05$, **$p < 0.01$, ***$p < 0.001$; $N = 450$; McFadden's Adjusted $R^2 = 0.26$; $\chi^2_{(52)} = 362.6$, $p < 0.001$

[a]Range 1–6

[b]Full-time = 1 month, part-time = 0.5 month

[c]Self-reported estimation of total household income (before taxes and deductions) adjusted for household size

[d]Range 23–102

in its corresponding independent variable, holding all other indicators constant. Finally, two key assumptions of multinomial logistic regression are as follows: (1) each nominal outcome cluster does not impact the effect of independent variables in other categories and (2) outcome clusters are distinguishable. Independence of irrelevant alternative (IIA) tests were non-significant and thus indicate that the IIA assumption is not violated. Likewise, Wald tests of whether two outcomes can be combined were all significant, indicating that no clusters should be combined.

The results in Table 2.2 demonstrate that respondents who graduated from high schools in metropolitan areas have a lower relative risk (e.g., lower odds) of being in Clusters 3, 4, and 5. That is, graduating from a metropolitan area increased the likelihood of entering university directly. Likewise, a higher GPA decreased the relative risk of being in one of the university transfer clusters. Gender, parental education, and graduating high school with the requirements for university entrance were not statistically significant when comparing Cluster 1 to all other clusters.[2] An examination of postsecondary outcomes reveals that participants who spent less time attending postsecondary institutions were more likely to be members of Clusters 2, 3, or 4. Confirming the descriptive statistics above, participants in Clusters 4 and 5 were less likely to hold baccalaureate degrees or higher by 2016. A comparison of work and income outcomes demonstrates that rates of full-time employment, household income, management responsibilities, or occupational prestige are not statistically significant when comparing Cluster 1 to all other clusters. Nevertheless, individuals in Cluster 4 have a slightly higher likelihood of part-time employment compared to Cluster 1.

Discussion and Conclusion

Educational systems can be designed to keep individuals out or to invite them in. The vertically segregated system adopted in the 1960s in British Columbia, Canada was designed to do both. The vertically segregated

---

[2] Statistically significant in multinomial regression is based on the cluster of comparison. For example, if Cluster 2 was chosen as the reference, there would be a significant gender and parental difference for Cluster 4.

nature of the system sorted individuals into either non-university institutions or universities. Nevertheless, the articulation component allowed for a considerable amount of inter-institutional transfer. Over the years of the *Paths on Life's Way* project, the transfer component has expanded dramatically. As featured in Cluster 2, the nature of transfer has changed to the extent that a number of individuals have participated in reverse transfer; that is, they have transferred from universities to non-university institutions. Nowadays, it is common to consider all public postsecondary institutions within the British Columbia constellation as both sending and receiving institutions. This phenomenon was not envisioned by the original architects of the system.

To what extent do ascriptive characteristics have "dissipating" or "lingering" effects on these outcomes? According to our findings, we argue that there is evidence of both effects. Almost 96% of respondents had attended postsecondary institutions sometime between 1988 and 2016 and 59% had earned at minimum baccalaureate credentials, which could be argued to be evidence of dissipating effects. However, lower levels of participation and degree completion are reflected in comparably lower levels of median household income 28 years after high school graduation for Clusters 3, 4, and 5. Having spouses with earned bachelor's degrees or greater, known as assortative mating, is highest in Cluster 1. As such, Cluster 1 members tend to be in high income families who are able to pool and share resources (Esping-Andersen 2009; Schwartz 2013, p. 452). Also, it is an increasingly troubling form of social reproduction. Also demonstrating this cumulative impact, median occupational prestige scores are highest for the three clusters with high levels of earned baccalaureate degrees.

The lingering effect of gender is reflected in non-university participation—at least initially—which supports Charles and Bradley's (2002) hypothesis that expansion of non-university sectors of higher education with the "ideals of universalism do more to undermine vertical segregation" (p. 574) by diverting women away from elite institutions. Our findings suggest that the gender effect is compounded by geographic location: women from urban/rural and remote communities appeared to be less likely than men to move to more metropolitan locations to commence university study directly out of high school. Frenette (2004) demonstrates that the mean earnings in Canada over a 20-year period were $728,000 for men with baccalaureate credentials; for women with the same credentials, the figure is $442,000. In other words, even women with earned bachelor's degrees earn substantially less than men with the same credentials. Also, as Foley and Green (2016) point out, earnings by women with university degrees are considerably higher than earnings by women who have graduated from the non-university sector. Women with non-university credentials are even more disadvantaged and these effects are clearly lingering.

At the beginning of this paper we asked, *how does a vertically segregated articulated system of higher education have an impact on the educational, occupational, and other life course outcomes of individuals from young adulthood through to middle age?* As evidenced in varying ways for all clusters, the structure of the system facilitated both participation in and transfer among institutions, which in turn had an impact on other life outcomes. If baccalaureate degree completion serves as evidence of high academic quality and standards, then the higher education system in British Columbia, in relation to the *Paths* sample, has been a success. No less than 29% in any cluster earned this credential. However, the system works in tandem with ascriptive characteristics to determine by which cluster one is defined. Multivariate analyses highlight that high school GPA and having grown up in a metropolitan area continued to have significant effects in terms of cluster determination 28 years after high school graduation.

In closing, it must be noted that the respondents to all phases of the 28 years of the Paths project could be considered the "best case scenario" in that they were all high school graduates and that the sample is slightly biased toward women, higher achievers in high school, and postsecondary graduates. Despite the limitations of the sample, differences among clusters in educational and occupational outcomes remain.

References

Abbott, A. (1990). A primer on sequence methods. *Organization Science, 1*(4), 375–392.

Andres, L. (2002). *Paths on life's way. Phase II follow-up survey, 1993. Five years later (revised)*. Vancouver: Department of Educational Studies, University of British Columbia.

Andres, L. (2009). The cumulative impact of capital and identity construction across time: A fifteen year perspective of Canadian young women and men. In K. Robson & C. Saunders (Eds.), *Quantifying theory: Bourdieu* (pp. 75–88). Berlin: Springer.

Andres, L. (2015). Taking stock of 50 years of participation in Canadian higher education. In M. Shah, A. K. Bennett, & E. Southgate (Eds.), *Widening higher education participation: A global perspective* (pp. 15–33). Oxford: Elsevier.

Andres, L., & Dawson, J. (1998). *Investigating transfer project. Phase III. A history of transfer policy and practice in British Columbia* (Research report prepared for the BC Council on Admissions and Transfer). Vancouver: BC Council on Admissions and Transfer.

Andres, L., & Krahn, H. (1999). Youth pathways in articulated systems: Enrolment and completion patterns of urban young men and women. *Canadian Journal of Higher Education, 19*(1), 47–82.

Andres, L., & Offerhaus, J. (2012). *The mosaic of post-secondary institutional attendance: A twenty-two year perspective.* Vancouver: BC Council on Admissions and Transfer. Retrieved from http://edst.educ.ubc.ca/sites/edst.educ.ubc.ca/files/faculty_uploads/u20/BCCAT

Arrow, K. (1973). Higher education as a filter. *Journal of Public Economics, 2*, 193–216.

Bidwell, C. E., & Friedkin, N. E. (1988). The sociology of education. In N. Smelser (Ed.), *Handbook of sociology* (pp. 449–470). Beverly Hills: Sage.

Brint, S., & Karabel, J. (1989). The diverted dream. In *Community colleges and the promise of educational opportunity in America, 1900–1985*. New York: Oxford University Press.

Charles, M., & Bradley, K. (2002). Equal but separate? A cross-national study of sex segregation in higher education. *American Sociological Review, 67*(4), 573–599.

Clark, B. (1960). *The "cooling-out" function in higher education.* New York: The Free Press.

Clark, B. (1973). Development of the sociology of higher education. *Sociology of Education, 46*(1), 2–14.

Cowin, J. R. (2017). *Public policy and the structural development of postsecondary education in British Columbia, Canada, 1960–2015* (Unpublished PhD dissertation). University of British Columbia, Vancouver. Retrieved from https://open.library.ubc.ca/cIRcle/collections/ubctheses/24/items/1.0342720

Davies, S., & Guppy, N. (1997). Fields of study, college selectivity, and student inequalities in higher education. *Social Forces, 75*(4), 1417–1438.

Esping-Andersen, G. (2009). *The incomplete revolution. Adapting to women's new roles*. Cambridge: Polity Press.

Foley, K., & Green, D. A. (2016). Why more education will not solve rising inequality (and may make it worse). In D. A. Green, W. C. Riddell, & F. St-Hilaire (Eds.), *Income inequality: The Canadian story* (pp. 347–298). Montreal: The Institute for Research on Public Policy (IRPP).

Frenette, M. (2004). Access to college and university: Does distance to school matter? *Canadian Public Policy, 30*(4), 427–443.

Halpin, B. (2014). *Sequence analysis tools for Stata* (Working paper no. WP2014-03). Ireland: Department of Sociology, University of Limerick. Retrieved from https://ulir.ul.ie/bitstream/handle/10344/3783/Halpin_2014_SADI.pdf?sequence=2

Hilbe, J. M. (2009). *Logistic regression models*. Boca Raton: CRC Press.

Hosmer, D. W., Lemeshow, S., & Sturdivant, R. X. (2013). *Applied logistic regression* (3rd ed.). Hoboken: Wiley.

Krahn, H., Howard, A. L., & Galambos, N. L. (2015). Exploring or floundering? The meaning of employment and educational fluctuations in emerging adulthood. *Youth & Society, 47*(2), 245–266.

Macdonald, J. (1962). *Higher education in British Columbia and a plan for the future*. Vancouver: University of British Columbia.

Mare, R. D. (1980). Social background and school continuation decisions. *Journal of the American Statistical Association, 75*, 295–305.

Müller, W., & Karle, W. (1993). Social selection in educational systems in Europe. *European Sociological Review, 9*(1), 1–23.

OECD. (2011). *Divided we stand – Why inequality keeps rising*. Paris: Organisation for Economic Cooperation and Development (OECD). Retrieved from http://www.oecd.org/social/inequality.htm

Pullman, A., & Andres, L. (2015). Two sides of the same coin?: Applied and general higher education gender stratification in Canada. *Comparative Social Research, 31*, 239–265.

Schwartz, C. R. (2013). Trends and variation in assortative mating: Causes and consequences. *Annual Review of Sociology, 39*(1), 451–470. Retrieved from http://www.annualreviews.org/doi/abs/10.1146/annurev-soc-071312-145544

StataCorp. (2015). *Stata statistical software: Release 14*. College Station: StataCorp.

Statistics Canada. (2016). *Education indicators in Canada: An international perspective*. Ottawa: Minister of Industry. Retrieved from http://www.statcan.gc.ca/pub/81-604-x/81-604-x2015001-eng.htm

Studer, M., Ritschard, G., Gabadinho, A., & Müller, N. S. (2011). Discrepancy analysis of state sequences. *Sociological Methods & Research, 40*(3), 471–510.

Triventi, M. (2013). Stratification in higher education and its relationship with social inequality: A comparative study of 11 European countries. *European Sociological Review, 29*(3), 489–502.

Turner, R. (1960). Sponsored and contest mobility and the school system. *American Sociological Review, 25*(6), 855–867.

3

Supporting Students' Learning: The Power of the Student–Teacher Relationship

Debra Cureton and Phil Gravestock

Higher Education Context in the UK

In 2014–15 there were 164 UK higher education providers (excluding further education colleges) in receipt of public funding (Universities UK, http://www.universitiesuk.ac.uk/facts-and-stats/Pages/higher-education-data.aspx). Figures from the Higher Education Statistics Agency (HESA) (http://www.hesa.ac.uk/) indicate that there were 1,435,415 full time undergraduate students studying higher education in the United Kingdom in 2015/16. Of these students, 55.4% were female and 44.6% were male; 12.3% had a known disability; 75.5% were White, 7.0% were Black, 11.3% were Asian and 5.4% were classed as 'Other' (including mixed).

D. Cureton (✉) • P. Gravestock
University of Wolverhampton, Wolverhampton, UK
e-mail: D.Cureton@wlv.ac.uk

© The Author(s) 2018
M. Shah, J. McKay (eds.), *Achieving Equity and Quality in Higher Education*, Palgrave Studies in Excellence and Equity in Global Education,
https://doi.org/10.1007/978-3-319-78316-1_3

Introduction

The basis of the evidence for this chapter stems from two projects funded by the Higher Education Academy (HEA). The first of these (Disparities in Student Attainment—DiSA) was conducted by Cousin and Cureton (2012) which considers differential outcomes in student success, and suggests that student success is affected by a number of components that fall into four interlinking categories. As these categories are not discrete it is important to consider how each can influence each other and most importantly how each of these influence and are influenced by the student–teacher–learning relationship. The four components are:

1. Relational Factors. This relates to the features influencing students' connectivity to their fellow students, the people who teach them, the departments in which they learn and the university in which they study. This connectivity relates strongly to the concept of student belongingness, which has been discussed extensively within the school sector (see Goodenow 1993; Anderman and Freeman 2004) and more recently in higher education (see Lee and Davis 2000; Tinto 2007; Martin and Dowson 2009; Trowler and Trowler 2010; Thomas 2012). There are a variety of factors that can influence the quality of learning relationships, which include students' perceptions of the level and types of respect that they are being offered and, in particular, whether students believe they are recognized as an 'individual'.
2. Aspects of Pedagogy. This refers to the inclusivity of the learning environment. It focuses mainly, but not exclusively, on the inclusivity of the curriculum.Cousin and Cureton (2012) observed that the focus for the majority of students and teachers fell on the accessibility of assessments, the related support on offer and how this impacts on student success; however, the findings also provided insights into what students appreciate about the curriculum, those who teach it and how this facilitates their success. Not surprisingly, this area of the research also proposes a strong link between accessible assessment process, facilitative learning environments and productive learning relationships.

3. Psycho-social Processes. A number of psychological and sociological processes have the potential to influence student success and can lead to marginalization if not challenged. This area relates to the Theory of Opportunity and challenges the manifestation of society's conceptions of who should be educated and whether the processes and knowledge of higher education are expressed in an accessible way. These include students' understanding of higher education as expressed through their pre-expectations and current expectations, and whether these are met. If a student feels that their expectations of higher education are not being met this can generate violations of their psychological contract (Cureton 2016), which is a set of powerful unspoken rules of engagement with a university. Violations of this contract can lead to psychological wounds, a lack of engagement, lower productivity and in severe cases can lead to withdrawal (Rousseau 1996). The findings also relate to the development of students' academic identity and provide useful insights into aspects of how students understand themselves in relation to their formal and informal education. These factors are recognized by Wenger (1998) and Falk and Balatti (2003) as ones that influence how students integrate into the academic community of practice. This process can be disrupted by students' fear of stereotype threat: the fear that those around them are thinking and behaving in a way that conforms to traditional stereotypes about particular social groups (Steele and Aronson 1995; Shih et al. 2011). Needless to say, this may not only impact on students' academic identity, but can also impact on their sense of belonging and can in turn affect the quality of learning relationships.
4. Social and cultural capital. This is the knowledge that students bring with them into higher education and can help them to negotiate and understand the physical and social structures of the environment or the habitus (Bourdieu 1987). It recognizes that for students to transition effectively into higher education they must construct new knowledge from the knowledge that they already possess. Cousin and Cureton (2012) observed that some students are challenged by the inaccessibility of the structure and practices of higher education, which impeded their agency or ability to act in an autonomous manner. In particular, student pre-expectations of higher education and

how realistic these are is important within this process. If students' pre expectations of higher education are unrealistic, they can form both psychological and physical barriers in their transition from further to higher education. Combining this with students' reports that they don't understand higher education systems or language, which hinders their ability to understand and action the rules of academic engagement, it is not surprising that students can struggle to understand the difference between further and higher education and transition successfully into and through higher education.

The second project focused on creating dialogue to challenge marginalization and was conducted by Cureton et al. (2017) as part of the Paul Hamlyn Foundation *What Works? Student Retention & Success* initiative, working with the HEA and Action on Access. The programme focused on increasing retention, progression and student success through induction, active learning or co-curricular initiatives that enhance students' sense of belonging. The programme investigated how the implementation of an inclusive student-led assessment process would impact positively on retention and success. The inclusive assessment process provides a clear, concise and understandable assessment brief and a set of guidelines to support student-led sessions to unpack and understand assignment briefs. As this work encourages an inclusive approach, it also provides a process to help reduce differential degree outcomes. As differences in the perceived sense of belonging between students categorized as Black and Minority Ethnic (BME) and their white counterparts was observed in this work, an institutional-wide belongingness study was carried out to understand the development of belongingness as a student progresses through their degree and the differences that occur as a result of demographic differences.

What Factors Influence the Student–Teacher Relationship?

Although traditional learning theories suggest that learning and performance are singular activities based within the individual (Hirst 2009), the concept of the learning relationship is not new. Drawing on historical philosophical and educational theories about the process of learning, learning relationships are evident, albeit implicit, within the principles proposed by Socrates, Rousseau, Dewey and Piaget, all of whom proposed a rich tradition of learning through dialogue, where the teacher promotes knowledge enhancement through the use of questions and exchange (Harding and Thompson 2011). These ideas move learning from the personal domain to the social domain, which highlights the need to recognize the affective and relational aspects of learning as much as the pedagogic environment. This concept is recognized in the American Psychological Association's (APA) research-validated Learner-centered Psychological Principles (APA 1997), which highlight the importance of attending to both the personal and the technical domain of learning to promote motivation, learning and achievement for all learners. It is also a central concept in Wenger's work around 'Communities of Practice' as the theory identifies that members of a community of practice are involved in a series of relationships that are established and developed over time (Lave and Wenger 1991). Moreover, the relational aspects involved in communities of practice allow members to undertake larger or more complex activities and projects than if they were working alone. This not only encourages greater individual growth, knowledge and skills acquisition, it binds people together and helps to facilitate stronger relationships and trust.

Ideas about how the social and dynamic aspects of pedagogy might operate is exemplified in Hirst's (2009) research that integrates Vygotsky's (1978) model of learning with Wenger's (1998) notion of Communities of Practice and Bronfenbrenner's (2001) Bioecological System Theory to explain the interactions and relationships a student has within their environment. Bioecological System Theory originally considered child development in relation to how layers of society can potentially impact on their learning. Bronfenbrenner proposed four systems within the environment. By placing the student at the centre of the system, Hirst (2009) illustrated how each system could impact on socially-oriented learning and the role that learning relationships play within this process at several levels.

1. Microsystem—the institutions and groups that immediately and directly impact on a learner's development (for example, family, educational system and peers). Students learn through their face-to-face relationships within the learning environment. Wenger's Communities of Practice model also operates at this level and provides information on how these microsystem relationships enable or disable participation and therefore learning
2. Mesosystem—the interaction between a learner and elements of the microsystem level (for example, between the learner and their learning system or the interaction between learners and their peers). Hirst proposes that Wenger's (1998) notion of participation within a Community of Practice is central to student learning in the mesosystem. The theory behind Communities of Practice provides a framework to explore how participation and therefore learning is enabled or disabled depending upon the different types of relationships with aspects of the setting that the students engage in. For example, the links between a student's university life and home life could be either facilitative or a barrier.
3. Exosystem—the links between an individual's social setting and their immediate context. For example, changes in the home learning environment or changes in their educational environment. An example of this might be how university practices and policies can impact upon students' relationships and how policy and practice may enable or disable students' participation and therefore their learning.
4. Macrosystem—the predominant culture and its contexts. Hirst believed that exploration of this level highlighted the wider cultural and political imperatives that operate at a sector level. This influences the students' relationships, participation and learning in many ways. For example, government promotion of widening participation in higher education means that there is now greater diversity in the undergraduate student body.

The above highlights that student learning is not a singular and individual activity. By reviewing the social and cultural domains in which pedagogy is applied, it becomes evident that learning relationships are multi-layered and multifaceted and therefore the student–teacher learning relationship is not discrete nor takes place within a vacuum. This

Case Study: Belongingness, Place and Space

The university implemented Mantz Yorke's Belongingness Scale and conducted focus groups to consider the role of place and space in students' sense of belongingness. The responses to the questionnaires were analyzed by the campus and faculty where students studied. This analysis highlighted that students who mostly study on smaller, discretely-identified and branded campuses have an enhanced sense of belonging compared with those who study on larger campuses or those without defined boundaries. This analysis also found that there was an interaction between campus and faculty, indicating that students who have identifiable home buildings have a higher sense of belonging. These findings were further explored via focus groups, which found that although belongingness was primarily affective and relational, some levels of belonging were located in buildings and the students' base campus. 'Our building' and 'our rooms' were important to students. It appears that students have an affective link to these rooms and feel an ownership and pride about the facilities they hold. It was felt that 'our spaces' 'allow students to interact with each other' (female student, second year) and encourage students to develop relationships and gain support. Students who did not have an 'our space' did not miss it but made their own 'our space': 'yeah we go to the library and meet there' (male student, third year). All agreed that 'mixing spaces that are not social learning space are important to meeting people and feeling that you belong; it gives students a reason to stay' (male student, second year).

Students also noted that although space was important in the development of belongingness, it also has negative implications. Having your own space can facilitate 'the occurrence of cliques and they just make you feel like you don't belong' (female student, second year). In terms of academic activities, students noted that although students 'don't like it, they want to be pushed to mix with other students on their course' (male student, third year); they recognized the importance of meeting others, experiencing diversity and learning from others' experiences and felt that having the space to meet and interact both socially and academically was important. Students agreed that 'seminars are important in encouraging the development of belonging, because small groups and seminars are important ways to mix, meet others and feel that you belong' (female student, first year). Students commented that the rooms that seminars take place in often '... stop us from mixing. When the tables are set out in rows you can't move around so you end up working with the people that you chose to sit by. You just don't mix with other people' (male student, second year). As a solution, students proposed that having time and space in the curriculum and places where cross-university gatherings can take place, was important to encouraging student belonging. For example, 'The International Fayre was good; you meet people from all over the world. Having places on campus, and time in the curriculum to develop relationships and work with peers, is really important' (female international student, second year).

suggests that engagement in a learning relationship can be enabled or disabled through processes in the environment which impact upon the student, the teacher or both.

In their report for the Higher Education Funding Council for England (HEFCE) Mountford-Zimdars et al. (2015) reviewed the sector intelligence relating to differential degree outcomes. They concluded that in order to consider student success factors, the influences within and outside the university environment had to be taken into account. Mountford-Zimdars et al. (2015) recognized that the macro, meso and micro systems influence the inclusivity of the learning environment and therefore the interactions that take place within it. Mountford-Zimdars et al. (2015) also acknowledge that these levels impact on curricula and learning, relationships between staff and students, social, cultural and economic capital and psychosocial and identity factors, all of which Cousin and Cureton (2012) suggest impact on the quality of learning relationships.

Curricula and Learning

Drawing on Cureton et al. (2017) and Cousin and Cureton (2012), an inclusive curricula and learning environment are the gateway to supportive learning relationships for all students. An inclusive learning environment supports students' academic and social engagement, whilst inclusive curricula encourage academic engagement. It is through these activities that students commence their journey toward gaining a sense of belonging (Cureton 2016) and are retained and attain in higher education (Singh 2011). In particular, an inclusive approach to assessment is crucial not only to retention and success but to encouraging and supporting the development of the student–teacher relationship. Cousin and Cureton (2012) observed that good assignment briefs reduce student anxiety, raise their confidence in their ability to achieve and, crucially, impact on attainment. When reflecting on why accessible assessment practices, in particular assessable assignment briefs, influence the student–teacher learning relationship, it is important to consider the work of Howell-Richardson (2012), who identified that students often believe that there is a hidden 'trick question' within assignment briefs and it is the role of the student to uncover the 'golden key' in order to deliver the 'right answer' required by the assessment brief. Obviously this is not the case and so when students approach their lecturers to ask advice in regard to assessment they repeatedly ask the same questions in an attempt to expose the 'golden key'. This is a fruitless task as there is no 'golden key' and students feel that lecturers are deliberately being evasive while lecturers are frustrated by being repeatedly asked the same questions. Through this interaction, students and their teachers are engaged in a fracas on a pedagogic battlefield which, if the dynamic is not identified and dealt with, could damage the quality of the learning relationship.

Relationships Between Staff and Students

The second area that influences student success at the micro, meso and macro levels is the learning relationship between staff and students (Mountford-Zimdars et al. 2015). Murphy (2009) highlights that social relationships encourage a student in their transition to becoming a 'fish in water' as academic relationships support students' academic and social integration into higher education. This is a notion that is also promoted by phase one of the *What Works?* Programme, which not only stresses the importance of the learning relationship in student success, but also recognizes the importance of building early and good social relationships with other students and staff (Thomas 2012). This is important because it not only supports transition but also promotes the perception of caring and reliable support which is crucial in underpinning pedagogical strategies that create a safe educational setting to stimulate and challenge students. Field and Morgan-Klein (2012) note that staff and student relationships provide both practical support and symbolic value, as they foster intellectual development and encourage a sense of belonging in higher education.

Access to learning relationships might be hampered for some groups of students, which reduces their opportunities to be successful (Cousin and Cureton 2012). One of these barriers is students' fear of stereotype threat. This is the students' fear that the lecturer may apply a stereotype to them that is based on appearance and that they may behave according to the beliefs they hold about the stereotype, rather than from what they know about the individual (Cousin and Cureton 2012). This is partially supported by Frumkin and Koutsoubou (2013) who found that BME students in further education reported that if teaching staff demonstrated that they were knowledgeable about a student's culture it led to them feeling an increased sense of inclusion.

Cousin and Cureton (2012) reported that both lecturers and students highlighted that good learning relationships are crucial to student success. Moreover, both lecturers and students identified three areas of importance that were facilitative in learning relationships:

1. The nature and quality of the learning relationship. The learning relationship should be positive, development-focused, inclusive, fair and respectful.
2. A demonstration of respect. Respect should be at the core of a learning relationship and that respect should be from student to lecturer and lecturer to student.
3. Open pathways of communication. Communication between students and lecturers should be encouraged and easy. Students did not mind how communication took place, as long as the questions they had were recognized as important and responded to.

An aspect of the learning relationship that was strongly related to the promotion of BME student success was termed 'the role of the interlocutor' (Cousin and Cureton 2012), or someone who takes part in a dialogue or conversation. In this case the dialogue or conversation is about a student's potential and often introduces the student to the concept of their potential to be successful, thereby opening their minds to the possibility that they are good students who have the opportunity to gain a good degree. The interlocutor therefore facilitates the student to continue a discourse around their ability to be successful beyond the lecturer's intervention: it is, in essence, aspiration-raising.

Case Study: Belongingness and Retention

The role of belongingness in retention was discussed in a number of guises. In its most explicit form, belongingness provided students with a sense of resilience, normative experience and a belief that they mattered to their peers and teachers during turbulent times.

Students discussed the role that their sense of belongingness played during the times that they questioned whether university was right for them. Some students discussed incidents that had led them to consider leaving university and how members of the academic community had intervened, which had led to a decision to stay. Much of this focus was on members of staff 'going beyond the call of duty' (female Students' Union—SU—Officer reflecting on her recent undergraduate experience), which led students to feel that they were cared about. The literature indicates that not having a sense of belonging is a critical factor in students leaving higher education (Thomas 2012); however, 'lecturers can generate belonging when it isn't present by being open to students, by showing respect; it's almost as if they are demonstrating that they see something worthwhile in you and that matters' (female, SU Officer). It is important to remember this at times when belongingness has been lost or was never felt in the first place: 'lecturers can lose students by being rude, unapproachable, unavailable, destructive rather than constructive, acting like they can't be bothered, like not answering questions and emails, or by providing generic feedback to students. And stereotyping us' (male student, BME, third year); however, just as belongingness can be lost it can also be retrieved or even built at any point of the student lifecycle. Discussing the lack of belongingness throughout the majority of his degree, one student talked about how he was 'enticed into being part of the group' by lecturers who 'reached out [to him] and made an effort to understand [him]'. By implementing an invitational approach and demonstrating that he saw the student as an individual, with potential, the lecturer was viewed as 'going beyond the call of duty', which in turn opened a door to developing trust and a facilitative learning relationship to develop. Or, as the student described it, 'he made an effort and no one did that before. He told me I had to go to lectures, they were important, I didn't know that right, so I started going to lectures. You know, when I went to lectures I started to feel I fitted in'.

Belongingness also supports students in developing their psychological resilience, self-confidence and their evolving academic identity. Again this increases their likelihood to weather stormy situations. A sense of belonging provides students with 'emotional and psychological strength' (female international student, third year), 'because it helps students build their confidence' (female student, third year), and it helps 'understanding of how to cope' (female student, second year); through which students 'find themselves; personally and academically' (female student, third year) thereby

(continued)

(continued)
facilitating the development of personal and academic identity. Students also talk of the normative value of having a sense of belonging and how it can 'normalize their university experience' especially when family and friends at home do not understand the demands of higher education: 'here [at university] you can talk to people about things that are going on and they understand and say yeah I know what it is like, it happened to me, but if I said it to my mum she has no idea what I'm talking about' (female student, third year). Through the normalizing experience, students are able to gain reassurance during times of stress: 'you have this huge sense of relief when someone says yeah we all feel like this sometime' (female student, second year).This also helps to generate a sense of safety that allows students to 'vent when it's all going wrong' (female student, third year). Moreover, having a sense of belonging was equated to having a sense of 'camaraderie' (female student, second year) in which students are 'sharing a journey, growing together and learning from each other' (male student, second year). The 'socialising' aspect of this provides 'a sounding board' (female SU representative) as well as helping student to 'settle in and feel part of the family' (female student, second year).

Psychosocial Aspects

The third area that can impact on the development of learning relationships falls in the psychosocial domain. The impact of stereotype threat, having a sense of belongingness and being seen as an individual are all psychosocial factors that can influence the development of a learning relationship; however, it is necessary to revisit the concept of being seen as an individual. Mountford-Zimdars et al. (2015) propose that avoiding the damaging psychological effects of not being seen as an individual is crucial to students' self-confidence, particularly if this relates to staff stereotyping students in ways that suggest that they have negative attitudes towards students' innate ability to achieve. Support for this idea is offered by both Dhanda (2010) and Stevenson (2012), both of whom propose that tutors' attitudes and expectations play a significant role in the process of success.

Just as psychosocial factors can affect learning relations, the quality of learning relationships can also affect psychosocial aspects of the learning environment. For example, interruptions in the formation of positive relationships with tutors and students can negatively affect the development of a coherent academic identity for students. This is a process of co-construction, which results from the on-going negotiations of the daily academic experience, interactions with others and students' reflections on those experiences (Lave and Wenger 1991; Wenger 1998; Eckert and Wenger 2005). In other words, the development of a coherent and authentic identity is reliant on the student being involved in rich, respectful and developmental interactions within the university environment and its inhabitants.

Social and Cultural Capital or Habitus

The final factor that can influence the development of learning relationships is students' understanding of habitus. Cousin and Cureton (2012) presented evidence that some students struggle to access the cultural and social knowledge that allows them to understand the rules of academic engagement, and more importantly the language used to communicate in higher education. This creates barriers to forming academic learning relationships for a number of reasons. Firstly, a lack of a common language and understanding of the meanings of key concepts in higher education makes communication between students and lecturers difficult. Secondly, not understanding habitus suggests that it is possible that students may not understand the value of academic learning relationships, or know how to or have the confidence to cultivate these. Traditionally, not understanding habitus has been tackled by providing mentoring relationships (Action on Access 2011; Dhanda 2010; NUS 2011), supporting family, friends and local communities to better understand higher education (Byfield 2008; Singh 2011; Cousin and Cureton 2012), and developing social or cultural networks to help break down barriers (Mountford-Zimdars et al. 2015).

Now that factors have been identified that can affect the development of successful learning relationships, it is important to consider how these are viewed by those involved and how differences in perception might impact on students and their success.

What Do Students Most Appreciate in Learning Relationships?

The DiSA project provided considerable evidence that could offer answers to this question. Firstly, what students most appreciate in learning relationships is strongly associated with the behaviours and attitudes that students most appreciate in their lecturers. With the specific focus on the attitudes and behaviours demonstrated by lecturers that encourage good inclusive quality learning relationships, students suggested that they appreciated lecturers who:

- were enthusiastic about the subjects that they taught and also demonstrated a passion for teaching;
- were good communicators and able to communicate clearly not only the complexities of the theoretical aspects of the discipline, but also the assignment expectations;
- listened to them and encouraged questions. Students wanted to be able to ask questions and receive answers. They did not mind how this was facilitated (e.g. lecture, online forum, email, office hours), as long as they felt heard and the questions were answered;
- generated respectful learning environments that recognized and valued the contributions of all students, especially if this demonstrated that the lecturers were valuing students' prior knowledge;
- were invitational and encouraged students into learning interactions with them; and
- saw students as individuals and valued their uniqueness rather than using group identities or stereotypes as a basis for their interactions. In other words students respected lecturers who did not generate a stereotype threat.

It is proposed that through these activities lecturers locate learning in both the affective and cognitive domains and utilize the strengths of both these areas in the creation of a dialogic classroom (Bowers 2005). Through these activities the learning relationship opens a door for students to access knowledge above and beyond their discipline-related activities, and provides access to the possibility of developing their academic skills knowledge as well as their cultural and social knowledge.

The question of whether students and teachers view learning relationships in similar ways, and whether there are potential effects on success if any differences in perception exist, can also be answered using evidence from the DiSA project.

In the case of students, learning relationships are defined as two-way. This is encapsulated by the students' belief that:

> We build a relationship and through this relationship we share information that will enable me to gain my degree. (female student, second year)

While lecturers believe that learning relationships are one-way and commonly define these in terms of:

> I provide you [the students] with the where with all to get your degree. (female, Senior Lecturer)

Again the data suggested that students saw respect as a two-way process whereas staff saw this as a one-way practice. Students' definition of respect is summarized as:

> I show you [the lecturers] and my fellow students respect; you show me respect. (male student, third year)

Whereas lecturers define respect in the learning relationship as:

> I create a respectful learning environment for your learning. (female, Lecturer)

These differences can have an impact on the quality of learning relationships which could relate to violations in the psychological contract and could result in students withdrawing their engagement and losing motivation. This could also damage students' trust in the lecturers, which could be very damaging as this is the foundation of all relationships; however, DiSA also identified the impact of matching expectations between students and their teachers. One part of the study considered the pedagogic approaches of lecturers in modules where there were no attainment gaps. The common pedagogic techniques employed by these lecturers were:

- activities to encourage good learning relationships;
- engendering respectful interactions;
- recognizing the student as an individual;
- encouraging good communication; and
- providing opportunities to discuss work.

There are strong overlaps between these activities and the attitudes and behaviours that students appreciated in learning relationships. This suggests that where there is consistency in expectations, success is likely to follow. It could therefore be argued that there is an affiliation between what students most appreciate in learning relations, students' and teachers' views of learning relationships and the impact of these on student success.

What Can We Do to Encourage Facilitative Learning Relationships?

Considering the above in light of what practitioners can do to facilitate learning relationships and the success of all students, it is suggested that interventions that affect the development of quality learning relationships should be taken seriously in all learning interactions. It is also imperative to ensure that lecturers' definitions of learning relationships match students' definitions and that differences in expectations are communicated explicitly. Interventions should explore students' expectations of their educational environment and encourage the development of shared expectations to help to ensure that students' psychological contracts are not violated in any way. Opportunities for dialogue are important and these conversations should be respectful of, and build on, students' prior knowledge and provide students with opportunities to enhance their social and cultural capital in order to help them better understand their new habitus. This has already been discussed in relation to the Theory of Learning, which proposes that for students to make an effective transition into higher education they must construct new knowledge from the foundations provided by knowledge that they already possess. Moreover, a core aim of pedagogic development should be the facilitation of heightening students' aspirations.

The role of the interlocutor in these processes is also very powerful. The interlocutor intervenes where students have the ability to gain a good honours degree, to help them take their first steps to recognize this and where possible to provide advice or mentorship to aid them in their development; however, this intervention could potentially support the enhancement of student success at every level. This effect is seen in the impact of the interlocutor in group settings, highlighting the role and importance of the use of positive language in the classroom and the impact that lecturers' positive expectations can have on an individual's confidence and on the likelihood of them developing a positive learning relationship with their teachers. This is further supported by the DiSA project that emphasized the importance of communicating high expectations and concluded that stretching students intellectually influences aspiration and engagement positively (Cousin and Cureton 2012). Evidence of the impact of positive expectations and related intellectual challenge on student success is plentiful and has formed recommendations in numerous research programmes (Berry and Loke 2011; Singh 2011). This has also been found to be powerful when emphasized in continuing professional development (CPD) programmes for academic staff (Sanders and Rose-Adams 2014), although the complexity of the relationship between aspiration-raising and student success should be recognized (Mountford-Zimdars et al. 2015).

Indeed complexity is prolific in this area of work and attention to intersectionality is crucial. For example, CPD for teaching staff should recognize ways in which pedagogy and learning relationships are profoundly shaped by inequalities of gender, race and class and should provide more resources and support to lecturers to enhance their ways of understanding this (Burke et al. 2013).

Moreover, while research suggests that aspirations may be higher among low socio-economic groups than is generally believed (Cummings et al. 2012), little is known about how this is shaped by gender and/or race and the role that these factors play in student success. It is, however, important to ensure that relevant information, advice and guidance is delivered at appropriate times, to help learners in their understanding of the pathways to achieving their ambitions (Mountford-Zimdars et al. 2015).

Having a sense of belonging is of upmost importance to both student success and the development of productive learning relationships. Cureton et al. (2017) suggest that students' sense of belonging is multi-layered and multifaceted and impacts on affective and cognitive aspects of learning and social aspects of higher education. Activities that inspire the development of relationships with peers and lecturers, as well as encouraging an alliance with the academic department that students study in, are essential. Again this should be the central aim of pedagogic development; however, the role of students' pre-expectations of higher education should not be overlooked and in particular how pre-expectations of higher education can influence the development of effective relationships. Both pedagogic development and CPD for staff need to support a better understanding of potential difference in the expectations between students and their teaching team, in order to ensure that students' psychological contracts are not violated.

Concluding Comment

The affective aspect of learning is an important and influential factor in students' opportunities to be successful in higher education; however, the affective domain is not discrete and is influenced by, and influences, psycho-social aspects of the learning environment, the curricula and learning, and cultural, social and economic capital. All these factors need to be taken in to consideration when evaluating and enhancing the student–teacher relationship.

References

Action on Access. (2011). *Social mobility through higher education: Promoting the success of all students*. Ormskirk: Action on Access. Retrieved from http://www.heacademy.ac.uk/resources/detail/action-on-access/Promoting_Success_of_all_Students.

Anderman, L. H., & Freeman, T. M. (2004). Students' sense of belonging in school. In P. R. Pintrich & M. L. Maehr (Eds.), *Advances in motivation and achievement: Vol. 13. Motivating students, improving schools: The legacy of Carol Midgley* (pp. 27–63). Greenwich: JAI Press.

APA (Americal Psychological Association). (1997). *Learner-centered psychological principles: A framework for school reform and redesign*. Washington, DC: American Psychological Association.

Berry, J., & Loke, G. (2011). *Improving the degree attainment of Black and minority ethnic students*. York: Higher Education Academy and Equality Challenge Unit.

Bourdieu, P. (1987). What makes a social class? On the theoretical and practical existence of groups. *Berkeley Journal of Sociology, 32*, 1–17.

Bowers, R. (2005). Freire (with Bakhtin) and the dialogic classroom seminar. *The Alberta Journal of Educational Research, 51*(4), 368–378.

Bronfenbrenner, U. (2001). The bioecological theory of human development. In U. Bronfenbrenner (Ed.), (2005) *Making human beings human: Biological perspectives on human development* (pp. 3–15). London: Sage.

Burke, P. J., Crozier, G., Read, B., Hall, J., Peat, J., & Francis, B. (2013). *Formations of gender and higher education pedagogies* (National Teaching Fellowship Scheme Final Report).

Byfield, C. (2008). *Black boys can make it: How they overcome the obstacles to university in the UK and USA*. London: Trentham.

Cousin, G., & Cureton, D. (2012). *Disparities in student attainment (DiSA)*. York: Higher Education Academy.

Cummings, C., Laing, K., Law, J., McLaughlin, J., Papps, I., Todd, L., & Woolner, P. (2012). *Can changing aspirations and attitudes impact on educational attainment?* York: Joseph Rowntree Foundation.

Cureton, D. (2016). The secret of their success. In G. Steventon, D. Cureton, & L. Clouder (Eds.), *Student attainment in higher education*. London: Routledge.

Cureton, D., Groves, M., Day, P., & Williams, C. (2017). *Supporting student success: Strategies for institutional change*. University of Wolverhampton. London: Paul Hamlyn Foundation. Retrieved from http://www.phf.org.uk/wp-content/uploads/2017/04/University-of-Wolverhampton-final.pdf.

Dhanda, M. (2010). *Understanding disparities in student attainment: Black and minority ethnic students' experience*. Wolverhampton: University of Wolverhampton. Retrieved from http://www2.wlv.ac.uk/equalopps/mdsummary.pdf

Eckert, P., & Wenger, E. (2005). Communities of practice in sociolinguistics. *Journal of Sociolinguistics, 9*, 582–589.

Falk, I., & Balatti, J. (2003). Role of identity in VET learning. In J. Searle, I. Yashin-Shaw, & D. Roebuck (Eds.), *Enriching Learning Cultures: Proceedings of the 11th Annual International Conference on Post-compulsory Education and Training* (Vol. 1, pp. 179–186). Brisbane: Australian Academic Press.

Field, J., & Morgan-Klein, N. (2012). The importance of social support structures for retention and success. In T. Hinton-Smith (Ed.), *Widening participation in higher education: Casting the net wide?* (Issues in Higher Education, pp. 178–192). Basingstoke: Palgrave Macmillan.

Frumkin, L. A., & Koutsoubou, M. (2013). Exploratory investigation of drivers of attainment in ethnic minority adult learners. *Journal of Further and Higher Education, 37*(2), 147–162.

Goodenow, C. (1993). Classroom belonging among early adolescent students: Relationships to motivation and achievement. *Journal of Early Adolescence, 13*, 21–43.

Harding, J., & Thompson, J. (2011). *Dispositions to stay – And to succeed*. Newcastle: Northumbria University.

Hirst, B. (2009, March 23–April 2). Learning in higher education – The impact of relationships. In *University of Huddersfield Research Festival*. University of Huddersfield.

Howell-Richardson, C. (2012). *Challenges in academic writing' project* (Unpublished research data). Coventry University: Centre for Academic Writing.

Lave, J., & Wenger, E. (1991). *Situated learning. Legitimate peripheral participation*. Cambridge: University of Cambridge Press.

Lee, R. M., & Davis, C. (2000). Cultural orientation, past multicultural experience and a sense of belonging on campus for Asian American college students. *Journal of College Student Development, 41*(1), 110–115.

Martin, A., & Dowson, M. (2009). Interpersonal relationships, motivation, engagement, and achievement: Yields for theory, current issues, and educational practice. *Review of Educational Research, 79*(1), 327–365.

Mountford-Zimdars, A., Sabri, D., Moore, J., Sanders, J., Jones, S., & Higham, L. (2015). *Policies & reports, practitioners, support, widening participation.*

HEFCE | King's College London, ARC Network and the University of Manchester.

Murphy, J. (2009). *The educator's handbook for understanding and closing achievement gaps*. Thousand Oaks: Corwin Press.

NUS. (2011). *Race for equality: A report on the experiences of Black students in further and higher education*. London: National Union of Students. Retrieved from http://www.nus.org.uk/PageFiles/12350/NUS_Race_for_Equality_web.pdf

Rousseau, D. M. (1996). *Psychological contracts in organizations: Understanding written and unwritten agreements*. Cambridge, MA: Sage.

Sanders, J., & Rose-Adams, J. (2014). Black and minority ethnic student attainment: A survey of research and exploration of the importance of teacher and student expectations. *Widening Participation and Lifelong Learning, 16*(2), 5–27.

Shih, M. J., Pittinsky, T. L., & Ho, G. C. (2011). Stereotype boost: Positive outcomes from the activation of positive stereotypes. In M. Inzlicht & T. Schmader (Eds.), *Stereotype threat: Theory, process, and application*. New York: Oxford University Press.

Singh, G. (2011). *Black and minority ethnic (BME) students' participation in higher education: Improving retention and success. A synthesis of research evidence*. York: Higher Education Academy.

Steele, C. M., & Aronson, J. (1995). Stereotype threat and the intellectual test performance of African Americans. *Journal of Personality and Social Psychology, 69*(5), 797–811.

Stevenson, J. (2012). *Black and minority ethnic student degree retention and attainment*. York: Higher Education Academy.

Thomas, L. (2012). *Building student engagement and belonging at a time of change in higher education*. London: Paul Hamlyn Foundation.

Tinto, V. (2007). Research and practice of student retention: What next? *Journal of College Student Retention: Research, Theory & Practice, 8*(1), 1–19.

Trowler, P., & Trowler, V. (2010). *Student engagement evidence summary*. York: The Higher Education Academy.

Vygotsky, L. S. (1978). *Mind in society: The development of higher psychological processes*. Cambridge, MA: Harvard University Press.

Wenger, E. (1998). *Communities of practice: Learning, meaning and identity*. Cambridge: Cambridge University Press.

4

Facilitating the Success of Students from Low SES Backgrounds at Regional Universities Through Course Design, Teaching, and Staff Attributes

Marcia Devlin and Jade McKay

Introduction

Over the last decade in particular, higher education in Australia has made notable strides towards strengthening the participation of students from low socioeconomic status (SES) backgrounds and those from regional and remote areas. These shifts have necessitated a rethink of current models and strategies and the development of more inclusive curriculum, assessment, and teaching to better facilitate the success of students from low SES backgrounds at regional universities.

The existing research on curriculum design, assessment, and teaching which best caters to diverse student cohorts is extensive (see for example

M. Devlin
Victoria University, Melbourne, VIC, Australia

J. McKay (✉)
Deakin University, Burwood, VIC, Australia
e-mail: jade.mckay@deakin.edu.au

Devlin et al. 2012; Devlin and O'Shea 2011, 2012; McInnis 2003). This wide body of research documents a plethora of suggested strategies and approaches to enable the retention and achievement of equity students in higher education. What is not so widespread, however, is research that explores these factors as they relate specifically to students affected by *both* low SES background and regionality (James 2000, 2001). The study from which this chapter has emerged set out to speak to this gap in the scholarship and contribute to the existing research.

This chapter provides the findings of a national study that explored the major factors that contribute to low SES background student success in regional areas. The key findings relating to high quality course design, teaching, and staff attributes are presented. The chapter begins by canvassing the current higher education landscape in Australia with a specific focus on issues of inclusion and participation. It then narrows the focus to two specific equity groups: students from low SES backgrounds who are also at regional and remote universities. The national study upon which this chapter is based is then detailed, encompassing: the project overview, the project team, the methodology, and the key findings. The remainder of the chapter concentrates on the relevant findings relating to course design, teaching, and staff attributes that contribute to facilitating the success of students from low SES backgrounds.

The Higher Education Landscape in Australia

Regional higher education institutions (HEIs) play a key role in the higher education landscape in Australia, making significant social, cultural, environmental, and economic developments and contributions to the regions in which they function. Prior research has canvassed the lower participation rates of people from regional, rural, and remote areas and this research reveals a "complex variety of factors that lead to differing participation rates across regions" including, "distance from a university campus; differences in aspirations and attitudes of regional students; Year 12 retention and completion, and the cost of university study" (DEEWR 2010, p. 3). While the population in capital cities and regional Australia are on the rise, unfortunately the same cannot be said about the rates of higher education attainment. Not only are these rates a significant equity issue for the individuals concerned, they also have notable implications for regional communities (RUN 2016). It is promising to note that, "The gap has started to narrow in recent years, largely due to the demand driven system of student funding, started in 2012, which allows universities to enrol as many eligible students as they wish in bachelor degrees" (RUN 2016). While the uncapping of student places has assisted regional universities to increase the number and proportion of low SES and regional students at university, there is still room for improvement. To this end, the study upon which this chapter is based set out to determine specific approaches and high-level factors that can assist students from low SES backgrounds at regional universities to succeed, as well as provide policy advice for decision makers in higher education.

Students from Low SES Backgrounds at Regional Universities

With few exceptions (Behrens et al. 1978; James 2001), there is limited research exploring the issues of participation, access, and retention for those higher education students affected by *both* low SES and rurality. Parker (2016), among others (Black 2015; Glenday 2014; Koshy 2014), posits that students from low SES backgrounds are:

> …distributed unevenly among different types of institutions, a situation that is well-documented… In Australia, the Group of Eight universities have the lowest percentage of low-SES students, followed by the Australian Technology Network universities. The distributions of low-SES students according to university type have not changed much since at least 2007. Of the change that there has been, it is the rural and regional universities that have done most of the heavy lifting, followed by the outer urban universities. (Parker 2016)

A recent Regional Universities Network (RUN 2013) report notes:

> Regional universities are said to be national leaders in enrolling and supporting students from low SES backgrounds: in 2011, 29 per cent of their

domestic students were from low SES backgrounds. The comparable figure for the national higher education system as a whole was 16 per cent (DIICCSRTE 2012). (RUN 2013, p. 14)

Wilks and Wilson (2012) found that there are clear intersections between demographics, financial factors, geographic location, and cultural and social capital in relation to the formation of students' perceptions, choices, and decisions about participation in higher education. They conclude, "In remote, rural, and regional settings *financial factors* strongly influence decisions around pre-Year 12 termination and going on to university" (Wilks and Wilson 2012, p. 80, emphasis added).

The national study detailed in this chapter contributes to the scholarship by offering an insight into the factors contributing to the success of students affected by both low SES and regionality.

The Study

The study from which this chapter is premised set out to:

- determine the major, high-level factors that contribute to retention and completion for domestic students from low SES backgrounds who are studying at regional universities;
- determine successful approaches to increasing the success of these students;
- provide guidance about how to begin addressing gaps in current approaches to supporting these students; and
- provide policy advice around priorities for potential new approaches to fostering success for low SES students studying at regional universities.

To determine what has been effective in increasing student participation, retention, and success, the following evidence was collected:

- an extensive review of prior research and relevant literature;
- interviews with 69 successful students from low SES backgrounds approaching completion of their studies at six regional universities; and

- interviews with 26 staff from these six universities deemed "experts" in how these students succeed.

This paper focuses on some of the key factors related to course design, teaching, and assessment that were found to contribute to student success.

Findings

Prior to presenting the three key findings relating to course design, teaching and staff attributes, it is necessary to contexualise the characteristics and sociocultural considerations as they relate to these students.

Student Characteristics

In previous research on the success of students from low SES backgrounds in higher education, Devlin et al. (2012) found that university staff understanding the circumstances of, and respecting, low SES students was key to student success. The circumstances and characteristics that staff need to be mindful of relate to the fact that these students are often "balancing financial pressures, family responsibilities and/or significant hours of employment with study" (Devlin et al. 2012, p. 4). These students may also be impacted by other issues including being first in family, having had poor educational experiences, lacking cultural capital and having limited support of their ambitions to study at the tertiary level (Devlin and McKay 2011).

Sociocultural Considerations

Evidence of "sociocultural incongruity" between students from low SES backgrounds and the higher SES of the institutions at which they were studying (Devlin 2013) were evident in both student and staff interviews. Stakeholders raised the matter of students' cultural capital, feelings of belonging, and academic know-how in their interviews. One stakeholder astutely explained:

It crosses onto the first gen family, as well, that students don't come with that backpack of 'already understanding' to the uni. I think that for students, particularly where a regional uni from low SES backgrounds and regional and rural areas, they mightn't have had the same opportunities and experiences that someone in a metro or in a really high, wealthy school. (SCU_STK_031)

Student success was found to be facilitated by staff being sympathetic to the interplay of both socioeconomic and geographic factors affecting these students:

But for the single mum who's got three kids who has a – children down consecutively with chicken pox or measles or whatever, they might miss two assessment tasks and then they're gone … So … those realities don't sit comfortably with the expectations of academic life. (UNE_STK_015)

I remember one particular student who was … a very sound academic student, but was a carer for her mother dealing with mental health issues, and those sorts of barriers kept drawing her out and kept making it difficult to complete assignments, even to get to class. (USC_STK_025)

I think they're probably the main ways that the university can help by being much more responsive to the needs of the students and recognising that they have unique needs when they come from low SES backgrounds particularly from regional areas where they might feel fairly isolated. (USQ_STK_121)

The research identified three key factors that may assist students from low SES backgrounds at regional universities to persist, progress, and succeed. These include: course design, high quality teaching, and particular staff attributes.

Course Design

Designing courses that respond to students' particular circumstances and needs was found to be a critical factor in the success of students. This finding echoes prior research (see McLoughlin and Oliver 2000; Warren 2002) which points to the importance of responsiveness and cultural awareness in the design process in order to provide learning environments which are sensitive to diversity and student needs. Our research identified that course design and staff approaches that take into account the realities of students' complex lives and competing priorities have the strong potential to contribute to student retention and success. Indeed, stakeholders interviewed as part of the study stressed the importance of inclusive, responsive course design that considers diversity and which is premised on inclusivity. One stakeholder explained that the curriculum and course design are "powerful" tools in facilitating the success of students. For course design to be inclusive of the unique needs and situation of students from low SES backgrounds at regional universities, it must address and consider: student expectations, student preparedness, building capacity to succeed, and critically, assessment.

Student Expectations

Seventy-three percent of stakeholders in our study saw expectations as critical to student success and many suggested that these students sometimes enter higher education with unrealistic expectations. A number offered insight into why this may be:

> *It's hard to have an expectation when you're unfamiliar. It's hard to have an expectation when you have no role model. It's hard to have an expectation when we don't clearly articulate what that expectation is or we articulate in such a way that it's not meaningful to these students who don't have the cultural capital. (UNE_STK_015)*
>
> *… if they are first in family, then they're probably less likely to have a realistic expectation of what university's all about… (USC_STK_021)*

A key part of ensuring student success is the need for institutions to make expectations clear to students from the outset. Students were found to appreciate having expectations of them being made explicit from the outset, and, significantly also report appreciating staff who had high expectations of them. Such considerations need to be factored into course design to ensure overall student progress and success.

Student Preparedness

A key factor found to contribute to the success of students was their preparedness for the realities of university study. While some regional low SES background students who were first in their family to attend university were prepared in some ways for study and university life, many had gaps in their understanding of what was expected of them as a university student. Building students' capacity for success and their confidence, including through making the implicit expectations of them explicit, were identified as key practices that assist students to succeed.

Eighty-one percent of stakeholders viewed being prepared as a key factor in success and interestingly, many viewed students from low SES backgrounds as more prepared than their middle-class peers:

> …they're probably better mentally prepared in terms of their expectations. How much work they're going to have to do, and that's what I've noticed with all students, low SES or not, it's that appropriate expectation of what they're going to have to do, what they're going to have to sacrifice, how hard they're going to have to work, is I think one of the key factors for success and with low SES… (UNE_STK_012)

However, other staff members viewed students from low SES backgrounds as less prepared because of their prior educational experiences, background and/or first in family status, commenting:

> I think some students from low SES backgrounds come to the university without possibly the backpack of competencies or experiences that other students may have - they may be the first in their family to come to university - so they don't always have that whole toolkit and understanding about university: who does what, who to talk to, what it looks like, what the hierarchy's like. (SCU_STK_031)

Thirty-five percent of stakeholders saw enabling programmes and preparatory courses as critical in adequately preparing students for university. These are a critical part of course design that are often seen as "add on" rather than fundamental to student success. The research indicated the potential benefit of these programmes being an integral part of course design, ideally embedded in programmes in a holistic approach seen to benefit *all* students; a finding reiterated in the existing research (Habel et al. 2016; Pitman et al. 2016; Shah et al. 2014).

Building Capacity to Succeed

Research suggests that students from low SES backgrounds entering university are often required to shift from being unfamiliar to being familiar with university-specific culture and practices. Students are required to become more competent and confident in the specific knowledge and skills necessary for university and to have the requisite self-efficacy and so-called "grit" necessary to succeed (see Chemers et al. 2001; Sandler 2000). Several stakeholders framed these shifts as "adaptation" claiming, "*I think it's the ability to adapt quickly, that's the single most important factor, because the environment that they're coming into is so different to what they would have come from. So, adaptability and coping strategies would be…most important*" (USQ_STK_120). Stakeholders saw a significant part of adaptation as helping students work through their identity issues and becoming "learners".

> *Well I think what we're doing in the programme is that to deal with kind of identity issues and identify them as a learner and what kind of barriers have you had in the past and how you can maybe rewrite those stories of your own identity. So I think a lot of it has to do with that kind of sense of self, of what you bring to the learning environment.* (USC_STK_026)

The issue of adaptation is made more difficult in relation to students from low SES backgrounds at regional universities given that a whole range of other barriers are at play, including socio-psychological factors like fear of failure (Leathwood and O'Connell 2003) and "imposter syndrome" or "imposter phenomenon" (Gardner and Holley 2011; Sonnak and Towell 2001). Stakeholders discussed the implications of complex interplay of factors:

I think there needs to be acknowledgement of how difficult it is if you're a first in family or coming from a background where you didn't necessarily expect to be at uni but here you are and that that's normal. I think that needs to be consciously and clearly articulated and normalised. Not just, "Oh hello. All the students here today, welcome to the university," like not really engaging with the fact that they're sitting there in that head space. That could be engaged really. You can do a three-minute presentation on imposter syndrome and just make fun of it and you can kind of crack that a little bit. Just, "If you experience this, don't back out. This is normal. You'll grow through it. You can adapt." (SCU_STU_133)

..often just saying, "It's okay you can do it, if you fail it's alright." It just helps to remove that pressure they put on themselves. (UNE_STK_012)

Also the better student will try to learn from, if they failed something, they'll try to learn from it and go on from there. Rather than be completely devastated, turn it all on to themselves and say basically I'm worthless. (USQ_STK_122)

While some students were prepared in some ways, many had gaps in their knowledge and were unsure of what was expected of them. Building students' capacity for success and their confidence, including through making the expectations of them explicit are practices that may assist students to succeed. Embedding this capacity-building in course design is a way to not only enable success for non-traditional students, but significantly, is also an effective way to ensure *all* students benefit (see Murphy and Fleming 2003; Thies et al. 2014).

Assessment

A critical aspect of course design is assessment. Assessment is a central feature of both teaching and the curriculum; powerfully framing how students learn and what they achieve (Boud and Dochy 2010). According to Boud and Dochy (2010, p. 1), "It is one of the most significant influences on students' experience of higher education and all that they gain from it." In an era of widening participation, a significant part of this is ensuring that assessment suitably caters to the diverse cohorts now entering higher education institutions. Montenegro and Jankowski (2017) argue that for assessment to meet the goal of improving learning for *all* students and authentically documenting what students know and are capable of, a culturally responsive approach to assessment which is inclusive and caters to diversity is required.

Assessment of student learning was a particularly strong theme in interviews focused on what helped students succeed, with sixty-eight percent of (47 of 69) students commenting on assessment as a factor in their success. Students stated:

Probably the memorable assignments are those ones that you struggle with but they're very applicable to the real world and you struggle because you can't quite make that leap but, once you get there, they are the most helpful things. Like, you learn the most about what you're going to need when you're out there. (SCU_STU_065)

Well-written assessment tasks for starters. Like I mentioned the ones that make the effort to have discussions about them as opposed to just posting a list of things you need to do. If there's even just a video that they've bothered to record to explain things a bit further than just an A4 piece of paper with what you need to do on there, that makes a huge difference to the success in achieving tasks. (USQ_STU_121)

I think the more feedback you get as a student… the better it is. (SCU_STU_067)

Of particular note were repeated references by stakeholders as to the necessity of relevance of assessment. One staff member summed up a common thread in a number of comments:

That is relevant and timely, linked to assessments that are intelligently designed and compassionately designed, not to terrify the crap out of the poor things. But to motivate them, awake their curiosity and give them a sense of achievement when they've finished it. So rather than making it this mind numbing, let's learn everything by heart and then you know, pour it all out again on paper in an exam. (SCU_STK_032)

> But most of all I think intelligent design of assessments. That move away from just writing a bloody essay, that are relevant to them. But that then would benefit everybody, not just the low SES. (SCU_STK_032)

Finally, when asked about the ways success could be better facilitated through assessment, as well as a variety of assessment tasks, students and staff highlighted the following factors: the importance of making the criteria explicit; and reasonable amounts of reading material given many work full time as well as studying.

As outlined in this section, designing courses that respond to students' particular circumstances and needs was found to be a critical factor in the success of this particular cohort of students. The research found that inclusive course design addresses and considers student expectations, student preparedness, builds capacity to succeed, and critically, comprises inclusive assessment which embraces diversity.

High Quality Teaching

In a time when the student body is continually diversifying, an inclusive and engaged approach to teaching and learning is increasingly essential. Needless to say, high quality teaching is a significant aspect of student learning and overall success. While countless researchers have explored what constitutes high quality and effective teaching, opinions vary as to the key factors that comprise effective teaching (Devlin and Samarawickrema 2010). In relation to students from low SES backgrounds at regional universities, effective, high-quality teaching is that which is inclusive.

Indeed, a widely accepted approach to facilitating the success of so-called "non-traditional" students that has been used with success is "inclusive teaching" (Devlin and McKay 2011), or teaching that embraces and caters to diversity (see Griffiths 2010; Devlin et al. 2012). David et al. (2010) and Roberts (2011) maintain that part of effective teaching is the adoption of pedagogical approaches that better cater to diversity. The present study found that teaching that was, and teachers who were, inclusive of the "real-world" of students from low SES backgrounds studying at regional universities were able to facilitate success for these students. It also found the following as key aspects of high quality teaching: inclusive pedagogical approaches, engagement through active and interactive learning, and flexibility.

Inclusive Pedagogical Approach

Adopting more inclusive pedagogical approaches has been found to help students from low SES backgrounds to succeed. In relation to being inclusive of online students, one student explained:

> *I think some lecturers seem to be more conscious of external students than others. I think in lecturing style particularly, sometimes lecturers might forget that they are recording and that people external like myself will be listening online. I think that's - yeah, hasn't been particularly hindrance but I do find sometimes the lecturers might be referring to material that they have in the classroom or in the lecture theatre, but we as external students obviously can't see on the recording. (UNE_STU_021)*

> *I think if there is that element of consistency and if you as a regional student feel like you have the same chance as the people on campus have you're a lot more willing to keep pushing through. (USQ_STU_121)*

Engagement Through Active and Interactive Learning

Throughout both staff and stakeholder interviews, one factor proposed as key to success was the engagement of students through active and interactive learning. Sixty-five percent of stakeholders shared the view that engagement in learning and teaching was critical to student success. Thirty-six percent of students referred to the importance of engagement in their learning, and saw active, interactive teaching approaches as critical to facilitate this. As students noted:

> …*all of them were very approachable and hands-on, so definitely hands-on teaching. Visual teaching helped me because I'm that kind of learner. And yeah, got you actively involved, like got you up and done group things or asked your opinion or got you up to have a play with something to understand the concept with science or maths or something like that, that you could do with the kids. So, not just sitting there receiving information at a desk, we were often moving around and standing around the room or sitting on the floor in a group and that sort of stuff. (USQ_STU_135)*

> *It's really good when they actually interact with you and actually makes you respond to their questions. (FED_STU_004)*

Flexibility

Flexibility has previously been heralded as a positively influencing factor in the academic experiences of non-traditional students (Devlin et al. 2012; Kehoe et al. 2004; Roberts 2011). The research points to the importance of open and flexible access (Schuetze and Slowey 2002), flexibility in relation to the curriculum (Miller and Lu 2003), adaptability/flexibility on behalf of teachers themselves (Devlin et al. 2012) and flexibility relating to timeframes, timetables, and deadlines (El Mansour and Mupinga 2007; Thomas 2002).

The issue of flexibility was a prominent theme in both staff and student interviews. This flexibility related to: assessment dates, deadlines, study load (part-time/full-time), access to teaching staff, ability to defer, online learning allowing students to access materials in their own time, ability to study at one's own pace, the option to study from home and save on travel costs, generous open times for the campus and computer labs, and special consideration/extensions.

Flexibility was viewed as particularly critical for those balancing work and study (65% of students), or dealing with study and having children and/or other family responsibilities (72.5% of students). Stakeholder respondents urged fellow academic staff to be sensitive to the complex issues experienced by these students:

I think we're notoriously bad for being inflexible as institutions. A lot of it has got to do with the scale of student numbers, enrolments. It tends to make us think that we can't bend the rules or we can't be very flexible without completely letting the whole place down. But I do think we need to be more responsive to individual needs and circumstances in a whole range of different ways. (USQ_STK_121)

This quote highlights the need for staff to understand that flexibility can be the difference for many of these students continuing and succeeding in higher education.

As discussed in this section, inclusive, high-quality teaching was found to entail an inclusive pedagogical approach, which engaged students through active and interactive learning, and was flexible and responsive to students' unique circumstances. We further found that teaching that was, and teachers who were, inclusive of the "real-world" of students from low SES backgrounds studying at regional universities were better able to facilitate success for these students.

Staff Attributes

A wide body of literature has explored the attributes of teaching staff that are most valued by students and which are seen to improve student learning and foster student success (Klassen et al. 2011; Ramsden 2003; Stronge et al. 2011). Effective teaching and teachers have also been researched relating to non-traditional students specifically, with a range of varied staff attributes identified as critical to student achievement (Devlin et al. 2012; Devlin and O'Shea 2011, 2012; Devlin and Samarawickrema 2010). The attributes identified in the present study are respect for students, empathic support, and approachability which are discussed below.

Respect for Students and Sensitivity to Low SES Issues

In the study from which this chapter has emerged, it was clear that staff understanding the impacts on low SES regional students of competing priorities was key to student success. Students provided multiple examples of how their life circumstances affected their ability to engage with university study. One student stated:

> I'm limited on how much time I can actually spend at the university too, with being a carer, I'm only allowed to be at university for a certain amount of hours a week while I'm caring for the others. So I structure my degree around how many hours I can actually spend on campus. That really is eaten up with tutorials and lectures. I'd like to go to the library a lot more and spend a lot more time there, but I just really can't. (USC_STU_053)

Thirty-five percent of stakeholders (9 of 26) similarly stressed the importance of understanding on the part of staff, and the accommodation of students' life circumstances. Typical comments included:

> … you get students who, for all sorts of reasons, start off with good intentions and then life gets in the way, life pressures, time pressure, money pressure, family pressure, work pressure. (SCU_STK_032)

> …you expect these quite simple things, it can be like, why are these things not done? You know, why is this assignment two weeks late? Or whatever. Why are they asking for an extension again on the day the assignment's due or whatever it is, but to have an understanding that for a lot of these people, they're struggling and a lot of the time they're not telling the full story about their circumstances, which are really hard. So … it's a balancing act between I guess being kind and compassionate. (UNE_STK_014)

Empathic Support

Stakeholders highlighted the necessity of "empathic support"; that is, support that takes into consideration the unique circumstances and needs of students from low SES backgrounds from regional areas. Empathic support, as described by stakeholders:

- takes into consideration the distinct needs of low SES regional students for flexibility;

- is support that empowers students to be enabled and self-supportive;
- stems from an inclusive approach that helps students feel they are part of an institutional/tertiary "family" (USC_STK_023);
- entails personal welfare checks where students know someone "cares" (CQU_STK_043); and
- is personalised and ongoing throughout a student's academic journey.

Empathic support was elucidated by stakeholders in the following way:

I think again it comes down to that empathetic support. It's a fine balance because you need to support people without doing everything for them. So supporting people to enable them to become independent and effective and confident. (UNE_STK_012)

In terms of supporting them, I think a lot of it comes down to empathy and encouragement and willing to support them on that journey. (USC_STK_024)

Approachable Staff

Previous research documents a raft of factors affecting general student health and wellbeing. These include staff-student relationships, especially staff receptiveness and approachability (Levett-Jones et al. 2009). Devlin et al. (2012) found the perceived approachability of staff a key factor in the success of students from low SES backgrounds. In the present study, students having access to staff who were perceived as "approachable" was a consistent theme in stakeholder interviews. Stakeholders thought the approachability of staff was essential to facilitating connectedness and overall student success.

…people will come and knock on my door and say to me 'I need a food voucher'; 'I need this, I need that' or '…I don't know what I'm doing'. Someone they can go to who they can trust, again it doesn't need to be an academic staff member but I think it's better if it is. (FED_STK_002)

> *That rapport, the connection, the human aspect of the learning experience, that we weren't these people that stood at the front with our black gowns on talking about hypothesizing things. Actually, we seemed like we were really approachable and I think that broke down all those barriers. (USC_STK_026)*

For students, teaching staff being accessible and approachable played a large part in helping them feel "connected". For those studying online, accessibility and approachability helped to ensure they were not disconnected from the university experience.

Staff Professional Development

A significant aspect of teaching effectiveness is staff development. The present study found evidence that regional universities have further work to do in terms of educating staff about the circumstances and needs of students from low SES backgrounds. Twenty-three percent (6 out of 26) of stakeholders pointed to the need for staff training, commenting:

> *I think academic staff…need better training around…this term 'low SES'. I know a lot of my colleagues honestly have got no idea and they have fixed ideas about what successful experiences of university are; they're fixated on things like literacy and numeracy as kind of you fix that problem and everything else is fixed whereas for low SES students that problem could actually be what I've talked about earlier, first and foremost housing, secure housing and safe housing, other issues that are around poverty, poverty is poorly understood and regional poverty is highly problematic… Poverty is not well understood by most academic staff. (FED_STK_002)*

> *I think educating staff about the complexity of the lives that students have and bring with them to … universities is important. (UNE_STK_013)*

> *Yeah, we could probably provide more professional development to some staff who perhaps haven't recognised the importance of the value of supporting students on an individual basis. (USQ_STK_121)*

The importance of understanding and responding to the particular circumstances and needs of students from low SES backgrounds at regional universities was foregrounded by both staff and students in our study. These factors were found to have a positive influence on the overall success of students.

As discussed in this section, staff attributes are a significant aspect of effective teaching and learning. Students in our study valued the impact of staff who respected them, had a sensitivity to low SES issues, offered empathic support and were both approachable and accessible. Obviously, a significant aspect of this is staff training and developing staff awareness and understanding relating to the multitude of issues and challenges affecting students from low SES backgrounds at regional universities.

Conclusion

In light of efforts to widen participation across Australian higher education, the study findings presented in this chapter offer insight into the critical factors required to facilitate student success. The importance of adequately supporting students in equity categories once they gain entry to university is essential if success is to be achieved. To this end, this chapter has presented the key findings to emerge from a national study that set out to explore the key success factors for students affected by both low SES and regionality. In line with prior research, the findings point to a raft of challenges and barriers affecting these students and the need for institutions, staff, and students to work together to facilitate student success. The study identified the critical success factors relating specifically to course design, teaching, and staff attributes that impact on student retention, progress, and success.

It was found that academic staff must foremost be informed and aware of the sociocultural incongruities which exist between these equity students and the institutions in which they study. To bridge these incongruities, course design must be responsive, flexible, and premised on inclusivity. Student expectations, levels of preparedness also need to be considered. This responsiveness, flexibility, and inclusiveness must also extend to assessment as our study points to the need for assessment to be relevant, varied in approach, and explicitly explained. High quality teaching was equally important, with both stakeholders and students stressing flexibility, inclusivity, active and interactive T&L as critical to student success. Finally, our study pointed to various staff attributes as key; these included, staff being respectful, exhibiting cultural awareness, being empathic, and being approachable.

Collectively, course design, teaching, and staff attributes were highlighted as major, high-level success factors by both students and stakeholders in our study. They were found to have a profound influence on students' educational experiences and achievement in higher education. These findings may prove useful to academics, policy makers, and institutional leaders concerned with students affected by both regionality and low SES.

References

Behrens, N., O'Grady, J., Hodgson, S., Hoult, P., & Hughes, A. (1978). *The Huon valley study: Opportunities and educational priorities in a Tasmanian country area*. Hobart: Education Department of Tasmania.

Black, T. S. (2015). *Education students' first year experience on a regional university campus* (Thesis, PhD/Research, Unpublished).

Boud, D., & Dochy, F. (2010). *Assessment 2020. Seven propositions for assessment reform in higher education*. Sydney: Australian Learning and Teaching Council (ALTC). Available at: https://lirias.kuleuven.be/bitstream/123456789/263461/2/Assessment-2020_propositions_final.pdf

Chemers, M. M., Hu, L. T., & Garcia, B. F. (2001). Academic self-efficacy and first year college student performance and adjustment. *Journal of Educational Psychology, 93*(1), 55.

David, M., Crozier, G., Hayward, G., Ertl, H., Williams, J., & Hockings, C. (2010). Institutional practices and pedagogies for social diversity. In M. David (Ed.), *Improving learning by widening participation in higher education* (Improving learning series, Chapter 7, pp. 180–201). London: Routledge.

Department of Education, Employment and Workplace Relations (DEEWR). (2010). *Regional participation: The role of socioeconomic status and access*. Canberra: AGPS. Available at: http://apo.org.au/files/Resource/regionalparticipation_report. pdf.

Department of Industry, Innovation, Climate Change, Science, Research and Tertiary Education (DIICCSRTE). (2012). Students: Selected higher education statistics, 2011 Student Full Year.

Devlin, M. (2013). Bridging socio-cultural incongruity: Conceptualising students from low socioeconomic status backgrounds in Australian higher education. *Studies in Higher Education, 38*(6), 939–949.

Devlin, M., & Samarawickrema, G. (2010). The criteria of effective teaching in a changing higher education context. *Higher Education Research & Development, 29*(2), 111–124.

Devlin, M., & McKay, J. (2011). *Inclusive teaching and support of students from low socioeconomic status backgrounds: A brief discussion paper.* Melbourne: Higher Education Research Group, Deakin University.

Devlin, M., & O'Shea, H. (2011). *Teaching students from low socioeconomic backgrounds: A brief guide for University teaching staff.* Melbourne: Deakin University.

Devlin, M., & O'Shea, H. (2012). Effective university teaching: Views of Australian university students from low socio-economic status backgrounds. *Teaching in Higher Education, 17*(4), 385–397.

Devlin, M., Kift, S., Nelson, K., Smith, L., & McKay, J. (2012). *Effective teaching and support of students from low socioeconomic status backgrounds: Resources for Australian higher education* (Final Report). Office for Learning and Teaching, Commonwealth of Australia.

El Mansour, B., & Mupinga, D. M. (2007). Students' positive and negative experiences in hybrid and online classes. *College Student Journal, 41*(1), 242.

Gardner, S. K., & Holley, K. A. (2011). 'Those invisible barriers are real': The progression of first-generation students through doctoral education. *Equity & Excellence in Education, 44*(1), 77–92.

Glenday, J. (2014, July 5). Regional universities wary of higher education reforms despite meeting with Education Minister Christopher Pyne. *ABC News.* Available at: http://www.abc.net.au/news/2014-07-05/federal-education-minister-visits-regional-universities/5573218

Griffiths, S. (2010). *Teaching for Inclusion in Higher Education: A guide to practice.* United Kingdom and All Ireland Society for Higher Education: Higher Education Academy.

Habel, C., Whitman, K., & Stokes, J. (2016). *Exploring the experience of low-SES students via enabling pathways.* Perth: National Centre for Student Equity in Higher Education (NCSEHE), Curtin University. Available at: https://www.ncsehe.edu.au/publications/exploring-the-experience-of-low-ses-students-via-enabling-pathways/

James, R. (2000). *Socioeconomic background and higher education participation: An analysis of school students' aspirations and expectations.* Canberra: Higher Education Division, DEST.

James, R. (2001). Participation disadvantage in Australian higher education: An analysis of some effects of geographical location and socioeconomic status. *Higher Education, 42*(4), 455–472.

Kehoe, J., Tennent, B., & Becker, K. L. (2004). The challenge of flexible and non-traditional learning and teaching methods: Best practice in every situation? *Studies in Learning, Evaluation, Innovation and Development e-Journal, 1*(1), 56–63.

Klassen, R. M., Tze, V. M., Betts, S. M., & Gordon, K. A. (2011). Teacher efficacy research 1998–2009: Signs of progress or unfulfilled promise? *Educational Psychology Review, 23*(1), 21–43.

Koshy, P. (2014). *Student equity performance in Australian higher education: 2007 to 2012*. Perth: National Centre for Student Equity in Higher Education (NCSEHE), Curtin University.

Leathwood, C., & O'Connell, P. (2003). 'It's a struggle': The construction of the 'new student' in higher education. *Journal of Education Policy, 18*(6), 597–615.

Levett-Jones, T., Lathlean, J., Higgins, I., & McMillan, M. (2009). Staff–student relationships and their impact on nursing students' belongingness and learning. *Journal of Advanced Nursing, 65*(2), 316–324.

McInnis, C. (2003). From marginal to mainstream strategies: Responding to student diversity in Australian universities. *European Journal of Education, 38*(4), 387–400.

McLoughlin, C., & Oliver, R. (2000). Designing learning environments for cultural inclusivity: A case study of indigenous online learning at tertiary level. *Australasian Journal of Educational Technology, 16*(1), 58–72.

Miller, M., & Lu, M. Y. (2003). Serving non-traditional students in e-learning environments: Building successful communities in the virtual campus. *Educational Media International, 40*(1–2), 163–169.

Montenegro, E., & Jankowski, N. A. (2017). *Equity and assessment: Moving towards culturally responsive assessment*. National Institute for Learning Outcomes Assessment. Available at: http://learningoutcomesassessment.org/documents/OccasionalPaper29.pdf

Murphy, M., & Fleming, T. (2003). Partners in participation: Integrated approaches to widening access in higher education. *European Journal of Education, 38*(1), 25–39.

Parker, S. (2016, February 24). How universities make inequality worse. *The Conversation*. Available at: https://theconversation.com/how-universities-make-inequality-worse-55155

Pitman, T., Trinidad, S., Devlin, M., Harvey, A., Brett, M., & McKay, J. (2016). *Pathways to higher education: The efficacy of enabling and sub-bachelor path-*

ways for disadvantaged students. Perth: National Centre for student equity in higher education (NCSEHE), Curtin University.

Ramsden, P. (2003). *Learning to teach in higher education*. London: Routledge.

Regional Universities Network (RUN). (2013, June). *Regional Universities Network: Engaging with regions, building a stronger nation* (Regional Universities Network, Vol. 1 Report). Canberra. Available at: http://www.run.edu.au/resources/RUN_regional_impact_study_vol_1.pdf

Regional Universities Network (RUN). (2016). *Clever regions, clever Australia: Policy advice for an incoming government*. Report. Available at: http://www.run.edu.au/resources/RUN_PolicyAdvice%20booklet%20final.pdf

Roberts, S. (2011). Traditional practice for non-traditional students? Examining the role of pedagogy in higher education retention. *Journal of Further and Higher Education, 35*(2), 182–199.

Sandler, M. E. (2000). Career decision-making self-efficacy, perceived stress, and an integrated model of student persistence: A structural model of finances, attitudes, behavior, and career development. *Research in Higher Education, 41*(5), 537–580.

Schuetze, H. G., & Slowey, M. (2002). Participation and exclusion: A comparative analysis of non-traditional students and lifelong learners in higher education. *Higher Education, 44*(3–4), 309–327.

Shah, M., Goode, E., West, S., & Clark, H. (2014). Widening student participation in higher education through online enabling education. *Widening Participation and Lifelong Learning, 16*(3), 36–57.

Sonnak, C., & Towell, T. (2001). The impostor phenomenon in British university students: Relationships between self-esteem, mental health, parental rearing style and socioeconomic status. *Personality and Individual Differences, 31*(6), 863–874.

Stronge, J. H., Ward, T. J., & Grant, L. W. (2011). What makes good teachers good? A cross-case analysis of the connection between teacher effectiveness and student achievement. *Journal of Teacher Education, 62*(4), 339–355.

Thies, L., Wallis, A., Turner, A., & Wishart, L. (2014). Embedded academic literacies curricula: The challenges of measuring success. *Journal of Academic Language & Learning, 8*(2), 43–59.

Thomas, L. (2002). Student retention in higher education: The role of institutional habitus. *Journal of Education Policy, 17*(4), 423–442.

Warren, D. (2002). Curriculum design in a context of widening participation in higher education. *Arts and Humanities in Higher Education, 1*(1), 85–99.

Wilks, J., & Wilson, K. (2012). Going on to uni? Access and participation in university for students from backgrounds of disadvantage. *Journal of Higher Education Policy and Management, 34*(1), 79–90.

5

A Case Study Using Developmental Education to Raise Equity and Maintain Standards

Michelle Hodara, Di Xu, and Julie Petrokubi

Introduction

Community colleges play a critical role in addressing the equity agenda in the United States (Cohen et al. 2014). As low-cost open-access institutions, these two-year colleges provide a key point of access to postsecondary education for millions of underrepresented students each year. Two-year institutions are much more likely to educate low-income, first-generation, and minority students than four-year institutions: Based on data from the US Department of Education (2011/12), Beginning Postsecondary Students Longitudinal Study, among first-time college students in 2011/12, 52 percent of two-year college students received Pell (federal aid for low-income students) compared to 43 percent of four-year college

---

M. Hodara • J. Petrokubi
Education Northwest, Portland, OR, USA
e-mail: michelle.hodara@educationnorthwest.org

D. Xu (✉)
University of California, Irvine, CA, USA

students, 61 percent of two-year college students were the first in their families to attend college compared to 40 percent of first-year four-year college students, and 48 percent of two-year college students were students of color compared to 40 percent of four-year college students.

Yet, academic access without academic progress is no more than an empty promise. Many community college students received inadequate secondary education or enter college after a long gap in their education. The most common approach that colleges use to address gaps in academic preparedness is to provide students with the opportunity to increase their skills and knowledge with further college-level coursework through "developmental" or "remedial" education. The typical developmental program consists of a sequence of multiple courses on related topics across several semesters (Grubb and Gabriner 2013). For example, in a three-course math sequence, the lowest level of developmental math covers arithmetic, the middle level beginning algebra concepts, and the highest level prepares students for college algebra. In developmental writing and reading, the lowest level courses cover basic writing and reading skills, such as constructing complete sentences and building vocabulary; the middle level courses focus on writing a coherent essay and identifying main ideas; and the highest level courses prepare students for college English, focusing on reading college-level texts and writing a college-level essay. Developmental education courses serve as prerequisites to college math and English, as well as other college courses. As a result, students at the lowest levels need to complete at least three semesters of developmental coursework before they can enroll in college math/English and courses that have college math/English prerequisites.

Developmental education is prevalent and costly. Nationally, about two-thirds of community college entrants are considered academically underprepared for college-level coursework and assigned to developmental education (Bailey et al. 2010). Developmental education imposes huge costs to institutions and students. Students spend an estimated $6.7 billion per year on such courses at community colleges (Scott-Clayton et al. 2014), but the credits earned from these courses do not count toward degree requirements. The cost to institutions for providing the developmental education instruction is even greater, which has been estimated at more than $1 billion each year (Noble et al. 2004). Despite the huge costs and high hopes around remediation to raise equity and at the same time maintain high standards for higher education, there is considerable uncertainty surrounding the effectiveness of this tactic in facilitating the academic progress and success of students who enter colleges with weak academic skills. What is the national scope of developmental education in the US? What does the current research say about the problems associated with developmental education and possible ways to reform it?

In this chapter, we provide a comprehensive overview of developmental education, the most commonly used strategy in United States community colleges to address the equity agenda through preserving the open-access mission while maintaining academic standards. The chapter starts with a descriptive overview about the extent of developmental education, followed by a thorough discussion of the impacts of developmental education coursework on student outcomes, and the problems associated with the traditional developmental sequence. We then review common strategies to reform developmental education to better support students and provide a case study of developmental education reform implementation in Oregon. The interviews with faculty and administrators provide insight for practitioners and researchers seeking to identify and implement promising strategies to support community college students.

National Scope of Developmental Education

Examining nationally representative data on the 2003/04 first-time college entrants reveals that 68 percent of students who entered a public two-year college took at least one developmental education course (Chen 2016). Developmental course-taking is much more prevalent in math than English: Among 2003/04 community college entrants, 59 percent took a remedial math course and 28 percent took a remedial English/writing or reading course (Chen 2016). U.S. high school students tend to struggle with math more than English; results from the Program for Internal Assessment (PISA) demonstrate that U.S. students rank below average in math but about average in English (OECD 2012).

While most community college students take developmental education, it is more prevalent among disadvantaged groups. Undertaking developmental education was more common among female students (71 percent compared to 65 percent of males), students of color (78 percent of Black students, 75 percent of Latino/Hispanic students, and 68 percent of Asian students compared to 64 percent of White students), and low-income students (76 percent of students who were in the lowest income group compared to 59 percent of those in the highest) (Chen 2016).

In terms of outcomes, students who take remedial courses are less likely to complete college. Among 2003/04 community college entrants, 63 percent of students who did not take developmental education were still enrolled (23 percent) or had earned a certificate, associate's, or bachelor's degree (40 percent), compared to 48 percent of students who took developmental education (14 percent were still enrolled and 34 percent had earned a degree or certificate) (Chen 2016). Yet, this may be expected given that developmental education students are considered academically underprepared and may fare even worse without the additional academic remediation coursework. Therefore, studies that intend to evaluate the impacts of developmental education would need to address the baseline differences between students assigned to developmental coursework and students who are determined as "college-ready".

Evidence Regarding the Effectiveness of Developmental Education

Impacts on Student Academic Outcomes

The typical methodological approach used by existing literature in assessing the impact of developmental education takes advantage of the traditional developmental education assignment process. A student matriculating at an open-access two-year institution is typically assigned to a set of courses that are deemed appropriate to his or her level of academic preparation. At most community colleges, this assignment has been typically based on standardized placement exams that measure English and mathematics skill levels (Hughes and Scott-Clayton 2011). Students who score above a cutoff are viewed as ready to take college level courses in that subject area, while students who score below the cutoff are referred to developmental coursework in that subject area.

Thus, researchers use the regression discontinuity design, which exploits the fact that similar students are assigned to developmental or college level coursework around a placement test score cutoff. The intuition behind this strategy is fairly straightforward: If we assume that nothing other than the developmental assignment varies discontinuously at the placement test score cutoff, we may attribute any observed discontinuity in outcomes at the cutoff to the developmental education assignment. For example, while we might expect fall-to-fall persistence be positively related to students' math placement test scores, there is no reason other than the developmental education intervention to expect a discontinuous jump in this relationship for students that fall right around the score cutoff.

Based on this methodological approach, the majority of existing studies fail to find any consistent positive impacts of developmental coursework on students' academic outcomes (such as college course performance, college persistence, transfer, and degree completion) (Bettinger and Long 2005, 2009; Calcagno and Long 2008; Martorell and McFarlin 2011; Scott-Clayton and Rodriguez 2015; Xu 2016). These studies took place in six different states, suggesting that they are applicable to a large number of higher education contexts (Jaggars and Stacey 2014). Because college systems define college readiness differently and, as a result, have different placement exam score cutoffs that assign students to college-level courses or developmental education, these studies also represent students with different levels of incoming ability (Bailey et al. 2013). For these reasons, causal research suggests that, on average, traditional sequences of developmental education do not improve the college outcomes of community college students.

While these studies do not find any significant harm imposed on students assigned to development education either, these "null" effects represent a waste of time and resources on the part of students, institutions, and taxpayers. Some researchers argue that one of the limitations with the majority of existing studies is that these studies mainly focused on evaluating the effectiveness of developmental education on students at the margin of needing it and did not consider the effect of developmental education on students who were identified to have very low skills. Would the least academically prepared students benefit from the additional developmental coursework?

A handful of studies have examined this issue and the existing studies fail to find any consistent evidence that students benefit from these lengthy sequences (Boatman and Long 2017; Hodara 2012; Xu 2016; Xu and Dadgar 2018). In fact, some studies identified negative impacts of being placed into a longer developmental sequence versus a shorter sequence on students' academic outcomes. For example, based on college administrative data from the Virginia community college system (VCCS), Xu (2016) compared the outcomes of students who scored barely above the cutoff scores for placement into different levels of developmental education with those who scored barely below. The results suggest that developmental courses do differ in their impacts by the level of assignment. Consistent with the existing literature, the estimated effects are generally small in magnitude and statistically insignificant for students on the margin of needing developmental coursework. In contrast, lower level (and therefore longer) developmental sequences lead to negative impacts on various academic outcomes for students with very low skills, including a lower first-year retention rate, a lower probability of ever attempting a college-level English course, a lower number of college-level credits earned, and a lower probability of earning any degree or certificate within five years of initial enrollment. These negative impacts of developmental education are also identified in another study that examines the impacts both of being assigned to and of enrolling in the lowest level developmental sequence in math in the same state (Xu and Dadgar 2018).

Impacts on Student Labor Market Outcomes

In contrast to the large volume of studies that examine the impact of developmental education on student academic outcomes, there is surprisingly little evidence on its impact on student labor market outcomes. The most relevant evidence on labor market returns to developmental education so far comes from two studies. Based on data from Texas, Martorell and McFarlin (2011) estimate the effect of developmental education on both student academic and labor market outcomes and find little evidence that the students who score close to the cutoff benefit from developmental education, either in terms of academic outcomes or labor market earnings.

One limitation of the regression discontinuity design, however, is that the analytical sample was restricted to a small proportion of students around the test score cutoff, which substantially limits the power to detect effects or the generalizability of the findings. In a more recent study by Hodara and Xu (2016), the researchers used longitudinal data from two state community college systems and used an individual fixed effects approach to address any unobserved characteristics that are constant over time. The results indicate that earning developmental reading and writing credits increased earnings due to an increased likelihood of employment, but had no direct impact on earnings among those who are already employed. Alternatively, developmental math is associated with a strong negative impact on earnings, especially those placed in the lowest level of math.

Challenges to Developmental Education

In general, given the time and costs associated with developmental education, the benefits received from these programs are far from satisfying. Why are these intensive programs ineffective? Why might long developmental sequences even hurt students' academic progress? To better understand these questions, it helps to look at two theoretical explanations for how developmental education might influence students' academic outcomes and motivation.

The theoretical framework for understanding the results of developmental education distinguishes between two main models (Scott-Clayton and Rodriguez 2015). The *Assistance Model* hypothesizes that developmental education helps students with inadequate preparation catch up with other students by developing their skills and knowledge to college-ready standards. As a result, while enrollment in developmental coursework may delay college progress at first, students should reap benefits over the long term, such as a greater chance of passing college-level courses and higher college persistence rate. However, this model is based on several assumptions that are yet to be substantiated:

(a) that there are well defined criteria for what students need to know to be ready for college level course, which could be effectively delivered through developmental coursework;
(b) that the assessment and assignment criteria to divide students into "developmental" and "college-ready" population correctly identifies students who can benefit from the developmental content; and
(c) that any benefit in acquiring the relevant knowledge and skills outweighs the additional financial and academic burden to the students, the additional opportunities for students to leak out of the system, and any stigma associated with being assigned to developmental education coursework (Scott-Clayton and Rodriguez 2015).

On the opposite end of this theoretical discussion is the *Hindrance model*, where any benefit from skills and knowledge development in the developmental courses, is outweighed because of one or more of the following costs to the students:

(a) direct economic costs of taking additional courses that do not contribute towards a degree or certificates;
(b) the cost of additional time spent in the classroom as well as delaying access to college level courses; and
(c) the psychological cost of feeling stigmatized for not being ready for college level coursework. Such negative psychological factors may be particularly strong among those who are prepared for college-level courses yet are placed into developmental education, which is referred to as "underplacement" (Scott-Clayton and Rodriguez 2015), which has been found to be fairly common across colleges (Scott-Clayton et al. 2014).

Moreover, the negative impacts of imposing such a burden on students may be even stronger if these courses do not develop students' skills. Indeed, qualitative evidence suggests that developmental education content is taught in a decontextualized way through drill-and-kill instruction and thus both curriculum and instruction are not aligned with college-level context, expectations, and tasks (Grubb and Gabriner 2013). As a result, these courses fail to "clarify for students the reasons for or the importance of learning these subskills" (Grubb and Gabriner 2013, p. 52), and may not effectively achieve the intended goal to prepare students for subsequent college coursework. Thus, the limited positive benefits of developmental education may be outweighed by the substantial direct, opportunity, and psychological costs of developmental education.

A Case Study of Current Reforms

In response to concerns about the effectiveness of developmental education, community colleges across the country have been working to improve developmental education by changing how they assess and place students, adopting reforms that accelerate students' progress through developmental education, and enhancing student services (Edgecombe et al. 2013; Hodara et al. 2012; Quint et al. 2013). The common strategies generally fall under reforms intended to decrease the need for developmental education or improve the outcomes of students once in developmental education (see Table 5.1). It is fairly common for a community college or state system to implement multiple strategies at the same time. In general, all these reformed approaches attempt to optimize the benefits of the *Assistance Model* of developmental education while minimizing the challenges of the *Hindrance Model*.

Early evaluations find that these new strategies are promising. An evaluation of modularization identified preliminary positive impacts on students' progress in developmental coursework after one year (Gardenhire et al. 2016). An examination of different forms of acceleration—compression and the corequiste model – in three different contexts found positive impacts on enrolling and passing the entry-level college course (Jaggars et al. 2015). Finally, there are also promising early outcomes for alternative developmental math pathways to college-level math for students pursuing non-Science Technology Engineering and Math (STEM) programs of study (Hern 2012; Rutschow and Diamond 2015; Yamada and Bryk 2016).

More research is needed to identify the long-term impacts of developmental education reform on student and institutional outcomes. Thus far, qualitative research has identified challenges to developmental education reform implementation (Edgecombe et al. 2013; Mayer et al. 2014; Price et al. 2015; Quint et al. 2013). This research suggests that many reforms reach only a small fraction of students and thus have a limited impact on institutional outcomes.

Table 5.1 Common developmental education reforms

Strategy	Problem it addresses	Brief description of reform
Decrease the need for developmental education through assessment and placement reforms	Too many community college students are needlessly or inaccurately assigned to developmental education	Early assessment and transition courses: High schools administer a standardized assessment in 11th grade that measures college and career readiness and provides courses in the senior year to students who are not on track to be college and career ready
		Summer bridge and brush-up courses: Colleges provide opportunities for students who place into developmental education to brush-up on skills, retake the placement exams, and place into college-level coursework prior to the start of college
		Multiple measures: Colleges assign students to coursework based on measures that provide additional, useful information about college readiness. For example, colleges may look at recent high school graduates' high school grade point average, grades in specific math and English courses, or performance on a state assessment to determine their readiness for college coursework

(continued)

Table 5.1 (continued)

Strategy	Problem it addresses	Brief description of reform
Improve the outcomes of developmental education students through acceleration	Long sequences and de-contextualized curriculum and instruction lengthen time-to-degree and lead to high attrition	Compression: Multiple developmental education courses are combined into a single term through curriculum redesign (e.g., reducing redundancies, better alignment with college-level course) Integrated reading–writing: Separate developmental reading and writing sequences are combined into a single sequence aligned with college English Corequisite model: The highest level developmental course is offered alongside the entry-level college course in that subject Modularization: Course is divided into discrete modules designed to improve a specific competency; students are required to complete and pass only the modules they need and no more Alternative math pathways: New shorter math sequences focus on quantitative literacy for students who do not need advanced math for their programs of study

Developmental Education Reform in Oregon

To better understand the conditions that support the implementation and eventual institutionalization of developmental education reforms, we conducted an in-depth case study of implementation at two community colleges in Oregon—a large college near an urban area and a small college in a rural area. We conducted interviews and focus groups with 16 faculty and administrators across the two colleges. These colleges provide an example of what developmental education reform looks like in practice and offer lessons for other institutions undertaking large-scale innovations.

Each college participated in a statewide working group focused on identifying and promoting best practices in developmental education redesign. Both colleges implemented multiple reforms, including multiple measures and accelerated developmental education sequences (shorter non-STEM math pathways, integrated reading–writing, and the co-requisite model). We identified four key strategies that contributed to the success of these large-scale implementation efforts: careful messaging, commitment and engagement of administrators and faculty, additional resources and capacity building, and leveraging external networks.

Careful Messaging Developmental education redesign is a paradigm shift that requires careful messaging by leadership to overcome resistance and ensure campus-wide support. Since redesign involves multiple departments, campus leaders had to communicate that developmental education was both a priority and an expectation. In framing their messages, campus leaders emphasized the basic value of developmental education for students and for the college overall. One administrator described the success of these efforts in building awareness and engagement:

> It used be just a teacher here or there working on it, or we put that responsibility on that teacher. Now, our campus is very aware of developmental [education]. They know these are the students that are really going to be supporting the school in terms of tuition and enrollment and numbers … Now we realize how significant they are in the entire financial health of the school, as well as academically helping these students who felt they didn't have much of a chance … [Administrator]

Indeed, some study participants indicated that aspects of developmental education redesign, such as the "holistic" approach, resonated with the "student-centered culture" on their campuses. On both campuses, study participants cited faculty turnover as opening the door for reform in some departments. New faculty were now being hired with an expectation that they will support developmental education, and being oriented to a culture where that is the norm.

However, many participants noted that "resistance" to redesign may create "conflict" once plans were implemented. Part of this resistance appears to be rooted in a lack of agreement on campus about what it means to be a "college-ready" student, with some faculty unwilling to integrate skill development into their content courses because they expect students to arrive ready to perform at a higher level. For example, one case study participant suggested that to reduce student costs, developmental education workshops should perhaps be offered prior to college enrollment.

Most commonly, participants suggested that developmental education redesign posed a challenge because implementation required them to break down "silos" and collaborate more frequently across departments. In particular, best practices such as the use of multiple measures for placement are blurring conventional roles by involving a wider range of staff in student advising and placement. While challenging, this "shift" has been mostly positive, both for campus culture and student achievement.

Commitment and Engagement of Administrators and Faculty The representation and engagement of diverse stakeholders is a cornerstone of successful developmental education redesign (Edgecombe et al. 2013; Price et al. 2015). In line with previous research, case study participants repeatedly returned to the idea that redesign is a "collaborative" process in which both faculty and administrators play an important role in building and sustaining the "momentum" necessary for reform.

Administrators typically viewed their role as seeding redesign efforts across campus and removing barriers for faculty and staff who may champion redesign with their peers. One administrator described cultivating an "institutional growth mindset" that fostered innovation and continuous improvement. On both campuses, administrators told stories of "self-generating" faculty who "asked questions, sought out professional development opportunities, embraced redesign in their own practice, and then brought others along in their department." This approach is based on the idea that redesign can't be top down because faculty place a high value on autonomy and innovation:

> You really need to involve faculty from the beginning and not tell them that this is what's going to happen, but provide them with the data and find people who can be champions among the faculty who will help their peers along. [Administrator]

On both campuses, faculty in English and math—as well as other subjects such as basic skills development and English as a Second Language—championed redesign, piloted reforms, and provided coaching to their peers. Student services staff also embraced redesign. In focus groups and interviews, faculty and staff often described administrators as being "open" to changes they proposed in courses and supportive of their participation in professional development.

> For me, when I come up with an idea it's well-received, and we try it and see if it works. I haven't been shut down … I've experienced a lot of open, excited encouragement from administration. [Faculty/staff]

Campuses often struggle to implement redesign in the face of campus norms of autonomy and isolation (Edgecombe et al. 2013). Both Oregon colleges are responding to this challenge by creating new norms of collaboration and by encouraging innovation around redesign. These findings are in line with research on the importance of cultivating internal networks (Price et al. 2015) that may be used to support and scale redesign.

Additional Resources and Capacity Building Additional resources and capacity building help engage faculty and staff and sustain the redesign process. Innovation and collaboration take time. In addition to encouragement, both campuses provided tangible resources and incentives to support participation in redesign. This includes funding and time to participate in professional development conferences as well as state and national meetings related to redesign. Campuses also offer course releases and sabbaticals to provide faculty with the time to work together on projects such as the redesign of courses or the analysis of course-taking and performance trends. At one college, faculty applied for "innovation funds" to support several redesign projects.

> Another key at this college is we have an innovation fund process that every year, right after budgeting – it's been at least a minimum of $250,000 per year … everybody gets to submit funded projects to identify if they attach

to a larger priority related to the institution or beyond. In that same year [when we started using innovation funds for developmental education redesign] we had a lot of synergy. That was probably one of our more productive movement years. [Administrator]

In addition to funding, participants cite the need for capacity building to implement and sustain reform. This includes professional development for faculty and staff in taking on new responsibilities, as was noted in one focus group:

> Writing teachers are having to see themselves as reading teachers. They have to teach students with problems they have never seen before. They might not be able to identify students early enough who are not able to pass. [Faculty/staff]

Study participants cited a particular need for more on-campus professional development to "foster a culture of sharing and learning about pedagogy." Study participants on both campuses cited considerable challenges in keeping part-time faculty informed about developmental education redesign efforts, given the limitations of their schedule.

Capacity building also involves the creation of new positions to respond to the greater demands redesign places on advising, placement, and institutional research staff. In the case of multiple measures, in particular, participants from both campuses highlighted the need for additional staffing to implement these reforms:

> What we're finding out, though, is that we're understaffed because these processes now take longer. I'm going to be talking with you as opposed to just looking at test scores and placing you, so there's some budget issues with that. I need more advisors to do intake advising if we're going to be going to a multiple measure models then that requires additional conversations with the students. The implementation is the issue. We can talk about the theory behind it and the research and the best practices, but it's hard to implement. [Faculty/staff]

Leveraging External Networks External networks provide useful perspective, models, and resources that spark or reinforce campus-level reforms. Across the sample, participants cited the value of participating in external networks such as the statewide Developmental Education Redesign Work Group and national initiative Achieving the Dream. Administrators frequently described how these networks offered "outside" perspective that they were able to use to generate support for redesign on campus.

On one level, administrators used these networks to make the case to campus leadership, faculty, and staff about the value of developmental education redesign. Participating in these networks made the campuses feel like they were part of a larger movement in which developmental redesign was an "expectation" and "not just us." Administrators intentionally sent cross-campus teams to participate in these activities so that they could support each other in bringing back the momentum and ideas to their own campus:

> I'll tell you it's helped me a lot to be able to go to instructional council, go to a general faculty meeting, go to the senate and say, you know, the state is saying we need to do this. I think that's helped tremendously. Then, of course, the faculty that have been going to those meetings can stand up and say, 'Yeah, you're right. We're doing a lot of good things and we think this will be best for us.' When the other faculty hear their peers saying that, it holds a lot of weight. [Administrator]

Not only do faculty and staff leave network meetings feeling "energized" about the work they are doing on campus, they also gain access to new models, research, and resources to support their efforts.

In Oregon, we observed that by embracing norms of autonomy and fostering a culture of innovation, both colleges have been successful in implementing developmental education reforms in multiple areas simultaneously. The challenge now lies in institutionalizing reforms, so they reach the majority of students and begin to have an impact on institutional outcomes.

Conclusion

While current developmental reforms are promising, more rigorously conducted evaluations are still needed to understand their impacts on various student outcomes, their implementation fidelity, and their ben-

Table 5.2 Student-level and institution-level outcomes and measures to consider tracking

	Interim	Long term
Student-level outcomes	Increased pass rates of students in redesigned courses (compared to pass rates in traditional courses or in years prior to redesign) Increased enrollment and pass rates of students in redesigned courses in college-level math/English (compared to prior-year college-level math/English enrollment/pass rates of students who started in traditional courses) Increased retention of students who participated in first-year experience, college success courses, or redesigned courses (compared to students who did not participate or prior year retention)	Decreasing trend in developmental education referral rate over time Increasing institution-level trends in persistence and completion rates
Institution-level outcomes	There is a campus wide committee/group to guide reform and a plan in place to help align efforts and sustain reform There are supportive and transparent policies/procedures in place Outreach is conducted to staff and students to increase campus-wide awareness and engagement in reform Data are available in a timely and accessible manner to inform reform efforts There is an investment in resources to support scaling	Reform is common practice/policy There are enough redesigned courses for all students who are interested/placed into the course Developmental education sequences are shorter and aligned with college-level content and major/career pathways Student services reforms reach the majority of the target population

efits relative to costs. Additionally, it is important for colleges to conduct studies to document how a particular strategy is implemented and the costs associated with the implementation, as well as evaluate the impacts of each strategy on student academic progress and success, and to share the findings widely with other colleges. An important part of scaling a reform is to assess its effectiveness and to make necessary adjustments (Edgecombe et al. 2013). The case study colleges are using data to examine course pass rates and students' progression through the redesigned courses. They should continue to assess the impact of the redesign on long-term, institutional outcomes to determine whether the changes are transforming outcomes for the college as a whole. Additionally, we recommend tracking interim and long-term implementation outcomes to understand the extent to which reforms are scaling up and sustaining (Table 5.2).

To conclude, developmental education is key to supporting the progress of underprepared community college students but can act as a hindrance limiting access to college-level coursework, delaying students' time-to-degree, and increasing attrition. Assessment and placement reforms and acceleration can turn developmental education from an obstacle into a bridge into programs of study. We found four key strategies supported the implementation of redesign efforts at colleges in Oregon:

- Careful messaging about the value and purpose of developmental education reform
- Commitment and engagement of both administrators and faculty
- Additional resources and capacity building
- External networks

Additionally, by using data to ensure innovations are effective and institutionalizing these innovations there will be a potential to realize wide-scale changes in student persistence and completion.

References

Bailey, T., Jeong, D. W., & Cho, S.-W. (2010). Referral, enrollment, and completion in developmental education sequences in community colleges. *Economics of Education Review, 29*(2), 255–270.

Bailey, T., Jaggars, S. S., & Scott-Clayton, J. (2013). *Characterizing the effectiveness of developmental education: A response to recent criticism.* New York: Columbia University/Teachers College/Community College Research Center.

Bettinger, E. P., & Long, B. T. (2005). Remediation at the community college: Student participation and outcomes. *New Directions for Community College, 129*, 17–26. http://eric.ed.gov/?id=EJ761022

Bettinger, E. P., & Long, B. T. (2009). Addressing the needs of underprepared students in higher education: Does college remediation work? *Journal of Human Resources, 44*(3), 736–771. http://eric.ed.gov/?id=EJ846143

Boatman, A., & Long, B. T. (2017). Does remediation work for all students? How the effects of postsecondary remedial and developmental course vary by level of academic preparation. *Educational Evaluation and Policy Analysis, 40*(1), 29–58.

Calcagno, J. C., & Long, B. T. (2008). *The impact of postsecondary remediation using a regression discontinuity approach: Addressing endogenous sorting and noncompliance* (NBER Working Paper No. 14194). Cambridge, MA: National Bureau of Economic Research.

Chen, X. (2016). *Remedial Coursetaking at U.S. Public 2- and 4-Year Institutions: Scope, Experiences, and Outcomes* (NCES 2016-405). U.S. Department of Education. Washington, DC: National Center for Education Statistics. Retrieved August 1, 2017, from http://nces.ed.gov/pubsearch

Cohen, A. M., Brawer, F. B., & Kisker, C. B. (2014). *The American Community College* (6th ed.). San Francisco, CA: Jossey-Bass.

Edgecombe, N., Cormier, M. S., Bickerstaff, S., & Barragan, M. (2013). *Strengthening developmental education reforms: Evidence on implementation efforts from the scaling innovation project* (CCRC Working Paper No. 61). New York: Columbia University, Teachers College, Community College Research Center.

Gardenhire, A., Diamond, J., Headlam, C., & Weiss, M. J. (2016). *At their own pace. Interim findings from an evaluation of a computer-assisted, modular approach to developmental math.* New York, NY: MDRC. Retrieved from https://www.mdrc.org/publication/their-own-pace.

Grubb, W. N., & Gabriner, R. (2013). *Basic skills education in community colleges: Inside and outside the classroom.* New York, NY: Routledge.

Hern, K. (2012). Acceleration across California: Shorter pathways in developmental English and math. *Change: The Magazine of Higher Learning, 44*(3), 60–68.

Hodara, M. (2012). Language minority students at community college: How do developmental education and English as a second language affect their educational outcomes? (Doctoral dissertation, Columbia University, 2012). *Dissertation Abstracts International, 73*(8-E).

Hodara, M., & Xu, D. (2016). Does developmental education improve labor market outcomes? Evidence from two states. *American Educational Research Journal, 53*(3), 781–813.

Hodara, M., Jaggars, S. S., & Karp, M. M. (2012). *Improving developmental education assessment and placement: Lessons from community colleges across the country* (CCRC Working Paper No. 51). New York, NY: Columbia University, Teachers College, Community College Research Center. http://eric.ed.gov/?id=ED537433

Hughes, K. L., & Scott-Clayton, J. (2011). Assessing developmental assessment in community colleges. *Community College Review, 39*(4), 327–351.

Jaggars, S. S., & Stacey, G. W. (2014, January). *What we know about developmental education outcomes (CCRC Research Overview).* New York: Columbia University/Teachers College/Community College Research Center. Retrieved April 22, 2014, from http://ccrc.tc.columbia.edu/media/k2/attachments/what-we-know-about-developmental-education-outcomes.pdf

Jaggars, S. S., Hodara, M., Cho, S.-W., & Xu, D. (2015). Three accelerated developmental education programs: Features, student outcomes, and implications. *Community College Review, 43*(1), 3–26.

Martorell, P., & McFarlin, I. Jr. (2011). Help or hindrance? The effects of college remediation on academic and labor market outcomes. *Review of Economics and Statistics, 93*(2), 436–454.

Mayer, A., Cerna, O., Cullinan, D., Fong, K., Rutschow, E. Z., & Jenkins, D. (2014). *Moving ahead with institutional change: Lessons from the first round of Achieving the Dream community colleges.* Retrieved January 1, 2016, from MDRC website: http://www.mdrc.org/publication/moving-ahead-institutional-change

Noble, J. P., Schiel, J. L., & Sawyer, R. L. (2004). Assessment and college course placement: Matching students with appropriate instruction. In J. E. Wall & G. R. Walz (Eds.), *Measuring up: Assessment issues for teachers, counselors, and administrators* (pp. 297–311). Greensboro: ERIC Counseling & Student Services Clearinghouse and the National Board of Certified Counselors.

Organisation for Economic Co-operation and Development (OECD). (2012). *United States 2012 PISA results.* https://www.oecd.org/unitedstates/PISA-2012-results-US.pdf

Price, D., McMaken, J., & Kioukis, G. (2015). *Case-informed lessons for scaling innovation at community and technical colleges.* Retrieved from Equal Measure website: http://www.equalmeasure.org/ideas/report/case-informed-lessons-for-scaling-innovation-at-community-and-technical-colleges/

Quint, J. C., Jaggars, S. S., Byndloss, D. C., & Magazinnik, A. (2013). *Bringing developmental education to scale: Lessons from the developmental education initiative.* Retrieved January 1, 2016, from MDRC website: http://www.mdrc.org/sites/default/files/Bringing%20Developmental%20Education%20to%20Scale%20FR.pdf

Rutschow, E. Z., & Diamond, J. (2015). *Early findings from the new mathways project.* New York: MDRC.

Scott-Clayton, J., & Rodriguez, O. (2015). Development, discouragement, or diversion? New evidence on the effects of college remediation. *Education Finance and Policy, 10*(1), 4–45.

Scott-Clayton, J., Crosta, P. M., & Belfield, C. R. (2014). Improving the targeting of treatment: Evidence from college remediation. *Educational Evaluation & Policy Analysis, 36*(3), 371–393.

U.S. Department of Education. (2011/12). *Beginning Postsecondary Students Longitudinal Study, First Follow-up (BPS:12/14).* Computation by NCES QuickStats on 8/29/2017. Washington, DC: National Center for Education Statistics.

Xu, D. (2016). Assistance or obstacles? The impact of different levels of English remediation on underprepared students in community colleges. *Educational Researcher, 45,* 496–507.

Xu, D., & Dadgar, M. (2018). How effective are community college remedial math courses for students with the lowest mathematics skills? *Community College Review, 46*(1), 62–81.

Yamada, H., & Bryk, A. S. (2016). Assessing the first two years' effectiveness of statway: A multilevel model with propensity score matching. *Community College Review, 44*(3), 179–204.

6

Vision 20:20 and Indigenous Health Workforce Development: Institutional Strategies and Initiatives to Attract Underrepresented Students into Elite Courses

Elana Taipapaki Curtis

Introduction

Widening access to highly competitive and restricted health professional programmes of study such as medicine, pharmacy and optometry remains a challenge for many tertiary institutions and countries worldwide. Indigenous, under-represented ethnic minorities and lower socio-economic communities are currently underserved by the current health workforce. Accepting a health workforce that fails to reflect the communities it aims to serve is unfair, unjust and is likely to be contributing to the creation and maintenance of contemporary ethnic inequities in health and healthcare (Curtis 2016). Tertiary educational institutions have an important role to play in the recruitment, admission, bridging/foundation edu-

E. T. Curtis (✉)
University of Auckland, Auckland, New Zealand
e-mail: e.curtis@auckland.ac.nz

cation, retention and graduation of students from indigenous and ethnic minority communities. Whilst secondary educational factors are undoubtedly a major driving factor in health workforce inequities, tertiary interventions can (and should) address a large number of the barriers to participation within these health professional programmes. This chapter explores the interventions associated with the *Vision 20:20* initiative within the FMHS at the University of Auckland, Aotearoa, New Zealand (NZ). A commitment to a widening participation agenda for indigenous Māori and Pacific students over the last 40 years has contributed to the University of Auckland's recent graduation of one of the largest cohorts of Māori and Pacific medical graduates worldwide. This success reflects a number of effective practices that can act as potential exemplars for other tertiary institutions and countries wishing to contribute to a social justice agenda within indigenous health workforce development.

Health Workforce Development

Health workforce development represents one area of response to address indigenous inequalities in health (Curtis 2016). Despite being a well-documented and significant issue, the challenge of providing a comprehensive indigenous and ethnic minority health workforce within a NZ context continues. For example, Māori and Pacific peoples are underrepresented, relative to overall population proportions, in the:

- Medical workforce (2.9% Māori, 1.8% Pacific compared to 95.3% European) (Ministry of Health 2014).
- Dental workforce (2.8% Māori, 1% Pacific compared to 53.5% NZ European) (Dental Council of New Zealand 2010) (Ministry of Health 2014).
- Pharmacy workforce (1.5% Māori, 0.9% Pacific compared to 52.3% NZ European/Pākehā (Pharmacy Council of New Zealand 2014).
- Optometry workforce (1.8% Māori, 1.5% Pacific compared to 52.2% NZ European) (Ministry of Health 2011).
- Nursing workforce across all DHB regions (6.6% Māori, 2.5% Pacific compared to 90.7% European) (Ministry of Health 2014).

- Midwifery workforce (5.2% Māori compared to 88.9% European) (Ministry of Health 2014).

The only area where Māori and Pacific are represented in proportions equivalent to their overall population within the health workforce is within the non-regulated workforce sector that includes lower paid occupations of kaiāwhina and support roles (i.e. 15% Māori and 8% Pacific) (Ministry of Health 2014).

Educational Inequities

Large secondary and tertiary educational inequities for Māori and Pacific students exist within NZ. Of concern, secondary schools are standing-down more Māori students than any other ethnic group and Māori and Pacific students have double the absence rate compared to European and Asian students (Ministry of Education 2015c). Māori have the lowest proportion of students remaining at school to age 17 and both Māori and Pacific students experience lower than OECD-average levels for science proficiency (Ministry of Education 2015a). In addition, Māori and Pacific are overrepresented in low decile (lower socio-economic) schools in NZ (i.e. 33% of Māori and 22% of Pacific are enrolled in a decile one primary or secondary school compared to 7% of European students) (Ministry of Education 2015c).

School deciles are a funding mechanism, used by government, that indicate the extent that a school draws their students from low socio-economic communities (Ministry of Education 2015b). Work by the Starpath Project at the University of Auckland has shown that there is a statistically significant correlation between school decile and achievement of a University Entrance (UE) qualification necessary for movement into degree-level tertiary study. For example, students from decile ten (higher socio-economic) secondary schools were three times more likely to leave school with the UE qualification than students from decile one (lower socio-economic) secondary schools (Madjar et al. 2009). The association between school decile and tertiary access is of major concern for Māori and Pacific potential to access tertiary education. This association is repeated internationally with tertiary participation being significantly lower for students from lower socio-economic backgrounds (Whitehead et al. 2013).

Educational inequities continue into tertiary education. Māori and Pacific students experience lower tertiary participation rates and Māori are the least likely to transition directly from high school to tertiary study compared to other ethnic groups. The proportion of Māori and Pacific people who hold a bachelor degree or above is much lower than non-Māori non-Pacific (Ministry of Education 2015a). Specific inequities include (Ministry of Education 2015a):

- Between the years of 2003 and 2013, Māori experienced the greatest decrease in tertiary participation (4.4 percentage points) compared to Asian (4.1 percentage points) and European/Pākehā (1.9 percentage points). In contrast, Pacific tertiary participation increased during this time period by 0.2 percentage points.
- Between 2010 and 2011, Māori and Pacific students were less likely to transition to tertiary education directly (68% and 65% respectively) compared with 90% of Asian students and 77% of European/Pākehā.
- In 2011, Māori and Pacific students had the lowest first year retention rate (74% and 79% respectively) compared to 89% for Asian and 84% for European students.
- In 2008, 9% of Māori and 8% of Pacific aged 25–64 years held a bachelors degree or above compared with 24% of their non-Māori non-Pacific counterparts.

University of Auckland and Vision 20:20

The University of Auckland is situated within central Auckland and is one of New Zealand's largest universities delivering undergraduate and postgraduate programmes to over 30,000 students (The University of Auckland 2015). Teaching and research are delivered over eight faculties and two large scale research institutes (The University of Auckland 2015).

The FMHS was established in 1968 as The University of Auckland School of Medicine. Originally dedicated to medical education, it now offers five undergraduate degree programs: the Bachelor of Health Sciences (BHSc), Bachelor of Medicine and Bachelor of Surgery (MBChB), Bachelor of Nursing (BNurs), Bachelor of Pharmacy (BPharm) and more recently Bachelor of Optometry (BOptom) (The University of Auckland 2013).

The Faculty has demonstrated a long-standing commitment to addressing Māori and Pacific health workforce development via the provision of a Māori and Pacific entry quota since 1972, Māori and Pacific bridging/foundation since 1999 and Māori student recruitment since 2003. Developed in the late 1990s, Vision 20:20 articulated a high-level, strategic equity statement for the FMHS to achieve and support Māori and Pacific health workforce development. Under Vision 20:20, the Faculty has a stated commitment to increase the proportion of the Māori and Pacific health workforce to 10% by the year 2020. Today, Vision 20:20 represents a Faculty initiative consisting of the three major programmes targeting Māori and Pacific student recruitment, admission, bridging/foundation education and retention. These programmes include:

- The Whakapiki Ake Project (WAP) (Māori secondary school recruitment);
- The Māori and Pacific Admission Scheme (MAPAS) (Māori and Pacific admission and student support for students enrolled in undergraduate and postgraduate programmes within the FMHS); and
- Hikitia Te Ora—Certificate in Health Sciences (CertHSc) providing Māori and Pacific bridging and foundation education. A one-year programme of study focused on bridging students with academic gaps into first year health professional degree-level study.

Understanding the process of health workforce development and the way this is reflected within the Vision 20:20 initiative is helped by the use of a pipeline framework (Ratima et al. 2007a; The Sullivan Commission

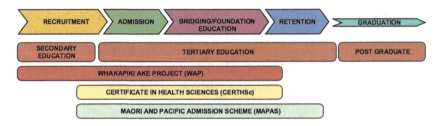

Fig. 6.1 Vision 20:20 pipeline

2004). The following conceptual pipeline is specific to the Vision 20:20 context (Fig. 6.1).

The number of Māori and Pacific students enrolled within the Faculty has increased significantly over the recent years. In semester one 2017, there were 477 Māori and Pacific students enrolled within FMHS undergraduate programmes with 71 in the CertHSc programme, 121 in health science (BHSc), 239 in medicine (MBChB), 20 in nursing (BNurs), 6 in pharmacy (BPharm), 6 in optometry (BOptom) and 14 students in various conjoint degrees. Between the years 2002 and 2009, 17% of the medical student intake were Māori and Pacific students admitted via the MAPAS pathway (Curtis et al. 2017).

The achievement of FMHS students (particularly within the Certificate in Health Sciences and medicine) has also improved with the faculty having one of the largest increases in successful course completion rates for Māori students within the university moving from 78.5% in 2007 to 94.6% in 2014. The Pacific completion rate within the FMHS increased from 81.9% to 88.6% across the same timeframe (University of Auckland 2015).

Effective Practices for Indigenous Health Workforce Development

Twelve recommendations for 'effective practice' are presented. These recommendations draw on research undertaken by Vision 20:20 to examine the areas of recruitment, admission, bridging/foundation education and retention for Māori and Pacific health workforce development.

Recruitment

Effective Practice 1: Recruitment Must Target Academic Requirements for Health Professional Study

Research findings highlight the importance of secondary education outcomes in the health workforce pipeline (Curtis et al. 2012b). In order to progress into health professional study, indigenous students must have access to, and achieve well in, science, mathematics and English-related subjects. Despite MAPAS applicants representing a cohort of students wanting health professional study, our research has identified that these applicants are not always 'university ready' and often require an alternative academic pathway in order to acquire the academic building blocks necessary for entry, and success within, our health professional programmes of study (Curtis et al. 2015b).

Recruitment strategies must ensure that this educational reality is acknowledged and addressed. Hollow et al. (2006) have identified similar issues for American Indian and Alaska Native students enrolled in medicine at the University of Washington in Seattle (Hollow et al. 2006). Early educational experiences were the most frequently mentioned sources of support for the students interviewed. However, a small number of students also noted that 'poor-quality education, especially in science, was a barrier to their pursuit of a medical career' (Hollow et al. 2006, p. S66). Brunson et al. (2010) review recruitment strategies within their context of dentistry and argue for an increased focus on the closing of preparatory gaps.

Reviewing indigenous pathways into professional occupations, Anderson (2011) notes the importance of tertiary recruitment strategies to provide additional academic development to support indigenous students to become competitive by the end of their secondary schooling. Successful educational interventions will need to move beyond a focus on remediation and ensure that indigenous students with potential are adequately prepared for professional study contexts. Anderson (2011) argues for universities to refocus indigenous student recruitment to include interventions to build the secondary school cohort so that they can successfully transition into higher education.

Effective Practice 2: Recruitment Must Offer a Comprehensive Suite of Recruitment Interventions

Research findings reinforce the importance of providing a comprehensive suite of recruitment interventions that can target indigenous students at different points of their journey along the workforce pipeline (Curtis et al. 2012b; Ratima et al. 2007b). Early exposure interventions, offered within multiple settings and contexts (both internal and external to the tertiary institution) are required. In addition to the academic support outlined above, recruitment programmes should consider a mix of school visits, secondary and tertiary enrichment programmes, advertising/marketing, secondary school financial support, targeting of careers advisors and interventions that are inclusive of indigenous communities (Curtis et al. 2012b).

It is important to note that the comprehensive nature of recruitment activity extends beyond the number and type of interventions provided. Our findings highlight the need for recruitment interventions to be grounded in indigenous realities (Curtis et al. 2012b). This includes purposeful framing of educational disparities as representing a product of historical and contemporary colonisation, the representation of indigenous-specific recruitment as reflecting indigenous student and community rights within a social justice agenda, and the active incorporation of opportunities for students to develop cultural and indigenous leadership skills.

Effective Practice 3: Recruitment Must Be Grounded in Indigenous Realities and Contexts

The recruitment literature discusses the importance of actively including parents, families and indigenous communities within early exposure activities as they have an important influence on student career choices (Curtis et al. 2012b). This approach is consistent with the collective ethos underpinning Māori and Pacific culture and should be incorporated into recruitment practices. Similarly, the use of cultural points of reference, access to indigenous leadership or role models and the ability to deliver recruitment activities appropriate to the socio-cultural and economic positioning of indigenous students and their families is encouraged (Curtis et al. 2015).

This recommendation is consistent with Mackean et al. (2007) who note that best practice elements in the recruitment of indigenous students include personal contact and community engagement involving both university and school visits (Mackean et al. 2007).

Effective Practice 4: Recruitment Should Be Linked to Equity Admissions Processes That Include the Provision of Alternative Pathways

Our findings from across the workforce pipeline highlight the importance of linking recruitment activities to the equity admission processes and alternative pathways offered by tertiary institutions. The experience of Vision 20:20, where indigenous students were recruited with inadequate academic preparation and encouraged to enter the CertHSc, resulted in poor student outcomes (Curtis and Reid 2013). These experiences assisted us to understand the interrelated nature of recruitment on admission processes, bridging/foundation education delivery and retention (and vice versa) (Curtis and Reid 2013; Curtis et al. 2014a). As a result, Vision 20:20 now represents a programme in which indigenised recruitment is embedded within the delivery of the equity admissions process, bridging/foundation programme and student retention activities.

To successfully recruit and retain indigenous people into medicine, the Australian Indigenous Doctors Association (2005, p. 45) argues that 'multiple and flexible pathways need to be developed that take into account peoples' life stages, educational and socioeconomic background and cultural context'. They note that the complexities of tertiary admission can deter some indigenous applicants therefore indigenous recruitment that is aligned with the delivery of admissions processes is recommended (Australian Indigenous Doctors Association 2005). Ratima et al. (2007a, p. 167) also describe the delivery of alternative pathways as being an important recruitment tool, noting:

At the organisational level, bridging courses were identified as recruitment facilitators. Bridging courses are offered by most tertiary institutions, and will continue to be important facilitators of Māori participation in the workforce for some time

Admission

Vision 20:20 has confirmed the internal validity of the MAPAS admissions process and that this process has been positively associated with first-year academic outcomes (Curtis et al. 2015a, b). Based on these findings, which are now reflected in the delivery of Vision 20:20 interventions, three effective practices for admission are recommended.

Effective Practice 5: Admissions Processes Should Focus on Identifying the 'Best Starting Point' for Success

Central to the MAPAS admissions process is the alignment of assessment to identify an applicant's 'best starting point' for entry towards their intended health career. This approach to student admission reflects the educational disparities experienced by Māori and Pacific students within NZ and the mismatch between programme entry criteria and the potential to succeed once admitted (Curtis et al. 2015b).

The science of 'picking stayers' (p. 548) or indigenous students who will be successful within health professional programmes of study is a challenge for most universities (Lawson et al. 2007). In addition to academic ability, the literature supports the assessment of motivation, support structures and an applicant's ability to balance study with family and community commitments (Australian Indigenous Doctors Association 2005; Lawson et al. 2007). However, it is acknowledged that the science behind this process is imprecise:

> …*it is difficult at times to decide on a background that guarantees completion, and we have had remarkable success stories from a range of academic backgrounds.* (Lawson et al. 2007, p. 548)

This is particularly relevant for mature applicants considering a career in health. The MAPAS admissions process, inclusive of a Multiple Mini Interview, Mathematics and English testing, facilitates a level of objective assessment of the ability of mature applicants to succeed. This is important given the findings of Ratima et al. (2007a, b, p. 174) who note:

There were some concerns among research participants that tertiary education institutions are better equipped to recruit students directly from school, and are less adept at targeting and providing support for mature students considering a career in health.

The MAPAS admissions process was found to be important given the complex, lived realities of many indigenous students (including mature applicants). Within the MAPAS admissions process, these complex, lived realities of indigenous students are explicitly explored and investigated. This information is used to assess the appropriateness of student admission *and* the delivery of student support services. Therefore, the MAPAS admissions process was found to provide an important site of negotiation where the potential 'misfit' between the lived realities of indigenous students and institutional resources for support are examined and addressed.

Effective Practice 6: Admissions Processes Should Assess Applicants Holistically Using Both Cognitive and Non-cognitive Selection Tools

Vision 20:20 research findings suggest that there is value in providing a comprehensive admissions process for indigenous students that is inclusive of both cognitive and non-cognitive selection tools (Curtis et al. 2015a, b). These findings also provide evidence for the value in adapting the Multiple Mini Interview for use within a holistic, equity-targeted admissions process.

Consistent with previous research, the MAPAS admissions process was found to highlight the need for universities to establish 'a more flexible and inclusive selection and admission policy emphasising personal qualities and experience as well as academic ability' (Powis et al. 2007, p. 1239).

Powis et al. (2007) support the assessment of non-academic qualities and skills noting the importance of using methods and instruments that are 'reliable and valid, fair and equitable, and which are free of cultural, racial and gender bias' (Powis et al. 2007, p. 1242). The use of the Multiple Mini Interview, within an equity-targeted admissions process, is seen to align with this recommendation as it is likely to remove bias (by using more than one interviewer) and provides guidelines for interviewer assessment (Powis et al. 2007). The Multiple Mini Interview has been shown to provide practically relevant, positive predictive correlations for future performance within medicine (Eva et al. 2004, 2009; Siu and Reiter 2009).

Effective Practice 7: Admissions Processes Should Be Inclusive of Alternative Pathways and Points of Entry

As previously noted for recruitment, the provision of an equity-targeted bridging/foundation programme can contribute to redressing educational and social disparities experienced by Māori and Pacific students within NZ. Universities committed to achieving equity targets within an indigenous rights framework should provide alternative points of entry including bridging/foundation education and a comprehensive admissions process should be provided to support student selection into the programme(s) on offer.

Middleton (2008) reinforces the importance of the secondary education and higher education interface. The provision of 'enabling programmes' is acknowledged as being a mechanism that can enhance student success and retention in higher education (Middleton 2008). Given this reality, it is important that tertiary admission processes link to and offer alternative points of entry for indigenous students to increase the potential for socio-academic success within the institution. James (2007) also acknowledges the role of enabling programmes in widening access for indigenous students and argues for tertiary institutions to select students more flexibly by being less reliant on academic ranking scores (James 2007). As noted by Zepke and colleagues within their guidelines for effective tertiary practice, some students 'may need to be counselled out of taking a particular course' (Zepke et al. 2005, p. 21). They acknowledge the importance of providing sound academic advice rather than focusing on increasing student numbers as 'the drive for "bums on seats" does not lead to good retention' (Zepke et al. 2005, p. 21).

Bridging/Foundation

Alongside the previous recommendations for bridging/foundation education to be aligned with recruitment and admission processes, two additional effective practices specific to bridging/foundation are recommended.

Effective Practice 8: Bridging/Foundation Education Should Provide a Comprehensive and Holistic 'Learning Community'

It is arguable, that alongside changes made to student selection, the development of a 'learning community' within the CertHSc programme contributed positively to improving student outcomes (Curtis et al. 2014a).

According to Malnarich (2005, p. 52), learning communities 'create the kind of learning environments that engage students in the hard, persistent, and challenging work associated with academic success'". Malnarich (2005) outlines a number of recommendations for successful learning communities that can be observed within the characteristics of the CertHSc model including the infusion of an intellectually rigorous, inclusive curriculum with high expectations, the design of developmentally appropriate assessments, and the inclusion of student participation in the creation of knowledge. In particular, the CertHSc learning community allowed for previously noted 'curricular choices that intentionally introduce non-Western experiences, language, and values into the classroom in order to disturb what people "know" to be true' (Malnarich 2005, pp. 59–60). The decolonised nature of the CertHSc environment is likely to be a contributing factor to positive academic outcomes seen for both Māori and Pacific students and aligns with Malnarich's assertion that learning community students 'are invited to explore diversity and engage in comparative cultural analysis that upsets essentialist and monocultural notions of "truth"' (Malnarich 2005, p. 60).

The learning community approach was also found to align with available evidence that identifies the factors leading to successful bridging/foundation education (Trewartha 2008). Examples include a pedagogy that has a focus on improving the quality of the learning process, valuing and accommodating the cultural capital of students, provision of an inclusive and affirming classroom environment and staff collaboration across disciplines to support the delivery of well managed and comprehensive student assessment (Trewartha 2008). Within our research, the close integration of MAPAS student support staff and activities within the CertHSc programme is key to the success of our learning community approach. These findings offer new documentation for the delivery of indigenous-appropriate learning communities where cultural and indigenous-specific student support expertise are interwoven with academic and broader programme operations.

Effective Practice 9: Bridging/Foundation Education Requires High Quality Teaching and Learning Delivered Within a Constructively Aligned Curriculum

Associated with the development of the learning community approach outlined above, the importance of high quality teaching and learning and the requirement for a constructively aligned curriculum within bridging/foundation education is recommended. Vision 20:20 evidence indicates that CertHSc programme changes in response to these issues have contributed to the dramatic improvements in student outcomes observed within the CertHSc (Curtis and Reid 2013; Curtis et al. 2012a, 2014a).

Biggs (2014, p. 5) describes constructive alignment as 'an outcomes-based approach to teaching in which the learning outcomes that students are intended to achieve are defined before teaching takes place'. Teaching is then developed to engage students in effective teaching and learning activities linked to those objectives and student assessment tasks are designed to assess whether the objectives have been attained (Biggs 2014). Biggs (1999, p. 73) notes that:

Constructive alignment is common sense, yet most university teaching is not aligned. This is possibly because many academics, holding traditional transmission theories of teaching that ignore alignment, simply haven't seen the need to question their assumptions.

Retention

Vision 20:20 findings contribute to the growing literature base demonstrating the importance and effectiveness of providing comprehensive support services for indigenous students within tertiary education contexts (Curtis et al. 2014b). Student support services delivered within culturally appropriate contexts were predominantly helpful to student retention. In contrast, the undergraduate programme environment was identified as being both helpful and hindering to success with some students experiencing 'unsafe' teaching and learning practice. The teaching of indigenous health to all students will assist in the development of a culturally competent student body (and workforce) that in turn is hypothesised to support indigenous student retention. Based on these findings, three effective practices are recommended for retention.

Effective Practice 10: Retention Requires Comprehensive Student Support Service for Māori and Pacific Students

The research findings highlight the helpful impact of student support services that provide indigenous-specific study and meeting spaces, additional study resources and dedicated support staff able to respond to both academic and pastoral student needs. The provision of culturally appropriate cohort bonding activities supported retention by creating a sense of belonging and connectedness for indigenous students (Curtis et al. 2014b).

The New Zealand Tertiary Education Committee notes that 'a culturally appropriate and relevant learning environment is consistently identified in the literature as fundamental to Māori doing well in tertiary settings' (p. 11) (Chauvel and Rean 2012). Key factors for success include the provision of culturally specific learning spaces and peer mentoring where Māori learners are 'socially and academically connected to support through regular interactions with academic staff, role models and peers' (p. 12) (Chauvel and Rean 2012). Greenwood and Te Aika (2008) suggest that the development of spaces 'where Māori values operate, where Māori knowledge is valued, where iwi are welcomed and where Māori people can be at home' (p. 11) are core factors related to the association between the provision of indigenous-specific spaces and successful Māori student retention (Greenwood and Te Aika 2008).

Mayeda et al. (2014) explored similar issues for both Māori and Pacific students. Their findings also stress the importance of having safe spaces for ethnic minority students within predominantly white, westernised, institutions. Identified as 'ethnic counter spaces' (p. 175), Māori and Pacific students are able to provide one another with emotional and cultural support, to learn in ways that draw from their cultural backgrounds (without feeling judged by non-Māori non-Pacific peers or educators) and may experience an increased sense of institutional inclusion (Mayeda et al. 2014). Airini et al. (2011, p. 83) note the importance of having a place to gather both informally and formally as Māori and Pacific students because:

Such spaces created havens in which minority culture, language and identity could be normal, and learning, support, and success could occur through lenses of culture, language and identity. Without space, students felt stressed, isolated, and lacking in confidence.

Alongside the creation of ethnic counter spaces, the literature also acknowledges the importance of student support services. Gorinski and Abernathy (2007, p. 232) suggest that support services assist in the creation of positive relationships necessary for retention success:

Students' relationship with the institution is negotiated through the people and services that provide clear guidelines to institutional expectations of them, development of learning skills and success in their studies. The confidence that student support is central to the core business of the institution (not the add-on for the deficient) may be a determining factor in effective participation and retention.

Effective Practice 11: Retention Requires a Culturally-Inclusive Teaching and Learning Environment

Successful retention of Māori and Pacific learners requires targeted student support services, however the total teaching and learning environment is also important. Tertiary institutions that can provide a culturally-inclusive teaching and learning environment do better in terms of supporting Māori and Pacific student retention (Chauvel and Rean 2012).

Gorinski and Abernathy (2007, p. 230) argue for total curriculum transformation in order to reduce student alienation. They suggest that:

> *Māori (and minority) students need to see themselves reflected in the curriculum through acknowledgement of their prior learning, their values and experiences, their traditions and cultural icons, in order to effectively engage with the curriculum and develop commitment to their study and achievement.*

Chauvel and Rean (2012) note the importance of integrating culturally relevant content and pedagogy as it is affirming of cultural (and self) identity that has been associated with academic success. Airini et al. (2011, p. 79) showed that Māori and Pacific students perceived their success to be 'linked to experiences in which university educators facilitated learning through links between university studies and culture'. The absence of links to culture acted as barriers to academic success (Airini et al. 2011).

However, other research cautions against the inclusion of cultural content if framed from a stereotypical positioning. Mayeda et al.'s (2014, p. 175) findings suggest that when cultural content was included within the curriculum, lecturers often 'perpetuated a deficit model, framing racialised disparities through victim-blaming'. Identifying these experiences as 'everyday colonialism and racism', Mayeda et al. (2014, p. 176) call for teaching staff to 'adjust curricula in ways that encourage indigenous and related minority students to discover their ethnic identities' and 'be supported in forging positive ethnic identities'. If this occurs, student retention is likely to improve. As identified by Zepke and Leach (2005, p. 52), student departure is influenced by 'their perceptions of how well their cultural attributes are valued, accommodated and how differences between their cultures of origin and immersion are bridged'.

Effective Practice 12: Retention Is Aided by the Development of Cultural Safety and Cultural Competency of Non-indigenous Students

The research showed that the experience of re-presenting the indigenous health curriculum to ensure that all students are prepared to meet the challenge of improving Māori health and reducing health inequities is expected to support indigenous student retention (Curtis et al. 2014a).

Related to the recommendation above, positive curricula representations of Māori and Pacific individuals and society should help to expose non-indigenous students to alternative frameworks that may require them to 'unlearn' previously accepted 'truths' about New Zealand history and society (Curtis et al. 2014a). Evidence of stigmatisation of quota pathways and assumptions of preferential treatment have been reported by Māori and Pacific students as being 'quite demoralising' with students feeling less empowered to 'speak out' or 'draw attention to themselves' (Mayeda et al. 2014, p. 175). If unlearning occurs, non-indigenous students may be encouraged to self-reflect (integral to cultural safety) and a greater understanding of Māori and Pacific cultural diversity may be achieved (DeSouza 2008). In this context, it is expected that peer–peer racism experienced by Māori and Pacific students may reduce, leading to increased indigenous student retention.

Supporting non-indigenous students to increase cultural competency and cultural safety is expected to contribute to an environment that will reduce experiences of 'everyday colonialism and racism' (Mayeda et al. 2014). As previously noted, this is important as access to a culturally inclusive teaching and learning environment has been shown to improve indigenous student retention (Chauvel and Rean 2012).

Discussion

At the heart of health workforce development is education. As previously outlined, New Zealand's education system historically, and presently, empowers and privileges non-Māori, Pākehā, students to achieve positive academic outcomes. In contrast, Māori and Pacific students experience an alienating and restricted environment of learning that contribute to large inequities observed in both secondary and tertiary educational settings. Arguably, it is these educational inequities that drive disparities in health workforce capacity and capability observed for Māori and Pacific communities within the NZ context.

Addressing the educational drivers of inequity is important. This requires a focus not only on why and how the education system works so that indigenous students are underrepresented within tertiary contexts, but an equally important focus on why our universities operate in ways that ensure non-indigenous students are over-represented in both participation and performance. Wheelan (2009) describes the social inclusion policies of tertiary education within an Australian context as promoting a 'focus on the under-representation of students from disadvantaged backgrounds' (p. 262) whilst rarely calling attention 'to the over-representation of students from more privileged background. What results is the casting of disadvantage as "attributes that are lacking in students from disadvantaged backgrounds, thus obscuring the social conditions that structure disadvantage and privilege"' (Wheelan 2009, p. 262).

Clearly framing her views on tertiary equity from a social justice perspective, Wheelan (2009) supports the need for 'distributive justice' where there is a restructuring of privilege and disadvantage to better support disadvantaged students to access high status professional occupations and therefore 'social power' (p. 262) (Wheelan 2009). This is particularly important for elite universities and professional programmes of study that have historically mediated access for students from privileged backgrounds (Crampton et al. 2012). In addition, recent data analyses suggest that there is a need to look beyond increasing access *into* health professional programmes by ensuring there are adequate supports in place to support successful movement *through* to graduation and completion (Curtis 2017). This work confirms that it is possible to admit significant numbers of indigenous students into medicine via equity pathways and have most successfully complete the programme despite entering with lower academic qualifications.

Conclusion

Vision 20:20 represents a programme of investment *into* indigenous health workforce development using tertiary and indigenous-led interventions. Incremental changes to the model of indigenous support, the provision of indigenous-appropriate recruitment activities, alternative pathways of entry via comprehensive bridging/foundation education and admission processes inclusive of social justice quotas for entry have all contributed to the success seen within the FMHS at the University of Auckland. This chapter provides a framework of effective practices to help other tertiary institutions intervene and uphold the rights of indigenous peoples worldwide. It is no longer appropriate to ignore the potential contribution tertiary institutions can provide with respect to health professional programme access and widening participation.

References

Airini, Curtis, E., Townsend, S., Rakena, T., Brown, D., Sauni, P., … Johnson, O. (2011). Teaching for student success: Promising practices in university teaching. *Pacific-Asian Education, 23*(1), 71–90.

Anderson, I. (2011). *Indigenous pathways into the professions*. Melbourne: University of Melbourne.

Australian Indigenous Doctors Association. (2005). *Healthy futures: Defining best practice in the recruitment and retention of Indigenous medical students*. Canberra: Australian Government: Department of Health and Aging.

Biggs, J. (1999). What the student does: Teaching for enhanced learning. *Higher Education Research & Development, 18*(1), 57–75.

Biggs, J. (2014). Constructive alignment in university teaching. *HERDSA Review of Higher Education, 1*, 5–22.

Brunson, W., Jackson, D., Sinkford, J., & Valachovic, R. (2010). Components of effective outreach and recruitment programs for underrepresented minority and low-income dental students. *Journal of Dental Education, 74*(Suppl. 10), S74–S86.

Chauvel, F., & Rean, J. (2012). *Doing better for Māori in tertiary settings*. Wellington: Tertiary Education Commission.

Crampton, P., Weaver, N., & Howard, A. (2012). Holding a mirror to society? The sociodemographic characteristics of the University of Otago's health professional students. *New Zealand Medical Journal, 125*(1361), 12–28.

Curtis, E. (2016). *Kohi Maramara. The effect of tertiary recruitment, admission, bridging/foundation education and retention on indigenous health workforce development* (Doctor of Medicine). University of Auckland, Auckland.

Curtis, E., & Reid, P. (2013). Indigenous health workforce development: Challenges and successes of the vision 20:20 programme. *Australian & New Zealand Journal of Surgery, 83*(1–2), 49–54.

Curtis, E., Townsend, S., & Airini. (2012a). Improving indigenous and ethnic minority student success in foundation health study. *Teaching in Higher Education, 17*(5), 1–14. https://doi.org/10.1080/13562517.2012.658559.

Curtis, E., Wikaire, E., Stokes, K., & Reid, P. (2012b). Addressing indigenous health workforce inequities: A literature review exploring 'best' practice for recruitment into tertiary health programmes. *International Journal for Equity in Health, 11*(13), 1–15.

Curtis, E., Reid, P., & Jones, R. (2014a). Decolonising the academy: The process of re-presenting indigenous health in tertiary teaching and learning. In F. Cram, H. Phillips, P. Sauni, & C. Tuagalu (Eds.), *Māori and Pasifika higher education horizons* (Vol. 15, pp. 147–166). Bingley: Emerald Group.

Curtis, E., Wikaire, E., Kool, B., Honey, M., Kelly, F., Poole, P., ... Reid, P. (2014b). What helps and hinders indigenous student success in higher education health programmes: A qualitative study using the Critical Incident Technique. *Higher Education Research & Development, 34*(3), 486–500. https://doi.org/10.1080/07294360.2014.973378.

Curtis, E., Stokes, K., Wikaire, E., & Reid, P. (2015). Recruiting via Hui-ā-Rohe: How the Whakapiki Ake Project has increased engagement with Māori students, their whānau (families) and communities. In O. Mazel & C. Ryan (Eds.), *LIME good practice case studies* (Vol. 3, pp. 16–23). Melbourne: University of Melbourne.

Curtis, E., Wikaire, E., Jiang, Y., McMillan, L., Loto, R., Airini, & Reid, P. (2015a). Quantitative analysis of a Māori and Pacific admission process on first-year health study. *BMC Medical Education, 15*(196), 1–17.

Curtis, E., Wikaire, E., Jiang, Y., McMillan, L., Loto, R., Airini, & Reid, P. (2015b). A tertiary approach to improving equity in health: Quantitative analysis of the Māori and Pacific Admission Scheme (MAPAS) process, 2008–2012. *International Journal for Equity in Health, 14*(7), 1–15. https://doi.org/10.1186/s12939-015-0133-7.

Curtis, E., Wikaire, E., Jiang, Y., McMillan, L., Loto, R., Poole, P., ... Reid, P. (2017). Examining the predictors of academic outcomes for indigenous Māori, Pacific and rural students admitted into medicine via two equity pathways: A retrospective observational study at the University of Auckland, Aotearoa New Zealand. *BMJ Open, 7*(8), e017276.

Dental Council of New Zealand. (2010). *Dental council workforce analysis 2009*. Wellington: Author.

DeSouza, R. (2008). Wellness for all: The possibilities of cultural safety and cultural competence in New Zealand. *Journal of Research in Nursing, 13*(2), 125–135.

Eva, K., Rosenfeld, J., Reiter, H., & Norman, G. (2004). An admissions OSCE: The multiple mini-interview. *Medical Education, 38*, 314–326.

Eva, K., Reiter, H., Trinh, K., Wasi, P., Rosenfeld, J., & Norman, G. (2009). Predictive validity of the multiple mini-interview for selecting medical trainees. *Medical Education, 43*(8), 767–775.

Gorinski, R., & Abernathy, G. (2007). Māori student retention and success: Curriculum, pedagogy and relationships. In T. Townsend & R. Bates (Eds.), *Handbook of teacher education: Globalization, standards and professionalism in times of change* (pp. 229–240). Dordrecht: Springer.

Greenwood, J., & Te Aika, L. (2008). *Hei Tauira: Teaching and learning for success for Māori in tertiary settings*. Wellington: Ako Aotearoa.

Hollow, W., Patterson, D., Olsen, P., & Baldwin, L. (2006). American Indians and Alaska natives: How do they find their path to medical school? *Academic Medicine, 81*(Suppl. 10), S65–S69.

James, R. (2007). *Social equity in a mass, globalised higher education environment: The unresolved issue of widening access to university*. Melbourne: Centre for the Study of Higher Education. Retrieved from http://cshe.unimelb.edu.au/people/james_docs/Richard%20James%20Dean's%20Lecture%20Series%20Sept2007.pdf

Lawson, K., Armstrong, R., & Van Der Weyden, M. (2007). Training indigenous doctors for Australia: Shooting for goal. *Medical Journal of Australia, 186*(10), 547–550.

Mackean, T., Mokak, R., Carmichael, A., Phillips, G., Prideaux, D., & Walters, T. (2007). Reform in Australian medical schools: A collaborative approach to realising indigenous health potential. *Medical Journal of Australia, 186*(10), 544–546.

Madjar, I., McKinley, E., Jenssen, S., & Van Der Merwe, A. (2009). *Towards university: Navigating NCEA course choices in low-mid decile schools*. Auckland: Starpath Project, The University of Auckland.

Malnarich, G. (2005). Learning communities and curricular reform: "Academic apprenticeships" for developmental students. *New Directions for Community Colleges, 129*(Spring), 51–62.

Mayeda, D., Keil, M., Dutton, H., & 'Ofamo'oni, I. (2014). "You've gotta set a precedent". Māori and Pacific voices on student success in higher education. *AlterNative, 10*(2), 165–179.

Middleton, S. (2008, July). *Beating the filters of failure: Engaging with the disengaged in higher education*. Paper presented at the Higher Education Research & Development Society Association (HERDSA) 2008 International Conference, Rotorua, New Zealand. Retrieved from http://www.herdsa.org.au/wp-content/uploads/conference/2008/media/Stuart%20Middleton.pdf

Ministry of Education. (2015a). *Education counts*. Retrieved September 4, 2015, from http://www.educationcounts.govt.nz/indicators

Ministry of Education. (2015b). *Education counts*. Retrieved November 25, 2015, from http://www.education.govt.nz/school/running-a-school/resourcing/operational-funding/school-decile-ratings/

Ministry of Education. (2015c). *School rolls*. Retrieved November 25, 2015, from https://www.educationcounts.govt.nz/statistics/schooling/student-numbers/6028

Ministry of Health. (2011). *Monitoring the regulated Māori health workforce*. Wellington, New Zealand: Author. Retrieved from http://www.health.govt.nz/publications/monitoring-regulated-maori-health-workforce

Ministry of Health. (2014). *Health of the health workforce 2013 to 2014: A report by health workforce New Zealand*. Wellington: Author.

Pharmacy Council of New Zealand. (2014). *Pharmacy Council of New Zealand workforce demographics as at 30 June 2014*. Wellington: Author.

Powis, D., Hamilton, J., & McManus, I. (2007). Widening access by changing the criteria for selecting medical students. *Teaching and Teacher Education, 23*(8), 1235–1245.

Ratima, M., Brown, R., Garrett, N., Wikaire, E., Ngawati, R., Aspin, C., & Potaka, U. (2007a). *Rauringa Raupa: Recruitment and retention of Māori in the health and disability workforce*. Auckland: Taupua Waiora: Division of Public Health and Psychosocial Studies, Faculty of Health and Environmental Sciences, AUT University.

Ratima, M., Brown, R., Garrett, N., Wikaire, E., Ngawati, R., Aspin, C., & Potaka, U. (2007b). Strengthening Māori participation in the New Zealand health and disability workforce. *Medical Journal of Australia, 186*(10), 541–543.

Siu, E., & Reiter, H. (2009). Overview: What's worked and what hasn't as a guide towards predictive admissions tool development. *Advances in Health Sciences Education, 14*, 759–775.

The Sullivan Commission. (2004). *Missing persons: Minorities in the health professions. A report of the Sullivan Commission on diversity in the healthcare workforce.* Atlanta: The Sullivan Commission.

The University of Auckland. (2013). *2014 Faculty of Medical and Health Sciences undergraduate prospectus.* Auckland: Author.

The University of Auckland. (2015). University of Auckland key statistics 2010–2014. Retrieved September 9, 2015, from https://cdn.auckland.ac.nz/assets/central/about/the-university/documents/Website%20Key%20stats%20Pdf-%20EFTS%20&%20FTE%20-2010-2014.pdf

Trewartha, R. (2008). Innovations in bridging and foundation education in a tertiary institution. *Australian Journal of Adult Learning, 48*(1), 30–49.

University of Auckland. (2015). *University of Auckland equity profile 2014. Compiled by the staistical consulting centre for the equity office – Te Ara Tautika.* Auckland: University of Auckland.

Wheelan, L. (2009). Do educational pathways contribute to equity in tertiary education in Australia? *Critical Studies in Education, 50*(3), 261–275.

Whitehead, G., Shah, M., & Nair, C. (2013). Equity and excellence are not mutually exclusive: A discussion of academic standards in an era of widening participation. *Quality Assurance in Education, 21*(3), 196.

Zepke, N., & Leach, L. (2005). Integration and adaptation. *Active Learning in Higher Education, 6*(1), 46–59.

Zepke, N., Leach, L., Prebble, T., Campbell, A., Coltman, D., Dewart, B., … Wilson, S. (2005). *Improving tertiary student outcomes in their first year of study.* Wellington: Teaching and Learning Research Initiative.

7

Social Inclusion or Social Engineering? The Politics and Reality of Widening Access to Medicine in the UK

Kirsty Alexander and Jennifer Cleland

Introduction

The movement to 'widen access' (WA) to those who have not traditionally participated in Higher Education is a global issue, and currently a 'hot topic' for educators, politicians and policy-makers in the UK. The focus of WA is in part determined by each country's historical and current social issues. For example, US WA initiatives may particularly aim to attract students from under-represented minority (URM) ethnicity and racial groups (Castillo-Page 2012; Lakhan 2003), whilst in Canada and Australia medical schools also aim to recruit those from rural or indigenous communities (Behrendt et al. 2012; Dhalla et al. 2002; Puddey et al. 2014). In the UK, the medical profession has been applauded for

---

K. Alexander • J. Cleland (✉)
Centre for Healthcare Education Research and Innovation (CHERI),
School of Medicine, Dentistry and Nutrition, University of Aberdeen,
Aberdeen, Scotland
e-mail: jen.cleland@abdn.ac.uk

© The Author(s) 2018
M. Shah, J. McKay (eds.), *Achieving Equity and Quality in Higher Education*,
Palgrave Studies in Excellence and Equity in Global Education,
https://doi.org/10.1007/978-3-319-78316-1_7

widening access to include greater ethnic and gender diversity (Milburn 2012) and for creating increasingly 'fair' selection procedures for these groups (Mathers et al. 2016b). However, medicine remains under the spotlight with regards to the lack of progress in widening the profession's socioeconomic diversity.

Currently home applicants and entrants to UK medical schools remain clustered in higher socioeconomic groups. Only 5.1% of UK applicants come from the least affluent 10% of households, with that number being as low as 1.8% in some regions. These percentages drop further when it comes to achieving a place in medical school (Steven et al. 2016). Other indicators suggest that the percentage of medical students from 'working class' backgrounds (those with parents in semi-skilled or unskilled occupations) may even be falling (Cleland et al. 2012a).

Medical schools work in a multifaceted landscape of competing pressures—many of which are in tension with greater inclusion. In this chapter we explore the reasons why medical schools are under pressure to diversify their cohorts and the initiatives they currently deploy to attract and support applicants from under-represented or disadvantaged groups. We discuss why these initiatives have had limited success, including schools' concerns about maintaining a reputation for excellence and a lasting adherence to the principles of academic meritocracy. We conclude by discussing whether some of the tensions which block progress within WA might be reconciled, and how this might be done. In so doing, we call for medical schools, as well as the wider educational contexts in which they are situated, to consider systemic and cultural change to tackle WA.

Context

In the UK, the vast majority of tertiary education is provided by state-funded universities. (There is only one, small, private medical school in the UK at the time of writing this chapter.) The vast majority of students enter medicine after high school (i.e., with school-leaving qualifications) onto a 5-year course, with this considered the 'standard' route into medical education. In an effort to increase the diversity of the medical school population, a number of accelerated (four-year) graduate entry medicine (GEM) programmes have been established since 2000 (Medical Workforce Standing Advisory Committee 1997). These now train 10% of the UK's medical students (Kumwenda et al. 2017b).

As in all countries, entry to medicine is highly competitive. While competition or selection ratios vary by medical school, on average around half of those who apply as school-leavers receive an offer/place (Mathers et al. 2016b). The selection ratios are higher for those applying to GEM programmes at approximately 4:1 (Kumwenda et al. 2017b). Successful applicants must demonstrate very high educational achievement; strong performance in aptitude tests, application statements and interviews; and, increasingly, must demonstrate that they possess personality traits befitting a career in medicine such as compassion, team working skills and integrity (Medical Schools Council 2017).

Collectively UK medical schools currently accept approximately 6500 new students each year (of which over 90% are UK-domiciled at the time of application (MacKenzie et al. 2016)). Medical student numbers are regulated by the government and are expected to rise by approximately 23% in the next few years (with most, but not all, of these additional places being available in England) (Roberts and Bolton 2017). This increase has been proposed partially in response to the dual concerns raised later in this chapter: the lack of participation of those from lower socio-economic groups in medicine; and the challenge for the state education system (medical schools) to meet the needs of its state-funded and state-controlled National Health Service (NHS).

Barriers to Widening Access in UK Medicine

It is widely acknowledged that applicants from URMs/disadvantaged groups may face additional challenges when considering, preparing, or submitting a competitive application to medicine. These additional challenges may therefore place some applicants at an unfair disadvantage in comparison to others during the selection process. For WA initiatives to be successful, it is first important to understand how a complex and intertwining network of factors may contribute to an applicant's disadvantage and how these challenges might be addressed.

Disadvantage is initially evident when examining the inequalities between applicants' pre-university educational experiences (Chowdry et al. 2013; Nicholson and Cleland 2015). Worldwide, high academic achievement is a key requirement of all competitive medical courses, and worldwide, students in higher socioeconomic groups outperform students in lower groups in school exit examinations (Bowes et al. 2013; Chowdry et al. 2013; Gorard et al. 2006).In the UK, inequalities in attainment by socioeconomic group are already evident in primary school (Chowdry et al. 2013), showing that differentiated achievement starts early. As a result, a selection process centred strongly around academic attainment can be biased in favour of those in higher socioeconomic classes, who generally have access to higher achieving and better resourced schools (Cleland et al. 2012a). For example, primary and high schools may be able to access different amounts of material resources and information, which influences how much support they can offer students who wish to apply to competitive professional subjects such as medicine (Southgate et al. 2015). As a result, many students who are able and motivated may still lack important knowledge about the admissions procedures or requirements (Kamali et al. 2005; Robb et al. 2007).

Moreover, a school's culture regarding academic attainment, work ethic and aspiration to certain careers also plays a large role in students' choices (Archer and Leathwood 2003; DFES 2003; Gorard et al. 2006; Reay et al. 2001; Slack 2003). There is increasing evidence that students in some UK state schools may be discouraged from considering or applying to medicine by school factors, including school culture and teachers' expectations (McHarg et al. 2007; Medical Schools Council 2014a; Robb et al. 2007; Southgate et al. 2015).

These inequalities are starkly evidenced in schools' application rates to highly selective universities and to competitive subjects such as medicine (Hemsley-Brown 2015; Medical Schools Council 2014b). In England, 100 'elite' schools (3% of all schools) provided 11.2% of admissions to highly selective universities, and 31.9% of admissions to Oxford and Cambridge (Sutton Trust 2011). Applications to medicine are also highly differentiated by school: 80% of UK applicants come from only 20% of UK schools, and half the schools in the UK sent no applicants to medicine in recent years (Medical Schools Council 2014b).

Of course, schools are just one piece of the jigsaw, as larger societal influences, peer and familial expectations, as well as a student's beliefs about their own ability also strongly influence students' educational and career choices (Bridges 2006; DFCSF 2008; Hill et al. 2004; Miller and Cummings 2009; Robb et al. 2007).

Financial concerns about the cost of tuition fees and living costs whilst a student may also deter capable applicants, and particularly those from poorer backgrounds who are more likely to be worried by the burden of 'debt' (Callender and Jackson 2008; Minty 2015). Although tuition fees for medicine are equivalent per year to studying any other subject at university (due to government subsidies), the course is considerably longer, and may require additional costs (Cleland et al. 2012a). There is substantial evidence that students from poorer backgrounds may also prefer to stay in the family home whilst studying to limit costs (Hughes et al. 2008; Mangan et al. 2010), which may severely restrict the medical schools available to them, especially if they live rurally.

Overall, the choice to attend university generally, and medicine particularly, may be seen as presenting more risk for a student from a non-traditional background, both culturally and financially (Archer and Hutchings 2000; Archer and Leathwood 2003). As discussed, a complex and intertwining set of factors may lead students to this conclusion. Justifiably, UK medical schools feel they are unable to counterbalance the large inequalities in applicants' pre-entry experiences through their efforts alone (Cleland et al. 2015). Large-scale and joined-up interventions and investment at a political level are needed for real improvements to inequality and social mobility (Sutton Trust 2017). Nonetheless, some of the negative perceptions held about medicine may be justified, as studies suggest medical school is not always welcoming to diverse students (Beagan 2005; Greenhalgh et al. 2004; Orom et al. 2013), nor do systems provide them with enough support to concentrate on their studies (BMA Medical Student Committee 2015). As a result, there are still potential applicants who feel that medicine is not a suitable career choice for someone from their background (Greenhalgh et al. 2004; Mathers and Parry 2009) and this must continue to be addressed.

Why Is Widening Access Important in Medicine?

In the UK, there are two main arguments to justify WA to medicine: the first is to increase social mobility; the second to improve healthcare provision. These drivers mirror those in many other countries which face similar challenges regarding a lack of diversity in the medical profession.

In relation to the first, the UK has long-standing and increasing levels of inequality in income (Eurofound 2015), health (RCPCH 2017) and education (Jerrim and Shure 2016), coupled with limited social mobility (Sutton Trust 2017)—considered the means to break 'the transmission of disadvantage from one generation to the next' (Nicholson and Cleland 2015, p. 231).

The concept of social mobility is closely tied to ideas of meritocracy. 'Meritocracy' can be defined as 'a social system, society, or organization in which people have power because of their abilities, not because of their money or social position' (The Cambridge English Dictionary 2017). Meritocratic systems are strongly cherished for their perceived fairness, productivity, and for the opportunities they offer individuals within all social strata. However, although the meritocratic approach is the preferred philosophy of education in the UK (Sheeran et al. 2007), there are limits to its effectiveness.

As discussed above, the level of educational, social, cultural and financial resources and opportunities an applicant possesses, or is able to access, before they apply to medicine may still set them at a considerable disadvantage in a competitive, and apparently 'meritocratic' application system. Despite much investment in WA activities to address these disadvantages, to remove barriers, and to attract and support able but disadvantaged students into medicine, the proportion of medical students from lower socio-economic groups has remained static over many years (BMA 2009) (see later for further discussion). Indeed, a high profile report for the Social Mobility and Child Poverty Commission stated that:

'medicine … has a long way to go when it comes to making access fairer, diversifying its workforce and raising social mobility' (Milburn 2012).

The second reason to 'widen access' to the medical profession addresses the need to build a healthcare workforce that reflects and understands the needs of patients from diverse cultures and in diverse locations.

There is increasing recognition that a more diverse student cohort may benefit the workforce and medical school learning environment. Amongst other strengths, diverse students are understood to contribute a better understanding of diverse populations (Guiton et al. 2007; Morrison and Grbic 2015; Saha et al. 2008; Whitla et al. 2003), multilingualism (Flores 2000), as well as resilience and persistence to overcome barriers (Cleland and Medhi 2015; Jardine 2012). Diversity in the workplace may not only improve the competence of staff, but also provide the workforce with more practitioners who choose to work in underprivileged communities, locations and specialties (Bailey and Willies-Jacobo 2012; Cooter et al. 2004; Dowell et al. 2015; Komaromy et al. 1996; Larkins et al. 2015; Puddey et al. 2014; Walker et al. 2012a, b).

The topic of workforce planning is currently high on the political agenda in the UK as there are significant doctor shortages in many specialties and localities (NHS Improvement 2016; UKFPO 2016). As in many western countries, demands on healthcare provision in the UK are changing as the population becomes increasingly multicultural and ageing (Office of National Statistics 2011), and technological advances increase the level of care it is possible to offer and 'disrupt' traditional roles with potentially dramatic reforms (Gorman 2017). The UK faces additional challenges when matching doctor supply to community needs, especially as medical graduates' choice of progression routes through training no longer fit predicted models (Cleland et al. 2016; Scanlan et al. 2017). In 2016, almost half of medical graduates either took a 'break' or left the workforce after completing the UK's two year 'Foundation Programme' (the broad training programme medical school graduates are required to undertake before they are eligible for general practice (family medicine) or specialty training) (UKFPO 2015). Although in the past graduates commonly took a 'break' at this point (especially to work overseas) (Smith and Low 2012), the current scale of the phenomenon, and the increasing number who do not return to the UK health service (NHS) (UKFPO 2016) has naturally led to concerns over a 'brain drain' within the UK and disrupted service provision. Moreover, the government's planned rise in medical student numbers alone may not be a solution to this issue—increasing the supply of doctors does not, in itself, better match that resource to accommodate areas of need (Gorman 2017).

A greater understanding about how socioeconomic factors (amongst many others) might relate to willingness to stay and practise in the UK is therefore becoming ever more pressing. It is worth noting however, that the relationship between lower socioeconomic status and higher desire to work in underserved areas is complex and often compounded by a multitude of factors (Griffin et al. 2016; O'Connell et al. 2017). Moreover, programmes that most successfully provide for rural areas have had three crucial support mechanisms: government investment; strong leadership; and lack of training places in neighbouring big cities (Gorman 2017), as well as a focus on exposing their students to underserved localities (Phillips et al. 2017).

The UK undergraduate medical education landscape is thus in a period of significant change, as it adapts to shifting population demographics and demands, significant political changes and decisions, as well as to changes in the preferred career paths of graduates. WA to the profession is thus seen as one way to meet and help improve the skills, efficiency and distribution of the workforce into the future.

How Are These Calls for Diversity Played Out in the UK?

It is important to understand how the different arguments for WA are conceptualised by UK medical schools as these concepts influence the design and implementation of WA initiatives, as well as how they are presented and judged to be successful (Jones and Thomas 2006; Sheeran et al. 2007; Stevenson et al. 2010).

First, it is crucial to acknowledge that there is a tension between the political drivers to WA and the (equally politically driven) competitive nature of neoliberal university education in the UK. The UK Higher Education system is becoming increasingly competitive, and universities must compete for funding, students and prestige within a stratified marketplace. This puts increasing pressure on universities and medical schools to promote a reputation of excellence, high quality experience and exceptional standards (see for example: Fairclough 1993; Molesworth et al. 2011). Yet, concurrently UK devolved governments are also putting increasing pressure on universities to widen access, setting them ambitious diversity targets (DBIS 2016; Scottish Government 2016). WA, with its aims of broader inclusivity and participation, can thus be seen at odds with the market pressure to convey more mainstream forms of excellence and of exclusivity and selectiveness in admissions.

When considering UK Higher Education as a whole, studies found large differences between the portrayals of WA given by more 'elite' institutions, in comparison to less selective or more recently established universities (Bowl and Hughes 2013; Graham 2013). Overall, selective institutions chose to continue to promote themselves as 'elite' with only vague statements about key WA activities (Bowl and Hughes 2013). Moreover, institutions' self-presentations with regard to inclusivity were seen to change over time in response to sector and policy changes: in the years between 2007 and 2011 the selective universities in Graham's study seemed to adopt a slightly more welcoming tone towards underrepresented groups, whereas less selective institutions moved away from promoting themselves as a 'WA institutions' to foregrounding their 'excellence' and 'quality' (Graham 2013).

Like the wider universities to which they belong, UK medical schools vary in terms of their culture, history, location and capital and use their reputations and resources strategically to differentiate themselves from their competitors (Brosnan 2010). There are clear differences between UK medical schools' curricula, image and aspirations, which also impact on their stance towards, and enactment of widening access. For example, a UK-wide study interviewing medical school Admissions Deans revealed significant differences in the schools' attitudes towards, and interpretations of, WA policy (Cleland et al. 2015). Many felt that they could not reconcile the political goals of WA (often referring to calls to improve the workforce through diversity), with their school's aims and interests (selecting through academic meritocracy). Maintaining the highest standards of academic excellence and thereby selecting the 'best' students and doctors was thus seen in tension with efforts to increase diversity, particularly in the current medical education system that does not sufficiently compensate for, or reward, WA efforts which pose both cost and risk to the institution (Cleland et al. 2015) (see later for further discussion).

A subsequent discourse analysis of UK medical school WA webpages found similar tensions (Alexander et al. 2017). The argument (discourse) of widening access for social mobility through academic meritocracy was very strongly promoted, especially when linked to the use of WA as a tool to find and select 'the best and brightest' from a wider range of applicants. More traditional forms of excellence, such as academic achievement and ability, were promoted. Although all schools predominately used this argument, differences remained between the ways it was conceptualised and used. Some schools claimed that introducing WA initiatives did not reduce quality standards, whilst others argued that initiatives increased the effectiveness of selection through widening the application pool, and improved fairness by removing barriers to 'level the playing field'. Schools thus differed in whether they proposed that WA initiatives for social mobility did not diminish, or actually improved, the quality of admissions through academic meritocracy.

In contrast, the argument (discourse) for widening access as a means to improve the efficiency of the workforce was significantly marginalised on UK medical school WA webpages and the alternative strengths that diverse or underrepresented students might bring to the profession were not discussed. As a result, these attributes were not communicated as valuable (Alexander et al. 2017). Overall, a differentiated field of opinions towards WA was revealed, although once again, UK medical schools strongly espoused their belief in academic meritocracy and were hesitant to propose the benefits of a diversified workforce.

How Do Medical Schools Implement WA Policies?

In this section we will briefly review some of the WA initiatives currently utilised by UK medical schools and discuss their effectiveness. We will also consider how these initiatives link to the concepts of WA for 'social mobility within academic meritocracy' or for 'workforce improvement through diversity', and how they relate to the tensions described in the previous section.

Pre-entry Activities

All UK medical schools undertake 'outreach' activities to raise awareness and interest in medicine among communities that would not traditionally produce large numbers of applicants. Typical outreach initiatives include university staff visiting high schools to provide information about subject choices and application procedures to pupils and teachers. Other outreach schemes involve near-peer 'mentoring', or events in which pupils are invited to the medical school for a 'taster' of life as a medical student, for example by student shadowing or summer schools. Overall, pre-entry activities aim to address some of the disadvantages and challenges students from lower socioeconomic backgrounds may experience when considering medical school (for a good overview see Medical Schools Council 2014a).

UK medical schools' goals for pre-entry activities appear to centre on increasing the social mobility of their participants (Alexander et al. 2017). By aiming to compensate for the disadvantage of targeted individuals from URMs/disadvantaged groups, these initiatives encourage WA participants to acquire additional or more 'appropriate' skills, knowledge and aspirations to make them 'suitable' for admission to medicine. These activities are framed as necessary 'top-up opportunities' to allow selected individuals to succeed within the current system of academic meritocracy.

However, these activities have been criticised for using a 'deficit model' which concentrates on the deficiencies of individual learners rather than fully acknowledging or tackling the barriers in their environments, including those posed by medical schools themselves (Jones and Thomas 2006; O'Shea et al. 2015; Sheeran et al. 2007; Smit 2012). Emphasising the deficiencies of those from underrepresented backgrounds may unintentionally further reinforce individuals' perceptions of difference and disadvantage, and in fact counter efforts to encourage them, or to help them to recognise their suitability for the profession (Alexander et al. 2017; Fahey Palma and Cleland 2017; Frost and Regehr 2013; Gartland 2014; Greenhalgh et al. 2004; Razack et al. 2015).

Although sufficient evidence exists to indicate these pre-entry activities do have a positive effect on the recruitment of diverse students to medicine, their impact has typically been poorly evaluated and existing studies do not 'expand the understanding or provide generalizable messages' in relation to what works and what does not (Nicholson and Cleland 2015, p. 234).

Widening Access Through Admissions Procedures

In recent years, UK medical schools have made changes to their admissions procedures with the stated goals of reducing bias and increasing fairness in selection. The most obvious change has been a move away from a reliance on academic achievement as the primary, or only, selection method. This has been replaced by use of a variety of tools to judge potential and ability to become a doctor (see MacKenzie et al. 2016) for a good overview of medical selection processes, and (Patterson et al. 2016) for a review of the effectiveness of various tools).

Attaining the required grades remains the first hurdle in medical admissions, and failure to do so is the most common cause of rejection. Yet—as discussed earlier—just looking at educational attainment may not accurately identify potential, given the association between systemic and social factors, and attainment (Williamson 2004).

In part to address this dilemma, UK medical schools first introduced the UKCAT test in 2006. The UKCAT test is an aptitude test which aims to measure whether an applicant possesses the cognitive ability, as well as the attitudes and behaviour, desirable for a clinician (UKCAT 2017). Aptitude tests are used globally for selection to medicine—for example in: Ireland (HPAT 2017); Australia (UMAT 2017); Canada and the USA (AAMC 2017)—as well as for a range of other professions (Bertua et al. 2005).

Aptitude tests were considered to be a useful tool to assist WA to medicine, as outcomes were thought to be influenced less by the socioeconomic and educational background of applicants, and because tests could not be 'coached' for to the same extent as traditional school exams (Cleland et al. 2012a). Although initial, smaller scale studies indicated this might be the case (Tiffin et al. 2012, 2014), emerging longitudinal work has not shown benefits to WA (Mathers et al. 2016a).

Medical schools are now encouraged to use 'contextual admissions' (CA) during the selection process (Medical Schools Council 2014b; Panel on Fair Access to the Professions 2009). The use of CA is intended to assess an applicant's potential to succeed in higher education by taking into consideration the context and circumstances in which their attainment to date has been achieved. In theory at least, this heralds a significant step towards seeking to select on ability rather than purely attainment and has considerable potential to reduce bias towards those in lower socioeconomic groups. However, in practice 'ability' is much harder to identify than 'attainment' is to assess—a major concern for many schools (Boliver et al. 2015; Cleland et al. 2014, 2015).

As a result, the national picture is complex and multifaceted: various different types of CA have been proposed for use by UK universities (see Boliver et al. 2015; Moore et al. 2013) for further detail) and large differences remain in how medical schools select their students. Moreover, these processes have been criticised for lacking transparency and clarity (Cleland et al. 2014). To date, there have been no studies examining the impact of CA on medical school admissions and there is much concern as to the reliability of the markers being used (Thomas et al. 2009). Moreover, the (unacknowledged) potential value of applicants selected via CA may be overshadowed by a focus on the worry of opening doors to students who have achieved slightly less well in terms of prior attainment, a perceived 'lowering of standards', and the potential negative impact this may have on school performance in league tables (Cleland et al. 2015). Unfortunately, given (in the UK at least) medical schools are notoriously poor at tracking their students in terms of evaluating the relative performance of students from different backgrounds; this attitude remains an unevidenced fear. Interestingly, recent evidence suggests that those entering with slightly lower academic tariffs and significantly lower outcomes on standard aptitude tests actually go on to outperform their more qualified counterparts from more privileged backgrounds (Kumwenda et al. 2017a). Further research and evaluation is needed to assess the 'added benefit' of medical school, and whether this differs by group.

Finally, similarly to pre-entry activities, CA initiatives may be subject to criticism for their focus on compensating for the 'deficit' of applicants from URMs/disadvantaged backgrounds (see for example Sheeran et al. 2007). Moreover, although these initiatives do initiate superficial systemic change, they are largely still underpinned by the argument of selection through academic meritocracy and advocate little cultural change towards WA.

Widening Access Through Alternative Entry Routes

Another approach to WA taken by UK medical schools has been to create specific routes of entry for URM/disadvantaged groups. These include: 'foundation years', or tailor-made preparation programmes (Curtis et al. 2014a); extended programmes (Garlick and Brown 2008); and graduate entry programmes (Medical Workforce Standing Advisory Committee 1997).

Foundation and extended programmes serve the dual purpose of offering an extra year of academic study, aimed at helping participants address gaps in their science knowledge and attainment, as well as a chance for students from diverse backgrounds to acclimatise to a university environment (Curtis et al. 2014b; Garlick and Brown 2008). These courses are generally considered to be successful and to add diversity to the schools' student cohort, however, they are costly to run and the number of places available are very small (Mathers et al. 2011). In addition, these programmes tend to be offered by less selective schools, suggesting that may continue to be seen to be incompatible with a reputation for 'excellence' (Cleland et al. 2012a). Finally, once again, these programmes may be seen as problematic, as they also seek to compensate for the 'deficit' of individuals within a system based on academic meritocracy.

Another 'alternative entry route' designed to WA has been the establishment of graduate-entry courses. These courses were founded on the premise that, as applicants with more varied life experience, higher numbers of graduate students would improve diversity within medicine, and perhaps they would be willing to work in underserved areas (Carter and Peile, 2007; Dowell et al. 2015; GP Taskforce 2014; Wilkinson et al. 2004).

In contrast to the aforementioned initiatives, justifications for these courses do appear to consider the argument (discourse) of WA for workforce improvement through diversity. As a result, they foreground the potential benefits mature students with prior degrees may bring to the profession and a number particularly promote career pathways towards generalists, rural medicine and healthcare improvement (for example Scottish Government Newsroom 2016).

The effectiveness of graduate-entry initiatives may be questioned however. Although student cohorts in graduate-entry only courses may be slightly more socioeconomically diverse, the small intake on these courses (10% of total UK medical students) means that they do not significantly aid WA to medicine (Mathers et al. 2011). Moreover, graduates who enter through 'standard entry routes' are not more socioeconomically diverse than school-leavers (Garrud 2011; Kumwenda et al. 2017b).

Enduring Issues and a New Way of Thinking About Widening Access to Medicine?

WA is a deeply contested area in educational policy and politics (Archer 2007; Francis et al. 2017) and the philosophical rationales supporting WA are not aligned (Sheeran et al. 2007). Uncertainty and conflicting messages have inevitably led to confusion 'on the ground' in medical schools and universities as to what WA should be 'for', how it should be 'done' and what the measures of 'success' should be (Cleland et al. 2015; Stevenson et al. 2010). These unresolved tensions are themselves a barrier to WA: restricting the responsibility for WA to a few committed individuals, causing frustration and the attribution of blame on others, and preventing widespread cultural change across the institution (Stevenson et al. 2010).

In this chapter we have discussed two competing arguments (discourses) for WA and explored how they are currently enacted in UK medical schools. Meritocratic selection on the basis of academic attainment and ability remains a cherished cornerstone of medical schools' selection procedures, and to date, WA efforts seem to have been predominately shaped around this model, emphasising the need to enhance the social mobility of disadvantaged individuals in this system. Such initiatives have, however, failed to significantly change the socioeconomic profile of UK medical school students.

We suggest this may be, at least in part, because these initiatives are primarily designed to fit into established models of selection, and do not embrace the required shift in attitudes at a cultural, professional, political or systemic level which would enable real progress in WA. The discourse of 'it ain't broke, so why fix it' in relation to medical admissions perpetuates within established approaches and attitudes, yet the reality of a polarized society and underserved health service loom large as indications of systems at crisis point (NHS Improvement 2016; Sutton Trust 2017). WA is certainly not the only solution to these issues, but emerging evidence suggests it may be an important part of the puzzle (see for example Dowell et al. 2015; Larkins et al. 2015; Milburn 2012). Medical schools must play an important role in shifting behaviour, attitudes and norms, however they cannot do this in isolation or without other parties moving in parallel—the impact of WA initiatives ultimately depends on stakeholders and systems aligning (Gorman 2017).

As in healthcare workforce planning (Gorman 2017), if no consensus on the desired endpoint for WA is reached, then pre-entry or entry level changes to medical school are difficult to assess or plan. Governmental targets requiring increased admission to underrepresented groups may be unavoidable, but medical schools are still relatively free to interpret and enact these as they choose (Cleland et al. 2015; Ball 1994, p. 19). Therefore, a consensus across all key stakeholders, including but not limited to medical schools, should be sought to clarify the desired overall endpoint for WA. Students are also stakeholders, so parents and applicants also need to 'buy-in' to any repositioning of medical education. This may be challenging in a society such as the UK—medical school is still considered to be for the elite and medicine to offer substantial personal choice and flexibility in terms of an ultimate career, rather than as a vocational course which aims to produce professionals who will meet the healthcare needs of the population.

Medicine is currently oversubscribed with qualified applicants, and many more who do not meet the current requirements aspire to this subject. In their role as gatekeepers, medical schools are able to prioritise who will join the profession. Despite ongoing research, choices about who to accept must be made with severely restricted information—relatively little is still known about how each selection procedure might affect eventual performance or choices as a doctor (Cleland et al. 2012a, p. 6). Nonetheless, fundamental choices can still be made. For example: should applicants who are more likely to graduate at the top of their class academically be prioritised? Or should applicants who are more likely to work in underserved areas be selected? Are these mutually exclusive or not? Where is the appropriate balance? The answers to these questions will determine the means as to how the answers are achieved, with consequences for both the processes and outcomes of WA.

The answers to these questions will also be strongly determined by the context in which medical schools operate and where most support from key stakeholders can be found. For example, if league tables reward schools that admit and graduate the highest academically achieving students (as they currently do) then the goal of academic excellence will be prioritised. If however, funding and prestige is available for courses that prioritise training medical students to ultimately work in underserved posts/regions (see for example, the graduate entry course discussed above), then promoting these courses may become more attractive.

Although there is some evidence within policy/governmental discourses that signal a move away from a deficit model of WA (see for example Scottish Government 2016, p. 31), for lasting change political targets for WA must be met by support financially, and by removing the perceived risks to repetition loss through WA within a competitive marketplace.

Finally, changes must be made within the profession itself to tackle current attitudes and hidden curriculums that dismiss or degrade general practice (family medicine), underserved specialties or rural posts as 'second best' (Baker et al. 2016; Edgcumbe et al. 2008). Medical schools can affect practical change here, as they exert significant influence on their graduates' choice of specialties and locations (Brosnan 2010; Cleland et al. 2012b; Walker et al. 2012a).

Conclusions

In this chapter we have explored the key drivers for WA, their comparative influence, enactment on the ground, and evaluated their success. We have also suggested systemic and cultural changes that could help preserve the good in the established system whilst embracing the changes necessary to better address the needs of UK society. This may be considered 'social engineering' but then, so could allowing the powerful in society (those who have access to good schools, professional cultures and ample finances) to dominate the status quo to the exclusion of others.

Innovative change sometimes only arises out of necessity. The UK is now experiencing severe levels of inequality (Eurofound 2015; Jerrim and Shure 2016; RCPCH 2017), a stagnation of social mobility (Sutton Trust 2017), and a growing healthcare workforce crisis (GP Taskforce 2014; NHS Improvement 2016). An effective model of WA may be one way to partially address these issues. We encourage a move away from an approach that selects certain individuals (targeted primarily because of their demographic traits) and aids them to better 'fit' and compete within academically orientated selection procedures. Instead we advocate a model of WA that redefines the parameters of 'merit' so that it is not only more inclusive and encompasses the benefits diversity brings to a workforce, but can also better serve the needs of the UK healthcare system. Achieving this depends on the Higher Education market adequately recognising and rewarding WA initiatives, as well as medical schools and the wider healthcare system working together to drive change (Cleland et al. 2015; Gorman 2017; Thompson 2008).

References

Alexander, K., Fahey Palma, T., Nicholson, S., & Cleland, J. (2017). "Why not you?" Discourses of widening access on UK medical school websites. *Medical Education, 51*(6), 598–611. https://doi.org/10.1111/medu.13264.

Archer, L. (2007). Diversity, equality and higher education: A critical reflection on the ab/uses of equity discourse within widening participation. *Teaching in Higher Education, 12*(5–6), 635–653. https://doi.org/10.1080/13562510701595325.

Archer, L., & Hutchings, M. (2000). "Bettering yourself"? Discourses of risk, cost and benefit in ethnically diverse, young working-class non-participants' constructions of higher education. *British Journal of Sociology of Education, 21*(4), 555–574. https://doi.org/10.1080/713655373.

Archer, L., & Leathwood, C. (2003). Identities, inequalities and higher education. In L. Archer, M. Hutchings, & A. Ross (Eds.), *Higher education and social class: Issues of exclusion and inclusions* (pp. 175–191). London: Routledge Falmer.

Association of American Medical Colleges (AAMC). (2017). *Taking the MCAT® exam*. Retrieved July 26, 2017, from https://students-residents.aamc.org/applying-medical-school/taking-mcat-exam/

Bailey, J. A., & Willies-Jacobo, L. J. (2012). Are disadvantaged and underrepresented minority applicants more likely to apply to the program in medical education-health equity? *Academic Medicine, 87*(11), 1535–1539. https://doi.org/10.1097/ACM.0b013e31826d6220.

Baker, M., Wessely, S., & Openshaw, D. (2016). Not such friendly banter? GPs and psychiatrists against the systematic denigration of their specialties. *British Journal of General Practice, 66*(651), 508–509. https://doi.org/10.3399/bjgp16X687169.

Ball, S. J. (1994). *Education reform: A critical and post-structural approach*. Buckingham: Open University Press.

Beagan, B. L. (2005). Everyday classism in medical school: Experiencing marginality and resistance. *Medical Education, 39*(8), 777–784. https://doi.org/10.1111/j.1365-2929.2005.02225.x.

Behrendt, L., Larkin, S., Griew, R., & Kelly, P. (2012). *Review of higher education access and outcomes for Aboriginal and Torres Strait Islander people.* Retrieved March 5, 2016, from https://docs.education.gov.au/system/files/doc/other/heaccessandoutcomesforaboriginalandtorresstraitislanderfinalreport.pdf

Bertua, C., Anderson, N., & Salgado, J. F. (2005). The predictive validity of cognitive ability tests: A UK meta-analysis. *Journal of Occupational and Organizational Psychology, 78*(3), 387–409. https://doi.org/10.1348/096317905X26994.

BMA Medical Student Committee. (2015). *Medical student finances and the effect on wider participation.* Retrieved July 5, 2017, from https://www.bma.org.uk/connecting-doctors/community_focus/m/mediagallery/185

Boliver, V., Gorard, S., & Siddiqui, N. (2015). Will the use of contextual indicators make UK higher education admissions fairer? *Education in Science, 5*(4), 306–322. https://doi.org/10.3390/educsci5040306.

Bowes, L., Thomas, L., Peck, L., & Nathwani, T. (2013). *International research on the effectiveness of widening participation.* Retrieved July 7, 2016, from http://www.hefce.ac.uk/pubs/rereports/year/2013/wpeffectiveness/

Bowl, M., & Hughes, J. (2013). Discourses of "fair access" in English higher education. *Widening Participation and Lifelong Learning, 15*(4), 7–25. https://doi.org/10.5456/WPLL.15.4.7.

Bridges, D. (2006). Ethics and education adaptive preference, justice and identity in the context of widening participation in higher education. *Ethics and Education, 1*(1), 15–28. https://doi.org/10.1080/17449640600584946.

British Medical Association (BMA). (2009). *Equality and diversity in UK medical schools.* Retrieved March 31, 2015, from www.nhshistory.net/bmastudentreport2009.pdf

Brosnan, C. (2010). Making sense of differences between medical schools through Bourdieu's concept of "field". *Medical Education, 44*(7), 645–652. https://doi.org/10.1111/j.1365-2923.2010.03680.x.

Callender, C., & Jackson, J. (2008). Does the fear of debt constrain choice of university and subject of study? *Studies in Higher Education, 33*(4), 405–429. https://doi.org/10.1080/03075070802211802.

Carter, Y. H., & Peile, E. (2007). Graduate entry medicine: High aspirations at birth. *Clinical Medicine, 7*(2), 143–147. https://doi.org/10.7861/clinmedicine.7-2-143.

Castillo-Page, L. (2012). *Diversity in medical education: Facts and figures.* Retrieved August 8, 2015, from https://members.aamc.org/eweb/upload/Diversity in Medical Education_Facts%20and%20Figures 2012.pdf

Chowdry, H., Crawford, C., Dearden, L., Goodman, A., & Vignoles, A. (2013). Widening participation in higher education: Analysis using linked administrative data. *Journal of the Royal Statistical Society: Series A (Statistics in Society), 176*(2), 431–457. https://doi.org/10.1111/j.1467-985X.2012.01043.x.

Cleland, J., & Medhi, M. (2015). *Optimism and grit: Key to success in the widening access student's journey into medical school.* Research paper presented at the Association for Medical Education Europe (AMEE) annual conference, September 5–9th, Glasgow, UK.

Cleland, J., Dowell, J., McLachlan, J., Nicholson, S., & Patterson, F. (2012a). *Identifying best practice in the selection of medical students: Literature review and interview survey.* London: General Medical Council. Retrieved April 9, 2016, from http://www.gmc-uk.org/Identifying_best_practice_in_the_selection_of_medical_students.pdf_51119804.pdf

Cleland, J., Johnston, P. W., French, F. H., & Needham, G. (2012b). Associations between medical school and career preferences in year 1 medical students in Scotland. *Medical Education, 46*(5), 473–484. https://doi.org/10.1111/j.1365-2923.2012.04218.x.

Cleland, J., Patterson, F., Dowell, J., & Nicholson, S. (2014). *How can greater consistency in selection between medical schools be encouraged? A mixed-methods programme of research that examines and develops the evidence base.* London: Medical Schools Council. Retrieved July 5, 2017, from http://www.medschools.ac.uk/SiteCollectionDocuments/Selecting-for-Excellence-research-Professor-Jen-Cleland-et-al.pdf

Cleland, J., Nicholson, S., Kelly, N., & Moffat, M. (2015). Taking context seriously: Explaining widening access policy enactments in UK medical schools. *Medical Education, 49*(1), 25–35. https://doi.org/10.1111/medu.12502.

Cleland, J., Johnston, P., Watson, V., Krucien, N., & Skåtun, D. (2016). What do UK doctors in training value in a post? A discrete choice experiment. *Medical Education, 50*(2), 189–202. https://doi.org/10.1111/medu.12896.

Cooter, R., Erdmann, J. B., Gonnella, J. S., Callahan, C. A., Hojat, M., & Xu, G. (2004). Economic diversity in medical education: The relationship between students' family income and academic performance, career choice, and student debt. *Evaluation & the Health Professions, 27*(3), 252–264. https://doi.org/10.1177/0163278704267041.

Curtis, S., Blundell, C., Platz, C., & Turner, L. (2014a). Successfully widening access to medicine. Part 1: Recruitment and admissions. *Journal of the Royal Society of Medicine, 107*(9), 342–346. https://doi.org/10.1177/0141076814538786.

Curtis, S., Blundell, C., Platz, C., & Turner, L. (2014b). Successfully widening access to medicine. Part 2: Curriculum design and student progression. *Journal of the Royal Society of Medicine, 107*(10), 393–397. https://doi.org/10.1177/0141076814538787.

Department for Business, Innovation and Skills (DBIS). (2016). *Success as a knowledge economy: Teaching excellence, Social mobility & student choice.* London. Retrieved January 5, 2017, from https://www.gov.uk/government/uploads/system/uploads/attachment_data/file/523546/bis-16-265-success-as-a-knowledge-economy-web.pdf

Department for Children, Schools and Families (DFCSF). (2008). *The impact of parental involvement on children's education.* Nottingham. Retrieved July 17, 2017, from https://www.ucy.ac.cy/nursery/documents/ThemaVdomadas/DCSF-Parental_Involvement_1.pdf

Department for Education and Skills (DFES). (2003). *The future of higher education.* London. Retrieved April 4, 2015, from http://webarchive.nationalarchives.gov.uk/20040117001247/dfes.gov.uk/highereducation/hestrategy/

Dhalla, I. A., Kwong, J. C., Streiner, D. L., Baddour, R. E., Waddell, A. E., & Johnson, I. L. (2002). Characteristics of first-year students in Canadian medical schools. *CMAJ, 166*(8), 1029–1035.

Dowell, J., Norbury, M., Steven, K., & Guthrie, B. (2015). Widening access to medicine may improve general practitioner recruitment in deprived and rural communities: Survey of GP origins and current place of work. *BMC Medical Education, 15*(1), 1–7. https://doi.org/10.1186/s12909-015-0445-8.

Edgcumbe, D. P., Lillicrap, M. S., & Benson, J. A. (2008). A qualitative study of medical students' attitudes to careers in general practice. *Education for Primary Care, 19*(1), 65–73. https://doi.org/10.1080/14739879.2008.11493651.

Eurofound. (2015). *Recent developments in the distribution of wages in Europe.* European foundation for the improvement of living and working conditions. Retrieved July 5, 2017, from https://www.eurofound.europa.eu/sites/default/files/ef_publication/field_ef_document/ef1510en1.pdf

Fahey Palma, T., & Cleland, J. (2017). "Aspirations of people who come from state education are different": How language reflects social exclusion in medical education. *Advances in Health Sciences Education*, First Online 24 January 2018. https://link.springer.com/article/10.1007/s10459-018-9809-2

Fairclough, N. (1993). Critical discourse analysis and the marketization of public discourse: The universities. *Discourse & Society, 4*(2), 133–168. https://doi.org/10.1177/0957926593004002002.

Flores, G. (2000). Culture and the patient-physician relationship: Achieving cultural competency in health care. *The Journal of Pediatrics, 136*(1), 14–23. https://doi.org/10.1016/S0022-3476(00)90043-X.

Francis, B., Mills, M., & Lupton, R. (2017). Towards social justice in education: Contradictions and dilemmas. *Journal of Education Policy, 32*(4), 414–431. https://doi.org/10.1080/02680939.2016.1276218.

Frost, H. D., & Regehr, G. (2013). "I am a doctor": Negotiating the discourses of standardization and diversity in professional identity construction. *Academic Medicine, 88*(10), 1570–1577. https://doi.org/10.1097/ACM.0b013e3182a34b05.

Garlick, P. B., & Brown, G. (2008). Widening participation in medicine. *BMJ, 336*(7653), 1111–1113. https://doi.org/10.1136/bmj.39508.606157.BE.

Garrud, P. (2011). Who applies and who gets admitted to UK graduate entry medicine? – An analysis of UK admission statistics. *BMC Medical Education, 11*(71). https://doi.org/10.1056/NEJMsa050004.

Gartland, C. (2014). *STEM strategies: Student ambassadors and equality in higher education*. London: Institute of Education Press, University of London.

Gorard, S., Smith, E., May, H., Thomas, L., Adnett, N., & Slack, K. (2006). *Review of widening participation research: Addressing barriers to participation in higher education*. Retrieved June 16, 2015, from http://dera.ioe.ac.uk/6204/

Gorman, D. (2017). Matching the production of doctors with national needs. *Medical Education*. [epub ahead of print] https://doi.org/10.1111/medu.13369.

GP Taskforce. (2014). *Securing the future GP workforce: Delivering the mandate on GP expansion*. London: Department for Health & Medical Education England. Retrieved July 24, 2017, from https://www.hee.nhs.uk/sites/default/files/documents/GP-Taskforce-report.pdf

Graham, C. (2013). Discourses of widening participation in the prospectus documents and websites of six English higher education institutions. *British Journal of Sociology of Education, 34*(1), 76–93. https://doi.org/10.1080/01425692.2012.692048.

Greenhalgh, T., Seyan, K., & Boynton, P. (2004). "Not a university type": Focus group study of social class, ethnic, and sex differences in school pupils' perceptions about medical school. *BMJ, 328*(7455), 1541–1544. https://doi.org/10.1136/bmj.328.7455.1541.

Griffin, B., Porfeli, E., & Hu, W. (2016). Who do you think you are? Medical student socioeconomic status and intention to work in underserved areas. *Advances in Health Sciences Education, 22*(2), 491–504. https://doi.org/10.1007/s10459-016-9726-1.

Guiton, G., Chang, M. J., & Wilkerson, L. (2007). Student body diversity: Relationship to medical students' experiences and attitudes. *Academic Medicine, 82*(10 Suppl), S85–S88. https://doi.org/10.1097/ACM.0b013e31813ffe1e.

Health Professions Admission Test (HPAT). (2017). *Home | HPAT Ireland*. Retrieved July 26, 2017, from https://hpat-ireland.acer.org/

Hemsley-Brown, J. (2015). Getting into a Russell Group university: High scores and private schooling. *British Educational Research Journal, 41*(3), 398–422. https://doi.org/10.1002/berj.3152.

Hill, N. E., Castellino, D. R., Lansford, J. E., Nowlin, P., Dodge, K. A., Bates, J. E., & Pettit, G. S. (2004). Parent academic involvement as related to school behavior, achievement, and aspirations: Demographic variations across adolescence. *Child Development, 75*(5), 1491–1509. https://doi.org/10.1111/j.1467-8624.2004.00753.x.

Hughes, A., Mangan, J., Vigurs, K., Slack, K., & Davies, P. (2008). *Knowing where to study? Fees, bursaries and fair access*. London: Sutton Trust. Retrieved July 17, 2017, from https://www.suttontrust.com/research-paper/knowing-study-fees-bursaries-fair-access/

Jardine, A. (2012). *Indicators of persistence and their influence on the first year experience of university students from low socio-economic backgrounds* (PhD thesis). Centre for the study of higher education, the University of Melbourne, Australia. Retrieved July 17, 2017, from http://hdl.handle.net/11343/37863

Jerrim, J., & Shure, N. (2016). *Achievement of 15-year- olds in England: PISA 2015 national report*. London. Retrieved July 5, 2017, from http://dera.ioe.ac.uk/27761/1/PISA-2015_England_Report.pdf

Jones, R., & Thomas, L. (2006). The 2003 UK government higher education white paper: A critical assessment of its implications for the access and widening participation agenda. *Journal of Education Policy, 20*(5), 615–630. https://doi.org/10.1080/02680930500222477.

Kamali, A. W., Nicholson, S., & Wood, D. F. (2005). A model for widening access into medicine and dentistry: The SAMDA-BL project. *Medical Education, 39*(9), 918–925. https://doi.org/10.1111/j.1365-2929.2005.02227.x.

Komaromy, M., Grumbach, K., Drake, M., Vranizan, K., Lurie, N., Keane, D., & Bindman, A. B. (1996). The role of black and Hispanic physicians in providing health care for underserved populations. *New England Journal of Medicine, 334*(20), 1305–1310. https://doi.org/10.1056/NEJM199605163342006.

Kumwenda, B., Cleland, J. A., Walker, K., Lee, A. J., & Greatrix, R. (2017a). The relationship between school type and academic performance at medical school: A national, multi-cohort study. *BMJ Open 2017, 7*, e016291. https://doi.org/10.1136/bmjopen-2017-016291.

Kumwenda, B., Cleland, J., Greatrix, R., MacKenzie, R., & Prescott, G. (2017b). Are efforts to attract graduate applicants to UK medical schools effective in increasing the participation of under-represented socioeconomic groups? A national cohort study. *BMJ Open,* 2017: 7: e016291.

Lakhan, S. E. (2003). Diversification of U.S. medical schools via affirmative action implementation. *BMC Medical Education, 3*(1), 6. https://doi.org/10.1186/1472-6920-3-6.

Larkins, S., Michielsen, K., Iputo, J., Elsanousi, S., Mammen, M., Graves, L., et al. (2015). Impact of selection strategies on representation of underserved populations and intention to practise: International findings. *Medical Education, 49*(1), 60–72. https://doi.org/10.1111/medu.12518.

MacKenzie, R., Cleland, J., Ayansina, D., & Nicholson, S. (2016). Does the UKCAT predict performance on exit from medical school? A national cohort study. *BMJ Open, 6,* e1011313. https://doi.org/10.1136/bmjopen-2016-011313.

Mangan, J., Hughes, A., Davies, P., & Slack, K. (2010). Fair access, achievement and geography: Explaining the association between social class and students' choice of university. *Studies in Higher Education, 35*(3), 335–350. https://doi.org/10.1080/03075070903131610.

Mathers, J., & Parry, J. (2009). Why are there so few working-class applicants to medical schools? Learning from the success stories. *Medical Education, 43*(3), 219–228. https://doi.org/10.1111/j.1365-2923.2008.03274.x.

Mathers, J., Sitch, A., Marsh, J. L., & Parry, J. (2011). Widening access to medical education for under-represented socioeconomic groups: Population based cross sectional analysis of UK data, 2002–6. *BMJ (Clinical Research Ed.), 342*, d918. https://doi.org/10.1136/bmj.d918.

Mathers, J., Sitch, A., & Parry, J. (2016a). Longitudinal assessment of the impact of the use of the UK clinical aptitude test for medical student selection. *Medical Education, 50*(10), 1033–1044. https://doi.org/10.1111/medu.13082.

Mathers, J., Sitch, A., & Parry, J. (2016b). Population-based longitudinal analyses of offer likelihood in UK medical schools: 1996–2012. *Medical Education, 50*(6), 612–623. https://doi.org/10.1111/medu.12981.

McHarg, J., Mattick, K., & Knight, L. V. (2007). Why people apply to medical school: Implications for widening participation activities. *Medical Education, 41*(8), 815–821. https://doi.org/10.1111/j.1365-2923.2007.02798.x.

Medical Schools Council. (2014a). *A journey to medicine: Outreach guidance.* London. Retrieved February 2, 2016, from http://www.medschools.ac.uk/SiteCollectionDocuments/MSC-A-Journey-to-Medicine-Outreach-Guidance.pdf

Medical Schools Council. (2014b). *Selecting for excellence: Final report.* London. Retrieved February 2, 2016, from http://www.medschools.ac.uk/SiteCollectionDocuments/Selecting-for-Excellence-Final-Report.pdf

Medical Schools Council. (2017). *Entry requirements for UK medical schools 2018.* London. Retrieved July 4, 2017, from http://www.medschools.ac.uk/SiteCollectionDocuments/MSC-Entry-requirements-for-UK-medical-schools.pdf

Medical Workforce Standing Advisory Committee. (1997). *Planning the medical workforce.* Third report. London: Department of Health. Retrieved July 24, 2017, from http://www.nhshistory.net/mwfsac3.pdf

Milburn, A. (2012). *Fair access to professional careers. The independent reviewer on social mobility and child poverty.* London. Retrieved December 2, 2015, from https://www.gov.uk/government/uploads/system/uploads/attachment_data/file/61090/IR_FairAccess_acc2.pdf

Miller, K., & Cummings, G. (2009). Gifted and talented students' career aspirations and influences: A systematic review of the literature. *International Journal of Nursing Education Scholarship, 6*(1), 1–26. https://doi.org/10.2202/1548-923X.1667.

Minty, S. (2015). Young people's attitudes towards student debt in Scotland and England. In S. Riddell, E. Weedon, & S. Minty (Eds.), *Higher education in Scotland and the UK: Diverging or converging systems?* (pp. 56–70). Croydon: Edinburgh University Press Ltd.

Molesworth, M., Scullion, R., & Nixon, E. (2011). *The marketisation of higher education and the student as consumer.* Oxon: Routledge.

Moore, J., Mountford-Zimdars, A., Wiggans, J., Gittoes, M., McArdle, S., Johnson School, D., & McCarthy, K. (2013). *Contextualised admissions: Examining the evidence.* Report to SPA the supporting professionalism in admissions programme. London: Arc Network Ltd. Retrieved July 26, 2017, from www.spa.ac.uk/sites/default/files/Research-CA-Report-2013-full.pdf

Morrison, E., & Grbic, D. (2015). Dimensions of diversity and perception of having learned from individuals from different backgrounds: The particular importance of racial diversity. *Academic Medicine, 90*(7), 937–945. https://doi.org/10.1097/ACM.0000000000000675.

NHS Improvement. (2016). *Evidence from NHS improvement on clinical staff shortages*. London: UK National Health Service. Retrieved July 26, 2017, from https://improvement.nhs.uk/uploads/documents/Clinical_workforce_report.pdf

Nicholson, S., & Cleland, J. (2015). Reframing research on widening participation in medical education: Using theory to inform practice. In J. Cleland & S. Durning (Eds.), *Researching medical education* (pp. 231–244). Chichester: John Wiley & Sons, Ltd. https://doi.org/10.1002/9781118838983.ch20.

O'Connell, T. F., Ham, S. A., Hart, T. G., Curlin, F. A., & Yoon, J. D. (2017). A national longitudinal survey of medical students' intentions to practice among the underserved. *Academic Medicine*, [epub ahead of publication]. https://doi.org/10.1097/ACM.0000000000001816

O'Shea, S., Lysaght, P., Roberts, J., & Harwood, V. (2015). Shifting the blame in higher education – Social inclusion and deficit discourses. *Higher Education Research and Development, 35*(2), 322–336. https://doi.org/10.1080/07294360.2015.1087388.

Office of National Statistics. (2011). *UK population census*. Retrieved June 23, 2016, from https://www.ons.gov.uk/census/2011census

Orom, H., Semalulu, T., & Underwood, W. (2013). The social and learning environments experienced by underrepresented minority medical students. *Academic Medicine, 88*(11), 1765–1777. https://doi.org/10.1097/ACM.0b013e3182a7a3af.

Panel on Fair Access to the Professions. (2009). *Unleashing aspiration: The final report of the panel on fair access to the professions*. London. Retrieved July 16, 2017, from http://webarchive.nationalarchives.gov.uk/+/http:/www.cabinet-office.gov.uk/media/227102/fair-access.pdf

Patterson, F., Knight, A., Dowell, J., Nicholson, S., Cousans, F., & Cleland, J. (2016). How effective are selection methods in medical education? A systematic review. *Medical Education, 50*(1), 36–60. https://doi.org/10.1111/medu.12817.

Phillips, J. P., Wendling, A. L., Fahey, C. A., & Mavis, B. E. (2017). The effect of a community-based medical school on the state and local physician workforce. *Academic Medicine*, [epub ahead of publication]. https://doi.org/10.1097/ACM.0000000000001823.

Puddey, I. B., Mercer, A., Playford, D. E., Pougnault, S., & Riley, G. J. (2014). Medical student selection criteria as predictors of intended rural practice following graduation. *BMC Medical Education, 14*(218). https://doi.org/10.1186/1472-6920-14-218.

Razack, S., Hodges, B., Steinert, Y., & Maguire, M. (2015). Seeking inclusion in an exclusive process: Discourses of medical school student selection. *Medical Education, 49*(1), 36–47. https://doi.org/10.1111/medu.12547.

Reay, D., Davies, J., David, M., & Ball, S. J. (2001). Choices of degree or degrees of choice? Class, 'race' and the higher education choice process. *Sociology, 35*(4), 855–874. https://doi.org/10.1177/0038038501035004004

Robb, N., Dunkley, L., Boynton, P., & Greenhalgh, T. (2007). Looking for a better future: Identity construction in socio-economically deprived 16-year olds considering a career in medicine. *Social Science & Medicine, 65*(4), 738–754. https://doi.org/10.1016/j.socscimed.2007.03.011.

Roberts, N., & Bolton, P. (2017). *Briefing paper 07914: Medical school places in England from September 2018*. House of Commons Library. London. Retrieved July 4, 2017, from http://researchbriefings.files.parliament.uk/documents/CBP-7914/CBP-7914.pdf

Royal College of Paediatrics and Child Health (RCPCH). (2017). *State of child health report* 2017. London. Retrieved July 5, 2017, from http://www.rcpch.ac.uk/system/files/protected/page/SoCH 2017 UK web updated.pdf

Saha, S., Guiton, G., Wimmers, P. F., & Wilkerson, L. (2008). Student body racial and ethnic composition and diversity-related outcomes in US medical schools. *JAMA, 300*(10), 1135–1145. https://doi.org/10.1001/jama.300.10.1135.

Scanlan, G., Cleland, J., Johnston, P., Walker, K., Krucien, N., & Skåtun, D. (2017). *Location and support are critical to attracting junior doctors: A discrete choice experiment.* Submitted for Publication.

Scottish Government. (2016). *The final report of the commission for widening access: A blueprint for fairness.* Edinburgh. Retrieved May 1, 2017, from http://www.gov.scot/Resource/0049/00496535.pdf

Scottish Government Newsroom. (2016). *Scotland's first graduate entry medical programme.* Edinburgh. Retrieved July 24, 2017, from https://news.gov.scot/news/scotlands-first-graduate-entry-medical-programme

Sheeran, Y., Brown, B. J., & Baker, S. (2007). Conflicting philosophies of inclusion: The contestation of knowledge in widening participation. *London Review of Education, 5*(3), 249–263. https://doi.org/10.1080/14748460701661302.

Slack, K. (2003). Whose aspirations are they anyway? *International Journal of Inclusive Education, 7*(4), 325–335. https://doi.org/10.1080/1360311032000110016.

Smit, R. (2012). Towards a clearer understanding of student disadvantage in higher education: Problematising deficit thinking. *Higher Education Research and Development, 31*(3), 369–380. https://doi.org/10.1080/07294360.2011.634383.

Smith, C., & Low, L. (2012). The gap between foundation years and specialty training. *BMJ Careers*. Retrieved July 24, 2017, from http://careers.bmj.com/careers/advice/view-article.html?id=20006722#

Southgate, E., Kelly, B. J., & Symonds, I. M. (2015). Disadvantage and the "capacity to aspire" to medical school. *Medical Education, 49*(1), 73–83. https://doi.org/10.1111/medu.12540.

Steven, K., Dowell, J., Jackson, C., & Guthrie, B. (2016). Fair access to medicine? Retrospective analysis of UK medical schools application data 2009–2012 using three measures of socioeconomic status. *BMC Medical Education, 16*(1), 11–21. https://doi.org/10.1186/s12909-016-0536-1.

Stevenson, J., Clegg, S., & Lefever, R. (2010). The discourse of widening participation and its critics: An institutional case study. *London Review of Education, 8*(2), 105–115. https://doi.org/10.1080/14748460.2010.487328

Sutton Trust. (2011). *Degrees of success university chances by individual school*. London. Retrieved July 14, 2017, from https://www.suttontrust.com/research-paper/degree-success-university-chances-individual-school/

Sutton Trust. (2017). *Social mobility 2017*. London. Retrieved July 14, 2017, from https://www.suttontrust.com/research-paper/social-mobility-2017-research/

The Cambridge English Dictionary. (2017). *Definition of meritocracy*. Retrieved July 25, 2017, from http://dictionary.cambridge.org/dictionary/english/meritocracy

Thomas, L., Storan, J., Wylie, V., Berzins, K., Harley, P., Linley, R., & Rawson, A. (2009). *Review of widening participation strategic assessments 2009*. Omskirk: Action on Access. Retrieved July 26, 2017, from https://www.heacademy.ac.uk/system/files/review_of_wp_assessments-2009.pdf

Thompson, D. W. (2008). Widening participation and higher education. Students, systems and other paradoxes. *London Review of Education, 6*(2), 137–147. https://doi.org/10.1080/14748460802185102.

Tiffin, P. A., Dowell, J. S., & McLachlan, J. C. (2012). Widening access to UK medical education for under-represented socioeconomic groups: Modelling the impact of the UKCAT in the 2009 cohort. *BMJ, 344*, e1805. https://doi.org/10.1136/bmj.e1805.

Tiffin, P. A., McLachlan, J. C., Webster, L., & Nicholson, S. (2014). Comparison of the sensitivity of the UKCAT and a levels to sociodemographic characteristics: A national study. *BMC Medical Education, 14*(7), 1–12. https://doi.org/10.1186/1472-6920-14-7.

UK Clinical Aptitude Test (UKCAT). (2017). *About us*. Retrieved July 26, 2017, from https://www.ukcat.ac.uk/about-us/

UK Foundation Programme Office (UKFPO). (2015). *F2 career destination report 2015*. Retrieved July 24, 2017, from http://www.foundationprogramme.nhs.uk/pages/resource-bank

UK Foundation Programme Office (UKFPO). (2016). *Career destination report 2016*. Retrieved July 24, 2017, from www.foundationprogramme.nhs.uk/download.asp?file=Careers_destination_2016.pdf

Undergraduate Medicine and Health Sciences Admissions Test (UMAT). (2017). *Home | UMAT*. Retrieved July 26, 2017, from https://umat.acer.edu.au/

Walker, J. H., Dewitt, D. E., Pallant, J. F., & Cunningham, C. E. (2012a). Rural origin plus a rural clinical school placement is a significant predictor of medical students' intentions to practice rurally: A multi-university study. *Rural Remote Health, 12,* 1908. Retrieved July 5, 2017, From https://www.ncbi.nlm.nih.gov/pubmed/22239835

Walker, K. O., Moreno, G., & Grumbach, K. (2012b). The association among specialty, race, ethnicity, and practice location among California physicians in diverse specialties. *Journal of the National Medical Association, 104*(1–2), 46–52. Retrieved July 4, 2017 from https://www.ncbi.nlm.nih.gov/pmc/articles/PMC3978451/

Whitla, D. K., Orfield, G., Silen, W., Teperow, C., Howard, C., & Reede, J. (2003). Educational benefits of diversity in medical school: A survey of students. *Academic Medicine, 78*(5), 460–466. Retrieved February 7, 2016, from https://insights.ovid.com/pubmed?pmid=12742780

Wilkinson, T. J., Wells, J. E., & Bushnell, J. A. (2004). Are differences between graduates and undergraduates in a medical course due to age or prior degree? *Medical Education, 38*(11), 1141–1146. https://doi.org/10.1111/j.1365-2929.2004.01981.x.

Williamson, H. (2004). *The Milltown boys revisited*. London: Berg.

8

University Strategies to Improve the Academic Success of Disadvantaged Students: Three Experiences in Chile

Oscar Espinoza, Noel McGinn, and Luis Eduardo González

Introduction

In the last two decades the world has witnessed a veritable explosion of university enrollments. Chile is no exception; beginning in the mid-1990s, sustained economic growth permitted government spending on primary and secondary education, resulting in greater demand for higher education.

O. Espinoza (✉)
Center of Advanced Studies, Universidad de Playa Ancha, Valparaíso, Chile

Center of Comparative Educational Policies, Universidad Diego Portales, Santiago, Chile
e-mail: oespinoza@academia.cl

N. McGinn
School of Education, Harvard University, Cambridge, MA, USA

L. E. González
Programa Interdisciplinario de Investigaciones en Educación (PIIE), Santiago, Chile

University enrollments have grown enormously, from 175,000 in 1983 to more than 1.2 million in 2015 (SIES 2015). Most of that growth has occurred in recently established private institutions, and most new students have come from lower income households and families with lower education levels (Espinoza and González 2013; CINDA 2010).

Contrary to expectations, however, expansion of access to higher education has so far had no impact on Chile's high level of income inequality, which remains the highest among developed nations (Espinoza 2002; Espinoza and González 2015; OECD 2016). This may be only a temporary phenomenon, for these reasons. Most of the new students have come from environments that may not have prepared them for university attendance (Concha 2009). These students have had lower completion (graduation) rates than continuing-generation students, with the consequence that the overall graduation rate has declined. Research in other countries indicates that university dropouts do not make a positive contribution to economic growth (Bound et al. 2010). Several universities in Chile have responded with efforts to prepare qualified but disadvantaged applicants to succeed in the university environment.

This chapter analyzes initiatives by three Chilean universities. These are: the Propedéutico Program of the University of Santiago (USACH); the Priority Admission System (SIPEE) of the University of Chile; and the PENTA Program of the Catholic University. The objective of the chapter is to assess the impact of these initiatives on student access and performance once enrolled.

The study used the exploratory case study method, combining data from primary and secondary sources. The former was obtained from the coordinators of the three programs, relying on semi-structured interviews to obtain data to assess the programs' impact. At the same time, we reviewed the programs' documentation and studies describing and assessing their experience.

The chapter begins with a brief review of research on types and causes of dropouts, distinguishing between factors used to predict student success and factors that can be used to design strategies to change a student's likelihood of success. We then describe the interventions, and their effectiveness in improving students' performance in the university. The chapter concludes with consideration of the range of options available to universities seeking to improve the academic careers of those who have been described as "vulnerable".

Background

Correlates of University Failure and Non-completion

The relationship between family socio-economic status (SES) and educational attainment has been well-documented for some time (Panos and Astin 1968; Sirin 2005). In the 1970s, university administrators in the United States noted that new enrollees whose parents had not attended university were less likely to succeed than were students with educated parents. The more vulnerable group was identified by university administrators as "first-generation" students (Adachi 1979).[1] Researchers then began to attribute a general decline in completion rates to the increase of first-generation enrollees (Billson and Terry 1982). First-generation students are more likely than their counterparts to be from a lower SES family, to have been raised in a lower income community, to belong to a minority ethnic group, to be a woman, and to have attended a lower quality secondary school (Kuh et al. 2006).

First-generation are different from continuing-generation students both in their antecedents as well as their behavior once in the university. A large volume of research has been carried out to identify factors that define the two groups (Aspelmeier et al. 2012; Banning 2014; Choy 2001; Engle and Tinto 2015; Ishitani 2006; Peabody 2013; Pike and Kuh 2005; Tym et al. 2004).[2] They do not necessarily differ in intellectual ability, but may command a different body of knowledge than that common among upper income groups.[3] As a consequence, their eventual

---

[1] Given higher levels of education in the United States, students are called "first-generation" only if both parents did not attend university.

[2] Most of the research available comes from the United States, and findings are not consistent across institutions or countries.

[3] Scores on curriculum-based achievement tests, for example, are more highly correlated with SES than are scores on tests of general intelligence.

failure can be explained as a lack of academic and social integration (Tinto 1975). They participate less in university life because they lack the cultural capital they would have received from educated parents (Bourdieu 1986; Lareau and Weininger 2003: Lohfink and Paulsen 2005; Banning 2014). This capital includes knowledge and understanding of: (a) what is required to succeed academically in university; (b) the university as a community and the function of its non-academic activities; and (c) sources of assistance in learning how to meet academic and social requirements and opportunities (Pascarella et al. 2004; Engle and Tinto 2015).

During their first year, vulnerable students are less likely to engage in academic and social activities, and less likely to learn the knowledge and skills required for academic success. In countries where universities have on-campus residents, these students are more likely to live at home (Gibbons and Shoffner 2004; Peabody 2013) and spend more hours in paid employment outside the university (Inkelas et al. 2007; Johnson 2010; Nunez et al. 1998). They are more often absent from class than their classmates (Gasper et al. 2012; De Clercq et al. 2013; Fowler and Boylan 2010), and participate less in class discussions; they use the library less often (Soria et al. 2015). They are less likely to talk with their professors (Kim and Sax 2009). They lack the "study habits" necessary to meet course demands (Lockhart 2004). They study less and spend less time preparing lessons (Credé and Kuncel 2008), and consequently fail and repeat courses (Collier and Morgan 2008).

In the face of failure, many students choose to quit the university, either to avoid the unpleasant experience of failure or to achieve the objectives that seem more achievable outside. Students with high academic performance are more likely to continue to graduation, even if actively employed outside the university. Students with low (but not failing) grades are likely to continue if they participated actively in student extracurricular activities (Johnson 2010).

The research cited above is consistent with the perspective that persistence and completion in the university is primarily a function of student agency. Consistent with this assumption, completion rates could be maintained or improved by screening out students with characteristics associated with failure. On the other hand, this would reduce the proportion of first-generation applicants who would be admitted.

An alternative perspective argues that first-generation students have difficulty in their first year in the university not for lack of intellectual ability, but because they lack the cultural capital required for academic success. The university as an institution was designed to serve students from upper class and well-educated families (Attewell et al. 2011; Gibbons and Shoffner 2004; Porter 2006; Stephens et al. 2017). In order to improve academic performance and raise completion rates, these policies and practices can and should be redesigned to match the more complex population seeking education (Kezar 2011; Thomas et al. 2003; Zepke and Leach 2010).

University actions to improve the success of disadvantaged candidates for enrollment differ in terms of whether they impact students directly, or change the structure and practices of others in the university. They differ in terms of whether they are remedial, that is, seek to make up for specific knowledge the student did not learn prior to entry into the university, or whether they address the learning how to learn in the university. Finally, they differ in whether the objective is to make the vulnerable first-generation student more like continuing-generation students, or to match the demands of university to the cultural capital of the new kind of student.

Colleges and universities in the United States and elsewhere have developed a variety of different strategies to reduce dropouts and increase graduation rates (ACUE 2015; Bradley and Blanco 2010; Hanover Research 2014; Mena 2015). These and other interventions are designed to affect students' ability to learn in the university setting and their motivation to do so. They differ in terms of when they engage students, prior to enrollment or once enrolled. One example of the former are the initiatives originally funded as part of the U. S. War on Poverty in 1968, designed to facilitate entrance and persistence of disadvantaged youth in higher education institutions. In addition to government-funded scholarships, these involve colleges and universities in running programs like Upward Bound, which engages secondary school students in counseling, guidance, tutoring and cultural activities intended to increase their likelihood of completing secondary school and succeeding in college (Balz and Esten 1998). Limited research has been done on the cost-effectiveness of this approach as compared to others, but the program enjoys strong support both from universities and students who have benefitted from it (U.S. Department of Education 2017).

Some universities (often funded through federal grants) offer anticipatory "Summer Bridge" programs to incoming students who are disadvantaged or first-generation. These provide tutoring, contact with professors, orientation to the university's facilities and non-academic activities designed to socialize the newcomers into the culture of the institution. Evaluations suggest that the programs are not highly successful. First-generation and other vulnerable students often do not participate in all voluntary activities, and there is no discernible impact on retention in later years (Bradley and Blanco 2010; Cabrera et al. 2013; Peabody 2013).

More successful are programs offered during the first year of study. One approach focuses on social integration combined with academic help. Older students (and some faculty) meet with new students to provide advice and encouragement. These "first-year experience" programs have been shown to improve learning outcomes and increase persistence (Porter and Swing 2006; Pan et al. 2008; Terenzini et al. 1996; Zhao and Kuh 2004). Much less successful are programs that require students to repeat failed courses. This remediation does little to improve student learning skills and reduces social integration. Although some students go on to complete the degree, many do not. The programs are expensive, both for the university and for students (Bettinger and Long 2009; Calcagno and Long 2008; Martorell and Mcfarlin 2011).

The life of a university student can be highly stressful. Stress reduces the individual's capacity to retain new information, reducing learning. A third approach to improvement of academic performance focuses on strengthening individual students' self-definition or self-identification, using a process called "values affirmation". A brief, psychological intervention, generally repeated during the first year, has a significant impact on confidence which leads to improved academic performance. The intervention focuses individuals' attention on themselves rather than on academic subjects. For example, women students in science courses were asked to write for 15 minutes about the values (such as friends and family) most important to themselves. This occurred at the beginning of the course and just before mid-terms. A control group wrote about their least important values. At the end of the course, women who had written about their most important values achieved significantly higher grades, and grades equivalent to those of male students who typically obtain higher grades in science courses (Miyake 2010). Similar results have been obtained in other value-affirmation experiments (Stephens et al. 2015; Tibbetts et al. 2016), including studies with first-generation students (Harackiewicz et al. 2014).

Programs Designed to Support Disadvantaged Students Entering University in Chile

Concern about the performance of vulnerable university students is a more recent phenomenon in Chile. The issue of expansion of education on income inequality surfaced in 2003, and by 2009 researchers began to focus in on the issues facing first-generation university students (Canales and De Los Ríos 2009; Castillo and Cabezas 2010; Fukushi 2013; Zandomeni et al. 2016). Their findings replicated what had been reported in the United States, with the exception that because Chilean universities are non-residential, living at home did not distinguish between first and continuing-generation students. One study demonstrated that once past the first year, first-generation students performed as well as their continuing counterparts (Soto 2016).

Chilean first-generation and vulnerable students with high secondary school grade point averages (GPAs) did as well in university as their counterparts, although they on average scored lower on the admission test which is based on secondary school curriculum knowledge. Propedeutic courses in the university were effective over time in enabling those first-generation students who remained after the first year to raise their performance levels (Leyton 2015).

Analysis of Cases

The Propedeutic Program of the University of Santiago

This program, initiated in 2007, was based on the belief that talent is equally distributed across social strata, and that talented students can be found in all schools, public, charter (or subsidized private) or (fee-charging) private, independent of their families' economic status. These students can be identified, in each school, by their high academic performance. Despite their ability to learn, however, these students enter university less well-prepared than students from the upper social strata who have attended more elite secondary schools. The program is consistent with the university's Institutional Mission, which promotes values of diversity, pluralism, inclusion and social responsibility.

To this end, the Propedeutic Program offers talented students from lower-income families, attending public or charter schools, a summer course in mathematics, language and "Personal Management". The course takes place on Saturdays during the second semester of the students' senior year in secondary school. Classes are taught by the university's professors (Figueroa and González 2013).

Participants are chosen from 4th year students attending a secondary school participating in the USACH program. Although all applicants admitted to the university must take the national university admission test (PSU), the scores of those applying to the Propedeutic Program are not taken into account. To be accepted, however, Propedeutic candidates must have maintained a GPA in the upper 10 per cent of their class in their present school during their first three years as a student. A "Weighted Admission Score" is based 60 per cent on the GPA during the first three years of secondary, 30 per cent on grades during their 4th year, and 10 per cent on grades in the Propedeutic course (Figueroa and González 2013). In other words, even though the program serves the most vulnerable population, the selection procedure is meritocratic and exclusive. At present six secondary schools send students to the program; seven schools were in the program during its first year (2007), and a high of 19 participated in 2014.

Propedeutic Program participants who complete the program are admitted to the undergraduate program in Science and Humanities. At the same time, these students must apply to the government's scholarship program (Sistema de Becas para la Educación Superior) and meet their requirements: 100 per cent attendance at the Propedeutic courses; submission of a letter of commitment from a parent or guardian; written commitment by the applicant; a passing grade in the Propedeutic courses; and a high GPA. This last measure is a weighted average of grades in years

1 to 3 of secondary (60%), grades in the last year (30%) and average grades in the Propedeutic (10%) (Figueroa and González 2013).

About half the students admitted to the Propedeutic Program enter the university each year, in the undergraduate program in Science and Humanities. Enrollments have grown from 46 in 2007 to 63 in 2012. At the same time, average PSU scores have increased from 436 to 552, indicating a significant change in the academic preparation of students entering through the Propedeutic channel. Even with this score increase, however, the Propedeutic students continue to score lower than those admitted by the regular process (Figueroa and González 2013).

As Table 8.1 shows, enrollments were stable in the first two years (2014–2015) but dropped almost 50 per cent in 2016. It is noteworthy that 92 per cent of the students admitted in 2014 were first-generation, and 73 per cent in 2016.

Also note that a high proportion of students admitted to the university through the Propedeutic continued in the second year. The retention rate was over 87 per cent in 2014 and 83 per cent in 2016 (Table 8.2).

The program has three objectives. First, it seeks to develop a model that, replicated by other institutions, would result in a more equitable and efficient higher education system. Second, this is to be accomplished

Table 8.1 Total number of students and first-generation students admitted to the USACH through the Propedeutic Program (2014–2016)

	2014	2015	2016
Total students	62	63	30
Total first-generation students	57	59	22

Source: Vicerrectoría de Desarrollo Institucional, USACH

Table 8.2 Number of students entering USACH through the Propedeutic who continued the following year (Retention rate for Years 2014–2016)

	2014	2015	2016
Total number of students	62	63	30
Total number of students continuing	54	49	25
(Retention rate)	(87%)	(78%)	(83%)

Source: Vicerrectoría de Desarrollo Institucional, USACH

by improving the inclusion and retention of talented youth who are socially vulnerable, contributing to equity for those who are disadvantaged by the current selection system. Third, the university hopes that this model of selection of students on the basis of class rank in secondary school will become a national policy.

These objectives have been achieved. There is now a Network of Propedeutic universities, made up of 19 institutions in Chile. Almost 500 students (who most likely would not have attended university) have been admitted to the University of Santiago. The Ministry of Education in 2015 began a pilot program to provide needy students with university access and support (PACE). The specific results expected are:

(a) Strengthening of links between the university and the social and cultural milieu of disadvantaged youth.
(b) Contribution to more equitable access to higher education.
(c) Incorporation of high school grades in the battery of instruments that universities use in their processes of selection.

Some research has been done on the academic performance of students who went through the Propedeutic Program. Koljatic and Silva (2013) compared the academic performance of Propedeutic students with that of others admitted to the USACH by the regular process. The Propedeutic students had lower grades during the first year, but their grades during the second year were similar to those of students admitted by the regular process. There were high dropout rates by Propedeutic students during the first and second year, but graduation rates were similar.

A different indicator of impact is the number of students who have graduated or been awarded degrees, more than 60 to this point. These students successfully completed two years of the common program and two or more years in the specific disciplines they followed.

Propedeutic students find their first year in the university difficult because of the low level of prior knowledge they bring from their secondary schools. The university has found it necessary to create a special unit that provides academic support of various kinds to these students. This is especially important during the first year, and less so in later years. Academic counseling is provided, which also helps the university detect other problems. Some of the students lack social-emotional skills that would enable them to participate more fully in university life and facilitate their academic work. In 2017 the university began a pilot project, "Constructing My Life Project", aimed at improving the social-emotional skills and practices of the Propedeutic students. At the same time, studies have been carried out to better understand the academic track of those who have finished the program (Figueroa and González 2013).

The program is evaluated annually in terms of student academic performance, retention rates and graduation rates. As noted, there is a follow up study of graduates and dropouts. These evaluations have contributed to modification of the program over time. For example, a special program was created to provide students selected into the university with an (additional) intensive course in mathematics.

The PENTA Program of the Catholic University

The Educational Program for Children with Academic Talent (PENTA) of the Catholic University began its activities in 2001. This initiative offers learning opportunities complementary to those available in school to academically talented students. These opportunities are designed to respond to the personal characteristics and learning needs of the students (PENTA-UC 2001a; López et al. 2002).

PENTA attends to outstanding students, identified by their general academic ability or a specific aptitude in language and writing, logic and mathematics, natural and/or social sciences (PENTA-UC 2001b). It seeks out a heterogeneous group of students, who come from different types of schools (public, charter or private), who are enrolled in grades six to 12. The students can remain in PENTA as long as they are in school.

The program carries out a process of identification and selection of talented youth over a period of five months and several stages. First is the identification of schools that will participate in the process. This is followed by training the teachers of these schools in the identification of talented students using the procedures and instruments developed by the program. The professors then nominate students who take the Raven

Progressive Matrices Test (a non-verbal measure of intelligence), and fill out questionnaires assessing self-esteem and achievement motivation. These instruments are administered by PENTA staff (Flanagan and Arancibia 2005).

PENTA solicits the voluntary cooperation of the university's professors in the design of courses in their specialization that would be of interest to high school students. Courses are offered on Saturdays during the academic year. Students can take one course per semester selected from a collection of course descriptions written by the professors. Courses not selected by a minimal number of students are not offered in the future.

Between 2003 and 2014 a total of 692 students have taken courses in PENTA, an average of 57 per year. Most (66.1%) of the students came from public schools, 27.6 per cent from charter schools and 6.3 per cent from private schools. Of the total, 92 per cent took the PSU (Table 8.3).

The data in Table 8.3 imply a clear increase in the number of public school graduates taking the PSU, establishing an essential equality among graduates of the three kinds of secondary schools. To demonstrate that this is attributable to participation in PENTA, researchers compared average PSU scores of participants with those of a control group of equal academic performance that did not participate in PENTA. The PENTA participants scored, on average, 42 points higher than the control group on the PSU mathematics test, 36 points higher on PSU language and 120 points in the gradepoint rank (PENTA-UC 2015).

Table 8.3 PENTA students completing the program by school origin (2003–2014)

Year	School of origin			Number completing program
	Public	Charter	Private	
2012	52	34	7	89
2013	57	35	7	99
2014	47	28	4	79
Total students 2003–2014	454	198	44	692
Total that have taken PSU				637

Source: PENTA-UC (2015)

Table 8.4 PENTA graduates entering higher education institutions between 2003 and 2014

Total graduates entering higher education	Traditional University	Non-traditional University	Foreign University	Professional Institute	Armed Forces or Police	Technical Training Centers
570	78.6%	15.8%	0.4%	4.6%	0.4%	0.2%

Source: PENTA-UC (2015)

Table 8.4 shows that three of every four PENTA students in the 2003–2014 period have entered one of the "traditional" universities. These universities, founded prior to the educational reform of 1980 (and which are members of the Council of Rectors of Chilean Universities (CRUCH)) offer scholarships funded by the government on the basis of PSU scores. Some 40 per cent of the students enrolled in the Catholic University, and 19.5 per cent in the University of Chile, the top-ranked universities in the country. Another 11.2 per cent enrolled in the University of Santiago and the other 29.3 per cent are distributed among 22 other universities. Slightly more than 15 per cent enrolled in one of the new private universities, principally in the Diego Portales University (3.7%) and 2.5 per cent in the Andres Bello University (PENTA-UC 2015).

To date, only 13.1 per cent of those graduating from PENTA and entering higher education have received their degree or graduated (PENTA-UC 2015). This low completion rate has two possible explanations: (a) a high dropout rate induced by the high cost of higher education, motherhood, or attractive employment, or; (b) a significant delay in graduation because of the length of some degree programs (e.g., medicine).

Other Impacts of PENTA

Former students are in agreement that the program helped them develop cognitive, academic and social-emotional skills. The program improved their study habits and their ability to express themselves in written and oral form. They report higher expectations for the future and the quality of life they will achieve, access to better-paid employment, and improved self-esteem. These expectations are shared by their parents (PENTA-UC 2015).

The Priority Admission System for Educational Equity of the University of Chile (SIPEE)

SIPEE began with an agreement taken in 2011 by the Senate of the University of Chile.[4] The decision was based on an earlier experience of the Faculty of Social Sciences, which in 2010 had set up a special admission process for students graduating from public secondary schools (Cupos Pro Equidad) (Universidad de Chile 2013).

SIPEE is a mechanism designed to promote the enrollment of students seeking admission who come from public schools and low-income households who do not achieve the PSU scores required by the regular admission process. The objective is to increase the participation of students with this profile in the student body of the university, to the extent that they are proportionally represented in comparison with students from other social strata and secondary schools.

The former admission process had used an open admission system with objective and well-defined selection criteria. All students had to score at least 600 (test mean is 500) on the PSU. SIPEE, on the other hand, established these criteria:

1. Student's household income had to be among the three lowest quintiles of the national distribution. This means that the students had to come from households in the lower 60 per cent of the income distribution.
2. Applicants had to have been enrolled four years (complete program) in a public (municipal) school.

---

[4] Antecedents to the creation of SIPEE include: in 2010 only 30% of the entering students were from public schools and 33.2% from private schools, while nationally 39.9% of all secondary graduates were from public schools and 7.2% from private schools. On the Index of School Risk (Indice de Vulnerabilidad Escolar, IVE), 27.2% of all students scored in the most severe rank, while only 1.5% of students admitted to the university were at that high level of risk (Senado Universidad de Chile 2014).

3. Applicants had to be enrolled in the 4th (or last) year of secondary school at the time of making application.
4. Students had to apply to the government's scholarship and loan program.[5]
5. Students had to maintain a GPA of 5.5 or better between the first and third years of secondary school (Universidad de Chile 2014).

The selection process takes three variables into account, in the following hierarchical sequence:

> First: Applications are ranked according to their score on the Index of School Risk. Students from schools in high risk areas (scores in upper quartile) are ranked first, followed by those whose risk score is between 76.5 and 53.4, with those scoring between 53.3 and 30 in the third rank.
>
> Second: Applicants are ordered according to their household's income quintile. Those in the lowest group are ranked first, then those in the second quintile from the bottom, followed by applicants in the third.
>
> Third: Applicants are ordered according to their secondary school grade point average. Students in the top 10 per cent in their school are first followed by those with lower GPAs. (Universidad de Chile 2014)

Students indicate their preference for a particular degree program offered by the University of Chile, and must obtain the minimum PSU score required by the program (Universidad de Chile 2014). Applicants who comply with these requirements are counted in the SIPEE quota when they matriculate.

Table 8.5 describes some aspects of this process of application and admission in SIPEE. The table shows that the number of openings has increased gradually, tripling over a five year period. SIPEE has generated increasing interest among secondary school graduates; applications have increased about 500 per cent between 2012 and 2016. The number of students enrolled through SIPEE has grown 300 per cent during the five year period, growing from 104 to 314 students admitted each year.

---

[5] Students admitted through SIPEE can finance their tuition costs with a scholarship from the Ministry of Education (and the National Scholarship System), or a scholarship provided by the university that admits them.

Table 8.5 SIPEE admission process (2012–2016)

Year	Number of faculties and programs	Number of openings	Number of applicants	Number enrolled through SIPEE
2012	7/10	131	895	104
2013	17/40	370	2497	200
2014	17/40	431	3722	301
2015	17/40	450	4426	301
2016	17/40	461	4423	314

Source: Universidad de Chile (2013, 2014); Dirección de Bienestar Estudiantil (2017)

The numbers make clear that SIPEE has grown stronger with the passing of time, and that its impact on at-risk students is without question. It is important to keep in mind that not all openings have been filled, for three major reasons. First, the program initially was not well known among 4th year secondary students. Second, it was not well known by school administrators and teachers. Third, the process of application implies a heavy load of paperwork for the students' families (Wegenreld 2015). Even so, access to the university by this means now accounts for 12 per cent of new first year students.

SIPEE requires a much lower minimum PSU score (as much as 130 points depending on the degree program) than the regular admission process. This compensates for the otherwise high selectivity of the university. By lowering the required score, the university can now admit intellectually talented students who, because of their family background or secondary education, cannot surmount the barrier of curriculum knowledge required by the PSU.

As a special admission process, SIPEE is not associated with support programs that help students to remain in the university and to graduate. It has, however, as an admissions process, made it possible to identify the need to support and help students who come from social and educational backgrounds that differ from those of the average student admitted. This has contributed to discussion about the role of teaching and professors in the integral formation of the student. It has called attention to the need to provide different paths to successful academic performance, and for greater flexibility within the university with regard to changes of career or degree program.

Table 8.6 Retention and completion rates of SIPEE students (2014–2016)

Year	Retention rate 2nd year of program	Number of graduates[a]
2014	85.0%	No graduates
2015	80.4%	No graduates
2016	83.8%	No graduates

Source: Dirección de Bienestar Estudiantil (2017)
[a]The first cohort of SIPEE students will graduate in 2017

As can be seen in Table 8.6, retention rates of SIPEE students in their second year are quite high, exceeding 80 per cent. This implies that SIPEE students have a high probability of finishing their university program successfully.

Castro et al. (2012) for their part, conclude that students admitted to the Psychology program of the University of Chile through the regular process had a higher level of academic performance than those admitted through SIPEE. The difference in GPAs was 0.3 during the first semester of the first year, and 0.6 in the second semester. A different study was carried out by the undergraduate department of the university. Using grades and pass rates for the courses in degree programs that participated in SIPEE during 2012–2014, the study found that students admitted solely on their PSU score did slightly better than the SIPEE students, but differences varied in amount across programs and year of admission (Departamento de +Pregrado de la Universidad de Chile 2014). Up to this point there has not been a thorough evaluation of the impact of SIPEE. There are, however, no signs of differences in student performance linked to the process of admission.

Expected Results

When beginning the SIPEE method the University of Chile anticipated that it would have three kinds of impact. Both the life project of the student as well as that of his/her family would change, increasing their expectations for personal development. Secondary schools, both staff and students, would raise their expectations for student performance. The university would promote a collaborative effort involving all the stakeholders, and that this would result in greater diversity and greater social integration (Devés 2014).

Conclusions

We do not yet have a full assessment of the impact of these efforts to improve access to higher education, especially for socially and economically disadvantaged students. To date there have been few studies of the academic performance of students admitted through these systems. We know little about their adjustment to university academic and social life. The initiatives are still relatively young, so we cannot assess their impact on the post-graduation performance of participants. There has not yet been an analysis of the long-term changes regarding university applicants, which universities are selected, and those admitted.

The number of disadvantaged students exposed to these special programs is only a tiny fraction of all students seeking higher education, too small to permit definitive statements about the programs' broad effect on academic standards and practices. On the other hand, anecdotal information suggests that (some) participating professors adjusted their content and teaching styles in response to their non-traditional students. Their innovations, and their students' achievements, were consistent with recent research claiming superior effectiveness for peer learning and project-based instruction as compared to traditional direct instruction methods. There was no evidence that these programs reduced learning outcomes.

The results of these three programs confirm findings of studies of similar (and earlier) initiatives in other countries. The conclusion drawn from those experiences (summarized briefly above) is that while it is possible to ameliorate the effects of lower SES (and accompanying factors) on development of academic ability, the long-term impacts of early childhood experience continue to be visible in adulthood. The initiatives taken by these universities in Chile should be seen, therefore, not as a panacea for profound social and economic inequality, but rather as an important contribution to society's array of instruments to promote social cohesion along with economic growth.

References

ACUE. (2015). *Linking college instruction to student attrition and graduation rates.* Washington, DC: ACUE – Association of College and University Educators. Retrieved from http://acue.org/linking-college-instruction-student-attrition-graduation-rates/

Adachi, F. (1979). *Analysis of the first generation college student population: A new concept in higher education.* Unpublished. University of Wyoming Division of Student Educational Opportunity, Larimie.

Aspelmeier, J. E., Love, M. M., Mcgill, L. A., Elliott, A. N., & Pierce, T. W. (2012). Self-esteem, locus of control, college adjustment, and GPA among first-and continuing-generation students: A moderator model of generational status. *Research in Higher Education, 53*(7), 755–781. https://doi.org/10.1007/s11162-011-9252-1.

Attewell, P., Heil, S., & Reisel, L. (2011). Competing explanations of undergraduate noncompletion. *American Educational Research Journal, 48*(3), 536–559. https://doi.org/10.3102/0002831210392018.

Balz, F., & Esten, M. (1998). Fulfilling private dreams, serving public priorities: An analysis of TRIO students' success at independent colleges and universities. *The Journal of Negro Education, 67*(4), 333–345. Retrieved from http://www.jstor.org/stable/2668134

Banning, J. (2014). First-generation college student dissertation abstracts: Research strategies, topical analysis, and lessons learned. *Journal of Education and Learning, 3*(2). https://doi.org/10.5539/jel.v3n2p14.

Bettinger, E., & Long, B. (2009). Addressing the needs of underprepared students in higher education. Does college remediation work? *The Journal of Human Resources, 44*(3), 736–771.

Billson, J., & Terry, M. (1982). *In search of the silken purse: Factors in attrition among first-generation students.* Retrieved from http://files.eric.ed.gov/fulltext/ED214431.pdf

Bound, J., Lovenheim, M., & Turner, S. (2010). Why have college completion rates declined? An analysis of changing student preparation and collegiate resources. *American Economic Journal: Applied Economics, 2*(3), 129–157. https://doi.org/10.1257/app.2.3.129.

Bourdieu, P. (1986). The forms of capital. In J. Richardson (Ed.), *Handbook of theory and research for the sociology of education* (pp. 241–255). Westport: Greenwood. https://doi.org/10.1017/CBO9781107415324.004.

Bradley, A. Jr., & Blanco, C. (2010). *Promoting a culture of student success: How colleges and universities are improving degree completion.* Atlanta: Southern Regional Education Board. Retrieved from http://publications.sreb.org/2010/10E02_Promoting_Culture.pdf

Cabrera, N., Miner, D., & Milem, J. (2013). Can a summer bridge program impact first-year persistence and performance? A case study of the new start summer program. *Research in Higher Education, 54*(5), 481–498. https://doi.org/10.1007/s11162-013-9286-7.

Calcagno, J. C., & Long, B. (2008). *The impact of postsecondary remediation using a regression discontinuity approach: Addressing endogenous sorting and noncompliance.* NBER Working Paper N°14194. Cambridge, MA: NBER.

Canales, A., & De Los Ríos, D. (2009). Retención de estudiantes universitarios vulnerables. *Calidad En La Educación, 30*, 50–83.

Castillo, J., & Cabezas, G. (2010). Caracterización de jóvenes primera generación en educación superior. Nuevas trayectorias hacia la equidad educativa. *Calidad En La Educación, 32*, 43–76. Retrieved from http://www.cl.undp.org/content/dam/chile/docs/pobreza/undp_cl_pobreza_publ2.pdf

Castro, P., Antivilo, A., Aranda, C., Castro, C., Lizama, C., Williams, J., & De Torres, H. (2012). El efecto de la implementación del 'cupo de equidad' en la carrera de Psicología de la Universidad de Chile. *Revista Inclusión Social y Equidad en la Educación Superior (ISEES), 10*, 161–174.

Choy, S. (2001). *Students whose parents did not go to college: Postsecondary access, persistence, and attainment.* Washington, DC: NCES. Retrieved from https://nces.ed.gov/pubs2001/2001126.pdf

CINDA. (2010). *Diagnóstico y Diseño de Intervenciones en Equidad Universitaria.* Santiago: CNDA.

Collier, P., & Morgan, D. (2008). Is that paper really due today? Differences in first-generation and traditional college students' understandings of faculty expectations. *Higher Education, 55*, 425–446. https://doi.org/10.1007/sl0734-007-9065-5.

Concha, S. (2009). Sujetos rurales que por primera generación acceden a la universidad y su dinámica de movilidad social en la Región del Maule. *Calidad En La Educación, 30*, 122–159.

Credé, M., & Kuncel, N. (2008). Study habits, skills, and attitudes: The third pillar supporting collegiate academic performance. *Perspectives on Psychological Science, 3*(6), 425–453. Retrieved from http://www.jstor.org.ezp-prod1.hul.harvard.edu/stable/pdf/40212266.pdf

De Clercq, M., Galand, B., Dupont, S., & Frenay, M. (2013). Achievement among first-year university students: An integrated and contextualised approach. *European Journal of Psychology of Education, 28*(3), 641–662. https://doi.org/10.1007/s10212-012-0133-6.

Departamento de Pregrado de la Universidad de Chile. (2014). *Sistema de Ingreso Prioritario de Equidad Educativa*. Santiago: Departamento de Pregrado de la Universidad de Chile. [Powerpoint presentation.]

Devés, R. (2014, Noviembre 7). *El compromiso colectivo con la equidad y la calidad en la Universidad de Chile*. Presentación en I Congreso de Inclusión en Educación Superior, Universidad de Santiago.

Engle, J., & Tinto, V. (2015). *Moving beyond access: College success for low-income, first-generation students*. Washington, DC: The Pell Institute. Retrieved from http://files.eric.ed.gov/fulltext/ED504448.pdf

Espinoza, O. (2002). *The global and the national rhetoric of educational reform and the practice of (In) equity in the chilean higher education system, 1981–1998* (Doctoral Dissertation). School of Education, University of Pittsburgh, Pittsburgh.

Espinoza, O., & González, L. E. (2013, June). Access to higher education in Chile: A public vs. private analysis. *Prospects, XLIII*(2/166), 199–214. Retrieved from http://www.ibe.unesco.org/en/services/online-materials/publications/prospects.html

Espinoza, O., & González, L. E. (2015). Equidad en el Sistema de Educación Superior en Chile: Acceso, Permanencia, Desempeño y Resultados. In A. Bernasconi (Ed.), *Educación Superior en Chile: Transformación, Desarrollo y Crisis* (Capítulo XII, pp. 517–580). Santiago: Ediciones de la Universidad Católica de Chile.

Figueroa, L., & González, M. (2013). *Una Experiencia de Acceso Equitativo a la Educación Superior: "Propedéutico USACH-UNESCO"*. Santiago: Dirección Ejecutiva Programa Propedéutico.

Flanagan, A., & Arancibia, V. (2005). Talento Académico: Un Análisis de la Identificación de Alumnos Talentosos Efectuada por Profesores. *Psykhe, 14*(1), 121–135.

Fowler, P., & Boylan, H. (2010). Increasing student success and retention: A multidimensional approach. *Journal of Developmental Education, 34*(6), 2–4. Retrieved from http://www.jstor.org/stable/42775357

Fukushi, K. (2013). Una aproximación cualitativa al estudiante de primera generación en la educación. In Aequalis, *Acceso y permanencia en la educación superior: Sin apoyo no hay oportunidad* (pp. 114–142). Santiago: Aequalis. Retrieved from http://www.aequalis.cl/articulos/Acceso_04.pdf

Gasper, J., Deluca, S., & Estacion, A. (2012). Switching schools: Revisiting the relationship between school mobility and high school. *American Educational Research Journal, 49*(3), 487–519. Retrieved from http://www.jstor.org/stable/23249235

Gibbons, M. M., & Shoffner, M. F. (2004). Prospective first-generation college students: Meeting their needs through social cognitive theory. *Professional School Counseling, 8*(1), 91–97. Retrieved from http://www.jstor.org/stable/42732419

Hanover Research. (2014). *Strategies for improving student retention*. Washington, DC: Hanover Reseach. Retrieved from http://www.hanoverresearch.com/media/Strategies-for-Improving-Student-Retention.pdf

Harackiewicz, J., Canning, E., Tibbetts, Y., Giffen, C., Blair, S., Rouse, D., & Hyde, J. (2014). Closing the social class achievement gap for first-generation students in undergraduate biology. *Journal of Educational Psychology, 106*(2), 375–389. https://doi.org/10.1037/a0034679.

Inkelas, K., Daver, Z., Vogt, K., Leonard, J., & Kurotsuchi, K. (2007). Living-learning programs and first-generation college students' academic and social transition to college. *Research in Higher Education, 48*(4), 403–434. https://doi.org/10.1007/s11162-006-9031-6.

Ishitani, T. (2006). Studying attrition and degree completion behavior among first-generation college students in the United States. *The Journal of Higher Education, 77*(5), 861–885. Retrieved from http://www.jstor.org/stable/3838790

Johnson, E. (2010). *Engagement and persistence of first-generation college students: A quantitative study* (Doctoral Dissertation). Seatle University, Seattle.

Kezar, A. (2011). *Recognizing and serving low-income students in higher education: An examination of institutional policies, practices, and culture*. New York: Routledge.

Kim, Y., & Sax, L. (2009). Student–faculty interaction in research universities: Differences by student gender, race, social class, and first-generation status. *Research in Higher Education, 50*(5), 437–459. https://doi.org/10.1007/s11162-009-9127-x.

Koljatic, M., & Silva, M. (2013). Opening a side-gate: Engaging the excluded in Chilean higher education through test-blind admission. *Studies in Higher Education, 38*(10), 1427–1441. https://doi.org/10.1080/03075079.2011.623299.

Kuh, G., Kinzie, J., Buckley, J., Bridges, B., & Hayek, J. (2006). *What matters to student success: A review of the literature*. Commissioned Report for the National Symposium on Postsecondary Student Success: Spearheading a Dialog on Student Success, NCES, Washington, DC. Retrieved from https://nces.ed.gov/npec/pdf/kuh_team_report.pdf

Lareau, A., & Weininger, E. (2003). Cultural capital in educational research: A critical assessment. *Theory and Society, 32*(5/6), 567–606. Retrieved from http://www.jstor.org/stable/3649652

Leyton, D. (2015). La transición de la escuela a la educación superior en estudiantes provenientes de contextos vulnerados. *Cuaderno de Educación (Universidad Alberto Hurtado), 64*, 1–6. Retrieved from http://mailing.uahurtado.cl/cuaderno_educacion_64/pdf/articulo_64_la_transicion_de_la_escuela.pdf

Lockhart, P. (2004). *An investigation into the causes of student drop out behavior*. Glasgow: University of Glasgow. Retrieved from http://www.psy.gla.ac.uk/~steve/localed/docs/lockhart.pdf

Lohfink, M., & Paulsen, M. (2005). Comparing the determinants of persistence for first-generation and continuing-generation students. *Journal of College Student Development, 46*(4), 409–428. Retrieved from http://www.csun.edu/afye/documents/Lohfink-and-Paulsen-2005-determinants-of-persistence.pdf

López, V., Arancibia, V., & Bralic, S. (2002). Representaciones sociales en torno al talento académico: Estudio cualitativo. *Psykhe, 11*(1), 183–202.

Martorell, P., & Mcfarlin, I. (2011). Help or hindrance? The effects of college remediation on academic and labour outcomes. *The Review of Economics and Statistics, 93*(2), 436–454. Retrieved from http://www.jstor.org/stable/23015946

Mena, J. (2015). *Strategies and best practices to improve student retention and engagement in your university*. Santiago: U-Planner. Retrieved from https://cdn2.hubspot.net/hubfs/1533000/ebook/retention_ebook/Ebook_Retention_U-planner-in-english.pdf?utm_campaign=retention+ebook+eng&utm_source=hs_automation&utm_medium=email&utm_content=36713407&_hsenc=p2ANqtz-_o3IkqMu5EYUtdJF5WeBZBwWM-N8VHVmxysOUsBhtPp

Miyake, A. (2010). Reducing the gender achievement gap in college sciences: A classroom study of values affirmation. *Science, 330*, 1234–1237.

Nunez, A., Cuccaro-Alamin, S., Carroll, C., & Riley, R. (1998). *First-generation students: Undergraduates whose parents never enrolled in postsecondary education*. Washington, DC: NCES. Retrieved from https://nces.ed.gov/pubs98/98082.pdf

OECD. (2016). *Education at a glance*. Paris: OECD.
Pan, W., Guo, S., Alikonis, C., & Bai, H. (2008). Do intervention programs assist students to succeed in college?: A multilevel longitudinal study. *College Student Journal, 42*(1), 90.
Panos, R., & Astin, A. (1968). Attrition among college students. *American Educational Research Journal, 5*(1), 57–72. Retrieved from http://www.jstor.org/stable/1161701
Pascarella, E., Pierson, C., Wolniak, G., & Terenzini, P. (2004). First-generation college students: Additional evidence on college experiences and outcomes. *The Journal of Higher Education, 75*(3), 249–284. Retrieved from http://www.jstor.org.ezp-prod1.hul.harvard.edu/stable/pdf/3838816.pdf
Peabody, M. (2013). A critical analysis of the identification and treatment of first-generation college students: A social capital approach. *Kentucky Journal of Higher Education Policy and Practice, 2*(1). Retrieved from http://uknowledge.uky.edu/kjhepp
PENTA-UC. (2015). *Compendio de Resultados e Impactos Ex Alumnos PENTA UC*. Santiago: Programa Educacional para Niños con Talentos Académicos.
Pike, G., & Kuh, G. (2005). First- and second-generation college students: A comparison of their engagement and intellectual development. *The Journal of Higher Education, 76*(3), 276–300. Retrieved from http://www.jstor.org/stable/3838799
Porter, S. (2006). Institutional structures and student engagement. *Research in Higher Education, 47*(5), 521–558. Retrieved from http://www.jstor.org/stable/40197601
Porter, S., & Swing, R. (2006). Understanding how first-year seminars affect persistence. *Research in Higher Education, 47*(1), 89–109.
Programa Educacional para Niños con Talentos Académicos [PENTA-UC]. (2001a). *Informe de avance. Sistema de selección de alumnos* (Documento interno de uso restringido). Santiago: PENTA-UC.
Programa Educacional para Niños con Talentos Académicos [PENTA-UC]. (2001b). *Componente educacional. Sistema de selección e identificación de los alumnos* (Documento interno). Santiago: PENTA-UC.
Senado Universidad de Chile. (2014). *Política de Equidad e Inclusión Estudiantil. Aprobada por el Senado Universitario el 10 de julio de 2014*. Santiago: Universidad de Chile.
SIES (Servicio de Información de Educación Superior). (2015). *Informe Matrícula 2015 de Educación Superior*. Santiago: SIES, División de Educación Superior, Ministerio de Educación.

Sirin, S. (2005). Socioeconomic status and academic achievement: A meta-analytic review of research. *Review of Educational Research*, *75*(3), 417–453. Retrieved from http://steinhardt.nyu.edu/scmsAdmin/media/users/lec321/Sirin_Articles/Sirin_2005.pdf

Soria, K., Nackerud, S., & Peterson, K. (2015). Socioeconomic indicators associated with first-year college students' use of academic libraries. *The Journal of Academic Librarianship*, *41*(5), 636–643. https://doi.org/10.1016/j.acalib.2015.06.011.

Soto, V. (2016). Estudiantes de primera generación en Chile: una aproximación cualitativa a la experiencia universitaria First-generation students in Chile: A qualitative approach to university experience. *Revista Complutense de Educación*, *27*(3), 1157–1173. https://doi.org/10.5209/rev_RCED.2016.v27.n3.47562.

Stephens, N., Brannon, T., Rose Markus, H., & Nelson, J. (2015). Feeling at home in college: Fortifying school-relevant selves to reduce social class disparities in higher education. *Social Issues and Policy Review*, *9*(1), 1–24. https://doi.org/10.1111/sipr.12008.

Stephens, N., Dittmann, A., & Townsend, S. (2017). Social class and models of competence: How gateway institutions disadvantage working-class Americans and how to intervene. In C. Dweck, A. Elliott, & D. Yaeger (Eds.), *Handbook of competence and motivation: Theory and application* (2nd ed., pp. 512–528). New York: Guilford Press. Retrieved from http://www.nicolemstephens.com/uploads/3/9/5/9/39596235/stephens_dittmann_townsend_-_chapter_27.pdf

Terenzini, P., Springer, L., Yaeger, P., Pascarella, E., & Nora, A. (1996). First-generation college students: Characteristics, experiences, and cognitive development. *Research in Higher Education*, *37*(1), 1–22. Retrieved from http://www.jstor.org/stable/40196208

Thomas, L., Cooper, M., & Quinn, J. (Eds.). (2003). *Improving completion rates among disadvantaged students*. Stoke on Trent: Trentham Books.

Tibbetts, Y., Harackiewicz, J., Priniski, S., & Canning, E. (2016). Broadening participation in the life sciences with social-psychological interventions. *CBE Life Sciences Education*, *15*(3), es4. https://doi.org/10.1187/cbe.16-01-0001.

Tinto, V. (1975). Dropout from higher education: A theoretical synthesis of recent research. *Review of Educational Research*, *45*(1), 89–125. Retrieved from http://www.jstor.org/stable/1170024

Tym, C., Mcmillion, R., Barone, S., & Webster, J. (2004). *First-generation college students: A literature review.* Texas: TG. Retrieved from https://www.tgslc.org/pdf/first_generation.pdf

U.S. Department of Education. (2017). *50th anniversary of the Federal TRIO programs celebrating 50 years of providing hope and opportunity for success.* Washington, DC: U.S. Department of Education. Retrieved from https://www2.ed.gov/about/offices/list/ope/trio/trio50anniv-factsheet.pdf

Universidad de Chile. (2013). *Memoria 2010–2013. Equidad y Calidad: El Compromiso de la Universidad de Chile con el País.* Santiago: Oficina de Equidad e Inclusión, Universidad de Chile.

Universidad de Chile. (2014). *Decreto Exento N°0047335 de 02 de Diciembre de 2014 que Aprueba Normas para el Proceso de Admisión en Carrera y Programas de Pregrado.* Santiago: Universidad de Chile.

Wegenreld, V. (2015). *Evaluación del programa de difusión de los cupos del sistema de ingreso prioritario de equidad educativa, SIPEE* (Seminario de Tesis para optar al título de Ingeniero Comercial). Facultad de Economía y Negocios, Universidad de Chile, Santiago.

Zandomeni, A., Fernanda, M., Fabiana, A., & María, A. (2016). *El estudiantado de primera generacion en la FCE: Características sociodemográficas, recorridos académicos y laborales.* Paper presented at XII Jornadas de Investigacion, Universidad Nacional del Litoral, Santa Fé. Retrieved from http://www.fce.unl.edu.ar/jornadasdeinvestigacion/libro2016/32.pdf

Zepke, N., & Leach, L. (2010). Improving student engagement: Ten proposals for action. *Active Learning in Higher Education, 11*(3), 167–177. https://doi.org/10.1177/1469787410379680.

Zhao, C.-M., & Kuh, G. (2004). Adding value: Learning communities and student engagement. *Research in Higher Education, 45*(2), 115–138.

9

Widening Participation in Medicine in the UK

Paul Garrud and Clare Owen

Background

Higher education expanded gradually in the UK from 1960 (5% participation by young people aged 18–19) to 1995 (30%), then faster following the Dearing report (HMSO 1997) that called for a 'learning society' and the need for a highly skilled and educated workforce, reaching a peak of 57% in 2006 (OECD 2008). However, this increase was not accompanied by a substantial decrease in inequality: in medicine, in particular, the proportion of students coming from non-professional or managerial backgrounds scarcely changed, averaging just 25% in 2014. Analysis of university entry rates by subject (SEEG 2014) showed that medicine (including veterinary medicine) had the lowest proportion of students

---

P. Garrud (✉)
School of Medicine & Health Sciences, University of Nottingham, Nottingham, UK
e-mail: Paul.Garrud@nottingham.ac.uk

C. Owen
Medical Schools Council, London, UK

© The Author(s) 2018
M. Shah, J. McKay (eds.), *Achieving Equity and Quality in Higher Education*,
Palgrave Studies in Excellence and Equity in Global Education,
https://doi.org/10.1007/978-3-319-78316-1_9

from under-represented neighbourhoods (5% from POLAR 1 quintile; POLAR is a measure of the proportion of young people participating in higher education, neighbourhoods are classified into five quintiles on this basis, 1 = lowest level of HE participation to 5 = highest proportion). This large social disadvantage contrasted with the marked representation of women and people from ethnic minority communities in medical school (e.g. 55% women; 33% BME; GMC 2015).

In addition, commissioned research by Selecting for Excellence demonstrated that applicants to medicine came from a restricted number of secondary educational establishments: over the UK, about half of all schools or colleges had no applicants to medicine and 80% of all applicants came from just 20% of schools/colleges (Garrud 2014), that were most likely to be independent (rather than state-supported) and selective (e.g. grammar schools).

Critical national reports (Panel on Fair Access to the Professions 2009; Milburn 2012; Social Mobility Commission 2016) recommended concerted action to improve fair access to the professions, and in response the UK Medical Schools Council initiated the Selecting for Excellence project that concluded in 2014. The Selecting for Excellence final report (SEEG 2014) embodied commissioned research and a set of recommendations for action by government, the UK National Health Service, Health Education England, universities and medical schools. Medical Schools Council then established a Selection Alliance, with representatives from each public medical school and a governance framework, to implement these recommended actions: broadly, to widen access to medical school, and to make selection equitable, transparent, and evidence-based. Targets set in the Selecting for Excellence final report were to increase the proportions of medical students from the lowest two POLAR quintiles from 14% to 20% over a ten-year period (i.e. by 2023).

National Policy

UK educational policy since 1997 has included the widening of participation in HE as well as expansion of the sector. Two distinguishable elements are 'fair access'—ensuring that students from disadvantaged backgrounds have a fair chance to gain admission to the more selective institutions—and 'widening participation' (WP)—the recruitment of students who otherwise would not enter HE at all. Funding incentives have been introduced to encourage and support these initiatives over the last 20 years, for example the Office for Fair Access[1] with which English universities must reach annual agreements before they are allowed to charge additional tuition fees (i.e. > £6K per annum; most universities charging ca. £9K currently). Three performance indicators have been published annually, since 1999, by the England HE Funding Council: percentage of students educated in state schools/colleges; percentage of students coming from the lowest four socioeconomic groups (SEC 4–7, defined by parental occupation); percentage from low HE participation neighbourhoods (POLAR measure). However, these indicators have had little impact on the socioeconomic profile of applicants or entrants to medical school. One reason may be that the different measures identify different communities; this issue is discussed later.

Much of the impetus behind WP and improving social mobility was incorporated in measures passed into law by the 2017 UK Higher Education and Research Act (UK Higher Education & Research Act 2017). The preparation for this legislation proposed even more ambitious targets for WP (than Selecting for Excellence), viz: a doubling of the entrant proportions from POLAR 1 and 2 from 14% to 28%, and in a shorter period—by 2020 (see Table 9.1).

Table 9.1 POLAR data on current and proposed proportions entering medical school

POLAR quintile	Current medical student profile	Selecting for Excellence target profile – 2023	UK government target profile – 2020
1	5%	8%	28%
2	9%	12%	
3	17%		
4	23%		
5	45%		

POLAR: The participation of local areas across the UK in terms of the proportion of the young population that participates in higher education. Each quintile contains 20% of the young population and they are numbered from the lowest young participation—quintile 1, most disadvantaged—up to the highest—quintile 5, most advantaged

---

[1] Since 2017 the UK Office for Students.

Rhetoric and Resistance

Three related arguments have been deployed in the rationale for WP in higher education and in healthcare professional training specifically. First is equity and social justice: that the same educational opportunities should be available for young people from all communities and backgrounds; this is often buttressed by social mobility arguments. Second is the contention that increased diversity amongst the health professional workforce will improve healthcare—in essence that 'like will treat like': this line of thinking has lain behind many workforce-driven initiatives e.g. in under-served rural areas of Canada and Australia (Tesson et al. 2005). Thirdly, the case is made that students' training in more diverse educational settings improves their capability for managing patients from different cultures and backgrounds than their own (Mathers et al. 2011). Given the very restricted pool of medicine applicants in the UK (Garrud 2014) an additional consideration is that medical schools are likely to be missing young people who have the ability and qualities to be good doctors because they simply do not consider this a possible career.

Commissioned research (Cleland et al. 2015, 2016) shows that admissions deans (and no doubt faculty more generally) have been somewhat risk-averse in this area, reflecting concerns of two kinds. The first is that students from WP backgrounds may be less likely to succeed at medical school; this is a particular concern as the number of medical students in the UK is controlled by central government—hence any attrition represents a financial loss to medical schools. The other major concern is that the inclusion of WP students, who may enter with lower grades, in publically compiled 'league tables' (e.g. Complete University Guide 2017), that compare different universities (medical schools), may jeopardise reputation and ability to attract students. The case for more sophisticated league tables, that include WP indicators, as well as systematic research to evidence the progress and attainment of WP students at medical school and in their professional careers, is on-going. For instance, in the proposed UK Teaching Excellence Framework (DfE 2017) one metric used to assess quality is learning outcomes for students from disadvantaged backgrounds. In addition, evidence is growing that demonstrates students from disadvantaged backgrounds can succeed as well as, or in some cases outperform, their peers at medical school (Kumwenda et al. 2017; McManus et al. 2013).

Attraction Initiatives

Outreach

Planning for a national outreach initiative began with a scoping exercise that plotted outreach activities conducted by each medical school and their parent university for each secondary educational establishment in UK (MSC 2016; see Fig. 9.1).

This revealed a highly varied pattern of engagement: 33 UK medical schools were reaching about 50% of secondary schools or colleges; however, this also meant that a substantial proportion of secondary establishments were not engaged in outreach, and mapping demonstrated a number of 'cold spots' in regions of the country. In the secondary schools that were engaged, the annual number of engagements also varied considerably—many engaged with a single medical school/university, but a few with up to 19 different ones. The outcomes from the mapping were fed back to individual medical schools and locally. Medical schools have responded well to the provision of these data and are actively changing the way they deliver outreach: either by extending the areas that they cover or developing new schemes that will enable them to cover these 'cold spots'. The mapping exercise will be repeated in 2017/2018 allowing MSC to see the real impact of providing schools with these types of data.

Selecting for Excellence also commissioned two guides for medical schools to assist with outreach and support of students from WP backgrounds (Nursaw 2014a, b).

Pre-16

A collaboration with a national body—Primary Futures—led to a competition for medical students to design suitable health-related activities

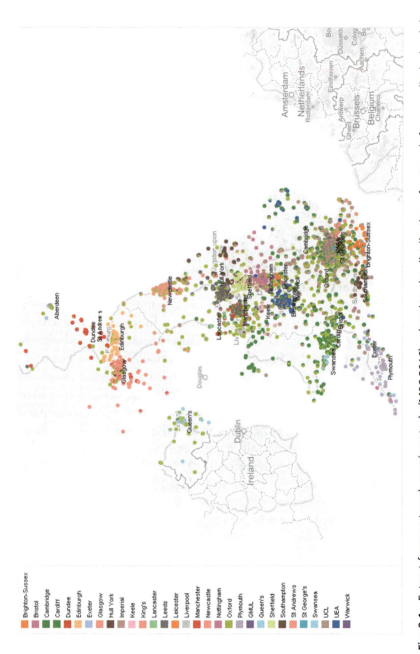

Fig. 9.1 Extract from outreach scoping study (MSC 2016)—showing the distribution of outreach from medical schools by secondary school and college in UK

for an outreach activity in primary schools (children aged 5–11 years in the UK), with the five winning lesson plans and materials published on the MSC website (MSC 2015). A long-term aim is to have every primary school visited annually by medical students.

Individual medical schools and universities were already working with many secondary schools, but this expanded post-'Selecting for Excellence' and was accompanied by some new initiatives. One example is a web-based chat project, 'I'm a Medic', targeting unengaged schools in the East Midlands, that provides live online chats (plus offline Q&A) between classes or groups of pupils and a team of six practitioners from primary care (Gallomanor 2017). The professionals answer questions put by the school pupils (14–16-years old) in a live chat, then answer further questions offline over a two week period. Participant pupils vote for the best practitioner who receives a cash prize to spend on outreach activities.

Post-16

For those school students in their last two years, typically taking advanced or higher level qualifications, outreach work has been more narrowly medicine-focussed. The MSC document 'A Journey to Medicine: Outreach Guidance' stresses that the type of outreach delivered will necessarily change depending on the stage an applicant is at in their journey to medicine. The post-16 stage focuses on consolidation activities to support individual learners to make successful applications to medicine. The guidance states that during this period medical schools should:

- Support the preparation for higher education including what a medical degree entails and how to access it.
- Ensure school and college students are aware of wider options and professions allied to medicine.
- Provide medicine-related curriculum support which provides challenge and stretch.
- Offer support to students to make an application to medical school including writing personal statements and preparing for interviews and admissions tests.

- Advise and guide staff within secondary schools and colleges and parents/carers on the medical application process.

Work Experience

Commissioned research by Selecting for Excellence (Nicholls et al. 2014) showed that access to clinical work experience (shadowing a health professional) was a major barrier for many potential applicants—particularly those with less social capital (e.g. no network contacts with current health professionals). Selecting for Excellence tackled this issue in three ways: first, by issuing consensus guidance about work experience clarifying that clinical work experience was not essential (since the profession could be researched in other ways) and that working directly with people in a caring or service setting would be most appropriate to gain communication and other social skills and to learn about one's own strengths and shortcomings (MSC 2014); secondly, by planning significant extension of clinical work experience opportunities in National Health Service organisations (e.g. hospitals and family practices) (SEEG 2014).

Following an initiative at Leeds medical school (Nicholls et al. 2018), Health Education England developed and published toolkits for NHS organisations providing work experience—one general guide and one specific to family practice (HEE 2015, 2016). This led at first to similar projects across Yorkshire, North East England, Wales and the East Midlands. Then, with support from the Royal College of General Practitioners, a national scheme to provide structured work experience in family practices, including toolkits, induction and debrief lesson plans, and reflective diaries began in 2017, involving 17 UK medical schools.

Teacher and Careers Advisor guidance

Another area identified as problematic by Selecting for Excellence was the deficient and often outdated knowledge about medical education and selection for medical school amongst secondary school teachers. Two responses to this have been undertaken: a series of regional conferences for teachers and careers advisors, and publication of a series of guides about preparing for and applying to medical school. 'A journey to medicine' (MSC 2017a) comprises five booklets covering 'Preparing your students', 'Routes into medicine', 'The UCAS application', 'The admissions process', and 'Results day and beyond' and was published online in March 2017 and marketed at conferences, by medical schools, and via national media.

Regional conferences for teachers and careers advisors were planned in eight areas of the UK, targeted at schools and colleges in the 'cold spots', those with lower than average academic attainment, and those unengaged in outreach activities. To date, four have taken place with circa 200 attendees and a mix of plenary sessions and experiential workshops covering topics such as access routes to medicine, multiple mini-interviews (MMI) and the UKCAT aptitude test. MSC are currently evaluating these, considering:

- The type of schools attending including the number and proportion of 'cold spot' schools drawn from the mapping exercise outlined earlier.
- The effectiveness of the event.
- The type of sessions that were deemed most useful.
- The teachers' knowledge of the resources available (and their likelihood to use them).
- The different models used by medical schools to recruit schools to the conferences, to deliver the event and the impact that these had.
- The impact on the host medical school and whether they intend to continue the relationship.

Gateway (WP) Medicine Programmes

In 2002 the first extended medicine programme designed to widen access to medicine began at Kings College London, where 42 students were admitted to a foundation year that led onto the standard five-year medicine degree. Since then a number of other 'gateway' courses that add an initial foundation year to a five year programme have been established, including Southampton (2004), Norwich (2007), and Sheffield (2011).

For 2018 entry, there are ten programmes offering over 200 widening access places of the approximately 8000 for medicine nationally. Whilst this is a welcome trend, it will not in itself achieve the national sector targets (Table 9.1) for increased participation by young people from disadvantaged backgrounds (in total these programmes could contribute 2.5–3% towards the 2020 national target of 28%).

Widening Participation Indicators

WP initiatives, by definition, seek to address under-representation from specific sectors or communities: their success, therefore, must be measured by robust indices that validly identify those sectors or communities. In past areas of action (e.g. gender, ethnicity) this has been less problematic than the current focus on socioeconomic disadvantage, particularly because several different types of indicator may be relevant: geographic (e.g. rural or coastal localities), educational (e.g. non-selective school), or personal/familial (e.g. family income). Detailed discussion of this can be seen in the SPA report 'Contextualised admissions: examining the evidence' (Moore et al. 2013). As already mentioned, the preferred UK Government measure is POLAR (Participation of Local Areas)—a geographical measure based on postcode and covering around 2–5000 households—but this is a fairly coarse-grained index. The majority of HE institutions, in contrast, have combined an individual measure (SEC, based on parental occupation) with POLAR to identify WP applicants. Specific WP programmes, such as the 'gateway' medicine programmes mentioned earlier, commonly employ detailed individual criteria that include household income (e.g. via eligibility for state benefits), refugee status and a history of being cared for outside the family. Another criterion used in contextualised admissions (i.e. adjusted selection criteria based on WP eligibility) is secondary school attended: a small number of UK medical schools operate this approach (e.g. Bristol, St Georges London) by listing the lowest 40% or 20% of schools based on average performance at level 4 (Advanced or Higher level).

It has been common to utilise multiple WP indices on the grounds that to do so will 'triangulate'—contributions of an additional criterion improving validity. Work undertaken by the MSC Selection Alliance (Curtis and Lambe 2017) does not support this assumption however: for example, 8% of state school educated students and 4% of privately educated medical students were found in the data to come from areas of the highest deprivation; and, within POLAR quintiles 1 and 2, 60% were classified as NS-SEC 1 and 2, that is with managerial or professional family backgrounds.

Admissions Initiatives

Information and Guidance for Prospective Applicants

Entry Requirements

One of the key findings of the Selecting for Excellence final report (SEEG 2014) was that applicants need better information and guidance to support them. The rationale behind this was that some prospective students will get good advice and guidance from skilled teachers or careers advisors whereas others, particularly those from a disadvantaged socio-economic background or poorer performing school, will not have access to this type of support.

From 2014, therefore, MSC has compiled each year the 'Entry Requirements for UK Medical Schools' (MSC 2017b). This booklet contains a high level view of the entry requirements for each course run by UK medical schools. Courses are split into four main types: standard 5–6 year courses, graduate-entry courses, medicine with a preliminary year (i.e. courses designed for those with high secondary educational qualifications, but without required science subjects), and medicine with a gateway year which are courses specifically for WP students.

For each course details are provided, via a standard pro-forma populated by individual medical schools, on their requirements for academic attainment, details of the aptitude test used (if any), work experience requirements, and how and what type of interview they run. There is also information about any WP activities the school runs, the number of applicants per interview, and places on the course. This gives applicants the chance to look quickly for the courses that best meet their individual level of attainment across multiple factors. They are encouraged to visit the medical school's website for more detailed information.

Journey to Medicine for Applicants

MSC has developed guidance for applicants on applying to UK medical school. A number of workshops with prospective applicants investigated what type and format of guidance they preferred. Early conclusions were that, as a first stage, MSC would produce a series of 15 'Infosheets' covering preparation, application, selection processes, and afterwards (MSC 2017c). They include quotes from current students and exercises for applicants to undertake to help prepare their applications. These short factsheets are easily printed and accessed online and will be useful for medical schools in outreach activities.

Further focus groups will inform the second phase of guidance development. Some resources that MSC is considering developing include YouTube videos and a MOOC.

Contextual Admissions (CA)

In 2016 MSC commissioned a research team led by Professor Jen Cleland to look at how contextual data is used in medical school admission and to suggest ways in which its use could be improved. The findings of the research (Cleland et al. 2016) found that there is no evidence to suggest that using a basket of measures of social disadvantage is effective. The team conclude: 'A combination of several weak CA markers does not automatically improve reliability and accuracy, nor does availability equate with usefulness and robustness.' Instead they recommended that comparing an individual applicant's academic performance to that of the average performance at their secondary school is a robust way of predicting success on a medicine course and well-supported by the published evidence.

Medical schools largely use a combination of contextual measures and their reasoning for this is that no single indicator can give an accurate measure of social background so each needs to be triangulated. Medical schools may be concerned that focusing on academic performance relative to school performance would not adequately identify candidates from a WP background. MSC is looking at the correlation between academic performance relative to school performance and other contextual markers as well as the relationship between markers described in WP Indicators. If there is a positive correlation between educational attainment markers relative to school performance, then this measure will prove extremely helpful in efforts to widen participation as it has a proven link to achievement on the course.

Weighting and Sequencing of Selection Criteria

Recently, MSC received the final report of commissioned research (Fielding et al. 2017) that looked at whether differences in admissions practices have an impact on student demographics. In particular, the team were asked to look at the impact of weighting one aspect of the selection process compared to another, for example aptitude tests being given more emphasis than prior academic attainment.

A retrospective analysis looked at what impact individual elements of the selection process had on the proportion of students admitted from target WP groups across 18 medical schools over an eight-year period. The group found no obvious changes in the proportion of admissions from each of the target groups.

The project then looked in more detail at data from five medical schools. Within each of these five schools, selection processes had changed in terms of the weightings of different selection criteria during the eight year period of study, but these changes did not map to any discernible changes in the proportion of students from the target groups. The conclusion was that current selection methods do not impact on WP and therefore there is no simple way to maximise the benefit to WP candidates by optimising weightings of the different criteria medical schools use at present.

Mentoring

The social and educational capital that prospective medical students can use to support their preparation and application varies enormously. As indicated earlier, attendance at one school compared to another may allow someone to meet and find out about several medical schools (or none), to find a teacher with experience in medical application (or not), and contacts to obtain work experience or advice and guidance from alumni. Thus one aim of many WP projects is to extend the opportunity for mentoring, advice, and guidance to applicants who may otherwise have none. The schemes are varied, but include some national mentoring (e.g. Social Mobility Foundation) and many local (e.g. a medical student Widening Access to Medicine Society) that use e-mentoring, often with moderation and safeguarding. Ambassador schemes (e.g. NHS Ambassadors; student ambassadors) are another source of advice, and, lastly, personal contact via a clinical observation placement (see Work Experience earlier) or Outreach events is also a mechanism. At present, however, there is little co-ordination, let alone monitoring of mentoring schemes, and it is not known how effective they are or how wide is their reach.

Multiple Mini-interviews

MMIs are an area that MSC is aware causes some apprehension for applicants and therefore MSC commissioned specific guidance for applicants on these. A candidate familiarisation tool has recently been released (MSC 2017d) comprising a general section of information about the structure of MMIs, what selectors are looking for, and advice about how to prepare for interviews, and a second section with commented videos of MMI stations. This tool is intended to ensure applicants are familiar with the format before the test.

Interviews have been used very widely as one selection tool for medical school. Currently all, bar one, UK medical schools interview prospective students after initial assessment of academic record and/or aptitude. The occupational psychology literature has demonstrated that many traditional forms of interview have poor validity and reliability (see Patterson et al. 2016), but one recent format—the multiple mini-interview (MMI), essentially a form of speed-dating in which eight or more interviewers each assess different domains in a series of brief, individual interviews with the candidate—promises substantially better reliability and validity (Pau et al. 2013; Rees et al. 2016). The impact of MMIs on equality and diversity has not yet been studied systematically and, hence, three developments have been started. Two concern training materials, with an online training package for interviewers that incorporates video material of MMIs and sections on best practice methods of judgment, and unconscious bias, and a shorter one for MMI candidates: these are now available for UK medical schools to train interviewers and familiarise candidates. A third strand is a collaborative programme between multiple medical schools to develop shared, standardised MMI stations and to use these to establish systematic evidence about the performance of different candidate groups, their reliability, and, ultimately, the extent to which this selection tool may predict aspects of professional career progression and performance, using the UK Medical Education database (UKMED 2016).

Discussion and Conclusion

This survey of the initiatives taken in the UK to widen access to medicine demonstrates several broad themes and supports a number of provisional conclusions.

First, a close alignment has developed between national policy and medical school endeavours in WP that includes shared targets, expanded outreach, and provision of guidance, amongst others. Second, systematic research of the published evidence and evaluation of current admissions practice is an essential precondition for the adoption of radical changes in selection. Third, widening access is a shared endeavour that requires multiple components and multiple agents. Though this chapter has focussed on UK medical schools and their representative national body, Medical Schools Council, it is clear that many other players are responsible for essential setting or facilitating conditions to successfully widen access: these agents include secondary schools/colleges, national government, professional bodies, compilers of league tables, employers, and student organisations, and, perhaps most neglected, families with little social or educational capital.

In conclusion, much has been done and much is being put into place. Commissioned research has shown that there must be a strong emphasis on attracting new applicants from schools and communities that have not aspired to produce doctors in the past. Although carefully evidencing and tuning selection processes so that they are equitable, transparent, and facilitate the entry of WP students is commendable, it will not on its own achieve the targets this sector of the academic community has set itself.

References

Cleland, J. A., Nicholson, S., Kelly, N., & Moffat, M. (2015). Taking context seriously: Explaining widening access policy enactments in UK medical schools. *Medical Education, 49*(1), 25–35.

Cleland, J., Nicholson, S., Patterson, F., Thomas, L., & Wilde, K. (2016, July). *The use of contextual data in medical school selection processes: A mixed-method programme of research* (Unpublished report to Medical Schools Council Selection Alliance).

Complete University Guide. (2017). *University subject tables 2018*. https://www.thecompleteuniversityguide.co.uk/league-tables/rankings?s=medicine. Accessed 31 July 2017.

Curtis, S., & Lambe, P. (2017, June). Unpublished report to Medical Schools Council Selection Alliance Executive Board.

Department for Education (DfE). (2017, October). *Teaching excellence and student outcomes framework specification*. https://www.gov.uk/government/publications/teaching-excellence-and-student-outcomes-framework-specification. Accessed 8 Dec 2017.

Fielding, S., Tiffin, P. A., Greatrix, R., Lee, A. J., Nicholson, S., Patterson, F., & Cleland, J. (2017, July). *Do differences in medical school admissions practices impact on student demographics?* (Unpublished report to Medical Schools Council Selection Alliance).

Gallomanor. (2017). *I'm a medic*. Imamedic.uk. Accessed 29 July 2017.

Garrud. (2014). *Help and hindrance in widening participation.* http://www.medschools.ac.uk/SiteCollectionDocuments/Selecting-for-Excellence-research-Dr-Paul-Garrud.pdf. Accessed 29 July 2017.

GMC. (2015). *Summary of 2014 Medical Schools Annual Return.* http://www.gmc-uk.org/Medical_School_Annual_Return_2014_Summary_Report_for_Publication.pdf_61816122.pdf_62533230.pdf. Accessed 31 July 2017.

Health Education England. (2015, May). *More than photocopying: Work experience – A toolkit for the NHS.* hee.nhs.uk/sites/default/files/documents/NHSWorkExperienceToolkitfinal.pdf. Accessed 17 July 2017.

Health Education England. (2016, July). *Doctor, doctor... How do I get work experience? GP work experience toolkit.* www.hee.nhs.uk/sites/default/files/documents/Toolkit%20for%20GPs.pdf. Accessed 17 July 2017.

HMSO. (1997). *The Dearing report: Higher education in the learning society.* http://www.educationengland.org.uk/documents/dearing1997/dearing1997.html. Accessed 29 July 2017.

Kumwenda, B., Cleland, J. A., Walker, K., Lee, A. J., & Greatrix, R. (2017). The relationship between school type and academic performance at medical school: A national, multi-cohort study. *BMJ Open, 7*(8), e016291.

Mathers, J., Sitch, A., Marsh, J. L., & Parry, J. (2011). Widening access to medical education for under-represented socioeconomic groups: Population based cross sectional analysis of UK data, 2002–6. *BMJ, 342,* d918.

McManus, I. C., Dewberry, C., Nicholson, S., & Dowell, J. S. (2013). The UKCAT-12 study: Educational attainment, aptitude test performance, demographic and socio-economic contextual factors as predictors of first year outcome in a cross-sectional collaborative study of 12 UK medical schools. *BMC Medicine, 11*(1), 244.

Medical Schools Council. (2014). *Work experience guidelines for applicants to medicine.* http://www.medschools.ac.uk/SiteCollectionDocuments/Work-experience-guidelines-for-applicants-to-medicine.pdf. Accessed 31 July 2017.

Medical Schools Council. (2015). *Who's in health? Example teaching sessions.* http://www.medschools.ac.uk/SiteCollectionDocuments/Whos-in-Health-example-teaching-sessions.pdf. Accessed 29 July 2017.

Medical Schools Council. (2016). *Implementing selecting for excellence; A progress update.* http://www.medschools.ac.uk/SiteCollectionDocuments/Selecting-for-Excellence-2016-update-MSC.pdf. Accessed 31 July 2017.

Medical Schools Council. (2017a). *A journey to medicine.* http://www.medschools.ac.uk/Publications/Pages/A-journey-to-medicine-series.aspx. Accessed 29 July 2017.

Medical Schools Council. (2017b). *Entry requirements for UK medical schools: 2018 entry.* http://www.medschools.ac.uk/SiteCollectionDocuments/MSC-Entry-requirements-for-UK-medical-schools.pdf. Accessed 29 July 2017.

Medical Schools Council. (2017c). *Infosheets for applicants to medicine.* https://www.medschools.ac.uk/studying-medicine/applications/resources-for-students-and-teachers. Accessed 8 Dec 2017.

Medical Schools Council. (2017d). *Multiple mini-interview familiarisation tool for candidates.* http://www.mscinterviewprep.co.uk/. Accessed 18 Dec 2017.

Milburn, A. (2012). *Fair access to professional careers: A progress report by the independent reviewer on social mobility and child poverty.* https://www.gov.uk/government/uploads/system/uploads/attachment_data/file/61090/IR_FairAccess_acc2.pdf. Accessed 29 July 2017.

Moore, J., Mountford-Zimdars, A., & Wiggans, J. (2013). *Contextualised admissions: Examining the evidence* (Report to SPA, the Supporting Professionalism in Admissions Programme). Cheltenham: SPA. https://www.spa.ac.uk/sites/default/files/Research-CA-Report-2013-full.pdf. Accessed 29 July 2017.

Nicholls, G., Wilkinson, D., Danks, N., & Stroud, L. (2014). *Work experience: A deterrent to applicants to medicine from a widening participation background?* http://www.medschools.ac.uk/SiteCollectionDocuments/Selecting-for-Excellence-research-Dr-Gail-Nicholls-et-al.pdf. Accessed 29 July 2017.

Nicholls, G., Wilkinson, D., & Bull, C. (2018). *Providing primary care work experience: Evaluating a national work experience pilot programme in general practice.* London: Royal College of General Practitioners. https://i.emlfiles4.com/cmpdoc/7/7/0/9/9/1/files/12697_rcgp_providing-primary-care-work-experience---march-2018-final.pdf. Accessed 16 April 2018.

Nursaw, C. (2014a). *A journey to medicine: Outreach guidance.* http://www.medschools.ac.uk/SiteCollectionDocuments/MSC-A-Journey-to-Medicine-Outreach-Guidance.pdf. Accessed 31 July 2017.

Nursaw, C. (2014b). *A journey to medicine: Student success guidance.* http://www.medschools.ac.uk/SiteCollectionDocuments/MSC-A-jouney-to-medicine-Student-success-guidance.pdf. Accessed 31 July 2017.

OECD. (2008). *Education at a glance: OECD indicators.* https://www.oecd.org/education/skills-beyond-school/41284038.pdf. Accessed 24 July 2017.

Panel on Fair Access to the Professions. (2009). *Unleashing aspirations: The final report of the panel on fair access to the professions.* http://webarchive.nationalarchives.gov.uk/+/http://www.cabinetoffice.gov.uk/media/227102/fair-access.pdf. Accessed 29 July 2017.

Patterson, F., Knight, A., Dowell, J., Nicholson, S., Cousans, F., & Cleland, J. (2016). How effective are selection methods in medical education? *Medical Education, 50*, 36–60.

Pau, A., Jeevaratnam, K., Chen, Y. S., Fall, A. A., Khoo, C., & Nadarajah, V. D. (2013). The multiple mini-interview (MMI) for student selection in health professions training – A systematic review. *Medical Teacher, 35*, 1027–1041.

Rees, E. L., Hawarden, A. W., Dent, G., Hays, R., Bates, J., & Hassell, A. B. (2016). Evidence regarding the utility of multiple mini-interview (MMI) for selection to undergraduate health programs: A BEME systematic review: BEME guide no. 37. *Medical Teacher, 38*, 443–455.

SEEG. (2014). *Selecting for excellence: Final report.* http://www.medschools.ac.uk/SiteCollectionDocuments/Selecting-for-Excellence-Final-Report.pdf. Accessed 24 July 2017.

Social Mobility Commission. (2016). *Social and ethnic inequalities in choice available and choices made at age 16.* https://www.gov.uk/government/uploads/system/uploads/attachment_data/file/574708/SMC_social_and_ethnic_inequalities_in_post_16_report.pdf. Accessed 29 July 2017.

Tesson, G., Curran, V., Pong, R., & Strasser, R. (2005). Advances in rural medical education in three countries: Canada, the United States and Australia. *Education for Health, 18*, 405–415.

UK Higher Education and Research Act. (2017). c.29. http://www.legislation.gov.uk/ukpga/2017/29/contents/enacted/data.htm. Accessed 24 July 2017.

UKMED. (2016). *The UK medical education database.* https://ukmed.ac.uk. Accessed 24 July 2017.

10

Affirmative Actions as an Instrument to Balance Access to Superior Education in Brazil: The Quotas Policy

Rubens Becak and Luis Felipe Cirino

Introduction

Until the beginning of the new millennium, tertiary education in Brazil was aimed almost exclusively to upper class people who were able to dedicate themselves to academic activities without compromising their living, something exceptional in a country which had low positions in several poverty rankings. Thus, only richer people could achieve more qualified professional positions, because they were the only ones who were able to dedicate more than ten years to study. Moreover, that reality contributes to the increase of social inequality in the country.

At the turn of the century there was a great boom in superior education in Brazil because of the exponential increase in course offers, mostly in private universities, enabling poorer people to access those institutions as the competition became huge.

R. Becak (✉) • L. F. Cirino
University of Sao Paulo, São Paulo, Brazil
e-mail: prof.becak@usp.br; luisfelipecirino@gmail.com

© The Author(s) 2018
M. Shah, J. McKay (eds.), *Achieving Equity and Quality in Higher Education*, Palgrave Studies in Excellence and Equity in Global Education, https://doi.org/10.1007/978-3-319-78316-1_10

After that boom, the results started to appear. Even we can find some news celebrating the widening access of superior education to poorer people, the quality of the offered courses did not contribute to the social upliftment purpose and consequently the best universities remained the exclusive destination for those who had better financial conditions.

In this context Law n. 12,711/12, commonly named "The Quotas Law" was enacted with the purpose of enabling the poorer people to gain access to a better-quality tertiary education. In its first article, the law highlights the need to separate half of all places in federal institutions tied to the Ministry of Education for students who attended public high schools.

The controversy in this legal diploma—besides the further diminishment of tertiary places for ruling class children—is based on the fact that those places are aimed at people who claim to be 'preto, 'pardo'[1] or indigenous' – the "PPIs".[2,3]

Hence, it is necessary to observe that the discrimination factor elected by the law determines two things to be true—an unfavorable social condition allied to skin color or certain ethnicity—exactly those which, historically and continually, have suffered subjugation in preference to a rich and white class.

This is a parallel public policy that does not compete with the "Income Quotas" applicable, only and exclusively, using social criteria which consider the household *per capita* income of the applicants.

The polemic of the "PPI quotas" and its legal diploma was so great that law was even questioned in judicial review by the Federal Supreme Court which, at the end, declared its constitutionality. Since then, several states have edited similar rules.

Therefore, the main purpose of this work is the analysis of the enforcement and effects of Law n. 12,711/12, which have been well entrenched by now in the Brazilian legal system.

---

[1] A Brazilian–Portuguese denomination to the "mixed people", the "brown" ones.
[2] The PPIs is the acronym used to refer to certain skin color or ethnicity as the blacks ("pretos" in Portuguese), brown (the "pardos") and indigenous (the índios).
[3] As well as those who have some disability.

Quotas Policy and the Principles of Equity

Before analyzing the quotas policy to access Brazilian universities, some considerations deserve to be stated regarding affirmation actions in general, especially and precisely, the central subject of this article.

University in Brazil has always been the exclusive domain of the ruling class, and not necessarily the intellectual one. Considering this, Oliveira et al. (2006, p. 9) observed that "over the course of History, the tertiary education institutes have been resisting most of the time to external pressure and radical transformations which will make them undergo basic changes".

The most recent reality of Brazilian universities remarkably shows the presence of richer ones in public schools. The admission process of the universities kept by the Federal Government[4] is eventually much more competitive than the process in private tertiary education institutes.

Thousands of places in private universities end up vacant. According to the data raised by Instituto Nacional de Estudos e Pesquisas Educacionais Anísio Teixeira (INEP) in 2015 only 2,385,861 of new places were taken from 5,667,128 offered places in private institutions. Consequently, a great paradox is being faced: places in public universities, mostly free of cost, go to the richer class of the population which, naturally, has the opportunity to attend more qualified basic school, at a high cost, whereas private institutes largely receive low-income students, many times the "PPIs".

At the same time, Brazil is fighting to increase the number of young people attending university. The Education National Plan intended to reach 30% of people aged between 18 and 24 in university education. However, this target is far from being reached (Kunsch 1992). Naturally, access to universities by the poorest is even more difficult, since it is necessary to combine studies with professional obligations.

In this way, The Economic Commission for Latin America and Caribbean—CEPAL has underscored the fundamental importance of education as an important tool of social and economic development, considering that the knowledge and skills acquired allow social uplifting

---

[4] In an exam called "vestibular".

for the individual. Thus, in a report published in 2007, the commission emphasizes tertiary education as an element that favors a better income distribution, affirming that "it is necessary to use different tools to enable access to college and university education through several affirmation actions which promote inclusion for young people who belong to traditionally excluded social groups".

In Brazil specially, which has been historically unbalanced, the need for affirmative actions in order to find balance in opportunities and reestablish the balance is truly imperative. According to the Brazilian Applied Economics Research Institute there were 22 million poor people in 2016, which equates to 11.2% of the population. The richest 1%, on the other hand, has 27.8% of the national income.[5]

Regarding the presence of different classes of the population in public and free universities, according to Ministry of Education data in 2014,[6] 36.4% of the students belonged to 20% of the richer families and only 7.6% of the students came from low-income families. As a result, considering all presented data, it is observed that reservation of places in universities for poorer people as well as underprivileged ethnic groups in Brazil fulfill the principle of equity, constitutionally ensured in head provision of the article 5 of the Federal Constitution promulgated in 1988.

The principle of equity has been mentioned by Rui Barbosa (1999, pp. 25–26) a long time ago when he addressed the class of 1920 of The Law School. As follows:

The nature part varies to the infinite. There are no equal things in the universe. Many look like each other. But all of them are different from each other. The branches of the same tree, the leaves of the same plant, the lines on a human finger, the drops of the same fluid, the motes of the same dust, the rays in a spectrum of the same star or solar ray. Everything from the stars in the sky to the microbes in our blood, from the nebulas in the outer space to the dew drops in the grassland.

---

[5] About this, BLATT states that "(…) poverty in Brazil has skin color, i.e., 44,1% of black population lived in household with less than half minimum wage per capita, while white people were 20,5%". In: BLATT, Ivo. A universidade do século XXI: lugar de excluSao ou de incluSao social? *UNIrevista*, vol. 1, n 2, abril 2006. URI/UNISINOS, Available in: http://www.fw.uri.br/publicacoes/revistach/artigos/capitulo_9.pdf.

[6] The latest full data in this topic.

In this social inequity, part of the nature inequity, is where the true law of equity is found. Anything else is folly created from envy, pride or madness. Treating equals unequally or unequals equally would be flagrant inequity, and not real equity. The human appetites conceived to invert the universal creation rule having the intention of not giving each one the same proportion of its value, but give everyone the same as if everyone were equals.

Beyond the Aristotelian interpretation of the principle of equity Bandeira de Mello (2012, p. 9) aims to clarify who are equals and who are unequals as well as who are the recipients, on the contrary, of the constitutional premise. Thus, he says that the important equity precept, as it has already been marked, is a rule intended both for the law enforcer and the lawmaker.

Regarding the principle of equity enforcement, Canotilho states that, "Being equal before the law does not mean same application of the law" being "the law itself should treat equally all citizens". Henceforth, the author emphasizes that "The principle of equity is meant to the lawmaker itself, binding them to creating an equal Law for every citizen" (2003, p. 417).

Miranda (2000, pp. 215–216) establishes a major and important difference between the principle of universality and the principle of equity. Despite having similar content, they express different legal values.

The principle (of universality), though inseparable from the principle of equity, does not blend with it. Everyone has all duties and rights—principle of universality; everyone (or in certain conditions or situations, only some) has the same duties and rights—principle of equity. The principle of universality is concerned with the rule recipients, the principle of equity with its content.

Discussing the principle of equity itself is the continuous underscoring of two different meanings: one negative and another positive. While the first seals privileges and discriminations, the second demands an equal treatment, considering the circumstances that avoid inequity, when verified, should be eliminated by the law enforcer, according to all constitutional rules, so that they are treated the way they should be (Miranda 2000, pp. 39–40).

Cademartori, in his work, divides the equity between formal and material. The first refers to the equity before the law; the second refers to the real equity where there is no discrimination. The author brings also an important classification regarding the nature of the fundamental rights and its interpretation by the principle of isonomy.

Patrícia Effting points out three different concepts of the principle of equity: nominalist, idealist and realist, stating that the last is satisfactory "as it understands the equal man as a human being, however, different in social relations" since "it says the equity and inequity coexist, as men are equal in essence, but different in a social context" (2012, p. 38).

Bandeira de Mello (2012, pp. 15–16) says that the principle of equity enforces unequal treatment on people, considering that the essential purpose of the law is providing unequal treatment. In that way, in all and any analyzed cases, the law erects something in differential element, that is "observed, in several qualified situations, some differential points which are emphasized in order to discriminate situations, instilling in each one correlated legal effects and thus, unequal".

The Brazilian Constitution treated equity as a principle and specialized it in rules aimed at relevant legal and social situations in order to reassert it. Several constitutional rules are based on the principle of equity, having a special focus on human dignity.[7,8]

The constitutional provisions provided in the article 5 head and item I, if considered in isolation, may lead to the wrong understanding that by the principle of equity people may not be legally unequal because of skin color, gender, religion or any other discriminatory factor apparently fortuitous, without logical correlation with the current grounds in the Federal Constitution.

Nevertheless it is not found like that "the insurmountable barrier shaped by the principle of equity. It is easy to demonstrate. Just set some

---

[7] "Men is different from all living beings, but stating that is not enough without real differences. They pursue a dignified existence which is one where all human conditions are respected. However, for this to happen, it is needed to recognize some rights. Therefore, all rights axiomatically related to a person is a fundamental right". Effting, op. cit., p. 38.

[8] See also articles 3°, III and IV, 5°, *head provision*, I and XLI, 7°, XXX and XXXI, 170, 193, 196 and 205.

hypotheses in which these attributes are essential for the discrimination to understand that, however, nothing goes against isonomy".[9]

So, it is possible to determine the differentiation by gender, skin color, religion, race and many other supposed criteria of diversity, whenever there is "a logic correlation between the chosen peculiarity in the object and the treatment inequity granted because of it, since such correlation does not contravene the Constitution" (Bandeira de Mello 2012, p. 17).

What is intended with the imperative enforcement of the principle of equity is the avoidance of fortuitous or unjustified comparisons. Hence, the difficulty of compliance: defining which discrimination factors, in fact, can justify the intended inequity.

In order to verify if there is a violation of the principle of equity, Bandeira de Mello points out that the acknowledgment of the differentiations that may not be made without breaking isonomy divides into three questions: (a) the first considers the element as the inequity factor; (b) the second underscores the logic correlation between the erected factor in criterion of discrimination and the inequity established in diversified legal treatment; and (c) the third points out the accordance between this logic correlation with the interests absorbed in the constitutional system, and thus legal (2012, p. 12).

Therefore, in order to not commit a violation against the principle of equity, it is necessary to have more than a simple abstracted logic correlation between the differential factor and the consequential differentiation. Moreover, a specific logic correlation is required, in accordance with the Federal Constitution, which translates into accordance or disagreement with the imperative requirements recognized in the Federal Constitution.

If the Aristotelian principle of equity says to treat the equals equally and the unequals unequally, proportionally to their inequalities, there is no logic in searching a differentiation in factors necessarily equal to every-

---

[9] The Author uses as an example a hypothetical situation of a public position competitive exam: "Assume that this exam is under supervision of research institutions and also evaluates physical abilities which will be used in measurements and studies of black people's sport specialty. It is obvious that white people will not be permitted to apply for this exam. And there will be no violation against the principle of isonomy excluding other people than the black ones. The proposed research, perfectly valid, justify the hypothetical differentiation. In order to do it, the government would not be obliged to do the same research with white, yellow or red people, or if extended to any of these races, to any race that is not provided in the exam" (Bandeira de Mello 2012, pp. 15–16).

one or, still, specific to a certain subject. That is why it is considered, in those situations, a violation of the principle of isonomy, provided in the Federal Constitution.

Even if the issued rule does not single out the individual reached by its effects, and, furthermore, defines the discrimination factor inherent to things, situations or people's qualities there is need of a logical correlation between the erected factor as the criterion of discrimination and the legal discrimination decided in accordance with it.

So, as a second requirement for defining the accordance with the precept of isonomy, there is need of a logical connection between the compared differential elements and the disparity of the disciplines established upon them, under the penalty of immediate and intuitive rejection of the validity of the rule.

There is, therefore, a violation of the principle of equity when the adopted discrimination factor, not only singles out certain individuals or relates to a fully neutral feature, it does not have a logical relation with the inclusion or exclusion for the granted benefit or with the inclusion or exclusion of the imposed encumbrance.

In other words: it violates the principle of isonomy, therefore, the stipulation of fortuitous or gratuitous discriminations which does not relate to the interests provided in the Federal Constitution and, more precisely, to the principles of the Public Administration.

Or, as it is well emphasized by Celso Antônio Bandeira de Mello, it is not possible that the law gives "(…) specified treatment, favorable or unfavorable, observing peculiar traits and circumstances of a category of persons if there is no rational adaptation between the differential element and the given regime" (Bandeira de Mello 2012, p. 39).

In order to have a perfect accordance with the principle of equity, beyond the impossibility of singling out the rule recipient and the necessary logical correlation between the discrimination factor which must originate from people, things and situations, and not in neutral elements, equally erected for all, it is imperative the full compliance with the elected discrimination and the interests protected by the Federal Constitution.

Although generally and logically justifiable, not all differences may be erected as a discrimination factor. The correlation needs to be relevant in a way that the chosen interests in the constitutional system are properly followed.[10]

Therefore, it is not enough that the differentiation factor has only logical correlation with the intended differentiation, without violating the isonomy. Not all logical reasons authorize the inequity, however, only that one that follows the interests of the highest legal system, under the penalty of conflicting with the principle of equity.

So, by all the reasons above, it is verified that the quotas policy intended to separate places for students belonging to underprivileged social classes and ethnical groups does not, whatsoever, violate the provisions of the Federal Constitution, but rather, it only intends to ratify the principle of equity.

Quotas Policy in Brazil

Historically, racial quotas meant separating places in public or private schools for specific groups according to racial criterion—aimed to people classified by race or ethnicity—or according to social criteria. Such systems emerged in India in the 1930s in a way that the quotas policy can be considered a true affirmative action with the purpose of reversing historical inequalities against certain groups.

In Brazil, the quotas policy is viewed as an attempt to diminish the excluding reality of university education, and also, as a secondary objective, it put on the agenda the discussion of democratization in higher education itself.

Despite this article being closely related to the quotas policy aimed at the university education—main objective of Law n. 12,711/12—in fact the search for more balanced opportunities was not restricted to education in Brazilian history.

In the 1950s, during President Getulio Vargas' term, a kind of affirmative policy was applied, though at the time this concept was not known

---

[10] That is why it is not possible to create restricted benefits for foreign groups instead of the national ones, even if those have, as a specified differentiation, high academic or technical qualifications because a situation like that violates the principle of an Independent State as provided in article 171, §§1° e 2°, of the Federal Constitution (Bandeira de Mello 2012, p. 43).

in that way. The Public Administration determined that the multinational companies settled in Brazil should reserve two thirds of the job vacancies for Brazilian workers.

A few years later, according to Law n. 5,465/68—historically known as the Cattle Law—the State determined that half the places in high schools and agriculture and veterinary schools should be reserved for farmers and their children, landowners or not, living in rural districts.

It was probably the beginning of affirmation actions in the educational area, a discussion which returned recently to the agenda, either because of the wide discussion made in Federal Supreme Court in the trial of ADPF[11] n. 186—further discussed below—or also, by laws being passed in different federal entities which started to demand the separation of places for certain student groups. Law n. 12,711/12 institutes a quotas policy for access to university education and has the clear objective to give people of certain ethnicity or skin color, historically underprivileged in Brazil, the possibility to attend the best universities in the country.

From a close analysis of rule, it is possible to verify that even before the passing of Law n. 12,711/12, there were applications of similar rules in universities in Brazil. In May 2012, months before the effective date of the law, 180 public education institutes (including universities, colleges and state institutes) offered some kind of affirmation action for poor, black or indigenous people. From all 59 federal universities, 32 offered quotas for students coming from public school, 21 for black and brown people, 19 for indigenous people and 7 for people with disabilities.

About three months after the data collection, the then President, Dilma Roussef, issued Law n. 12,711/12, which established a four-year period, until August 2016, for all federal education institutes to reserve at least 50% of their places for students who attended public high schools and, from those, half should go to students whose household income is up to one and a half times the minimum wage and, finally, part of those reserved places should go to people who claim to be black, brown or indigenous, following at least the same proportion appointed by IBGE in

---

[11] "Arguição de Descumprimento de Preceito Fundamental" one of the possible direct actions of constitutionality.

each Unit of the Federation where the tertiary education institutes are located.

It is important to underscore that, at the enactment of the law, its applicability was restricted to the 59 universities and 38 federal education, science and technology institutes that were under ministry supervision. Considering that, according to the data collected by the Education Ministry in 2016, there were 34,366 graduation courses in the country offered by 2407 tertiary education institutes, 298 were public and 2109 were private institutes, the range of application of the quotas policy is still small, but especially relevant considering that all federal institutes are public.

Overall, until August 2016, the law established that half of the places in federal tertiary education institutions should be divided among black, brown and indigenous students, as well as students from public schools, while the other 50% are open to competition which, during the four-year transition period provided in the law, could be disputed by the recipients of the quotas policy.

Even though the enforcement of Law n. 12,711/12 is restricted to federal tertiary education institutes, namely created and administered by the federal government, the required reservation of places for certain groups, in effect, was extended to other universities and colleges tied to other federal entities.

In that way, it is important to emphasize that Brazil, being a Federal State, distributes certain jurisdiction to each of the federal entities—particularly divided into four different spheres of sovereignty: the Union, the States, the Federal District and the Municipalities. Each one is autonomous so the requirements for entering each correspondent education institute are the responsibility of these legal entities.

Despite having autonomy, which makes compliance of the quotas policy in non-federal public institutes optional, many federal entities started to apply similar rules to Law n. 12,711/12.

The University of Sao Paulo (USP)—the most renowned in Brazil, created in 1934 by a Sao Paulo State decision[12]—implemented a quotas

---

[12] And so not included in the federal budget.

policywhere part of the places were intended for the same recipients of (Federal) Law n. 12,711/12.

For 2017, from all 8734 places offered in USP "vestibular", 1155 were given to students from public school and 586 to the "PPIs".

The quotas policy application, especially racial quotas, of USP aims to balance the participation of black, brown and indigenous population in the university atmosphere. Despite having 34.7% of Sao Paulo State population inserted in those categories, only 16.5% of the first-year students declare themselves "PPIs".[13]

It is also important to emphasize that after the University Council approved the partial participation in that system, each unit earned autonomy to define whether they would participate in the selection, how many places they would reserve, and eventually having the possibility to separate enrollments for black, brown and indigenous students or just the ones graduated from public schools.

Besides USP, many other public institutions not funded by the federal government, started to reserve, recently, places for students from underprivileged social classes. Moreover, most of them also reserve places for self-claimed black, brown and indigenous students.

Hence, despite the restricted application of the provisions of Law n. 12,711 to federal universities and institutions, it is a fact that the effects of the law reached many other federal entities which started to separate, through their tertiary education institutions, part of their places for the same recipients of that law.

ADPF No. 186 Trial

Having considered the quotas policy, it is important to emphasize that, despite many controversies raised by application of the law, The Federal Supreme Court—highest court of the judicial branch in Brazil—has already commented on it, during a trial of non-compliance argument of fundamental precept n. 186.

---

[13] According to the 2010 census, the last one made.

Before starting the discussion of the questions, there are some considerations to be stated about ADPF institution in order to understand the importance of the action in protecting the fundamental rights provided in the Federal Constitution.

ADPF is one of the actions that triggers the control of constitutionality concentrated in Brazil, the exclusive competent jurisdiction of the Federal Supreme Court, when the precedent to be confronted is the Federal Constitution. Among many other instruments that enable the control, ADPF specifically may have as objects, rules and laws preceding the Federal Constitution and, furthermore, enacted by municipal administrations, which does not happen in similar actions, as well as the Direct action of unconstitutionality (ADin) and the Action of declaration of constitutionality (ADC), which are restricted to federal rules (also state rules by ADin) enacted after the Federal Constitution.

That is why ADPF is a constitutional secondary action – which is comprised in the institute law—used to avoid or restore violation of a fundamental rule by the Government.

So, following that the Democratas Party (DEM) filled an ADPF n. 186—to put into question the quotas policy for student selection at University of Brasilia (UnB), years before the enactment of Law n. 12,711/12.

In short, the university decided to reserve 20% of the places for black and brown students and another 20% for indigenous people from all states of Brazil for ten years.

The arguments used to question the quotas policy in UnB, by the Democratas Party, were violation of the principle of dignity of the human person (provided in article 1, item III of Federal Constitution), repudiation of racism (principle that governs Brazil in international relations as provided in article 4, Item VIII of Federal Constitution), the principle of equity (provided in article 5, head provision) and also, supposed violation of universal right to education, present in many constitutional devices, from article 6 on.

The Federal Supreme Court unanimously upheld the legislation and repealed the ADPF. Some remarkable ministers expressed their votes in a convincing manner, such as, for instance Justice Lewandowski, for whom the quota policy adopted by the UnB has the purpose of establishing a diverse university atmosphere and overcoming historical inequalities in society, highlighting its transient use.

In this same sense, other ministers expressed that conviction, such as Justices Marco Aurelio and Cezar Peluso, who reaffirmed the necessary substantive observance of the principle of equity. To them this principle brings the ethical and legal responsibility of government and society by adopting public policies that approach this historical mistake, in an attempt to develop a process able to reach the desired material equity and, therefore, undo the historical injustice against black people in Brazil.

Despite using different arguments to base the constitutionality of the challenged rules, a close reading of the decision issued by the Federal Supreme Court reveals that the paradigm used by the court was the compliance of the principle of equity.

Therefore, it is verified that the Federal Supreme Court is in perfect agreement with the essential application of the principle of isonomy which is also strengthened with the compliance of the quotas policy in Brazil.

Conclusion

Thus, from the analysis of all that has been demonstrated in this article, it is verified that the quota policy is aligned with the necessary observance of the principle of equity and that, in Brazil, has brought significant results in reducing inequalities in the country.

The policy of quotas, therefore, has as its main objective the reduction of historical inequalities of the country, allowing greater access to public universities by people whose presence in that place has been an exception.

There were many questions about the constitutionality of normative instruments that instituted the quota policy. Most of the country's courts have understood the permanence of such provisions in the Brazilian legal system, in view of strict compliance with constitutional principles, especially equity.

In this sense, the country's main court has already affirmed its commitment to the constitutionality of different laws that institutionalized the quota policy in Brazil, highlighting the need for affirmative policies in order to effectively observe the principle of equity.

This position reflects the commitment of the judiciary to the observance of human rights, achieved at great cost, whose materialization in the country, unfortunately, depends on the jurisdictional activity, since it is common for the State to disregard strictly fundamental norms.

References

Bandeira De Mello, C. A. (2012). *O Conteúdo Jurídico do Princípio da Igualdade* (21st ed.). Sao Paulo: Malheiros.

Barbosa, R. (1999). *Oração aos Moços* (5th ed.). Rio de Janeiro: Casa de Rui Barbosa.

Blatt, I. A. (2006, abril). Universidade do século XXI: lugar de exclusão ou de inclusão social? *UNIrevista*, *1*(2). URI/UNISINOS, Disponível em: http://www.fw.uri.br/publicacoes/revistach/artigos/capitulo_9.pdf

Canotilho, J. J. G. (2003). *Direito Constitucional e Teoria da Constituição* (7th ed.). Coimbra: Almedina.

Effting, P. (2012). *A Finalidade do Princípio da Igualdade: a nivelação social – interpretação dos atos de igualar*. Sao Paulo: Conceito.

Kunsch, M. (1992). *Universidade e Comunicação na Edificação da Sociedade*. Sao Paulo: Loyola.

Miranda, J. (2000). *Manual de Direito Constitucional* (3rd ed.). Coimbra: Coimbra.

Oliveira, J., et al. (2006). *Políticas de acesso e expansão da educação superior: concepções e desafios*. MEC Ministério da Educação, INEP Instituto Nacional de Estudos e Pesquisas Educacionais Aluísio Teixeira. Brasília. Disponível em: http://www.publicacoes.inep.gov.br/arquivos/%7B4DDC9880-A5C8-433B58AB2CCE2284C49%7D_MIOLO%20TEXTO%20PARA%20DISCUSSAO%2023.pdf

11

The Conundrum of Achieving Quality Higher Education in South Africa

Sadhana Manik and Labby Ramrathan

Introduction

At the most recent American Educational Research Association's (AERA) annual meeting (April 2017), an explicit statement was made in terms of the current trends in HE, one of which relates to HE being the pipeline leading to jobs. Incidentally, more than 13 years ago, the South African Council on Higher Education (CHE), linked the concepts of access, success and quality in HE to obtaining a job. In the report titled 'Improving Quality in Higher Education: Whose Responsibility? '(CHE 2004, p. 2), the CHE which has a specialised quality committee (Higher Education Quality Committee) reported that 'As the costs of higher education escalate and the struggle intensifies to gain access to higher education and succeed in acquiring a qualification that opens up employment opportunities, the issue of the quality of higher education is becoming more

S. Manik (✉) • L. Ramrathan
School of Education, University of KwaZulu-Natal—Edgewood Campus, Durban, South Africa
e-mail: manik@ukzn.ac.za; ramrathanp@ukzn.ac.za

© The Author(s) 2018
M. Shah, J. McKay (eds.), *Achieving Equity and Quality in Higher Education*,
Palgrave Studies in Excellence and Equity in Global Education,
https://doi.org/10.1007/978-3-319-78316-1_11

urgent.' It is thus apparent that both internationally and at a local level for some time, there have been conversations on widening access to allow a more diverse student population that can achieve success in HE and to increase participation in the economy. It has been argued by Maguad (2009, p. 4) that HEIs cannot 'insulate' themselves from the 'economic pressures facing social institutions'. Whether all of this can be achieved with or without compromising quality is contentious, more so because 'quality' is a theoretically murky concept, itself shrouded in several layers of conception, interpretation and institutional understandings as we, the authors, later elucidate.

The above coupled with the more recent discourses on decolonisation and indigenising the curriculum as a way of improving the quality of curricula content in SA, implies that the intent and purpose of HE in SA (within the current globalised context) is again under interrogation. This adds a new platform for a nuanced and textured engagement with key concepts such as quality, access, curriculum and funding in HE. Additionally, the AERA 2017 annual meeting theme 'from knowledge to action' further alluded to the idea of going beyond intellectualism, suggesting that tangible outcomes of HE are being centred as the way forward. Together, this discourse on quality, HE as the pipeline for jobs and now the need for concrete outcomes in HE ushers in a novel vision for the widening access discourse in HE.

In this chapter, given the breadth of vantage points in the widening access discourse, we limit ourselves to unpacking just one dimension, namely that which links to HE institutional attempts at achieving quality. We present the current situation of widening HE in SA with a view to showing how this widening of access is being conceptualised and realised within arguments of quality and achieving success and the extent to which it merges into the re-purposing of HE locally (fitness for purpose). We then use case study examples from three universities within one province (microcosm) in SA to illustrate our central argument namely of there being a conundrum of achieving quality in HE in SA (macrocosm). The chapter unfolds with a brief quantitative analysis of access into HE nationally and this is followed by an engagement with selected literature that references the nature of the efforts, opportunities grasped and significant challenges that are playing out in the current context of widening access. The chapter concludes with some theoretical engagements that could help explain the current trajectory in achieving quality in HE in SA.

Contextualising the Widening of Access into Higher Education Through a Transformational Gaze

The history and ills of apartheid within SA have been documented as well as the impacts on HE in the literature (Brown 2006; Lange 2006; CHE Higher Education Monitor 9, 2010; CHE 2011; Lewin and Mawoyo 2014). In summary, however, for the purpose of this chapter, these ills include a race-based categorisation that was strategically contrived to discriminate and sustain white privileges by dominating blacks. This led to retrogressive life experiences for those disenfranchised by apartheid policies and structures. If a comparison is made to white education, the education of black people was appallingly neglected (Brown 2006). During apartheid, funding for black students was minimal and this was a parallel trajectory to reduced HE participation especially by the African population (Njuguna et al. 2008; Brown 2006) as politically they were being certificated for low-skilled jobs. It should be noted that Africans are considered a distinct group from the generic Black (also termed at times non-white) nomenclature which comprises African, Indian and Coloured—distinctly SA carved racial groups that were considered disadvantaged during the apartheid era. With the political transition to democracy, all systems and processes needed to be transformed to reflect a new vision and mission, free from discrimination and the harm caused by apartheid. The values-based constitution of democratic SA underpinned by human rights is the bedrock of a democratic political order, which began in 1994, with the vision of an equal society that could be achieved through redress and social justice of those disadvantaged by the apartheid system of governance. Manik (2017) argues that there is evidence that achieving social justice in education and society became a key prerogative and the widening of access into HE, a priority. Also, it must be noted that the policy framework of South African HE from 1995 was impacted upon by other necessities, apart from social justice, and these included 'international trends shaping higher education institutions in developed and developing countries' (Council on Higher Education (CHE) 2010, p. 2). For example, at a local level, the Education White Paper (1997) formed the foundation for change and it painted a vision for transforming HE in SA by widening access. Indeed this transformation for SA required dissolution of racial separation in HE and initiation of greater non-white student access into all public HEIs. In 1998, UNESCO highlighted massification in HE and it also called for greater student access. Thus, democratic SA shares joint concerns with numerous other countries, in respect of the need for transformation in HE. However, the face of transformation in HE within SA, has its own unique character and is still morphing, as is revealed below.

Access and Quality in Higher Education Locally

Theoretical Strands of Access

How student access into HE was conceptualised at the beginning of democracy in SA and how it is presently understood, has changed. Akoojee and Nkomo (2007) point to two distinctly separate conceptions of access in SA HE policies from 1994 onwards, namely that of allowing greater numbers of black students to enrol in HEIs, which previously denied them access. This is termed 'access as participation'. This was the initial political thrust of a new democratic SA HE. A more recent conception is that of facilitating black students who have enrolled to also achieve success in their studies ('access with success') and not merely allowing for their entry into HE. Whilst 'access as participation' comprised of efforts such as lenient enrolment policies in particular programmes, initial access with success efforts at university involved academic development programmes and funding efforts. The latter has since widened to numerous other endeavours, for example, supporting the specific needs of first generation students who are deemed to be the largest in the undergraduate sector (Heymann and Carolissen 2011). At the dawn of widening access into HE, a gaze on access policies at institutions was the focus and this has since given way to concerns about 'epistemological access' (Morrow 2007). It is argued that epistemological access could promote students' success and this is presently one of the dominant discourses that pervades HE transformation (see for example Dhunpath and Vithal 2012; Maphosa et al. 2014; Manik 2015b).

Theoretical Strands of Quality

The CHE which is the quality council on HE in SA, has published several different types of reports on the state of HE since 1994, an indication of an on-going commitment to placing quality concerns under the magnifying glass. The first was a systems report in 2004, ten years after the advent of democracy and the second on key local trends (impacted upon by international interests) was released in 2007 and yet another was published in 2009. In its latest offering, which comprises eight task team reports published in 2016, the chair of council, Themba Mosia says the report (which reviews HE after 20 years of democracy) aims 'to take stock of higher education in South Africa'. This is significant because it then positions SA HE along a particular continuum. Baijnath, who is the CEO of the CHE says (in this 2016 report), 'Higher education in South Africa in the post-apartheid era has never been more volatile than it is currently, some two decades into democracy, yet it is, contradictorily, perhaps the part of the entire education sector that has advanced most in terms of achieving national goals of quality, equity and transformation'. Clearly, an element of instability in HE is voiced, but there is also some optimism in his articulation of HE's progress on the way to achieving national targets encompassing quality, equity and transformation. What is evident here, from the CHE perspective, is that quality in the SA HE context is married to concepts of transformation and equity.

So, what exactly constitutes other conceptions of quality in HE? The literature is clear that it is a concept that is disputed (Harvey and Green 1993; Henard and Leprince-Ringuet 2008). No clear definition avails itself because as Harvey and Green (1993) contend, quality can be the end product (outcome) or it can be a journey (process). Henard and Leprince-Ringuet (2008, p. 2) expand on this explanation (in an OECD publication on Quality teaching in HE) stating that, 'quality can be regarded as an outcome or a property, or even a process, and because conceptions of teaching quality happen to be stakeholder relative'; they explain that these stakeholders can be teachers, students or evaluation agencies. In attempting to make sense of quality debates and achievements in HE in SA, it is necessary to also traverse to a time much earlier in the literature, when Harvey and Green (1993) attempted explaining five conceptions of quality. Later on, Akoojee and Nkomo (2007, p. 394) interpret their work to recognise four ways of considering what quality embodies by collapsing two of Harvey and Green's categories into one, namely that of 'exceptional' and 'perfection'. The five initial conceptions are 'quality as "exceptional" or as "perfection" (as exclusive/gold standard); quality as "fitness of and for purpose" (responding to identified aims); quality as "value for money" (responding to economic rationale and efficiency), and quality as "transformation" (moving from one state to another, implying an educational value add)'. These avenues of understanding directed at the phenomenon of quality in HE imply that the concept can mean different things depending on the perspective taken (Harvey and Green 1993) and we expand on these varying understandings of quality from stakeholders' perceptions in our discussions that unfold from the SA literature and from the case studies. Additionally, Akoojee and Nkomo (2007, p. 394) also contend 'education quality cannot be situated within politically or ideologically neutral criteria. Quality considerations are generally based on values, purposes and ends of the beholder'. It is for this reason of 'quality' being a politically and ideologically charged concept, that they proffer what they term 'a transformative notion of quality' which is premised on the 'quality for purpose' perspective of Harvey and Green (1993) and also informed by the work of Bergquist (1995). Bergquist 1995, p. 43) defined quality in HE from the perspective of an institution. Quality is, 'the extent to which an institution successfully directs adequate and appropriate resources to the accomplishment of its mission-related outcomes and that its programs make a significant and positive difference in the lives of people associated with it and that these programs are created, conducted, and modified in line with the mission and values of the institution'. Bergquist thus argues that quality can be achieved through open access of institutions and true access is not possible without paying attention to obtaining quality.

What is relatively clear, is that Akoojee and Nkomo (2007, p. 390) have located their work on SA HE from an institutional quality assurance perspective where the conception of quality is process oriented. They called for 'conceptions of access' which would 'need to be situated within appropriate definitions of quality' arguing that it would then allow 'institutions to track the responsiveness of measures to achieve national transformational objectives'. They thus 'called for a comprehensive quality assurance framework'. They (2007, p. 386) further advocated for ensuring quality assurance in academic development programmes which are seen as a way for institutional redress and meeting national access targets in transforming HEIs. Interestingly, their conception of achieving quality not only involves institutions framing quality within their own contexts and receptive to national goals but also self-evaluations of their efforts and the inclusion of an external evaluation, which are quality assurance institutional measures. Later, we discuss the efforts to achieve quality from different perspectives at three institutions and deliberate on whether they can be boxed into one or many of these avenues of understanding quality.

The Achievement of Quantitative Targets

In the South African context, approximately 17% of those students who complete their grade 12 (matriculation) school education, access HE across the 26 public funded institutions. This is in spite of the targeted enrolment plans of 20% in 2001 as indicated in the National Plan for Higher Education (Lewin and Mawoyo 2014). Early arguments claimed that 'policies have not really succeeded in achieving any real quantitative increase in black learners at higher education institutions nor have they increased their success rates' (see Akoojee and Nkomo 2007, p. 391). Some aspects of this view have since altered. The latest statistics as provided by the Centre for Higher Education Trust (CHET) (see Table 11.1 below) indicate that in 2015, approximately 985,000 students were

Table 11.1 Enrolments in South African Universities from 2009 to 2015 (CHET 2017)

		2009	2015
Headcount enrolments		837,776	985,212 (17.6% increase)
By race	African	547,686	696,154
	Coloured	55,100	62,186
	Indian	53,628	53,378
	White	178,190	161,739
By gender	Female	478,174	574,677
	Male	359,578	410,523
Success rates		73%	78%

enrolled in HE across the public universities, growing from 495,000 in 1994, which is almost double in a period of 21 years, thus a marker of significant progress. The enrolment of African students rose from 43% of the total enrolment in 1994 to 60% in 2015. Using the generic nomenclature of Black, the enrolment increased from 55% in 1994 to 81% in 2011 (Lewin and Mawoyo 2014), suggesting that participation of the previously denied population groups has increased to reflect the demographics of SA. But comparatively there are huge discrepancies that still exist. For example, Webbstock in the CHE report (2016, p. 07) highlights 2013 race-based participation statistics of '55% for Whites and 16% for African students', where participation rates are calculated based on the race-based population groups. Despite this, nine years since Akoojee and Nkomo's (2007) claim has seen the CEO of the CHE (Narend Baijnath) in a report (2016, p. ix) claiming that SA HE has achieved 'greater access and a radical change in the demography of its students, with an 80% growth in the number of African students'. It is thus evident that these positive trends in the demographic statistics signal an understanding of quality being attained to some degree if Bergquist's (1995) notion of opening up access to HE is the marker of quality achievement. However, there are areas of concern as further explained below.

Drawing from Table 11.1, it seems that the increase in headcount enrolment from the specific period 2009 to 2015 has only marginally increased. An average annual growth rate of 1.2% was recorded across all 26 public HE institutions within SA with some institutions recording a negative growth and some as high as 8.1% (CHET 2017). This marginal increase in annual growth rates suggests that widening access (as determined by a numerical increase) into public HE institutions within SA has either reached the infrastructural capacities or that institutions' rolling enrolment plans are being adhered to because of the state's subsidy (funding) that are based on these enrolment plans. Public HE institutions are funded on a model that privileges enrolments and success rates of students as they progress through their study period. Malaza in the CHE (2011) report highlights how the funding model is also influenced by the enrolment planning on a three- year cycle. (Badat 2014; CHE 2011 Report), explains that if institutions accept more students than their declared enrolment plans had projected, the institution does not get any additional funding (meaning that institutions have to take responsibility for the additional cost due to over-enrolments) and herein lies the twist in the narrative.

Interestingly, the marginal annual increase in headcount recorded during the period 2009 to 2015 is very different from that of the previous period 2000 to 2008. The total headcount enrolment across public HE had increased from 557,000 in 2000 to 816,000 in 2008 (CHET 2017) (enrolment numbers approximated to the nearest 1000), recording a 46% increase in enrolment over this period of 8 years. This percentage increase when compared to the percentage increase during the 2009 to 2015 period (17.6%) suggests that the widening of HE in SA was at its peak during the 2000 to 2008 period.

In spite of the above twist, located within the transformational and social justice discourses that unfolded since democracy, a race-based and gender-based enrolment analysis cannot be excluded as these were the main constructs of transformation in relation to access issues, especially within HE and in worksites. It can be argued that the massification of HE in SA has been occurring since early 2000. Increasing the numbers of black students and attracting women into previously considered male dominated fields such as science and engineering has become the rhetoric of planning at institutions. The CHE claimed that by 2004 'the student body had become representative in terms of its "racial" and gender composition and included also significant numbers of international students (CHE 2004, pp. 234–236)'. Additionally, the number of female students grew by approximately 20% and male students grew by approximately 14% over the period 2009 to 2015 (CHET 2017), suggesting that more female students are enrolling in HE institutions than male students, thus making inroads towards achieving a gender balance in the student demographics. In fact, garnering black women in STEM-related fields is considered a double achievement and something to be lauded about when they achieve success. Continual, and increasing, funding mechanisms for studies by target groups has been a feature. For example, the Vice Chancellor (University of KwaZulu-Natal email Communique 2017) sent a message marking Women's Day that noted the following: 'Today, UKZN boasts the first black woman with a PhD in Town Planning and…awarded funding to over 54% of the female student body population, with 72.67% being undergraduate students. As the University of KwaZulu-Natal, we want to continue playing a strategic role in developing women both for the betterment of our institution and society at large.'

Current Challenges and Shortfalls in Higher Education

There are several challenges and shortfalls which are proving to be sticky areas in the journey towards achieving quality in SA HE.

The Demand for Higher Education

While the statistics on HE enrolments are encouraging, the demand for HE is an ever increasing one. In each of the case study institutions presented in this chapter, the demand for places has far exceeded its first entry capacity. For example, the Durban University of Technology (in KwaZulu-Natal province) received approximately 89,000 applications for approximately 7000 places for first entry students in 2016. This institution has a capacity of approximately 27,000 students across all its programmes. This extremely high number of student applications is not unusual as media reports that most institutions in SA record, on an annual basis, applications in excess of four times the number of places available for first entry students.

Widening access into HE in SA is a process rather than an event. One of the processes of widening access into HE centres around finance on the part of potential students. The financial constraints experienced by students (Manik 2014; Van Zyl 2015) was again accentuated by the recent Fees Must Fall (#feesmustfall) campaign that saw the temporary closing down of most public universities as a result of heightened and sustained student protests against the rising cost of student fees and students' demand for free public HE studies. This campaign rendered a state of tentativeness to the academic programmes. A commission of inquiry was put in place by the national government to look into the plight of students and to explore possibilities for free HE. The outcome was a R 7 billion grant by government to fund students. Considering the historical past of SA and the inherent marginalisation of the majority of its citizens, the demand for free HE is another confounding drive at widening HE. The principle is to have full participation in the economy of the country and it's also a means to unshackle the stronghold of apartheid on the lives of the masses.

Student and Institutional 'Deficits'

Challenges related to staffing, curricula and students' preparedness at institutions have been deliberated over and collaborative efforts have been documented in several publications. Initially students were being targeted as being inadequately prepared/not prepared for HE and institutions labelled them, for example, using deficit terms such as 'at risk' and introducing specific programs (see for example Butler 2013; Moeketsi and Mgutshini 2014) to support these 'at risk' students. Some institutions have since begun acknowledging their role in students needing to achieve success (Dhunpath and Vithal 2012). Manik (2017, p. 202) asserted that given the multiple challenges in HE, 'national government and public HEIs in SA have demonstrated a commitment to boosting student success by investing in student support'. She argued that national government had demonstrated its commitment to student success by providing strategic funding for an assortment of support programmes. For example, the Department of Higher Education and Training provides teaching development grants to improve teaching and learning at institutions. Sosibo (2015, p. 149) maintains that 'projects that result' from this 'have a huge potential for improving quality in higher education'. The CHE also has a quality enhancement project, which promotes institutional sharing of best practices (Sosibo 2015). Additionally, specific programmes are crafted by public HE institutions to fulfil their own needs and also government goals. For example, The Siyaphumelela ('We succeed'), initiative aims to improve South African universities' ability to gather and then analyse data to improve the success of students. There are five universities thus far in this project and they are the Durban University of Technology, Nelson Mandela University, the University of Pretoria, University of the Free State and the University of the Witwatersrand. Support programmes are being analysed for their effectiveness in boosting student success. Manik (2017) has chronicled particular complexities and problems that are experienced in certain support programmes during the implementation phase citing studies written by Davids (2014), Sosibo and Katiya (2015) as well as Kilfoil (2017) who published work on HE institutional support initiatives and their related challenges in recent years. These relate to David's questioning of whether indeed the tutorial system is an adequate means of student support in its present form given the large numbers of students with particular needs. Sosibo and Katiya (2015) also honed in on their institution's challenges in addressing students' support requirements due to staff shortages, far too many 'at risk' students and the lack of support by some university departments. Recently, Professor Wendy Kilfoil (see Nkabinde 2017), a director at the University of Pretoria bemoaned the 'silo' approach to student record keeping which prevented trends being recognised and the need for timeous responses.

Methodology

The data that follows for this chapter has been obtained from three universities in KwaZulu-Natal (KZN), which is one of the nine provinces within SA. A single province was selected with a view to keeping the diversity of variables to a minimum in terms of potential student population, language diversity and school education experiences. The management of the school education system in SA is provincially controlled, suggesting that all public schools within the province of KwaZulu-Natal are under one administration within the provincial legislature of government. An urban university (U), an urban university of technology (UT) and a rural based comprehensive university (RU) were purposively selected as these three universities represent the three forms of universities that exist within SA. Geographically, urban and rural contexts have also informed the choice of institutions for this chapter. Data was produced through desktop research and a total of six interviews (and on-going email correspondence) with staff who are responsible for access and academic support at each of the selected institutions and it is weaved into creating the following narratives under the selected sub-headings. The participants selected were deemed to be most appropriate for the chapter as information about widening access and issues of quality were required.

The Three Case Studies in KZN: Efforts at Widening Access into Universities

This section of the chapter presents accounts related to access into universities as experienced over the last five years. These accounts are then analysed to show how the widening of access is an institutional intention, but opportunities for placement of students is the key determinant leading to placement. In addition, the access of students is largely still based on meritocratic principles with the quality of the student especially the conceptions of quality as perfection and quality as transformation (Harvey and Green 1993).

Strategic Student Selection into Programs

There are some study programmes which have race-based quota systems and within the race-based quotas, academic merit is used to select students into the programmes. The admission of students into public universities within KwaZulu-Natal is unique when compared to the universities in the other provinces where applications for placement are made directly to the institution. In KwaZulu-Natal a central applications office (CAO) manages the application process for all public universities in this province. Students make an application for admission through a single application form and a single application fee is paid for consideration of the student by the participating universities in KZN. Potential students would be required to make this application in the year prior to their admission. In the application form, potential students would be required to make a selection of the university and degree programme combination and a student can make up to six choices. For example, a student could apply to the University of KwaZulu-Natal (UKZN) for Civil Engineering degree as the first choice. S/he can take, as a second choice, studying Civil Engineering at Durban University of Technology (DUT). A third choice can be that of studying Civil Engineering at the University of Zululand (UNIZUL). In this case the student is applying to do the same degree at the three universities, with UKZN as being the first choice, DUT as being the second choice and UNIZUL as the third choice, leaving him/her with three further choices out of the six that are available for this potential student. These could include applications for other degrees within a single university. While there is some critique of this system of application (see Ramrathan 2013 who refers to this system of application as 'insidious institutional violence' to potential students), the rationality for this system of application is based on financial considerations of making several applications to several universities and on attempting to widen participation into any of the universities of choice.

The selection of potential students, once collated by the CAO and sent to all participating universities, is still the prerogative of the admitting university and it is considered on the basis of the grade 11 results or the mid-year results of grade 12 (where there is the High School exit examination). In selecting potential students, universities declare their minimum admission requirements as well as selection criteria that inform the selection process of potential students. Noting that most universities receive more than four times the number of first entry places available, the selection criteria becomes the guideline to the final selection and placement of students into programmes of study. Applicants that potentially meet the selection criteria for admission are given provisional offers into degree programmes and these provisional offers are realised upon them obtaining their final grades in the grade 12 national examinations. The selection criteria across the three universities include specific reference to academic ranking (e.g. students with the highest matric points are first to be selected), while the two urban universities include the ranking of their choice of university and degree programme. This suggests that the potential student's choice of institution and degree programme is an important consideration in whether the student is selected.

Student Recruitment and Institutional Capacity

All three universities have university staff who actively promote their university to communities and schools. A dedicated unit of professional staff within each of the institutions' student recruitment sections undertakes school visits in KZN with the intention of enlightening grade 11 and 12 learners. The following aspects are discussed: the programmes on offer and their admission and selection requirements and processes, the facilities and support services offered to students and the funding opportunities to support their studies, including merit recognition and rewards to students. HE marketing, adapted from business marketing strategies, has taken the centre fold in student recruitment, suggesting that recruiting potential students is a purpose-directed process. Considering that student success based on throughput analysis is the key to the financial stability of institutions, the three case study universities' drive in student recruitment is largely linked to attracting a larger pool of high academic achieving learners to their institutions, from whom they can select in terms of their institutional capacity. For example, at the rural case study university (RU) there is a larger number of students that have very good school grades, contrary to the popular view that students attending rural universities may not be high academic achievers. The explanation for this, as ascertained by the participant from the rural-based university, is that these students have been rejected by the urban universities, despite having good grades. They then take up places at the rural university because they have nowhere else to go. The urban universities (U and UT) consider applicants who have made their university the first and/or second choice in their CAO applications and many of these students that are enrolled at the rural-based university did not make the selection criteria of the urban universities. The above processes of recruitment, applications and selections into universities and degree programmes, thus perpetuates the meritocratic principles associated with access, selection and success of university students.

Academic ranking and institutional choice by potential students seem to drive the admission process within universities, suggesting that widening access is an on-going intention, the realisation of which is still dependent upon academic merit and institutional capacity. The intention is to widen the pool of potential students from which to select appropriate students into study programmes largely to address issues of institutional efficiencies related to student throughput. As indicated earlier, institutional rolling plans for admissions are linked to funding through state subsidies. These subsidies are calculated on the basis of enrolments and throughput rates. Hence, taking students who have good grade 12 results has the potential to increase throughput rates and institutions have the potential to get the major share of the state funding. Taking weaker students may bring down the throughput rates and this will have a negative impact on the institutions' finances. Hence selecting potentially good students from a larger pool of applicants would enhance the opportunity for the institution to get its total share of the state funding subsidy. Institutions can do this selection because of the limits to the number of potential students that they can take. Each institution has its rolling enrolment plan and is based on the institutional capacity. The opportunity to select promising students from the wider pool of applicants in relation to institutional capacities has resulted in what can be construed as the marginal increase of university students enrolled across South African universities since 2009. This suggests that widening access into HE in SA has reached a plateau (average of 1.2% annual increase in student enrolment from 2009 to 2015) and it will remain so until institutional capacities are increased. If Bergquist's (1995, p. 43) definition of institutional quality is now a yardstick for measurement, then these institutions (and other public HEIs in SA) are being strained in terms of 'resources'.

The above analysis provides an indication of attaining a plateau in widening access and its link to institutional quality based on capacity. A deep analysis of students within each of the institutions suggests that, with the exception of the rural-based university (which has a majority of Africans), students who are enrolled reflect the race-based demographics of the country. Going beyond the racially-based demographics, the number of first generation students, as reported by the participants, has increased substantially across all three institutions. In addition, they reported that a number of students from schools categorised as quintile 1 to 3 (meaning that these schools are amongst the poorest of schools and most deprived of conducive learning environments) have increased. This suggests that widening access has shifted away from just race-based enrolment to include students from disadvantaged school backgrounds, who, based on the predominantly meritocratic system of placement would not have been able to access HE. For example, approximately 42% of students enrolled at the medical school at the urban university (U), as reported by one participant, are from schools that were ranked 1 to 3 of the quintile ranking system. If place reservations were not made for these students, they would not have been considered in the selection process. The change in these kinds of demographic variables suggest that widening access into HE is on-going and opportunities for targeted race-based groups are changing for the better but these students have specific needs. More students from poor socio-economic backgrounds are increasingly accessing HE and this trend in enrolments has sparked the #feesmustfall campaign for SA to provide free HE to the poor (all KZN case study universities were affected).

A key question on widening access into HE is to ask how is this possible within the structural limitations of public HE that governs student enrolments? Student migration is a response to this question where private HE provisioning has begun expanding, thereby creating spaces within public HEIs for a greater intake of students from disadvantaged communities. Each of the participating institutions have made concerted efforts to market their institutions to marginalised communities through school visits, road shows and partnerships with local education departments with a view to increasing the participation rates of students from indigenous communities. The #feesmustfall campaign, and the review of funding students' studies for HE, is in line with the intentions of institutions to continue to reshape the population demographics of HE beyond race categorisations, in line with the transformation agenda of the country. Thus quality as the demographic alignment of the student population in HE with the existing population of SA along racial lines is being entrenched in the recent years.

Case Study Institutions: Staff, Student and Institutional Quality Within Higher Education Provisioning

The period 1994 to 2008 has shown the highest rates of increase in student enrolment within HE in SA, followed by a plateauing of university access in terms of numerical values. This early period of high rates of increase was also the same period when the institutional outlook was a student focus. The construct of student quality was utilised, believing that the deficits were in the realm of the students. This belief was reinforced by the introduction and proliferation of student support programmes, both in terms of academic support and personal, social and financial support across all three institutions. Institutional outlook has since changed to include introspection of institutions and staff.

Institutional Shifts

Initially access programmes were developed by institutions whereby potential students were supported during their school education so that they could develop their competence to succeed in universities (Ramrathan et al. 2007). Institutions developed induction programmes, stand-alone foundation programmes and integrated extended degree programmes that included elements of foundational learning. This trajectory from access programmes to stand-alone foundation programmes to extended programmes was largely in response to the efficiency, success and quality of these interventions. For example, in the urban case study institution (U), Ramrathan et al. (2007) found through a tracer study that while students enrolled for the access programmes, a relatively small number of the completers of these programmes accessed university, degree programmes of their choice or other possible HE study programmes. At the second urban-based university (UT), students were referred to partner institutions to provide access programmes with the intention of recruiting the graduates from these partner institutions into mainstream diploma programmes. This route to admissions and into diploma programmes, as reported by a participant, soon stopped due to a realisation that the students entering were still not coping and a higher failure rate was experienced. Student identity issues, student labelling and the low rate of access into intended programmes through the self-standing foundation programmes led to the introduction of extended learning programmes (e.g. the four-year Bachelor of Social Science degree) that have gained a stronghold within the university. Extended programmes are programmes where fundamental learning is incorporated into the degree structure, thereby extending the minimum number of years for the completion of degree by usually one year. This type of programme intervention to support the widening of access found favour by universities largely because of funding that was and still is provided by the national government through its HE funding formula. The extended programme was also favoured because it gave students direct access into the study programme from their first admission rather than accessing foundation programmes and then waiting for programme admissions (for many who did not gain access to their intended study programme).

Institutional research and institutional support formed the framework to identify students' needs for academic success in the last decade. Several research strategies like student engagement surveys, first year student experiences and more recently, the identification of gaps in student preparedness for HE studies has informed what should happen to provide quality learning spaces and opportunities to recruit, sustain and graduate students within minimum time to degree completion. The case study institutions have introduced an array of strategies in an attempt to address the challenges being faced. For example, the rural based university (RU) has a dedicated Teaching and Learning Centre which is responsible for the provision of services in four key categories: academic support to students, professional development to academic staff, promoting the scholarship of teaching and learning (SoTL) and integrating information communications technologies into teaching and learning. At the urban university (U), some individual departments are conducting their own analyses of their programme offerings and crafting an approach supported by government and institutional funding. For example, Higgins-Opitz et al. (2014) report on student monitoring (through academic development officers who also tutor students after assessing their academic needs) and student mentoring (on academic, social and personal issues) by their peers in a compulsory module that was experiencing poor pass rates in the Health Sciences Department.

Student Support Efforts

The urban case study institution has introduced an early warning system for students that appear to be in need of support, what they refer to as being 'at risk'. They (U) use what they call a 'traffic light' system as a support mechanism for university-wide tracking and informing students if they could be 'at risk' (Mngomezulu and Ramrathan 2015). The students are categorised according to various levels of risk using colours (red, amber and green) to denote their progression across modules. This is then available to students and support staff so that specific actions can be taken. The institution has academic development officers who meet with the students to chart a pathway for adequate progress. The rural institution (RU) has a similar system of identifying 'at risk' students but it is module-based and thus limited in providing an holistic picture of the student's progress. At UT, there is presently no early warning system but students are identified upon poor performance and support is offered to them. These interventions focus on the deficit being on the students and the school education system. Interestingly, the 2013 Council for Higher Education's proposal for a flexible undergraduate curriculum (CHE 2013) is also an example of this deficit thinking from a systems vogue.

There are other support mechanisms evident at the institutions, which appeal to other aspects of deficit (e.g. institutional) with discussions followed by actions emerging on how teaching and learning can be improved for enhanced quality in the institutions. For example, in the faculty of engineering at the urban institution (U), staff noticed a high attrition rate and introduced a plethora of support initiatives with a dynamic structure. These comprised peer instruction over the three-year programme, supplemental instruction and academic counselling of 'at risk' students; they also noted the influence of the institution's merger with other institutions that led to various changes. The discipline then engaged with students about these interventions and further refined their support instruments to include changes to the curriculum, staff's use of teaching methods and greater student engagement (Pocock 2012). There is additional institutional research emanating from the urban institution (e.g. Ramrathan 2013; Mngomezulu 2014; Mkhize 2017) which has alluded to factors within institutions that need to be engaged in providing a rich, sustainable quality HE environment for academic success. For example, Mkhize (2017) found that a lack of attention to cultural symbols was one of the reasons why students displayed lower levels of student engagement at university. Mngomezulu (2014) found, through her study, that students go through a cycle of alarm, denial, acceptance and then engagement with academic support. A caring, invitational and supporting environment results in the students realising their potential to succeed. Also, Ramrathan (2013) alludes to institutional factors of, amongst others, curriculum construction, pacing and assessments impacting on students' progress within their study programme. While the notion of academic success is also a contested concept, these kinds of institutional research have led to institutions reviewing their own teaching and learning environments and notions of where quality lies.

Staff Development

Another example in the participating institutions relates to staff capacity. At the urban institution (U), all teaching staff below senior lecturer level are required to take senate-approved university extended learning programmes for their personal and professional growth as a way of providing a quality teaching and learning environment for students. At another institution (RU), staff development workshops were flagged as a regular initiative. Additionally, two of the institutions shared a recent introduction (in the last few years) comprising of staff crafting their personal development plans which indicated the areas where they believe they require assistance to develop.

These kinds of interventions suggest that the focus of quality is shifting for these institutions in KZN from a student deficit lens to an institutional deficit lens. This shift is a significant one as it begins to interrogate HE studies in terms of its fitness for purpose (Harvey and Green 1993) and in terms of aligning itself to the needs of the country. A direct outcome of this shift is the re-purposing of HE, a global discourse that is unfolding as suggested by the global conference themes of World Education Research Association (WERA), American Educational Research Association (AERA) and South African Education Research Association (SAERA).

Conclusion

Given Bergquist's (1995) definition of quality in HE and Harvey and Green's (1993) conceptions of quality and the numerous CHE reports it is apparent that quality in HE as a phenomenon, is intensely complex. If quality is the transformation of a HE system and the meeting of equity targets, then quality has been attained to some degree only because the transformation of HE remains 'ongoing' and 'replete with tensions and paradoxes' (CHE 2004). It is evident that each of the case study public institutions in KZN are engaged in a reflexive process towards attaining fitness for purpose. They are addressing their challenges from different vantage points: staff, students and institutional with the help of limited government support. Achieving quality within a widening access framework in HE in KZN and in the rest of public HEIs in SA appears to have significantly evolved from efforts to 'fix' (Pym 2013) or repair the students to numerous efforts at developing staff and institutions. However, the challenges appear immense and complicated given the realities of an ever-changing HE context in SA. The challenging variables and strains are multiple. These include the relative notion of quality: by whom, for whom and in what educational spaces? There are institutional capacity and funding issues, the dominance of meritocratic selection processes and questions about the purpose of HE studies. All of these competing variables culminate in a quality conundrum amidst widening participation. Thus, the quest for achieving quality is a recurring challenge.

References

Akoojee, S., & Nkomo, M. (2007). Access and quality in South African higher education: The twin challenges of transformation. *South African Journal of Higher Education, 21*(3), 385–399.

Badat, S. (2014). *South African higher education in the 20th year of democracy: Context, achievements and key challenges.* Pretoria: HESA.

Bergquist, W. B. (1995). *Quality through access: Access with quality. The new imperative for higher education.* Upper Saddle River: Prentice Hall.

Brown, K. (2006). "New" educational injustices in the "new" South Africa: A call for justice in the form of vertical equity. *Journal of Educational Administration, 44*(5), 509–515.

Butler, G. (2013). Discipline specific versus generic academic literacy for university education: An issue of impact. *Journal for Language Teaching, 47*(2), 71–88.

Centre for Higher Education Trust (CHET). (2017). *South African higher education performance data 2009–2015.* Retrieved from https://chet.org.za/data/sahe-open-data#new_hepid

CHE. (2011). *Participation in higher education.* Available at http://www.che.ac.za/focusareas/highereducationdata/2011/participation. Accessed 23 Apr 2014.

Council on Higher Education. (2004). *Improving quality in higher education: Whose responsibility?* http://www.che.ac.za

Council on Higher Education. (2010). *Higher education monitor no. 9. Access and progression in South African higher education: Three case studies.* Pretoria: Council on Higher Education.

Council on Higher Education. (2013). *A proposal for undergraduate curriculum reform in South Africa: The case for a flexible curriculum structure.* Report of the task team on undergraduate curriculum structure. Pretoria: Council on Higher Education.

Council on Higher Education. (2016). *South African higher education reviewed: Two decades of democracy.* Pretoria: Council on Higher Education.

Davids, M. N. (2014). Traditional tutorial system – Fit for purpose or past its sell by date? University students' pedagogical experiences. *South African Journal of Higher Education, 28*(2), 338–354.

Department of Education. (1997). *Education white paper 3: A programme for the transformation of higher education.* Pretoria: Government Printer.

Dhunpath, R., & Vithal, R. (2012). *Alternative access to higher education: Under prepared students or underprepared institutions?* Cape Town: Pearson.

Harvey, L., & Green, D. (1993). Defining quality assessment and evaluation. *Higher Education, 8*(1), 9–34.

Henard, F., & Leprince-Ringuet, S. (2008). *The path to quality teaching in higher education.* Paris: OECD. Available at https://www1.oecd.org/edu/imhe/44150246.pdf.

Heymann, L., & Carolissen, R. (2011). The concept of "first generation student" in the literature: Implications for South African higher education. *South African Journal of Higher Education, 25*(7), 1378–1396.

Higgins-Opitz, S. B., Tufts, M., Naidoo, I., & Essack, S. (2014). Perspectives of student performance in the health sciences: How do physiology and professional modules compare. *South African Journal of Higher Education, 28*(2), 436–454.

Kilfoil, W. (2017, June 29). Presentation at Siyaphumelela ('We succeed') project conference in Johannesburg, South Africa. Retrieved from www.siyaphumelela.org.za/conf/2017/

Lange, L. (2006). Symbolic policy and 'performativity': South African higher education between the devil and the deep blue sea. In *Ten years of higher education under democracy.* Pretoria: Council on Higher Education.

Lewin, T., & Mawoyo, M. (2014). *Student access and success: Issues and interventions in south African universities.* Cape Town: Inyatelo.

Maguad, B. (2009, July 19–30). *Managing for quality in higher education: A biblical perspective.* In 40th International Faith and Learning Seminar held at Asia-Pacific International University Muak Lek, Saraburi, Thailand. Available at http://digitalcommons.andrews.edu/cgi/viewcontent.cgi?article=1062&context=autlc

Malaza, E. D. (2011). *Higher education South Africa- insight,* p. 3. Available at http://www.usaf.ac.za/wp-content/uploads/2016/09/HESA-Insight-No-3_September-2011.pdf

Manik, S. (2014). Shifting the discourse: Student attrition in the context of relative deprivations. *South African Journal of Higher Education, 28*(1), 148–163.

Manik, S. (2015b). Calibrating the barometer: Student access and success in South African public higher education institutions. *Alternation, 17,* 226–244.

Manik, S. (2017). What is being done? Ubuntu in student support programmes in public higher education institutions in South Africa. In M. Shah & G. Whiteford (Eds.), *Bridges, pathways and transitions: International innovations in widening participation* (pp. 189–208). Cambridge: Elsevier.

Maphosa, C., Sikhwari, T. D., Ndebele, C., & Masehela, M. (2014). Interrogating factors affecting students' epistemological access in a South African university. *Anthropologist, 17*(2), 409–420.

Mkhize, J. S. (2017). *Student engagement in the first year of study in undergraduate programmes in higher education.* Unpublished doctoral thesis, University of KwaZulu-Natal, Durban, South Africa.

Mngomezulu, S. D. (2014). *Academic intervention experiences of 'at-risk' students: A case of an undergraduate programme in a South African University.* Unpublished doctoral thesis, University of KwaZulu-Natal, Durban, South Africa.

Mngomezulu, S., & Ramrathan, L. (2015). Academic intervention experiences of 'at risk' students in a South African university. *Alternation, 17,* 116–141.

Moeketsi, R. M. H., & Mgutshini, T. (2014). A comparative time review of recruitment and retention at a university in South Africa. *African Journal for Physical, Health Education, Recreation and Dance, 20*(1), 246–264.

Morrow, W. (2007). *Learning to teach in South Africa.* Cape Town: HSRC Press.

Njuguna, N., Subotzky, G., & Afeti, G. (2008). *Differentiation and articulation in tertiary education systems: A study of twelve African Countries.* World Bank Working Paper, 145: 1–200. Washington, DC: World Bank.

Nkabinde, S. (2017, August 11). *Mining the power of data to boost student success.* University World News Global Edition Issue 469. Retrieved from www.universityworldnews.com/article.php?story=20170811075332643

Pocock, J. (2012). Leaving rates and reasons for leaving in an engineering faculty in South Africa: A case study. *South African Journal of Science, 108*(3–4), 1–8.

Pym, J. (2013). From fixing to possibility: Changing a learning model for undergraduate students. *South African Journal of Higher Education, 27*(2), 252–367.

Ramrathan, L. (2013). Towards a conceptual framework for understanding student drop-out from HEI's. *South African Journal of Higher Education, 27*(1), 209–220.

Ramrathan, P., Manik, S., & Pillay, G. (2007). Transformational access: The upward bound programme as a possibility for promoting access to HE. *South African Journal of Higher Education, 21*(4), 733–752.

Sosibo, Z. (2015). Support strategies for scaffolding students' acquisition of academic literacy skills: Experiences at a University of Technology. *Alternation, 7*, 142–167.

Sosibo, Z., & Katiya, M. (2015). Closing the loop between access and success: Early identification of at-risk students and monitoring as key strategies used by a South African university. *International Journal of Education Sciences, 8*(2), 271–279.

University of KwaZulu-Natal. (2017, August 8). Vice-Chancellor's electronic Communiqué for Women's Month 2017.

Van Zyl, A. (2015, May 18–22). University drop-out. *The Coastal Weekly*, p. 4.

12

Fees Regimes and Widening Access in the Four UK Nations: Are No-Fees Regimes Necessarily More Socially Inclusive?

Sheila Riddell and Elisabet Weedon

Introduction

Widening access is, at least at the level of policy rhetoric, a central focus of higher education across the UK, comprising the four nations of England, Scotland, Wales and Northern Ireland. The Scottish Government claims that, in comparison with the other jurisdictions, its approach to funding higher education is the most equitable. This chapter explores whether this is indeed the case. There are broad similarities between funding regimes in the four UK nations, for example, across the piece means-tested maintenance loans, based on family income, are available to cover living expenses. However, there are also major differences, the most significant of which is the availability of free tuition for Scottish-domiciled

---

S. Riddell • E. Weedon (✉)
Centre for Research in Education Inclusion and Diversity,
University of Edinburgh, Edinburgh, UK
e-mail: sheila.riddell@ed.ac.uk; Elisabet.Weedon@ed.ac.uk

students studying in Scotland. European full-time undergraduates also have the same rights as home students in all EU member states and therefore do not pay tuition fees in Scotland. By way of contrast, for students in the rest of the UK, including those studying in Scotland, tuition fees are charged, which may be covered by tuition fee loans issued by the government-backed Student Loans Agency. In Wales and Northern Ireland, the devolved administrations cover some of the cost of tuition fees, but in England the entire debt is incurred by the student. Loans to cover tuition fees and maintenance must be repaid after graduation once an individual's earnings reach a certain threshold, which varies by jurisdiction. At the time of writing, 9% of salary is deducted at source and interest is charged on the total loan. The debt is written off after a certain period of time—35 years in Scotland and 30 years in England. Full details of the loan systems in place in different parts of the UK are available in Table 12.1.

The Scottish Government has argued that the student funding system in Scotland is inherently fairer than arrangements elsewhere in the UK and has invested considerable political capital in promising that the policy of free tuition is not up for negotiation. On his final day as First Minister in 2014, Alex Salmond unveiled a commemorative stone at Heriot Watt University engraved with the words, 'The rocks will melt with the sun before I allow tuition fees to be imposed on Scottish students'. The abolition of the graduate endowment scheme (see Table 12.1) was, he said, his proudest achievement during his seven and a half year tenure as First Minister of Scotland. The underpinning assumption of this policy is that free tuition is most beneficial to those from the least advantaged backgrounds since this group has a disproportionate fear of debt. Rather than taking this as a self-evident truth, as has often been the case in Scotland, this chapter explores whether Scottish higher education is indeed more inclusive than systems in other parts of the UK, drawing on data published annually by the University and Colleges Admissions Service, as well as research commissioned by the Sutton Trust (Hunter Blackburn et al. 2016). Our findings are, we believe, relevant not just to the UK, but also to the rest of the developed world, as debate continues over the most effective and sustainable way of funding higher education.

Table 12.1 Undergraduate student support in the United Kingdom before and after devolution

1945–7	First national legislation empowering local authorities and ministers to support students in higher education. Greater provision of national and local state scholarships ensured many students received grants and had full fees paid, but no absolute entitlement. Separate primary legislation for Scotland and Northern Ireland, both showing some variation in the detailed approach, including more emphasis in Scotland on studying locally
1961–2	Following the Anderson Committee report, the introduction of full payment of fees (partially subject to means-testing until 1977) and means-tested grants, as an automatic entitlement on the award of a university place for the first time in any part of the UK. Separate primary legislation, regulations and administrative arrangements for Scotland and for Northern Ireland, but student entitlements essentially the same as for England and Wales
1990	Introduction of student loans to supplement living cost grants across the UK. 'Mortgage-style' repayment with only link to earnings the ability to seek 12 months' suspension of repayments
1998–9	Means-tested fee payment of up to £1000 introduced across the UK. No liability below £23,000; full liability from £30,000. Grants reduced, loan entitlements increased and extended at higher incomes. Loans become 'income-contingent', payable at 9% of all earnings over a threshold, initially £10,000
1999–00	Grants abolished completely across all of UK and replaced with higher loans
2000–1	Fee payments abolished for Scottish students studying in Scotland. £1000 fee continues for all other students in the UK
2001–2	Introduction in Scotland of post-graduation payment (the 'graduate endowment') of £2000, supported by income-contingent loan. National means-tested grants reintroduced for young Scottish students, up to £2000. Institutionally-administered grants introduced for Scottish mature students
2002–3	In Wales and Northern Ireland, means-tested grants re-introduced (for young and mature students) of up to £1500
2004–5	In England, means-tested grants re-introduced (for young and mature students) of up to £1000
2006–7	In England and Northern Ireland, variable fees of up to £3000 introduced, with dedicated income-contingent fee loan. Grant maximum increased to £2765. No change to fee arrangements in Wales. Income-contingent fee loan made available for Scottish and Welsh students studying in rest of UK. Annual fee payable by students from rest of UK in Scotland increased to £1700 (£2700 for medicine)

(continued)

Table 12.1 (continued)

2007–8	Graduate endowment abolished in Scotland. In Wales, £3000 fee introduced backed by income-contingent loan, but with an additional non-means-tested grant towards fees of £1845 to all Welsh students studying in Wales, reducing de facto fee liability. Grants increased to a maximum of £2700
2010–11	Fee grant abolished in Wales and means-tested maintenance grant increased to £5000. National means-tested grant re-introduced in Scotland for mature students, up to £1000
2012–13	In England, variable fees of up £9000 introduced, as before with dedicated income-contingent loan. Loan repayment threshold increased to £21,000 and loan interest rates increased. Grants increased to £3250. In Wales, variable fees of £9000 also introduced, but with a dedicated fee grant covering all fee costs over £3465 for Welsh students studying in any part of the UK, effectively capping fees at that level. Maximum grant raised to £5161. New loan rules adopted, as for England. In Scotland, variable fees with no legal maximum introduced for students from rest of the UK; loan increased to £9000 for Scottish students in rest of UK; free tuition retained for Scots in Scotland. In Northern Ireland, fees capped at £3465 for Northern Irish students in Northern Ireland, maximum fee loan increased to £9000 for NI students in rest of UK. Variable fees of up to £9000 introduced for students from rest of the UK
2013–14	Maximum grant for young students reduced from £2640 to £1750 in Scotland and mature student grant reduced to £750 and income threshold for grant reduced; tapered system replaced with steps. Minimum loan increased from £940 to £4500
2016–17	Abolition of maintenance grants for English students, with increase in means-tested maintenance loan

The chapter begins with an overview of the funding and support regimes in the different UK jurisdictions. We then examine the range of policy interventions which have been pursued in order to facilitate widening access by pupils from disadvantaged backgrounds. Finally, we examine statistical data to explore the success of the different regimes in attracting students from less advantaged backgrounds into higher education, questioning whether the Scottish no-fees system is more successful than those in other parts of the UK. It should be noted at the outset that cross-border comparisons should be treated with a degree of caution.

Education systems vary across the UK across a number of dimensions. For example, in all four jurisdictions the majority of those who go to university are aged 18. However, in Scotland a minority of young people go to university at age 17 after they have taken Level 6 examinations (Highers). Scotland also has more mature entrants than other jurisdictions. Area deprivation is measured differently across the UK, with the Scottish Government preferring to use the Scottish Index of Multiple Deprivation (http://www.gov.scot/Topics/Statistics/SIMD). The measure of deprivation most commonly used elsewhere is POLAR (Participation of Local Areas) (https://www.hesa.ac.uk/data-and-analysis/performance-indicators/definitions, which is based on the likelihood of university entry by young people from a given neighbourhood. This is also used in relation to Scotland, but is less satisfactory because it does not capture those young people who begin their higher education career in college. Despite these caveats, which apply to all international comparisons, we believe that much is to be gained by looking across, as well as within, national and international borders.

Policy Background

Over the past decade, as already noted, widening participation has been seen as a key policy objective within all four UK administrations. In both England and Wales, independent reviews have examined the best means of funding financially stable and accessible systems. In England, the Browne Review of higher education, published in 2010, and the White Paper which followed (DBIS 2011), envisaged greater institutional competition driven by the choices of individual students, who were increasingly envisaged as service consumers. English policy also recognised the need for market regulation to promote widening access (further discussion follows). The Higher Education Green Paper, *Fulfilling our Potential: Teaching Excellence, Social Mobility and Student Choice* (DBIS 2015) recommended that within the Teaching Excellence Framework (a new system of comparing and grading the quality of university teaching), institutions should be able to demonstrate that they are 'fulfilling widening participation expectations'. At the time of writing, it is envisaged that a newly created Office for Students will set targets for higher education providers failing to make progress on agreed widening participation goals.

In Wales, two consecutive reviews (Rees 2001, 2005) sought to identify funding systems which would be both fair and flexible. More recently, the *Review of Higher Education Funding and Student Finance in Wales* (the Diamond Review), emphasised the benefits of a thriving higher education system in terms of economic growth and social cohesion (Welsh Government 2016). Its recommendations on student funding were designed to ensure both sustainability and fairness, reflecting the principles of proportionate universalism.

Comprehensive reviews of tuition fees, student support and access measures have not as yet taken place in Scotland. As noted above, the Scottish Government has tended to argue that the absence of undergraduate tuition fees in Scotland guarantees the delivery of a fair system. For example, the White Paper on independence (Scottish Government 2013) used higher education as a prime example of Scotland's commitment to social justice and equality, arguing that 'free education for those able to benefit is a core part of Scotland's educational tradition and the values that underpin our educational system. One of the major achievements of devolved government in Scotland has been to restore this right to Scottish domiciled undergraduate students' (Scottish Government 2013, p. 198). While the Scottish Government claims that its system is based on 'the ability to learn rather than the ability to pay', the Westminster Government 'has pursued an increasingly market-driven approach to higher education, increasing tuition fees for undergraduate students to up to £9,000 per year'. More recently, the Scottish Government appears to have been less sanguine that free tuition would automatically produce a fairer system, reflected by its decision to set up a Commission on Widening Access in 2015. The Commission's terms of reference did not include the issue of tuition fees and student support more widely. However, both the interim and final reports painted a less than rosy picture of the extent to which the higher education system in Scotland was inclusive in practice, noting the dominance of the most prestigious higher education institutions by the most socially advantaged groups and the scale of inequality in participation which was described as 'unfair, damaging and unsustainable. Scotland has a moral, social and economic duty to achieve equality of access' (Scottish Government 2015, p. 8). However, the Commission stopped short of questioning why the no-fees approach was failing to deliver more equitable outcomes in comparison with other parts of the UK.

In Northern Ireland, the dominance of policy concerns connected with the peace process has meant that domestic issues, including higher education, have not taken centre stage. Nonetheless, Northern Ireland's first higher education strategy, *Graduating to Success*, was published in 2012, followed by a widening participation strategy entitled *Access to Success*, published in 2015 (DELNI 2012, 2015). As with the other reviews, a strong degree of policy continuity may be recognised in the reviews' four guiding principles: responsiveness, quality, accessibility and flexibility.

To summarise, there is broad agreement on the desirable end point of higher education policy in terms of achieving excellence and equity. However, there is wide disagreement in the funding approaches which will lead to the achievement of these goals, with Scotland adopting a distinctively different approach compared with the rest of the UK. In the following sections, we examine both policy measures and outcomes in the four UK jurisdictions.

Undergraduate Student Support

The affordability of higher education is one of the factors which is likely to have an impact on rates of participation overall, and in particular by students from less advantaged backgrounds. Table 12.1 summarises important developments in the funding of UK higher education since 1945. For around 50 years, the funding of higher education across the UK was broadly similar. Major differences began to emerge following administrative devolution in 1992, when the funding councils established in each jurisdiction adopted responsibility for resource distribution (Gallacher and Raffe 2012; Riddell et al. 2016). Following the establishment of the Scottish Parliament in 1997, divergence continued. In 2000, the Labour/Liberal coalition government in the Scottish Parliament abolished fees for Scottish students studying in Scotland, whilst the £1000 per annum fee continued to be charged to all other UK students. In 2001, a graduate endowment payment of £2000 was introduced in Scotland, supported by an income-contingent loan. The income threshold for the commencement of repayment following graduation was set at £10,000, but many groups were exempt including disabled students and those from low income households. In 2007, following an election campaign in which the SNP (Scottish National Party) promised to abolish student debt altogether, the graduate endowment was abolished by the new SNP minority administration. This, of course, accounted for only a small proportion of student debt, most of which was associated with maintenance costs. However, it acted as a powerful symbolic gesture used by the Scottish Government as a sign of the egalitarian nature of Scottish higher education.

By way of contrast, in the rest of the UK, tuition fees gradually increased. In 2012/13, variable fees of up to £9000 were introduced, with tuition fee grants available in Northern Ireland and Wales to lessen the fee burden for students residing in that particular jurisdiction. It is important to note that these fees were not payable up-front by home and EU students, who were eligible to take out government-backed loans, repayable on an income-contingent basis following graduation. In contrast to the sharply divergent policy on tuition fees, approaches to maintenance loans and non-repayable grants have been broadly similar across the UK. While means-tested non-repayable grants have been radically reduced (Scotland) or removed altogether (England), means-tested maintenance loans have become more freely available. The table below underlines the restlessness of this policy arena, with students and their families struggling to grasp its complexity (Minty 2016).

The focus on tuition fees in Scotland as the principal means of widening access has meant that less attention has been paid to other aspects of student funding, including the availability of maintenance grants and loans. As is evident from Table 12.1, the direction of travel across the UK in this area has been broadly similar, with a gradual reduction in non-repayable grant and an increase in the availability of repayable maintenance loans, both of which are based on an assessment of disclosed family income.

Only recently has research been conducted on the extent to which tuition fee and student support policies in Scotland are economically redistributive in their effect. Hunter Blackburn (2016) demonstrated that the greatest beneficiaries of free tuition have been those from more advantaged backgrounds. Students from more affluent Scottish families leave university with the least debt of any group in the UK, since they do not incur tuition fees if studying in Scotland and are likely to receive help with maintenance costs from their parents, thus avoiding maintenance loans. In other parts of the UK, students from all social backgrounds are likely to take out loans to cover tuition fees (albeit assisted by government support in Wales and Northern Ireland). The poorest students in the rest of the UK have until recently received more generous grants and institutional bursaries to offset living costs. Hunter Blackburn argued that although average student debt was lower in Scotland compared with other parts of the UK, until 2016 Scotland had the least redistributive system of the four nations (Hunter Blackburn 2016). However, the abolition of the maintenance grant from 2016/17 in England makes this system less redistributive than was previously the case.

The policy of free undergraduate tuition in Scotland also has implications for the amount of money which is available to spend on other parts of the education system. In 2016/17, the cost of university fees in Scotland was almost £1.5 billion. This compared with expenditure of about £0.5 billion on colleges and pre-school education respectively, and about £3.8 billion on primary and secondary schools, catering for the entire school population from 5–18. Because of the tuition fee loan system in the rest of the UK, which is not taken out of recurrent public expenditure, more money has been available to spend in pre-school, schools and colleges. However, at the time of writing, education expenditure is being cut across the UK and in England changes to the pupil formula mean that funding for specific regions, for example London, will be significantly reduced. The Institute for Fiscal Studies has calculated that between 2017 and 2020 there will be a cut of 6.5% in expenditure on 16–18 year olds in English schools, jeopardising some of the improvements in higher education access which have been made (Belfield and Sibieta 2017).

Government Regulation of Widening Access

The marketisation of higher education has been explicitly promoted in England through the charging of tuition fees and the repositioning of the student as consumer, which was a central theme of the Browne Review. The small administrations of Wales and Northern Ireland, though less enthusiastic in their support for the higher education market, have been carried along in England's wake, introducing tuition fees but with state amelioration for some groups particularly for Welsh students from poorer backgrounds. However, there has been considerable political resistance to these changes and the Higher Education Act 2004 was only passed by the then Labour Government on the condition that the proposed increase in student fees was accompanied by measures to regulate the market in order to protect the interests of students from less advantaged backgrounds. Under the terms of this legislation, the Office for Fair Access (OFFA) was established in England, with the remit of scrutinising universities' widening access plans and preventing an institution from charging higher fees if its widening access strategy was deemed inadequate. These sanctions were never used in practice, although in about a third of cases OFFA entered into negotiations with institutions to ensure the setting of more stringent targets. Similar regulatory institutions were established in Wales and Northern Ireland.

Statutory underpinning of widening access was instituted somewhat later in Scotland because it was believed that free tuition would automatically ensure fair access for all those 'with the ability to learn' (Gallacher and Raffe 2012). The Further and Higher Education (Scotland) Act 2005 explicitly prevented ministers from imposing terms and conditions on university admissions. However, the subsequent Green Paper entitled *Putting learners at the centre* (Scottish Government 2011) reflected a policy turn-around, proposing that institutions which failed to widen access should be subject to financial penalties. Since 2012–13, institutions have been obliged to submit widening access outcome agreements to the Scottish Funding Council (SFC). To date, as in England, the SFC has used encouragement rather than financial coercion, however both parties know that both carrots and sticks are in place and alter their behaviour accordingly. Some of the older universities have opposed direct government intervention in the widening access arena on the grounds that this unwanted interference restricts their autonomy (Riddell et al. 2016). The consensual character of Scottish higher education governance appears to be less secure than hitherto. In the following section, we provide a brief overview of approaches to widening access across the UK.

Measures Adopted by Universities to Widen Access

For the past two decades, initiatives to promote widening access across the UK have been broadly similar, focusing on measures such as outreach work in low participation communities and university-based summer schools. However, questions have been raised about the efficacy of these measures and the evidence used in their evaluation (Baker et al. 2006; Gorard and Smith 2006; Riddell et al. 2013). According to these researchers, evaluations tend to be descriptive rather than analytical, make unestablished causal connections and accept individual student views of particular programmes as providing hard evidence of their success. The interim report of the Commission on Widening Access also noted that 'current outreach activity may be having a limited impact on overall participation'.

Widening access initiatives have also been criticised for identifying lack of aspiration as the reason for lower rates of participation by those from poorer neighbourhoods. Kintrea et al. (2011) argue that this has led to a downplaying of structural problems, such as the under-supply of university places and the focusing of resources on individuals and schools in the most socially advantaged neighbourhoods. Despite the lack of firm evidence on the effectiveness of widening participation measures, and a possible misrecognition of the underlying problem, government and individual institutions continue to invest significant sums of money in widening participation, with broadly similar approaches used across the UK. Interestingly, particularly in the older universities, far greater resources have been dedicated to outreach work, rather than providing institutional support to students once they are enrolled in courses.

Contextualised Admissions

The use of more contextually sensitive admissions policies has been seen as a possible means of avoiding discrimination in the admissions process. Research by Lasselle et al. (2014) shows that students from low-progression schools admitted with lower grades may perform better than their counterparts from high participation schools with higher grades. Selective institutions may adjust admissions criteria, setting a minimum qualifications level for a particular course which all students must fulfil, but requiring students from socially advantaged schools to achieve higher qualifications. Whilst many institutions support the broad principles of contextualised admissions; there is little evidence that such practices are being widely used (Lasselle et al. 2014), partly because of fears of disadvantaging those from middle class backgrounds. Boliver's research suggests that those from more advantaged backgrounds are more likely to gain a place in a Russell Group university compared with those from less advantaged backgrounds, even when their qualifications are similar (Boliver 2013). Institutions may have been slow to adopt contextualised admissions approaches for fear of upsetting their traditional clientele, including young people (Minty 2016), who may believe strongly that everyone should be treated the same irrespective of social background.

The Role of Colleges in Widening Access

Diversification of higher education providers is a further policy intervention which may be used to widen participation. In Scotland and Northern Ireland, in contrast to Wales and England, colleges play an important role as higher education providers. In Scotland, about 17% of higher education, generally in the form of sub-degree programmes, takes place in the college sector, compared with 6% in England and 1% in Wales. Colleges have traditionally been effective in recruiting students from lower socio-economic backgrounds and offering more flexible routes, including articulation into the last two years of a university degree programme (Gallacher

2009, 2014). Following the allocation of additional funds by the Scottish Government and the creation of articulation hubs, there has been an increase in the number of students moving from college into the last two years of a university programme, increasing from 3019 in 2011–12 to 3469 in 2012–13 (Universities Scotland 2014). Overall, according to SFC data, about 47% of HN students in Scotland progress to degree level study at university, although only 22% of these are awarded full credit. Moving from a sub-degree programme in a college to a degree level programme at a university occurs much more frequently in some disciplinary areas and courses compared with others. For example, students studying for an HNC in social care at a college are unlikely to progress to degree level study, whereas computer studies students are more likely to do so.

Although Scottish colleges have been more successful than universities in recruiting young people from socially deprived backgrounds, Gallacher (2014) has drawn attention to both the upsides and downsides of such provision. As is the case in the US community college system, there is a danger that young people from lower socio-economic backgrounds are diverted into lower-status programmes leading to less well-paid jobs. As discussed in greater depth later in this chapter, more than half (58%) of young higher education entrants from the most disadvantaged areas study at colleges, making them two and a half times more likely to do so than those from the most advantaged areas (23%) (Social Mobility and Child Poverty Commission 2015). Articulation routes are typically from college to post-92 institutions, limiting access to high-status courses and routes into certain professions such as law and medicine. In addition, the type of teaching and learning which takes place in some college sub-degree programmes is based on developing practical and vocational skills, and students may struggle with the pedagogical and assessment demands of a university degree, making them more likely to drop out (Kadar-Satat and Iannelli 2016). As demonstrated in this report, the increase in higher education participation, particularly for students from poorer backgrounds, has been driven by the expansion of college rather than the university provision. Colleges are very important in terms of opening doors to previously excluded groups, but the danger is that students from less advantaged backgrounds are diverted away from more selective universities.

Targeted Places for Widening Access Students

Ear-marking places specifically for students from under-represented groups is another policy lever which has recently been used to good effect in Scotland. In October 2012, the SFC invited universities to submit proposals for additional funded places in a number of key areas including widening access and articulation. The aim of these additional places was to change the culture of recruitment from particular groups. In 2013–14, 727 undergraduate places were made available for widening access to the most selective universities, and 1020 undergraduate articulation places across 14 universities. The intention was to increase the number of places year on year at the institutions where they were originally allocated. However, in 2016, the SFC announced that this programme would not be continuing, and that in future individual universities would be responsible for the allocation of places to students from less advantaged backgrounds (Scottish Funding Council 2016, p. 4). As is evident from the figures presented later in this section, there was a marked growth in the recruitment of students from the most disadvantaged neighbourhoods (SIMD20) to the ancient universities following the introduction of the targeted places, with the University of Glasgow taking the largest number. Where there is very strong competition for places, reserving a certain number for young people from disadvantaged backgrounds seems to have been an effective way of increasing their representation. This is particularly the case in Scotland, where free tuition accounts for a high proportion of the government's total education budget, which cannot be readily increased due to squeezed public spending. In England, the decision to abolish the cap on student numbers from 2016/17 onwards has produced an expanding system which is more able to accommodate the growing demand for university places.

Raising Educational Attainment

The main reason for the under-representation of young people from socially disadvantaged backgrounds in higher education is that their levels of educational attainment are lower than those from more socially advantaged backgrounds. As illustrated by Fig. 12.1, the social class gradient in Scottish education becomes increasingly evident as students move into the post-compulsory education phase. Those from the most advantaged neighbourhood quintile are twice as likely to gain at least one pass at Higher grade (Level 6) compared with those in the least advantaged quintile. At Advanced Higher level, the gradient of achievement is even more marked, with four times as many young people from the most advantaged neighbourhoods obtaining a pass grade in one subject or more at Level 7 (Advanced Higher) compared with those from the least advantaged.

This social class gradient in achievement is common to all UK jurisdictions, however there are some differences between the nations which are

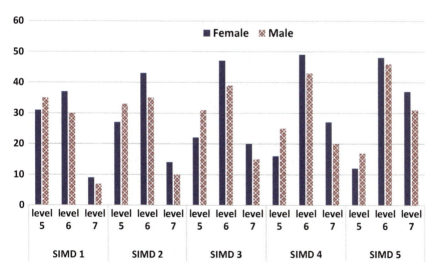

Fig. 12.1 Percentage of school leavers by highest qualification achieved at SCQF levels 5, 6 and 7, by SIMD 2012 quintiles and gender, 2014–15. (Source: Scottish Government data, Authors' own calculations)

Table 12.2 Indicators of educational attainment in the home nations

Measure	Source	England	Wales	Scotland	Northern Ireland
Percentage with five or more GCSEs A*-C or equivalent	GCSE exams or equivalent, 2010/11	80.5	67.3	78.8	75.3
Percentage with A*-C GCSE in Maths	GCSE exams or equivalent, 2006/07	54.6	50.0	48.3	54.7
Percentage with A*-C GCSE in English	GCSE exams or equivalent, 2006/07	60.2	58.9	69.8	62.9
Percentage of 17–18 year olds at school or in further and higher education	Labour force survey	72	Data not available	60	Data not available
Percentage of 17–24 year olds with no qualifications	Labour force survey, 2009	7.0	7.8	7.4	12.7
Percentage of 18 year olds with two or more A-levels or Highers	A-level results, 2011/12; higher results 2011/12	51.8	27.1	36.8	50.2

Source: Wyness (2013)

significant in terms of access to higher education by those from less advantaged backgrounds. As shown in Table 12.2, at lower levels, there are broad similarities between the four countries in terms of attainment. However, Wales and Scotland have a lower proportion of young people with two or more A levels or Highers, due to traditionally lower staying-on rates after the age of 16.

While levels of school attainment are of central importance in reproducing social inequalities in higher education participation, so too are subjects studied for 'A' level/Higher. UK universities specify not only the grades which must be achieved for admission to particular courses, but also the subjects which are required. As a guide to teachers, parents and pupils, Russell Group universities have identified the following as 'facilitating subjects': Chemistry, Physics, Biology, Maths and Further Maths,

English Literature, Modern and Classical Languages, History and Geography (Russell Group 2011). Using data from the Scottish School-Leavers' Surveys from the end of the 1970s to the first years of the twenty-first century, Iannelli (2013) examined the relationship between subjects chosen in upper secondary education and the social class differences in entry to higher education. She found that social inequalities in entry to higher education in Scotland are mostly explained by different subject choices made by pupils from different social class backgrounds. Subject choices are clearly not made in a social vacuum, but are shaped by cultural expectations and the array of available subjects within particular schools. Curriculum for Excellence emphasises the importance of pupil choice and the need for the curriculum to reflect pupil interests and aspirations. While a greater degree of choice may be motivating, there are also dangers that pupils from less advantaged backgrounds may choose or be channelled into vocational or 'non-facilitating' subjects, whilst pupils from more advantaged backgrounds are encouraged by parents and teachers to take more academic subjects.

Our comparison of UK higher education systems so far has highlighted both their broad similarities, for example, in terms of widening access initiatives, and differences, principally in relation to tuition fees. In the following section, we examine the extent to which this is reflected in better outcomes for students from less advantaged neighbourhoods in Scotland compared with other parts of the UK.

Social Inequalities in Participation Rates Across the UK

This section summarises some key findings from recent UCAS (University and College Admissions Service) reports on applications and acceptances to higher education institutions across the UK (UCAS 2016a, b). It should be noted that those applying to study sub-degree programmes in college (accounting for 17% of all Scottish and 6% of all English higher education provision) do not apply via UCAS, so these data do not reflect all higher education activity across the four nations.

Application Rates by Country of Domicile

With regard to the proportion of 18 year olds applying to enter higher education, (mainly degree programmes) via UCAS, Fig. 12.2 shows variations across the four countries between 2006 and 2016, although in each country there has been a marked increase in application rates. Northern Ireland has consistently had high application rates (about 48% of the age group), followed by England (about 35% of the age group). In 2016, Scotland and Wales had similar rates of application by 18 year olds (about 32%).

In 2011/12, following the trebling of tuition fees, there was a marked decline in applications in Northern Ireland and England, and to a lesser extent in Wales. This was in part due to decisions by prospective students to apply to university in 2011 to avoid tuition fees, rather than taking a gap year and applying after the confirmation of exam results. In subsequent years the upward trend in application rates continued, overtaking 2010 levels by 2014/15.

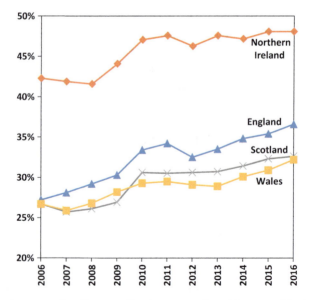

Fig. 12.2 January deadline application rates for 18 year olds by country, 2006–2016. (Source: UCAS 2016a)

In Scotland the pattern was somewhat different, with relatively stable application rates between 2010 and 2013. The slight increase in application rates in Scotland in 2010 was due to certain courses (nursing and education) being processed though UCAS for the first time.

Acceptance Rates by Country of Domicile

Figure 12.3 shows acceptance rates for the four countries in 2016, with Northern Ireland having a relatively low acceptance rate for 18 year olds compared with the other countries. This reflects the decision of Northern Irish policy makers to reduce the number of university places in response to budgetary pressures. The acceptance rate in Scotland (74%) is markedly lower than the equivalent figures for England (85%) and Wales (87%). This is a reflection of the cap on student numbers in Scotland, which has been lifted in stages in England. Student numbers are also controlled by the Welsh Government, but almost half of Welsh-domiciled students take up places in English institutions.

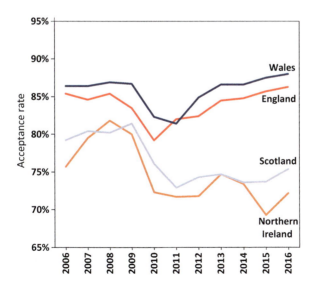

Fig. 12.3 Proportion of 18 year olds accepted for entry by UK country of domicile 2006–2016. (Source: UCAS 2016b)

Entry Rates by Country of Domicile

Scotland also has a lower proportion of 18 year olds entering university (about 23%) compared with the other three nations (Wales: 26%; England: 30%; Northern Ireland: 32%). Between 2013 and 2014, entry rates increased markedly for English and Welsh domiciled students, reflecting the early stages of the uncapping of student numbers. Whereas the proportion of 18 year olds entering university has steadily increased in Scotland, Wales and England, it has fluctuated in Northern Ireland reflecting budgetary pressures and shifting government policy (see Fig. 12.4).

It should be noted that the abolition of the graduate endowment in 2007 does not appear to have had an effect on the application, acceptance or entry rates of Scottish 18 year olds compared with observable patterns in other countries where tuition fees continued to be charged.

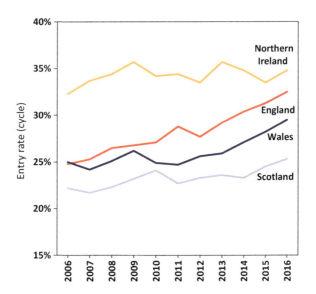

Fig. 12.4 Proportion of 18 year olds entering university by cycle and country of domicile, 2006–16. (Source: UCAS 2016b)

Social Inequality in Entry Rates by Area Deprivation and Country of Domicile

As shown by Fig. 12.5, Scotland has the lowest UCAS 18 year old entry rate for young people living in the most deprived areas. About 8% of Scottish domiciled 18 year olds from POLAR 3 Q1 (postcodes with the lowest university participation rates) enter university, compared with England (17%), Wales (15%) and Northern Ireland (14%). Scotland also has the lowest 18 year old entry rate for young people living in the most advantaged areas (Fig. 12.6).

The data presented above show that Scotland has relatively low application, acceptance and entry rates compared with the other home nations (although there is some variation in the position of the countries depending on the measure). Comparing Scotland with the other home nations, the abolition of the graduate endowment in 2007 did not appear to have a marked impact in encouraging students from poorer backgrounds to enter university. Scottish young people from the most advantaged areas are more than four times as likely to enter higher education compared

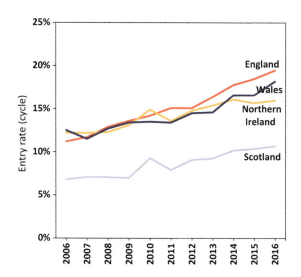

Fig. 12.5 18 year old entry rates for disadvantaged areas (POLAR3 Q1) by country of domicile, 2006–2016. (Source: UCAS 2016b)

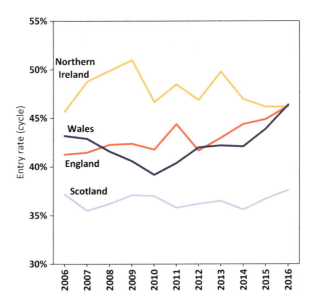

Fig. 12.6 18 year old entry rates for advantaged areas (POLAR3 Q5) by country of domicile, 2006–2016. (Source: UCAS 2016b)

with those from the least advantaged areas. There was an increase in the rate of entry between students living in both the most and least advantaged areas following the abolition of the graduate endowment in 2007, suggesting that this was not a critical factor in equalising participation rates. The staged lifting of the cap on student numbers in England from 2013 onwards appears to be having a positive impact on application, acceptance and entry rates. The lifting of the cap in England has also had an impact on participation by Welsh domiciled students, many of whom study in England. By way of contrast, the capping of student numbers in Scotland has led to more modest increases in participation rates.

Conclusion

Across the UK there is a strong stated commitment to widening participation to higher education for students from socially disadvantaged backgrounds. Widening access measures, such as outreach work and summer schools, have been broadly similar in character across the UK. The regulation of widening access via outcome agreements was instituted in England somewhat earlier than in Scotland because of the Scottish Government's belief that the absence of tuition fees would automatically produce a fair system, reflected in the mantra that higher education in Scotland is 'based on the ability to learn rather than the ability to pay'. Comparisons with other parts of the UK are important here, since the increase in tuition fees in the rest of the UK at the same time as their abolition in Scotland may be seen in terms of a natural experiment. Outcomes of this experiment suggest that the assumption that no-fees systems are the most socially inclusive may be misplaced. In the UK, Scotland has the lowest university entry rate compared to the three other jurisdictions and the lowest participation rate by those from the poorest backgrounds. Compared with those from the least advantaged neighbourhoods, young people from the most advantaged neighbourhoods in Scotland are four times as likely to enter university. By way of comparison, in England those from the most advantaged neighbourhoods are 2.4 times as likely to enter higher education compared with those from the least advantaged. As noted above, Scotland has tended to channel those from disadvantaged backgrounds into sub-degree programmes (Higher National Certificates and Diplomas) in colleges. About 50% of these students go on to complete a university degree, but only 25% gain full credit for the courses they have undertaken. As a result, students from poorer backgrounds may take six years to obtain an honours degree in Scotland (compared with the usual four years), potentially racking up high levels of debt in the form of maintenance loans.

With regard to international lessons, it would appear that the availability of loans, grants and bursaries may counteract the negative effect of tuition fees. In addition, the negative consequences of a free tuition system, in terms of limiting the number of available places, has a disproportionately negative impact on those from poorer backgrounds, since they are likely to have lower educational attainment for a range of social, economic and cultural reasons.

References

Baker, S., Brown, B., & Fazey, J. A. (2006). Individualisation in the widening participation debate. *London Review of Education, 4*(2), 169–182.

Belfield, C., & Sibieta, L. (2017). *Briefing note: The short- and long-run impact of the national funding formula for schools in England IFS BN 195*. London: Institute for Fiscal Studies.

Boliver, V. (2013). How fair is access to more prestigious UK universities? *British Journal of Sociology, 64*(2), 344–364.

Department for Business, Innovation and Skills (DBIS). (2011). *The returns to higher education qualifications* (BIS research paper 45). London: DBIS.

Department for Business, Innovation and Skills (DBIS). (2015). *Fulfilling our potential: Teaching excellence, social mobility and student choice*. London: DBIS.

Department for Employment and Learning Northern Ireland (DELNI). (2012, April). *Graduating to success: Higher education strategy for Northern Ireland*. Available at: https://www.economy-ni.gov.uk/sites/default/files/publications/del/graduating-to-success-he-strategy-for-ni.pdf

Department for Employment and Learning Northern Ireland (DELNI). (2015, April). *Access to success: An integrated regional strategy for widening participation in higher education*. Available at: https://www.economy-ni.gov.uk/sites/default/files/publications/del/Access%20to%20Success-An%20integrated%20regional%20strategy%20for%20widening%20participation%20in%20HE_0.pdf

Gallacher, J. (2009). Higher education in Scotland's colleges: A distinctive tradition. *Higher Education, 63*(4), 384–401.

Gallacher, J. (2014). Higher education in Scotland: Differentiation and diversion? The impact of college-university progression links. *International Journal of Lifelong Education, 33*(1), 96–107.

Gallacher, J., & Raffe, D. (2012). Higher education policy in post-devolution UK: More convergence than divergence? *Journal of Education Policy, 27*(4), 467–490.

Gorard, S., & Smith, E. (2006). Beyond the learning society: What have we learnt from widening participation research? *International Journal of Lifelong Education, 25*(6), 575–594.

Hunter Blackburn, L. (2016). Student funding in the UK: Post-devolution Scotland in a UK context. In S. Riddell, E. Weedon, & S. Minty (Eds.), *Higher education in Scotland and the UK: Diverging or converging systems?* Edinburgh: Edinburgh University Press.

Hunter Blackburn, L., Kadar-Satat, K., Riddell, S., & Weedon, E. (Eds.). (2016). *Access in Scotland: Access to higher education for people from less advanataged backgrounds in Scotland*. London: The Sutton Trust.

Iannelli, C. (2013). The role of the school curriculum in social mobility. *British Journal of Sociology of Education, 34*(5–6), 907–928.

Kadar-Satat, G., & Iannelli, C. (2016). *Beyond access to higher education: Widening access initiatives and student retention in Scotland*. Edinburgh: AQMeN, University of Edinburgh.

Kintrea, K., St Clair, R., & Houston, M. (2011). *The influence of parents, places and poverty on educational attitudes and aspirations*. Joseph Rowntree Foundation. http://www.jrf.org.uk/sites/files/jrf/young-people-education-attitudes-full.pdf

Lasselle, L., McDougall-Bagnall, J., & Smith, I. (2014). School grades, school context and university degree performance: Evidence from an elite Scottish institution. *Oxford Review of Education, 40*(3), 293–314.

Minty, S. (2016). Getting into higher education: Young people's views of fairness. *Scottish Educational Review, 48*(1), 48–62.

Rees, T. (2001). *Investing in learners: Coherence, clarity and equity for student support in Wales*. Cardiff: Independent Investigation Group on Student Hardship and Funding in Wales. Available at: http://gov.wales/dcells/publications/policy_strategy_and_planning/furtherandhighereducation/fehereviews/investinginlearners/investinginlearnerse.pdf?lang=en

Rees, T. (2005). *Fair and flexible funding*. Cardiff: Welsh Assembly Government. https://core.ac.uk/download/pdf/4155205.pdf

Riddell, S., Edward, S., Boeren, E., & Weedon, E. (2013). *Widening access to higher education: Does anyone know what works? A report to universities Scotland*. Edinburgh: University of Edinburgh, Centre for Research in Education Inclusion and Diversity (CREID).

Riddell, S., Weedon, E., & Minty, S. (Eds.). (2016). *Higher education in Scotland and the UK: Diverging or converging systems?* Edinburgh: Edinburgh University Press.

Russell Group. (2011). *Informed choices*. Retrieved from http://www.russellgroup.ac.uk/informed-choices/

Scottish Funding Council. (2016). *Outcome agreements for universities - indicative allocation for 2016–17*. Edinburgh: Scottish Fundng Council. http://www.sfc.ac.uk/web/FILES/Announcements_SFCAN042016_OutcomeAgreementsforuniversitiesindic/SFCAN042016_HE_indicative_funding_2016-17.pdf

Scottish Government. (2011). *Putting learners at the centre*. Edinburgh: Scottish Government.
Scottish Government. (2013). *Scotland's future*. Edinburgh: Scottish Government.
Scottish Government. (2015). *Commission on widening access: Interim report*. Edinburgh: Scottish Government.
Social Mobility and Child Poverty Commission. (2015). *State of the nation and child poverty in Great Britain*. London: Social Mobility & Child Poverty Commission.
Universities and Colleges Admissions Service (UCAS). (2016a). *UK application rates by the January deadline: 2016 cycle*. Cheltenham: UCAS.
Universities and Colleges Admissions Service (UCAS). (2016b). *End of cycle report 2016*. Cheltenham: UCAS.
Universities Scotland. (2014). *Delivering for Scotland: The third round of outcome agreements for higher education*. Edinburgh: Universities Scotland.
Welsh Government. (2016). *Review of higher education funding and student finance arrangements in Wales*. Cardiff: Welsh Government.
Wyness, G. (2013, October 28). Presentation to the education in a devolved Scotland: A quantitative analysis, *attainment and inequality seminar*, University of Edinburgh.

13

High Status Professions, Their Related Degrees and the Social Construction of 'Quality'

Erica Southgate, Susan Grimes, and Jarrad Cox

> *For equity to have real teeth, proportional representation also needs to apply across institution and course types. Short of this, it will be difficult to argue that the policy or at least its equity intent, has been successful.*
> *(Gale 2012, p. 246)*

Introduction

The global massification of higher education is underway (Altbach 2013). In Western contexts, this phenomenon has seen an increase in students who have been traditionally underrepresented in universities (Schuetze and Slowey 2002; Shah et al. 2015). However, certain bastions of inequity still persist: students from specific equity groups, particularly those from low socioeconomic status (LSES), first-in-family (FiF), rural, mature-aged, Indigenous and certain ethnic and cultural backgrounds,

---

E. Southgate (✉) • S. Grimes • J. Cox
School of Education, University of Newcastle, Callaghan, NSW, Australia
e-mail: erica.southgate@newcastle.edu.au

remain underrepresented in elite universities and in high status degrees (Gale and Parker 2013; Reay et al. 2009). High status degrees are pathways into prestigious professions such as medicine, law, information technology and engineering. These professions are ranked highly in occupational prestige scales (Ganzeboom and Treiman 1996; McMillan et al. 2009) and are generally held in esteem across nations (Treiman 2013). While acknowledging that social mobility can have 'hidden costs' (Cole and Omari 2003; Friedman 2014; Southgate et al. 2017a), there are substantial social, economic and health benefits to individuals, their families, the nation and the professions themselves, when high status occupations become socially diverse (Causa and Johansson 2010; Milburn 2012).

This chapter proceeds from a position that quality and equity are not mutually exclusive (Whiteford et al. 2013) and is organised into two sections. The first section provides a snapshot of some key literature on social diversity and high status professions and their related university degrees. Specifically, it offers observations on the assumptions of 'quality' underpinning access to high status degrees and elite professions. The second section presents original research on the experiences of FiF students undertaking medical education: internationally, medicine is considered the most prestigious of all professions (Ganzeboom and Treiman 1996; McMillan et al. 2009; Rosoff and Leone 1991). Specifically, the study pointed to some of the ways medical students from 'humble' backgrounds understand and experience ideas about 'quality'. The chapter concludes by arguing that there is much critical work to be done to de-naturalise notions of 'quality' in relation to such elite contexts.

High Status University Degrees and the Idea of 'Quality'

Different countries have different rates of social mobility. For example, Australia has relatively higher social mobility compared to the UK or US (Causa and Johansson 2010). Despite Australia's relatively high social mobility, students from non-traditional backgrounds, even those with substantial academic ability, are far less likely to be enrolled in Australian high status degrees (Southgate 2017a). In the Australian context, Koshy (2016) suggests that for proportional representational parity or equal share of enrolment to population, university participation data would need to reflect the following domestic student profile for equity groups: 2.4% students from remote geographic backgrounds; 25.4% from regional backgrounds; 25% from LSES backgrounds; and, 2.3% Indigenous students. Table 13.1 illustrates that students from these equity groups do not meet the proportional representation benchmark for elite Fields of Education (FoE) and that they are much more likely to be enrolled in non-elite universities (Other) than elite institutions (Group of Eight (Go8)).

It is at the discretion of each university which student they accept into their degrees. This includes students from equity groups and the high status degrees. The Australian higher education sector has broadly supported increasing the representation of students from equity group background, including the Go8 universities (Group of Eight 2010, p. 9). Table 13.2 shows students from equity groups as a proportion of the undergraduate FoE cohort in both Go8 and Other university categories. Students from equity groups comprise a much higher proportion of the FoE student cohort in Other universities than in the Go8 institutions. While undergraduate students from equity groups are a minority within high status FoE, in the elite context of Go8 universities they are usually a very small minority indeed. This snapshot of participation indicates that students from equity groups are far more likely to be accepted into a high status degree in non-elite universities and that these students make up a remarkably small percentage of their FoE cohort in Go8 universities.

From an equity perspective, such patterns of unequal proportional distribution require concerted attention including a pressing need for elite universities to address their role in stymieing social mobility. If the Go8 universities are genuinely committed to equity, as some of their documentation suggests, then they would need to demonstrate this by substantially increasing the proportion of their student cohort who are from equity groups, particularly for high status degrees. It would also entail government to commit to annual public release of fine grain statistics, in this case access, participation and success data related on broad

Table 13.1 2015 domestic undergraduate student enrolment in FoE by equity group

FoE	Equity group	% Enrolled in FoE		
Engineering and Related Technologies (n = 56,674)	Remote (451)	0.80	Go8 Other	0.15 0.64
	Regional (8907)	15.72	Go8 Other	2.44 13.28
	LSES (9637)	17.00	Go8 Other	2.58 14.42
	Indigenous (370)	0.65	Go8 Other	0.07 0.58
Information Technology (n = 25,686)	Remote (77)	0.30	Go8 Other	0.02 0.28
	Regional (3181)	12.38	Go8 Other	0.90 11.49
	LSES (4477)	17.43	Go8 Other	1.46 15.97
	Indigenous (234)	0.91	Go8 Other	0.05 0.86
Architecture and Urban Environment (n = 12,696)	Remote (0)	0.00	Go8 Other	0.00 0.00
	Regional (7)	0.06	Go8 Other	0.00 0.06
	LSES *	*	Go8 Other	* *
	Indigenous (0)	0.00	Go8 Other	0.00 0.00
Law (n = 40,903)	Remote (216)	0.53	Go8 Other	0.05 0.48
	Regional (4033)	9.86	Go8 Other	1.12 8.74
	LSES (3936)	9.62	Go8 Other	0.92 8.70
	Indigenous (459)	1.12	Go8 Other	0.09 1.03
Medical Studies (n = 11,014)	Remote (84)	0.76	Go8 Other	0.22 0.54
	Regional (1768)	16.05	Go8 Other	5.92 10.13
	LSES (1132)	10.28	Go8 Other	3.47 6.81
	Indigenous (211)	1.92	Go8 Other	0.39 1.53

*Less than 5 students

Table 13.2 2015 domestic undergraduate enrolment by equity group as a proportion of FoE cohort at Go8 and Other universities

FoE Enrolment by University Type	Equity group	% of Go8 FoE Cohort	% of other FoE Cohort
Engineering and Related Technologies	Remote	0.52	0.91
Go8 (n = 16,700)	Regional	8.28	18.82
Other (n = 39,974)	LSES	8.77	20.44
	Indigenous	0.25	0.82
Information Technology	Remote	0.11	0.33
Go8 (n = 3774)	Regional	6.09	13.47
Other (n = 21,912)	LSES	9.96	18.72
	Indigenous	0.37	1.00
Architecture and Urban Environment	Remote	0.00	0.00
	Regional	0.00	0.07
Go8 (n = 2812)	LSES	*	*
Other (n = 9884)	Indigenous	0.00	0.00
Law	Remote	0.27	0.59
Go8 (n = 7759)	Regional	5.89	10.79
Other (n = 33,144)	LSES	4.87	10.73
	Indigenous	0.46	1.28
Medical Studies	Remote	0.48	1.01
Go8 (n = 5048)	Regional	12.92	18.71
Other (n = 5966)	LSES	7.57	12.57
	Indigenous	0.85	2.82

*Less than 5 students

and narrow FoE related to high status degrees and by type of university sector (elite and non-elite).

Significantly, this pattern of stark underrepresentation of students from equity groups in high status degrees endures despite the implementation of widening participation policies, the provision of school-based career education, access to ever-expanding online information, and the considerable investment by universities in pipeline and school-based outreach programs, and other interventions such as 'taster' days, summer schools and e-mentoring.

Factors influencing social stratification and reproduction are complex and can be traced to: familial and community dynamics that inform career horizons, aspirations and norms; to the inequitable practices, processes and 'deficit' assumptions that are evident in school and tertiary education systems; and to the conscious and unconscious bias firmly embedded in high status professions (Southgate 2017a). It is important to embed the issue of access to high status professions within a structural dynamic of severe economic and educational disadvantage and sociocultural marginalisation. This includes recognising the detrimental impacts of child poverty on the quality of learning opportunities available to students. As McLachlan et al. (2013) suggest:

> A child's earliest years fundamentally shape their life chances. Gaps in capabilities between children from socioeconomically disadvantaged families and their more advantaged peers appear early in life. Starting school 'behind the eight ball' can begin a cycle of disadvantage that sets a trajectory for poorer outcomes later in life. (p. 2)

Decades of international research consistently show that the socioeconomic and ethnic segregation of schools has a profoundly negative impact on the academic achievement of students (Darling-Hammond 2014; Perry and McConney 2010; Rumberger and Palardy 2005; Strand 2014). By the end of the 4th grade, in the US for example, African American, Latino, and poor students of all races are two years behind their wealthier, predominantly white peers in reading and math, and by 8th grade are three years behind, and by 12th grade, have slipped four years behind (Teachers College, Columbia University n.d.). Similarly, in the Australian context, students from LSES, Indigenous and remote backgrounds are between 3–4 years behind in literacy and numeracy achievement compared to students from high SES backgrounds (Cobbold 2017).

This achievement gap adversely impacts on a student's ability to complete high school with the level of achievement that would make them competitive for direct access to university study. This has been well documented in the US, with SAT score distribution reflecting distinct patterns of racial inequality across generations (Reeves and Halikias 2017). Achievement gaps are apparent in Australia where young people gain direct access from school to university degrees by achieving an Australian Tertiary Admission Rank (ATAR) (University Admissions Centre n.d). Around 57% of students achieve an ATAR but only 36% of those are from the lowest SES decile compared to 83% for the top decile (Lamb et al. 2015). Only a very small minority of Indigenous students are eligible for university entry through an ATAR (in 2008 this was 8% compared with 46% of non-Indigenous students) (Wilks and Wilson 2015). The average ATAR for those in the lowest SES decile is 67/100 compared to 84/100 in the highest decile, making students from LSES backgrounds far less able to compete for places at university in general and putting high status degrees with their exceptionally high ATAR effectively out of reach for all but a tiny minority of students from disadvantaged backgrounds (Lamb et al. 2015). Generally, the higher the prestige of the degree, the higher the ATAR admission requirement (with variation between elite and second-tier universities). For example, depending on the institution, an ATAR for medicine or law would be between 92–99/100. Tellingly, Gale (2012) remarks: 'ATAR is more indicative of socioeconomic status than it is of a student's academic potential' (p. 246). ATARs are not indicative of a student's potential to become an outstanding doctor, lawyer or engineer.

Indeed the achievement gap barrier is more indicative of the impact of the quality of schooling available to students than their potential or talent. Naylor and James (2015) sum up the situation:

> (L)ow SES schools are less likely to be able to afford high achieving teachers or replace them in emergencies, sufficient teaching resources, sufficiently rich learning environments, less likely to have their students complete Year 12 (the final year of high school), and are less likely to provide access to the core academic curricula required for access to university. (p. 7)

Pitman et al. (2015) warn against higher education policy-makers (and we would add universities' administrators and Faculty) giving preference to an 'input definition of educational quality' (p. 622). An input approach prioritises what students bring with them into higher education and is inherently biased against students who, through no fault of their own, have not had access to superior educational opportunities. In the case of school-leavers the main 'quality' input is their test score/rank such as ATAR (for class and racial bias in the US SATs and in graduate admissions see Soares (2011) and Garces (2014) respectively). If universities are serious about equity, they need to re-examine or moderate the use of such inputs especially when they become the primary barrier to access to degrees. This is particularly important in light of evidence that non-traditional students can and do succeed in degrees with high admissions standards especially when given alternative pathways and when admissions criteria are adjusted (Lawson et al. 2007).

Three recent studies from the UK provide insight into how an input approach reproduces social stratification within the professions. Kirby's (2016) *Leading people 2016: The educational backgrounds of the UK professional elite* highlights how the UKs most prestigious professions 'remain disproportionately populated by alumni of private schools and Oxbridge, despite these educating only a small minority of the population (estimates suggest about 7% attended private schools, less than 1% Oxbridge)' (p. 2). Furthermore, in medicine 61% of 'top doctors', defined as those who have received a fellowship of the Royal College of Physicians, were educated at independent schools, nearly one quarter at grammar schools (22%), and the remainder (16%) at comprehensive schools (p. 2). 40% of 'top doctors' were educated at Oxbridge and 60% at one of the top 30 universities in the UK (Kirby 2016, p. 2). Similarly, in law, 74% of the top judiciary were educated at independent schools and the same proportion (74%) went to Oxbridge (Kirby 2016, p. 2). Access to elite universities in the UK is very low for students from poor backgrounds (Social Mobility Commission 2016). While some countries such as Australia and Canada have higher rates of social mobility than the UK and the US (Causa and Johansson 2010), it is imperative that any nation that seeks to promote social mobility undertake this type of analysis over time in order to hold a light to the way that education systems are implicated in the maintenance of privilege.

The second study explored non-educational barriers to entry into elite legal and financial services firms (Ashley et al. 2015). This qualitative research found that there was a strong tendency within these companies to recruit new employees from a narrow range of elite universities where higher SES students made up the majority of the student body. The research found that the concept of talent (a synonym for a high quality candidate) was class-based and that this bias drove discriminatory practice:

> (E)lite firms define 'talent' according to a number of factors such as drive, resilience, strong communication skills and above all confidence and 'polish', which participants in the research acknowledge can be mapped on to a middle-class status and socialisation. (Ashley et al. 2015, p. 6)

The authors suggest that the idea of a 'talented' graduate was treated as unproblematic by elite firms, when it is in fact a highly ambiguous concept, and that firms elide on 'proxy measures of potential associated with middle-class status, thus accentuating rather than reducing, non-educational barriers to entry and, possibly, career progression' (Ashley et al. 2015, p. 6).

Laurison and Friedman (2015) explore career progression for non-traditional graduates in elite professions. They contend that the framing of the social mobility 'problem', as one of access into university, detracts attention away from the professional journey of people from disadvantaged backgrounds. They contend that social mobility research should also examine objective indicators, post-graduation, such as earnings and occupational position. Utilising a large data set from the UK Labour Force Survey, Laurison and Friedman (2015) found that in professions such as medicine and law there were distinct patterns of 'micro-class reproduction' where children with parents in these occupations were 21.6 and 18.9 times respectively more common in the occupation than the population as a whole. Moreover, there was a substantial earnings difference among those in the highest positions of elite occupations linked with social origin: the upwardly mobile earned *far less* per week than those who were from the same prestigious occupational group as their parents (the 'micro-stable'). This phenomenon is a 'class ceiling', with women experiencing the double disadvantage of the glass and class ceiling. The authors recommend further research that untangles why this disadvantage persists, including qualitative research on how upwardly mobile individuals are evaluated within elite occupations, particularly in relation to their class-based embodied dispositions or habitus (Bourdieu 1977).

These studies provide tantalising insights into the role of elite professions in maintaining their socio-economic homogeneity (and hegemony). Kirby (2016) highlights powerful dynamics of social reproduction, where those that attend elite schools and very elite universities not only gain unparalleled access to high status professions but are consistently recognised by their peers as being at the pinnacle or 'top' of the profession. Being recognised as a top quality doctor by one's peers is both a perpetuation and amplification of existing privilege. Ashley et al. (2015) conclude that often elite firms select 'talented' candidates based on middle class dispositions captured in the nebulous quality of 'polish'. While there is a literature on conscious and unconscious bias in employment and promotion decisions (Ashley and Empson 2013; Isaac et al. 2009; Rivera 2012), high status professions require close scrutiny especially when the idea of a talented, quality candidate is so narrowly defined. Classificatory judgements about quality have material impacts on the career options and progression of upwardly mobile individuals. Even after beating the odds to gain access to a high status degree, and go on to employment in the profession, people from working class backgrounds, particularly women, may find they are assessed as being of lower quality and therefore worth considerably less remuneration over a lifetime compared with their peers from the 'micro-stable' group (those whose parents were from elite occupations) (Laurison and Friedman 2015). These studies illustrate how the concepts of 'quality', 'talent' and being the 'top of the top' are influenced by social class and gender dynamics that stubbornly persist even with social mobility.

The Construction of 'Quality' in Medical Education: Observations from a Case Study of First-in-Family Students

There is a relatively small but interesting literature on the experiences of non-traditional students in elite degrees (for example, Cole and Omari 2003; Granfield 1991). Medical education provides an interesting case for examination because internationally medicine is ranked as the most prestigious of all professions (Ganzeboom and Treiman 1996; McMillan et al. 2009). The impetus to widen access to medical education dates back several decades (Fox 1979) and has been primarily driven by a social accountability framework which proposes that medical schools should select 'best talent' that reflects the social diversity of the communities that doctors serve, and as a pragmatic means for addressing doctor shortages in underserved communities (Duvivier and Stull 2011; Garlick and Brown 2008; cf. Garces (2014) on the US affirmative action approach). Medical school admissions data from the US (Fenton et al. 2016), Canada (Association of Faculties of Medicine of Canada 2012), Australia

(Department of Education 2014), and the UK (Cleland et al. 2012), point to a very low intake of non-traditional students, with minimal improvement over time. For example, Australian medical schools enrol 10–16% of students from LSES backgrounds compared with approximately 46% from middle SES and 38% from high SES backgrounds (Department of Education 2014; Southgate 2017a). Remarkably, despite investment in widening participation initiatives over a number of years, the proportion of students from LSES backgrounds in UK medical schools declined from 14% to 11% (Cleland et al. 2012).

Research on the experiences of non-traditional students in medical education is growing. This literature examines the perceptions of non-traditional students on the likelihood of pursuing a career in medicine and the journey into university and through the degree (Beagan 2005; Brosnan et al. 2016; Greenhalgh et al. 2004; Robb et al. 2007; Southgate et al. 2015; Wright 2015). It is an important literature because it provides an understanding of the ways inequalities inhabit educational settings and, more notably, a window into how some students succeed in gaining access to the most elite degrees against significant odds (Southgate et al. 2017).

Our qualitative study of the experiences of students who were the first in their family to go to medical school highlights how the idea of 'quality' not only underpins the input-focused admissions process but was implicated in the construction of the professional self (Brosnan et al. 2016; Southgate 2017b; Southgate et al. 2017). The study, conducted in one Australian medical school, consisted of semi-structured interviews with 21 domestic undergraduate students which focused on: motivation and pathway to medicine; experiences of medical education; barriers and enablers; and future aspirations. The sample exhibited characteristics of non-traditional students including an overall LSES profile with the majority (14/21) residing in postcodes in the bottom 50% of areas in the Index of Relative Socioeconomic Disadvantage (Australian Bureau of Statistics 2013). Nine participants were aged in their late teens to early 20s, with 12 participants aged in their mid-20s to mid-30s. Sixteen were female and five male. Seven identified as Indigenous and 14 came from a rural or regional area.

Most students described their journey into medical school as circuitous and protracted. They all travelled great 'social' distance from their 'humble' family backgrounds into the elite world of medicine. Only two students had taken a direct route from high school with five taking a 'gap' year or two in which they took time to decide what they would like to do. Another five (mostly Indigenous) students entered via an enabling program. The remaining participants had either completed or partially completed a degree and/or were in the workforce for some time before deciding to apply to medical school. To quote one female participant, their life trajectories were neither 'simple' in terms of a linear 'normal' biography (Kohli 2007, p. 258), or 'lovely', in the sense of being carefree and straightforward. One Indigenous student captured the sentiment of the group when she described getting into medicine 'the hard way'.

For the majority of students the long, indirect route into medical education was a result of an intricate interplay of factors. Medical admissions processes are complicated, multi-phased and expensive. Student can stumble at any one of the hurdles including: not meeting the very high 92–99/100 ATAR; not getting a high enough score on the separate Undergraduate Medicine and Health Science Admission Test (UMAT); or doing poorly at the interview stage. Often students do not have teachers or family members with the knowledge and resources required to assist them in preparing for and negotiating such complex processes (Southgate et al. 2015). As the literature reviewed in the previous section demonstrated, students generally did not experience the quality of schooling required to achieve a very high ATAR. Stumbling at any one of the admissions hurdles is not an indication of the quality of the student or their potential talent as a doctor. Rather, it could be argued, it is an indictment of a higher education system that (consciously or unconsciously) maintains hurdles to keep certain types of students out of prestigious degrees.

In some cases, there are alternative entry or pipeline programs (for example to increase the number of Indigenous doctors [(Lawson et al. 2007)) that acknowledge that there are quality candidates who may not be able to meet all the stringent admissions standards but who would make fine doctors. These programs are however relatively rare perhaps because they require a radically different mind-set, adequate resourcing and a will to change. Some proponents of equity in medical education argue that the postgraduate rather than the undergraduate route is best for increasing social diversity. However, there is mixed evidence, at best, on whether postgraduate degrees really do achieve the goal (James et al. 2008; Mathers et al. 2011) and much more research is required before this claim can be substantiated. Furthermore, this argument does not take into account the hardship endured by those from less privileged backgrounds when they are required to considerably extend their university study and delay their earning capacity and career progression.

Perhaps one of the most interesting aspects of the FiF students was the way in which some participants were told by teachers that they were not capable of university study, let alone going to medical school. An Indigenous female student recounted the following experience:

> I wanted to do it (medicine) as a kid but I was told at high school that it was never going to be possible so I went to (post-school vocational education)…My high school principal told me I was going to be a typical Aboriginal drop out with lots of babies…I would have been 15 or 14 at the time.

Many students spoke of medicine as an unattainable dream and of not feeling they were good enough to become a doctor. It often took years to overcome these feelings of inferiority, of feeling that they were not the right 'class' of person to be a doctor:

> I guess I just didn't see myself in that class of people, because in my mind they were a different class of people…so how dare I consider putting myself in that category…(I)t was something I wouldn't dare to dream. (Non-Indigenous female)

These feelings of lacking the sort of *qualities* needed to become a doctor are not just a reflection of individual self-perception. Instead, they indicate a collective characteristic of FiF medical students: a shared understanding that certain groups are not really 'entitled' to aspire to medicine, even if they have demonstrated significant academic achievement and life accomplishments. Indigenous participants were especially explicit in naming how social class and racism influenced their sense of entitlement:

> Yeah well at first I thought I didn't realise I was good enough to get into something like medicine…and I guess yeah it's just such a good career. No one in my family has ever done anything like that before…(H)aving the background I have too, being Aboriginal, you don't really feel like you're entitled to something as good as this. (Indigenous female)

Students used language about themselves that reflected a sense of diminishment and deficit. For instance, students referred to themselves as 'a bit of a scummo', 'a bit rough around the edges' and 'not very polished'. They contrasted these negative qualities to those of other medical students who were viewed as 'a different breed' or different 'calibre of people', 'pretty clean cut', 'a lot more polished', 'bright' and 'highly intelligent'. This phenomenon of differentiating the (less privileged) self from other (more privileged) students resonates strongly with Ashley et al.'s (2015) observations on the types of middle-class characteristics valued in elite professions, including equating quality and talent with 'polish'. On a more positive note, many viewed their working class or cultural dispositions and knowledge as potentially very valuable in professional practice:

> If you understand my background you'll understand a fraction of who I am. …Very humble. Low socioeconomic status, surrounded by people who typically have low levels of education, low levels of money, poor health resulting from that. I understand (where patients are) coming from…I understand why it might be a health disaster because there's the cigarettes and there's the Centrelink (government welfare) benefits don't pay very much…I've lost my job…Yeah I understand it. (non-Indigenous male)

> (Other students) get shocked when I talk about … where I live at the moment … The whole opposite side of the street has now become (public) housing … so I see a lot of shit … That's hopefully an advantage … So I might have to be a slightly more refined version of myself as a doctor. But I think with the patients I'll still be okay and with my family, I'll still be much the same' (non-Indigenous female).

The FiF study highlighted tensions students felt between not being 'very polished' and a recognition that being 'a bit rough around the edges' would have professional benefits. These narratives capture how the notion of 'quality' in medical education is both deeply embedded in middle class and (white) assumptions about what makes a 'good' doctor and the way in which non-traditional students can challenge this bias within medical education.

Concluding Remarks

There is nothing natural about the concept of 'quality'. In higher education, 'quality; is a social construct that shifts across time and place and according to particular structural and historical forces' (Saarinen 2005, 2010; Stensaker 2007). When universities give preference to an input model of quality based on test scores and ranks, they effectively disadvantage students from low-income school communities who through no fault of their own did not receive the type education required to gain the extraordinarily high grades necessary to be competitive in the high status degree admission process. The higher education sector know this because there is evidence that students who gain entry into degrees, such as medicine, through enabling and alternative pathways make excellent professionals. This has been demonstrated with programmatic approaches that have successfully improved access to medical education for Indigenous people (Curtis et al. 2012; Lawson et al. 2007). Furthermore, elite professions themselves play a key role in maintaining barriers when they use middle-class proxies such as 'polish' to recruit 'quality' or 'talented' candidates (Ashley et al. 2015). Students from non-traditional backgrounds in high status degrees wrestle with these same middle-class and white conceptions of 'quality' and 'talent', but some offer alternative constructions of quality which emphasise the professional value of maintaining the dispositions, knowledge and skills that they have brought with them from their 'humble' backgrounds. Understanding where and how such students end up in elite professions after graduation is vital if the whole equity story is to be revealed (Laurison and Friedman 2015).

References

Altbach, P. (2013). *The international imperative in higher education*. Rotterdam: Springer.

Ashley, L., & Empson, L. (2013). Differentiation and discrimination: Understanding social class and social exclusion in leading law firms. *Human Relations, 66*(2), 219–244.

Ashley, L., Duberley, J., Sommerlad, H., & Scholarios, D. (2015). *A qualitative evaluation of non-educational barriers to the elite professions*. Retrieved July 25, 2017, from http://dera.ioe.ac.uk/23163/1/A_qualitative_evaluation_of_non-educational_barriers_to_the_elite_professions.pdf

Association of Faculties of Medicine of Canada. (2012). *The future of medical education in Canada*. Ottawa: AMFC.

Australian Bureau of Statistics. (2013). *2033.0.55.001 – Census of population and housing: Socioeconomic indexes for areas (SEIFA), Australia, 2011*. Canberra: Commonwealth Government of Australia.

Beagan, B. L. (2005). Everyday classism in medical school: experiencing marginality and resistance. *Medical Education, 39*(8), 777–784.

Bourdieu, P. (1977). *Outline of a theory of practice*. Cambridge: Cambridge University Press.

Brosnan, C., Southgate, E., Outram, S., Lempp, H., Wright, S., Saxby, T., … & Kelly, B. (2016). Experiences of medical students who are first in family to attend university. *Medical Education, 50*(8), 842–851.

Causa, O., & Johansson, A. (2010). Intergenerational social mobility in OECD countries. *OECD Journal: Economic Studies, 2010*. Retrieved November 17, 2016, from, http://www.oecd.org/eco/labour/49849281.pdf

Cleland, J., Dowell, J., McLachlan, J., Nicholson, S., & Petterson, F. (2012). *Identifying best practice in the selection of medical student*. London: General Medical Council.

Cobbold, T. (2017). *What's behind Australia's tottering PISA results: A review of Australia's PISA results*. Retrieved July 24, 2017, from http://www.saveourschools.com.au/national-issues/whats-behind-australias-tottering-pisa-results

Cole, E., & Omari, S. (2003). Race, class and the dilemmas of upward mobility for African Americans. *Journal of Social Issues, 59*(4), 785–802.

Curtis, E., Wikaire, E., Stokes, K., & Reid, P. (2012). Addressing indigenous health workforce inequities: A literature review exploring 'best' practice for recruitment into tertiary health programmes. *International Journal for Equity in Health, 11*(1), 1–15.

Darling-Hammond, L. (2014). Closing the achievement gap: A systemic view. In J. V. Clarke (Ed.), *Closing the achievement gap from an international perspective* (pp. 7–20). Dordrecht: Springer.

Department of Education. (2014). *Undergraduate applications, offers and acceptances, 2014 report and appendices*. Canberra: Department of Education.

Duvivier, R. J., & Stull, M. J. (2011). Advocacy training and social accountability of health professionals. *The Lancet, 378*(9807), e17.

Fenton, J. J., Fiscella, K., Jerant, A. F., Sousa, F., Henderson, M., Fancher, T., & Franks, P. (2016). Reducing medical school admissions disparities in an era of legal restrictions: Adjusting for applicant socioeconomic disadvantage. *Journal of Health Care for the Poor and Underserved, 27*(1), 22–34.

Fox, R. C. (1979). *Essays in medical sociology*. New York: Wiley-Interscience.

Friedman, S. (2014). The price of the ticket: Rethinking the experience of social mobility. *Sociology, 48*(2), 352–368.

Gale, T. (2012). Towards a southern theory of student equity in Australian higher education: Enlarging the rationale for expansion. *International Journal of Sociology of Education, 1*(3), 238–262.

Gale, T., & Parker, S. (2013). *Widening participation in Australian higher education*. Retrieved July 29, 2017, from http://www.ncsehe.edu.au/wp-content/uploads/2013/10/2013_WPeffectivenessAus.pdf

Ganzeboom, H. B., & Treiman, D. J. (1996). Internationally comparable measures of occupational status for the 1988 international standard classification of occupations. *Social Science Research, 25*(3), 201–239.

Garces, L. M. (2014). Aligning diversity, quality, and equity: The implications of legal and public policy developments for promoting racial diversity in graduate studies. *American Journal of Education, 120*(4), 457–480.

Garlick, P. B., & Brown, G. (2008). Widening participation in medicine. *British Medical Journal, 336*(7653), 1111.

Granfield, R. (1991). Making it by faking it: Working-class students in an elite academic environment. *Journal of Contemporary Ethnography, 20*(3), 331–351.

Greenhalgh, T., Seyan, K., & Boynton, P. (2004). "Not a university type": Focus group study of social class, ethnic, and sex differences in school pupils' perceptions about medical school. *British Medical Journal, 328*(7455), 1541–1547.

Group of Eight. (2010). *Group of eight framework for evaluation of equity initiatives*. Retrieved July 21, 2017, from https://go8.edu.au/sites/default/files/docs/go8equity_initiative_evalfwork.pdf

Isaac, C., Lee, B., & Carnes, M. (2009). Interventions that affect gender bias in hiring: A systematic review. *Academic Medicine: Journal of the Association of American Medical Colleges, 84*(10), 1440.

James, D., Ferguson, E., Powis, D., Symonds, I., & Yates, J. (2008). Graduate entry to medicine: Widening academic and socio-demographic access. *Medical Education, 42*(3), 294–300.

Kirby, P. (2016). *Leading people 2016: The educational backgrounds of the UK professional elite*. London: Sutton Trust.

Kohli, M. (2007). The institutionalization of the life course: Looking back to look ahead. *Research in Human Development, 4*(3–4), 253–271.

Koshy, P. (2016). Equity policy in Australian higher education: Past, present and future. In M. Hill et al. (Eds.), *Closing the gap: Bridges for access and lifelong learning* (pp. 277–302). London: Forum for Access and Continuing Education.

Lamb, S., Jackson, J., Walstab, A., & Huo, S. (2015). *Educational opportunity in Australia 2015: Who succeeds and who misses out*. Melbourne: Mitchell Institute.

Laurison, D., & Friedman, S. (2015). *Introducing the class ceiling: Social mobility and Britain's elite occupations*. London: London School of Economics.

Lawson, K. A., Armstrong, R. M., & Van Der Weyden, M. (2007). Training indigenous doctors for Australia: Shooting for goal. *Medical Journal of Australia, 186*(10), 547–550.

Mathers, J., Sitch, A., Marsh, J. L., & Parry, J. (2011). Widening access to medical education for under-represented socioeconomic groups: Population based cross sectional analysis of UK data, 2002–6. *British Medical Journal, 342*, d918.

McLachlan, R., Gilfillan, G., & Gordon, J. (2013). *Deep and persistent disadvantage in Australia*. Canberra: Productivity Commission.

McMillan, J., Beavis, A., & Jones, F. L. (2009). The AUSEI06: A new socioeconomic index for Australia. *Journal of Sociology, 45*(2), 123–149.

Milburn, A. (2012). *Fair access to professional careers*. Retrieved November 17, 2016, from https://www.gov.uk/government/uploads/system/uploads/attachment_data/file/61090/IR_FairAccess_acc2.pdf

Naylor, R., & James, R. (2015). Systemic equity challenges: An overview of the role of Australian universities in student equity and social inclusion. In M. Shah, A. Bennett, & E. Southgate (Eds.), *Widening higher education participation: A global perspective* (pp. 1–13). Amsterdam: Elsevier.

Perry, L., & McConney, A. (2010). School socio-economic composition and student outcomes in Australia: Implications for educational policy. *Australian Journal of Education, 54*(1), 72–85.

Pitman, T., Koshy, P., & Phillimore, J. (2015). Does accelerating access to higher education lower its quality? The Australian experience. *Higher Education Research & Development, 34*(3), 609–623.

Reay, D., Crozier, G., & Clayton, J. (2009). 'Strangers in paradise'? Working-class students in elite universities. *Sociology, 43*(6), 1103–1121.

Reeves, R., & Halikias, D. (2017). *Race gaps in SAT scores highlight inequality and hinder upward mobility*. Retrieved July 24, 2017, from https://www.brookings.edu/research/race-gaps-in-sat-scores-highlight-inequality-and-hinder-upward-mobility/

Rivera, L. A. (2012). Hiring as cultural matching: The case of elite professional service firms. *American Sociological Review, 77*(6), 999–1022.

Robb, N., Dunkley, L., Boynton, P., & Greenhalgh, T. (2007). Looking for a better future: Identity construction in socio-economically deprived 16-year olds considering a career in medicine. *Social Science & Medicine, 65*(4), 738–754.

Rosoff, S. M., & Leone, M. C. (1991). The public prestige of medical specialties: Overviews and undercurrents. *Social Science & Medicine, 32*(3), 321–326.

Rumberger, R. W., & Palardy, G. J. (2005). Does segregation still matter? The impact of student composition on academic achievement in high school. *Teachers College record, 107*(9), 1999–2045.

Saarinen, T. (2005). From sickness to cure and further: Construction of 'quality' in Finnish higher education policy from the 1960s to the era of the Bologna process. *Quality in Higher Education, 11*(1), 3–15.

Saarinen, T. (2010). What I talk about when I talk about quality. *Quality in Higher Education, 16*(1), 55–57.

Schuetze, H. G., & Slowey, M. (2002). Participation and exclusion: A comparative analysis of non-traditional students and lifelong learners in higher education. *Higher Education, 44*(3/4), 309–327.

Shah, M., Bennett, A., & Southgate, E. (2015). *Widening higher education participation: A global perspective*. Amsterdam: Elsevier.

Soares, J. (Ed.). (2011). *SAT wars: The case for test-optional admissions*. New York: Teachers College Press.

Social Mobility Commission. (2016). *State of the nation 2016: Social mobility in Great Britain*. Retrieved July 27, 2017, from https://www.gov.uk/government/publications/state-of-the-nation-2016/

Southgate, E. (2017a). *Fair connection to professional careers: Understanding social difference and disadvantage, institutional dynamics and technological opportunities*. Perth: National Centre for Student Equity in Higher Education. Retrieved December 21, 2017, from https://www.ncsehe.edu.au/wp-content/uploads/2017/09/Southgate_Fair-connection-to-professional-careers.pdf

Southgate, E. (2017b). Stigma and the journey of extreme social mobility: Notes on the management of discreditable identities in an elite university degree. In S. B. Thomson & G. Grandy (Eds.), *Stigma in the organizational environment*. New York: Palgrave Macmillan.

Southgate, E., Kelly, B. J., & Symonds, I. M. (2015). Disadvantage and the 'capacity to aspire' to medical school. *Medical Education, 49*(1), 73–83.

Southgate, E., Brosnan, C., Lempp, H., Kelly, B., Wright, S., Outram, S., & Bennett, A. (2017). Travels in extreme social mobility: How first-in-family students find their way into and through medical education. *Critical Studies in Education, 58*(2), 242–260.

Stensaker, B. (2007). Quality as fashion: Exploring the translation of a management idea into higher education. In D. F. Westerheijden, B. Stensaker, & M. J. Rosa (Eds.), *Quality assurance in higher education: Trends in regulation, translation and transformation* (pp. 99–118). Dordrecht: Springer Netherlands.

Strand, S. (2014). School effects and ethnic, gender and socio-economic gaps in educational achievement at age 11. *Oxford Review of Education, 40*(2), 223–245.

Teachers College Columbia University. (n.d.). *The academic achievement gap: Facts & figures*. Retrieved July 24, 2017, from http://www.tc.columbia.edu/articles/2005/june/the-academic-achievement-gap-facts--figures/

Treiman, D. J. (2013). *Occupational prestige in comparative perspective*. Amsterdam: Elsevier.

University Admissions Centre. (n.d.). *Frequently asked questions about the ATAR*. Retrieved July 18, 2017, from https://www.uac.edu.au/future-applicants/faqs/atar/

Whiteford, G., Shah, M., & Sid Nair, C. (2013). Equity and excellence are not mutually exclusive: A discussion of academic standards in an era of widening participation. *Quality Assurance in Education, 21*(3), 299–310.

Wilks, J., & Wilson, K. (2015). A profile of the aboriginal and torres strait Islander higher education student population. *Australian Universities' Review, 57*(2), 17–30.

Wright, S. (2015). Medical school personal statements: A measure of motivation or proxy for cultural privilege? *Advances in Health Sciences Education, 20*(3), 627–643.

14

How Can Contextualised Admissions Widen Participation?

Stephen Gorard, Vikki Boliver, and Nadia Siddiqui

Background

There are 164 higher education (HE) providers (139 universities and 25 colleges) in the UK, catering for around 2.3 million students. For traditional undergraduates, entry to HE is based on prior attainment at Key Stage 5 (KS5), currently taken by only just over half of the relevant age cohort. Applications are managed by the independent University and College Admissions Service (UCAS), but the actual places are offered by the universities themselves. Most students completing KS5 are capable of obtaining a place in HE somewhere, even with few or even no qualifications, and over 33% of the relevant age cohort continue directly to HE. The more prestigious universities are highly selective. All of this means that entry to HE in the UK is socially and economically stratified, to about the same extent as continuation to

---

S. Gorard (✉) • V. Boliver • N. Siddiqui
Durham University, Durham, UK
e-mail: s.a.c.gorard@durham.ac.uk

KS5 already is (Gorard et al. 2007; Chowdry et al. 2013). HE is even more stratified internally, because of the links between high attainment and some SES indicators (Broecke 2015).

The two main strategies for widening participation (WP) in HE have previously been outreach work by HE providers to encourage young people from disadvantaged backgrounds to apply to university, and efforts within the secondary and further education sectors to improve the pre-university academic attainment of students from disadvantaged backgrounds in order to increase the pool eligible for university admission. A third WP strategy is now being widely promoted—the use by universities of contextual data about prospective students' socioeconomic and educational circumstances to inform admission decision-making (Office for Fair Access 2015), usually by reducing the grade requirements for entry. Contextualised admissions (CA) policies are therefore a kind of positive discrimination within the current setup (Clayton 2012). Across the UK HE sector, many universities currently take into account the socioeconomic context of applicants' attainment when deciding whom to shortlist, interview, make standard or reduced offers to, or accept at confirmation as 'near-misses' (Moore et al. 2013; Universities Scotland 2016), and even more plan to use contextual data in the future.

The context indicators in widespread use are often chosen because they are readily available, without consideration of the possible alternatives (SPA 2015). Yet, in order to be effective, the indicators must be accurate, appropriate and complete. This chapter looks at a range of available indicators, and the evidence for their use in CA.

Methods

This chapter is based on two sources of data (with fuller accounts of the methods and findings in Gorard et al. 2017a, b). The first is a large-scale scoping review of research published between 2000 and 2016 in the English language. Electronic searches yielded around 120,000 reports, and screening reduced the number of full relevant research reports to 231. These were either large-scale empirical pieces, appropriately designed, with clear descriptions, or detailed discussions of the merits and difficulties of any potential indicator(s). The second source of data is the National Pupil Database (NPD), with records for all pupils at state-funded schools in England who ended their compulsory schooling in Key Stage 4 (KS4) in the years 2006, 2012, and 2014–2015, linked to their post-16 sixth-form or equivalent study (KS5), and where possible to their applications, courses and outcomes in HE (the HESA dataset) for those that applied to university at traditional age. There are around 600,000 students in each year cohort. The records include the student background characteristics, school details, and attainment for every year that they were at school, college or university in England.

The possible variables for use with CA must be easily and cheaply available to decision-makers at the time of application to HE. They must be true indicators of disadvantage, accurate, reliable, and have few or no missing values. Their deployment must also lead to increased fairness in admissions, and not to a different form of injustice, such as denying a limited place to a more deserving applicant, and ideally it should not substantially lower the overall retention, degree completion and degree classification rates of the universities concerned. Of course, no indicator will be perfect in all of these respects but these are the interlocking criteria by which they can be judged.

Indicators Not Available at Admissions Stage

The range of possible indicators that could be considered for CA is almost limitless, but however attractive they may sound, most are of no practical use. Most commonly, they are not available to the admissions authorities in a secure form. They include whether an applicant is a young carer for others, has suffered a recent bereavement or similar disruption, and their sexuality. There are several problems with reliance on all such self-reported items, including the fact that the definitions and thresholds used by different applicants will be different and, most importantly, that once it is known that reporting one of these issue leads to preferential offers at university there will be some gaming of the system. At present, many of the same problems arise with chronic ill-health (other than disability/special needs) and gender status. Our review found no good evidence relating to transgender students and attainment at school or HE, for example. None of these indicators appears in NPD or similar official datasets at present, and there are important ethical and legal problems concerning confidentiality and the protection of the data subjects.

The latter also applies to family income/tax credits. Official data on family income is not readily available. Self-reported family income data can be available to university admission authorities via UCAS, but only *after* the institution has made a decision on the application, and with a very high proportion of missing data. Students in receipt of the Education Maintenance Allowance (EMA) are considered disadvantaged, but this scheme is no longer operating in England.

At present none of these should be used as part of a valid approach to contextual admissions.

Indicators with Little or No Promise

The review showed that many of the common tools long-used for admissions, such as additional entry tests, interviews and setting tasks for applicants, may actually lead to more bias in offers and entry than using prior attainment (Yates and James 2013; Gill and Benton 2015).

Probably the most commonly used indicators for CA should not be used. These are the neighbourhood characteristics of where an applicant lives, whether based on low local participation in HE (POLAR), or indices of multiple deprivation (IMD, IDACI, Townsend). The problems of using the modal characteristics of where someone lives rather than their individual characteristics are many and serious. First, it is a kind of fallacy (Do et al. 2006; Harrison and McCraig 2015). Most disadvantaged applicants do not live in the most disadvantaged areas (e.g. around 60% of the most disadvantaged residents are not in the 20% lowest POLAR wards), whereas a substantial minority of the wealthiest residents do. Some local area indicators are based on as many as 6000 residents, who will vary considerably. The approach works especially badly in rural areas with population density, and in areas with high population density where rich and poor can live very close together.

An area measure can anyway only be used if the address of the applicant is known. In practice a large proportion of this address data is missing, which affects all such indices. For example, the school-age NPD has around 11–13% of student addresses (postcodes) missing in each year, and it is well-established that data is never missing by chance. Missing addresses are more common for recent immigrants, refugees, homeless and travellers, among others. For example, a total of KS4 1183 students were missing IDACI scores in 2015 (the year when most of them sat for 16+ examinations), and they are much more likely to be from poor families eligible for free school meals (FSM), certain ethnic minorities, with special educational needs (SEN) or disability, or to have been recent arrivals in their schools (Table 14.1). They also have markedly lower attainment than average, at every stage including KS2 (age 11) and KS4 when they decide whether to continue in formal education at age 16.

Therefore, ignoring cases with missing addresses when deciding which students are disadvantaged would be unjust because some of the most deprived and so most deserving of assistance would be put aside in favour of others. However, using the fact of missing data as an indicator in itself would also be unjust and would offer assistance to some of the least deprived students (who may simply have transferred from another home country of the UK). It would also provide an incentive for families not to provide clear data to schools and universities. And this missing data means that the neighbourhood scores themselves, even for those people whose postcodes are known, will tend to be biased since the characteristics of those residents missing addresses will also be missing from the averages of the local residents' characteristics.

Table 14.1 Percentage of students with specified characteristics with and without IDACI scores, England 2015

	Missing address	All students
FSM-eligible	21	14
SEN (any)	24	17
Joined school in last two years	8	3

Additionally, in order for the area measures to be accurate for all residents there must be accurate records on all other relevant factors for all residents as well, but if such data actually exists then it is clearly more appropriate to use the data from individuals (as in Table 14.1) and not only about where they live. Even for the cases that do exist, and do have addresses, much of the data is self-reported and so unverified anyway (such as ethnicity, via the Census of Population). It would also be possible to 'game' indicators based on postcode since wealthy families may be able to obtain an address in a disadvantaged neighbourhood for the purposes of increasing their child's university admissions chances (similar to what has happened in school choice and allocation processes). It is also not clear which address should be used to reflect childhood and current disadvantage—for mature students, the most recent or longest inhabited for younger students, and so on.

ACORN and MOSAIC are area measures based on smaller geographical units, such as 10–15 households, but the same issues arise. And in addition, both are commercial products and neither is freely available to universities without paying.

Another widespread indicator of possible disadvantage used by universities that should not be used is the nature of the school attended. Most of the same counter-arguments relevant to area indictors also apply to school-level indicators. Treating the modal characteristics of the students in a school, as though they were true of every individual in that school, is again an ecological fallacy. It is not clear whether it is the most recent school or the one attended for longest that is most relevant, and this is also open to games-playing (as when private pupils transfer to state-funded sixth forms).

One apparently simple school characteristic is its type, and the most common distinction is drawn between applicants from state-maintained and fee-paying schools. But using categories such as private school conflates the major public schools with cheap small sectarian schools. It ignores the fact that many special schools are private, and some mainstream private schools have attractive facilities for children with SEN. In fact, special schools more generally appear to provide a good example of a school type with lower attaining students and low progression to HE, but they are largely ignored for CA purposes. This approach does not really relate to mature students, or those educated outside mainstream school settings, such as the home-schooled. And it disadvantages the small number of private school attendees who could be among the poorest in society, and attending via a free place, bursary, scholarship or assisted place. In any year there are a considerable number of students in NPD with unknown schools (6532 out of a cohort of 590,000 in 2015). Where data are available, these students with missing schools are clearly more disadvantaged, and have markedly lower than average attainment and progress. There is no clear peer-mix effect.

So, as with area of residence, type of school attended is not justified as a contextual indicator, and similar problems arise for the average level of attainment, average poverty, and prior HE participation rates in a school. Using a modal characteristic for an area or school can be a very misleading guide to individual disadvantage, and can lead to at least as much injustice as the stratification that WP is intended to reduce.

Indicators that Are Not Clearly About Disadvantage

There are a number of possible indicators listed by advocates of CA that *are* about the individuals themselves, but are not necessarily indicative of disadvantage in education.

For UK residents applying to HE, the clearest 'non-traditional' route is that taken by mature students using prior experience as an alternative to KS5 or similar prior qualifications. First degree mature students are often, perhaps unintentionally, ignored in policy pronouncements and even research about WP to HE, which tends to focus on existing, traditional age full-time participants to the exclusion of all other relevant parties and comparators (Gorard 2013). In general, those with non-traditional entry qualifications tend to achieve higher degrees (Hoskins et al. 1997). Mature students also tend to do better after HE than their younger peers in terms of subsequent graduate employment and salaries (Woodfield 2011). What is not clear is why being older *per se* should be treated as disadvantaged.

Immigrant groups vary considerably in their access to and success in HE, and some face clear barriers (Erisman and Looney 2007). Recent immigrant status would currently have to be based on self-report and is not an indicator available to HEIs before decision on application. It is not clear that being a recent immigrant is necessarily an indication of educational or social disadvantage. A student from an English-speaking professional family moving to the UK from the US, for example, would not be considered disadvantaged but would be a recent immigrant.

A recent refugee or asylum seeker is, *ceteris paribus*, more likely to be disadvantaged than a recent immigrant more generally, but this is still not necessarily so. Currently, HEIs only receive this data from UCAS after an institution has made a decision on the application, and the data is based only on how applicants chose to classify and identify themselves in their UCAS applications. A substantial number select 'I prefer not to say', and so there would be considerable missing data as well as uncertainty if this were used for CA. Our review found no large-scale or authoritative evidence relevant to this indicator.

Having English as an additional language (EAL) can be an indicator of disadvantage given that instruction in the UK is generally in English. However, in most respects EAL students and the rest are very similar. EAL students are noticeably less likely to be recorded as having SEN but more likely to be non-White and to have arrived in their current school recently. They have lower than average KS2 results at primary age, but make considerably more progress than average, and have higher than average KS4 and KS5 results. They are then more likely to continue to KS5 (63% compared to 52% of first-language English speakers in 2008), and achieve good grades at A-level or equivalent. Being an EAL student is usually only a temporary disadvantage and for some individuals it is not even that. The NPD specifies the first language of the home or family, but a substantial minority of cases (9% or more) are missing a valid value in NPD. None of this makes EAL a good indicator for CA.

Participation by ethnic minorities, overall, but not necessarily in the more prestigious universities, is higher than might be expected from the target population (Chowdry et al. 2008; Gallagher et al. 2009). However, the level of degree completion is then sometimes lower even after age, prior attainment and subject of study are accounted for (Broecke and

Nicholls 2007). Black and Chinese minority students are most likely to have withdrawn from their course after one year (HEFCE 2013; Woodfield 2017). It would probably be necessary to disaggregate ethnic minority groups in order to use this indicator to widen participation in an effective manner. Some ethnic groups, such as Chinese, are well represented across the HE sector of the UK. Others, such as Black Caribbean origin students, are disproportionately in less selective or less prestigious HEIs, and others again such as travellers and White UK are under-represented in HE as a whole.

In NPD and the UK population census, missing ethnicity is the largest 'ethnic minority' classification. As with any indicator, the missing cases tend to be the most disadvantaged, with the lowest probability of continuing in education after the age of 16, and the lowest chance of any level of academic qualification at age 18 (Table 14.2). In general, ethnic minority students are more likely than the majority White students to continue to KS5, gain minimal A-level equivalent grades (EE+), and gain the kind of high grades needed for entry to the most selective universities (ABB+). On average, Black students are currently finding it hardest to convert participation into the highest grades.

It is not clear how much any disadvantage is about ethnicity itself and how much about it is acting as a proxy for other forms of disadvantage (Strand 2011). Some studies suggest that ethnicity has only a minor link to educational outcomes once other factors such as SES are accounted for (Gorard and See 2013), and others suggest that some apparently disadvantaged groups actually do better in some respects after controlling for social class and other factors (Van Dorn et al. 2006).

Table 14.2 Percentages of students continuing with post-16 education, by ethnicity, England 2008

	Any other	Asian	Black	Chinese	Mixed	Missing	White	Total
Continued post-16	61	67	58	84	55	49	51	53
Achieved EE+	51	57	48	77	47	41	44	45
Achieved CCC+	34	37	27	62	32	27	30	31
Achieved ABB+	23	25	16	50	23	19	22	22

Ethnicity does not have a clear legal definition, and even in official statistics such as NPD or the population census it can only be based on self-report. It has a large and growing number of categories, that either fail to capture the real variation or produce unwieldy schemes and tiny cell sizes (Williams and Husk 2012). The term is used in different and contradictory ways (Salway et al. 2010), based on common ancestry, memories of a shared past, a shared cultural identity which might include kinship, or religion, language, shared territory, nationality or physical appearance (Lee 2003). The classification is heavily dependent on the identification of sole ethnicities, with the mixed categories clearly intended to be for a minority. But it is hard to contend that there are many individuals who do not have a mixed ethnic origin of some kind. All of this does not make it a particularly reliable or valid indicator.

For all of the indicators above it is not clear that they are true indicators of disadvantage, although they will include some very disadvantaged applicants who should be picked up in other ways using more valid indicators.

Indicators Only Available for Applicants

At time of admission, universities can have access to a number of variables about individuals that could denote relative disadvantage from the application forms. Unfortunately, many of these are only available for applicants which means that we cannot tell whether any of the groups indicated are under- or over-represented in HE compared to the more general population of young people (for whom figures do not exist). They are also all only self-reported, and have considerable missing data even for the applicants. These indicators include the otherwise promising parental education, and parental occupation or social class. The proportion of HE applicants who did not state a parental (or other) occupation on their application has been growing over time to 26% of all HE applicants in 2007 (Harrison and Hatt 2009). This makes 'unknown' the largest social class group.

In general, indicators only available for the self-selected body of young people who enter and survive KS5 and then apply to a university in England are not to be preferred as a general solution to CA.

Individual Indicators with More Promise

In some respects, the indicator that an applicant has spent time living in care is not much better than some of those above. The indicator covers time spent by the applicant in local authority care, and is linked to the worst educational outcomes in the UK. This indicator has a relatively simple, binary and official definition, and where known this indicator is sent to universities with application data. However, at present the information is only self-declared by the candidate, and is otherwise unverified, and a lot of relevant data is missing or unclear. Such information is likely to yield both positive and negative misclassifications. It would be better if this data could be made available from official records to a responsible central authority. This indicator covers only a relatively small number of cases, and any that are verified could simply be tagged for CA.

Young people with SEN or disabilities tend to have lower average attainment and make lower average progress in any phase of schooling (Table 14.3). In 2015, no students had a missing value recorded for SEN (although there are an increasing number of missing values when going back through each prior year at school for these students). Not surprisingly, students with the most serious SENs have the lowest average attainment and make the least progress. Students with any SEN are clearly more disadvantaged than those without, on most available indicators, and this is especially so for students with statements.

Table 14.3 Mean attainment scores of students by SEN category, England 2015

	No SEN	SEN no statement	SEN with statement	Total
KS2 average points	21	17	11	20
KS1 to KS2 value-added	+0.22	−0.43	−0.65	+0.10
KS4 capped points	330	225	114	308

Table 14.4 Percentages of students continuing with post-16 education, by SEN, England 2008

	No SEN	SEN
Continued post-16	60	19
Achieved EE+	52	15
Achieved CCC+	36	8
Achieved ABB+	26	5

This means that SEN students will, on average, be less likely to proceed to HE. SEN students are much less likely than average to continue in education post-16, and even less likely to obtain the sort of qualifications permitting uncomplicated entry to HE under the current system (Table 14.4). 26% of non-SEN students achieved ABB+ at KS5 in 2008, compared to less than 3% of those with statements of SEN. Whatever provision for help those statements put in place it is clearly not enough to allow easy access to HE. All of this makes SEN a promising indicator for CA.

Compared to the school and more general population, students flagged as disabled are actually slightly over-represented in UK HE (Gorard 2008), are fairly evenly distributed across HEIs, and increasingly completing their first degrees successfully (Pumfrey 2008).

SEN is not a simple binary indicator and does not have a clear legal definition (Florian et al. 2004). It includes mental health difficulties, mobility issues, sensory impairment and unseen disabilities. A student with mild dyslexia should not be treated the same as one with both severe visual impairment and mobility problems. It would be fairer to disaggregate this indicator into a number of categories of risk concerning participation in HE, and the kinds of support HEIs provide after admittance. There are serious concerns about the accuracy of SEN labelling, whether in classification or recording (Douglas et al. 2012). Multiple challenges are often ignored in recording the most serious one or two for any individual (DfES 2003).

The accurate 'identification' of these challenges can itself be stratified by other indicators of relative disadvantage. Historically, SEN and especially the identification of learning or behavioural problems have been more prevalent among lower SES students. This stratification may be partly accurate, reflecting multiple disadvantages, but it may also be linked to differential diagnosis. Students in disadvantaged or more social segregated school settings are more likely to be diagnosed as having a behavioural disorder, for example, whereas those in more advantaged settings may be treated as being merely 'naughty' (Gorard and See 2013). However, this historical trend has changed with the rise of dyslexia and similar unseen disabilities. A disability statement based on dyslexia yields an increased chance in the competitive education system for the child (such as extra time in examinations), and it is clearly the middle-classes in the UK who have taken most advantage of this (Tomlinson 2012). An overall disability flag indicator, most especially a self-declared one, is therefore vulnerable to abuse. All of these issues mean that SEN is a promising CA indicator but cannot be adopted wholesale without further work.

Eligibility for free schools meals (FSM) relates to applicants from the poorest families in England, while they are at school—any family entitled to income support, income-based jobseekers allowance, child tax credit, the first four weeks of working tax credit following unemployment, the guaranteed element of state pension credit, employment and support allowance, and/or where part VI of the Immigration and Asylum Act 1999 applies. It is a reasonably secure and verified indicator of official relative poverty. Recording and reporting of it is a legal requirement for all state-funded schools, and the FSM-status of each child is held as part of the NPD to which HE institutions could have annual access. The measure is therefore available for nearly all relevant young people, irrespective of whether that person applies to HE or not. FSM is one of the most comprehensive and accurate measures of SES available.

It is clear that students eligible for FSM at any stage of schooling are more disadvantaged on average in all other respects as well. They are more likely to be recent arrivals, from ethnic minorities, with EAL, and special needs. FSM students have lower attainment at all stages of schooling, and they make less progress between Key Stages (Table 14.5), and the longer they have been eligible by age 16 the lower their attainment is.

Table 14.5 Mean scores of students by FSM, England 2015

	No FSM	FSM	Total
KS2 total points	41	35	40
KS4 capped points	319	243	308

Table 14.6 Percentages of students continuing with post-16 education, by FSM, England 2008

	Non-FSM	FSM
Continued post-16	56	31
Achieved EE+	48	25
Achieved CCC+	33	13
Achieved ABB+	25	8

Due to lower attainment at age 16, FSM students are far less likely to continue to KS5, and so apply to HE at age 18 (Table 14.6). They are less likely to obtain the minimum entry qualifications for HE, and far less likely to get the higher grades required by the most selective universities. FSM may be the best single indicator of relative disadvantage for use as a CA variable.

However, it is still not without some problems as an indicator (Boliver et al. 2016). For example, every year the NPD has around 11% of cases with unknown FSM status, of which around 7% are in fee-paying schools which do not have to complete the school census (Gorard 2012). A small number of children will be home-schooled or otherwise simply missing from the register, rather than in fee-paying schools. Some of these can be assumed to be among the poorest in society. The remaining 4% of students missing data on FSM-eligibility in state-funded schools would also be ignored and so disadvantaged by a system that used FSM as a context variable for HE admissions. It has been shown from what we do know about these students that they could be among the most disadvantaged in society—with the lowest known rate of qualification. Many are in special schools (while many of the rest are mobile students such as Travellers, or recent arrivals such as asylum seekers, perhaps without official papers). Given the level of inclusion of children with special needs in mainstream settings, those in special schools are more often those with very severe learning and other challenges. All of these groups could be among the most deserving of consideration in a contexualised admissions system, yet would be ignored if they were missing FSM data, and FSM was the criterion used.

Individual Indictors Currently Ignored

In England, almost all children attend school with an age cohort of whom the oldest was born on 1st September of one year, and the youngest was born almost a year later on 31st August of the following year. The precise age of a child or young person within their school year cohort has been shown to be strongly linked to their success in attainment, later life, and their wider personal development. This becomes a continuing problem, because although the relevance of an age gap of one year might seem less at age 18, the young person has by then had 12 or more years of schooling as the youngest, least mature, and maybe the smallest person in their year. The summer-born students are less likely to be picked for competitive sports and more likely to be bullied.

Students who are younger in the year are more likely to be labelled as having a special educational need (SEN). This is presumably because of their lower average attainment throughout their school career, which casts further doubt on the validity of SEN as an indicator. At every phase of schooling, older students have higher average attainment than younger students in almost direct proportion to their difference in age within their year group (Table 14.7). This is an inherent but probably unavoidable unfairness caused by an arbitrary date of entry to school.

Given that the level of recorded disadvantage is the same for each month of birth, only age can explain this systematic difference in attainment. The simplest way to deal with this would be to routinely age-standardise all attainment scores (Gorard 2015). Age would then be an easy to handle CA variable that would reduce unfairness for summer-born children (but perhaps not eliminate it entirely because of the enduring impact of early experiences). Age is a clear, valid and reliable indicator, collected officially, available from all applicants, and it can be easily

Table 14.7 Mean attainment scores of students by age in months (January 2015), England 2015

	184	185	186	187	188	189	190	191	192	193	194	195
KS2 points	19.5	19.7	19.8	19.9	19.9	20.1	20.3	20.1	20.2	20.4	20.6	20.7
KS4 capped	301	304	305	307	308	308	308	309	310	312	315	316

Table 14.8 Percentages of students continuing with post-16 education, by sex, England 2008

	Male	Female
Continued post-16	48.3	57.3
Achieved EE+	40.5	49.7
Achieved CCC+	26.3	35.3
Achieved ABB+	18.7	26.1

verified. Age is probably the single best CA variable available for use. Age in year is currently ignored because it is not seen as an issue for WP.

Male and female students are, as would be expected, very similar in levels of poverty, ethnic origin, first language, age in year, and school mobility. However, males are much more likely to be labelled as having SEN, and have markedly lower attainment results at all phases of schooling. Substantially fewer male than female students continue in education post-16, and fewer again attain any KS5 qualifications (Table 14.8). These differences cannot be explained by students' differential background, and if sex were almost any other characteristic it would already have been proposed and used widely for CA. The variable is a relatively clear one (perhaps the second clearest available after age), routinely collected and available to HEIs at time of admission. As with age, there is an argument that all attainment results should be sex-standardised, using student sex for CA. This would help to balance the intakes to HEIs better.

Conclusions

If we continue to use prior attainment to select students for HE then the HE system will inevitably have much of the same stratification as prior attainment patterns do. The problem is that students move through the phases of education becoming more socially stratified with every choice or transition, including the option to drop out of education entirely (Lucas 2001; Gorard and See 2009). CA could reduce this to some extent, if used wisely, and it is recognised that it cannot be based on invalid, unverified and partial indicators. Although the situation is different for different institutions and subject areas, the evidence from existing student data is that lowering standard admission offers by a few grades (at A-level or equivalent) would have only a very small impact on student retention and outcomes at selective universities (Boliver et al. 2017).

However, CA is not intended to be a replacement for work to reduce the impact of disadvantage on educational outcomes earlier in life. Many potential students do not even continue to KS5. This is where the key difference *must* be made.

Meanwhile, the safest and clearest indicators are the sex (male) and age in year (summer born) of a student. And, because they are unstratified by other factors such as poverty and ethnicity, using them for CA cannot introduce other unintended problems. But neither of these is currently considered in WP.

Otherwise, the best general indicator is eligibility for free school meals (poverty), and this is best computed as the number of years a student has been known to be eligible (Gorard 2016). A decision would have to be made about what to do with cases missing a value, perhaps by combining FSM and other indicators such as refugee status. Having a special educational need is also a promising indicator, but doubts are raised about its validity and it anyway covers a wide range of factors, some of which are already dealt with by the education system. Very few students registered as living in care continue in education post-16, and this indicator could be used safely and to advantage. The rest, including area measures, school type, performance relative to school, ethnicity and first language are generally not safe to use and may worsen representative participation in other ways.

Acknowledgements This work was funded by the ESRC: grant numbers ES/N012046/1and ES/N01166X/1.

References

Boliver, V., Gorard, S., & Siddiqui, N. (2016). Will the use of contextual indicators make UK HE admissions fairer? *Education Sciences*, 5(4), http://www.mdpi.com/2227-7102/5/4/306

Boliver, V., Gorard, S., Powell, M., & Moreira, T. (2017) *Mapping and evaluating the use of contextual data in undergraduate admissions in Scotland* (Report to the Scottish Funding Council).

Broecke, S. (2015). University rankings: Do they matter in the UK? *Education Economics, 23*(2), 137–161.

Broecke, S., & Nicholls, T. (2007) *Ethnicity and Degree Attainment* (Research Report no. 92). Department for Education and Skills, London. http://webarchive.nationalarchives.gov.uk/20130401151715/http://www.education.gov.uk/publications/eOrderingDownload/RW92.pdf

Chowdry, H., Crawford, C., Dearden, L., Goodman, A., & Vignoles, A. (2008). *Understanding the determinants of participation in higher education and the quality of institute attended: analysis using administrative data* (IFS Report). http://www.ifs.org.uk/publications/4279

Chowdry, H., Crawford, C., Dearden, L., Goodman, A., & Vignoles, A. (2013). Widening participation in higher education: analysis using linked data. *Journal of the Royal Statistical Society, 176*(Part 2), 431–457.

Clayton, M. (2012). On widening participation in higher education through positive discrimination. *Journal of Philosophy of Education, 46*(3), 414–431.

DfES. (2003). *Consultation: Classification of special education needs*. London: DfES.

Do, P., Parry, J., Mathers, J., & Richardson, M. (2006). Monitoring the widening participation initiative for access to medical school: Are present measures sufficient? *Medical Education, 40*(8), 750–758.

Douglas, G., Travers, J., McLinden, M., Robertson, C., Smith, E., Macnab, N., Powers, S., Guldberg, K., McGough, A., O'Donnell, M., & Lacey, P. (2012). *Measuring educational engagement, progress and outcomes for children with special educational needs: A review*. Trim, Ireland: National Council for Special Education (NCSE). http://ncse.ie/research-reports

Erisman, W., & Looney, S. (2007). *Opening the door to the American dream: Increasing higher education access and success for immigrants*. http://files.eric.ed.gov/fulltext/ED497030.pdf

Florian, L., Rouse, M., Black-Hawkins, K., & Jull, S. (2004). What can national data sets tell us about inclusion and pupil achievement? *British Journal of Special Education, 31*(3), 115–121.

Gallagher, J., Niven, V., Donaldson, N., & Wilson, N. (2009). Widening access? Characteristics of applicants to medical and dental schools, compared with UCAS. *British Dental Journal, 207*, 433–445.

Gill, T., & Benton, T. (2015). *The accuracy of forecast grades for OCR A levels* (Cambridge Assessment Statistics Report Series no.90). http://www.cambridgeassessment.org.uk/Images/243087-the-accuracy-of-forecast-grades-for-ocr-a-levels-in-june-2014.pdf

Gorard, S. (2008). Who is missing from higher education? *Cambridge Journal of Education, 38*(3), 421–437.

Gorard, S. (2012). Who is eligible for free school meals?: Characterising FSM as a measure of disadvantage in England. *British Educational Research Journal, 38*(6), 1003–1017.

Gorard, S. (2013). An argument concerning overcoming inequalities in higher education, Chapter 11. In N. Murray & C. Klinger (Eds.), *Aspirations, access and attainment in widening participation: International perspectives and an agenda for change*. London: Routledge.

Gorard, S. (2015, October 17). The easy way to help kids born in summer keep up at school. *New Scientist*, p. 29.

Gorard, S. (2016). *Challenging perceptions of a north south regional divide in school performance in England*, BERA Annual Conference, Leeds, September 2016.

Gorard, S., & See, B. H. (2009). The impact of socio-economic status on participation and attainment in science. *Studies in Science Education, 45*(1), 93–129.

Gorard, S., & See, B. H. (2013). *Overcoming disadvantage in education*. London: Routledge.

Gorard, S., with Adnett, N., May, H., Slack, K., Smith, E., & Thomas, L. (2007). *Overcoming barriers to HE*. Stoke-on-Trent: Trentham Books.

Gorard, S., Boliver, V., Siddiqui, N., & Banerjee, P. (2017a). *Which are the most suitable contextual indicators for use in widening participation to HE?* (Research Papers in Education). http://www.tandfonline.com/doi/pdf/10.1080/02671522.2017.1402083?needAccess=true

Gorard, S., Siddiqui, N., & Boliver, V. (2017b). An analysis of school-based contextual indicators for possible use in widening participation. *Higher Education Studies, 7*(2), 101–118.

Harrison, N., & Hatt, S. (2009). Knowing the 'unknowns'. *Journal of Further and Higher Education, 33*(4), 347–357.

Harrison, N., & McCraig, C. (2015). An ecological fallacy in higher education policy. *Journal of Further and Higher Education, 39*(6), 793–816.

HEFCE. (2013). Non-continuation rates at English HEIs: Trends for entrants 2005–06 to 2010–11. Available at: http://www.hefce.ac.uk/pubs/year/2013/201307/

Hoskins, S., Newstead, S., & Dennis, I. (1997). Degree performance as a function of age, gender, prior qualifications and discipline studies. *Assessment and Evaluation in Higher Education, 22*, 317–328.

Lee, C. (2003). Why we need to re-think race and ethnicity in educational research. *Educational Researcher, 32*(5), 3–5.

Lucas, S. (2001). Effectively maintained inequality: Education transitions, track mobility, and social background effects. *American Journal of Sociology, 106*(6), 1642–1690.

Moore, J., Mountford-Zimdars, A., & Wiggans, J. (2013). *Contextualised admissions: Examining the evidence.* Cheltenham: Supporting Professionalism in Admissions Programme.

Office for Fair Access. (2015). *Strategic Plan: 2015–2020.* Bristol: OFFA.

Pumfrey, P. (2008). Moving towards inclusion? The first-degree results of students with and without disabilities in higher education in the UK: 1998–2005. *European Journal of Special Needs Education, 23*(1), 31.

Salway, S., Allmark, P., Barley, R., Higinbottom, G., Gerrish, K., & Ellison, G. (2010). Researching ethnic inequalities. *Social Research Update, 58*, 1–4.

Strand, S. (2011). The limits of social class in explaining ethnic gaps in educational attainment. *British Educational Research Journal, 37*(2), 197–229.

Supporting Professionalism in Admissions. (2015). *SPA's use of contextualised admissions survey report 2015 (with HEDIIP).* Cheltenham: Supporting Professionalism in Admissions.

Tomlinson, S. (2012). The irresistible rise of the SEN industry. *Oxford Review of Education, 38*(3), 267–286.

Universities Scotland. (2016). *Futures not backgrounds, Edinburgh: Universities Scotland.* http://www.universities-scotland.ac.uk/wp-content/uploads/2016/09/10537-%E2%80%A2-Futures-Not-Backgrounds-web.pdf

Van Dorn, R., Bowen, G., & Blau, J. (2006). The impact of community diversity and consolidated inequality on dropping out of high school. *Family Relations, 55*, 105–118.

Williams, M., & Husk, K. (2012). Can we, should we, measure ethnicity? *International Journal of Social Research Methodology, 16*(4), 285–300.

Woodfield, R. (2011). Age and first destination employment from UK universities: Are mature students disadvantaged? *Studies in Higher Education, 36*(4), 409–425.

Woodfield, R. (2017). Undergraduate students who are required to withdraw from university: The role of ethnicity. *British Educational Research Journal.* https://doi.org/10.1002/berj.3259.

Yates, J., & James, D. (2013). The UK clinical aptitude test and clinical course performance at Nottingham: A prospective cohort study. *BMC Medical Education, 13*, 32. https://doi.org/10.1186/1472-6920-13-32.

15

Governmental Supports for Students in Turkey: Beneficiary Perspective on the Use of Financial and Social Support in Higher Education

Yasar Kondakci, Kadir Beycioglu, Yusuf İkbal Oldac, and Hanife Hilal Senay

Introduction

Ensuring adequate higher education provisions to disadvantaged students has been an ongoing discussion in several different disciplines such as sociology, political sciences, public administration and educational sciences. As a result, there has been an increasing number of calls to multiply and widen the services provided for disadvantaged students (Perna and Titus 2004; Richardson 2012; Shah et al. 2011). The issue of disadvantaged

---

This study was supported by Middle East Technical University's Scientific Research Funds (Project Code: BAP-05-02-2016-005)

Y. Kondakci (✉) • Y. İ. Oldac • H. H. Senay
Middle East Technical University, Ankara, Turkey
e-mail: kyasar@metu.edu.tr

K. Beycioglu
Dokuz Eylul University, Izmir, Turkey

© The Author(s) 2018
M. Shah, J. McKay (eds.), *Achieving Equity and Quality in Higher Education*, Palgrave Studies in Excellence and Equity in Global Education,
https://doi.org/10.1007/978-3-319-78316-1_15

students embodies a critical look at concepts of equity and social justice. In higher education, researchers have tried to identify the disadvantaged groups regarding students' access to universities and colleges (Atuahene and Owusu-Ansah 2013). In the context of education, race and ethnicity, sexual orientation, disabilities, culture and social class, gender, socio-economic status (SES), spatial and program-based disparities have been indicated as the key issues hindering education for certain groups in society (Gardner and Holley 2011; Grebennikov and Skaines 2008; Hofman and Van Den Berg 2003; Shah and Widin 2010; Swail et al. 2003). Despite the increasing interest in the issue of disadvantaged students, in many countries there are systemic or un-systemic practices hindering the access of disadvantaged students to higher education (Perna 2006; Perna and Titus 2004). Schendel and McCowan (2016) put forward that higher education systems around the globe face two important challenges: demands for equitable expansion and difficulties of maintaining quality during the expansion progress. According to the authors, while these challenges are hard to tackle in every country, these challenges are characteristically different in low- and middle- income countries.

Challenges in Higher Education of the Disadvantaged Students

Previous literature has identified several issues regarding educational provisions towards disadvantaged groups. First of all, limited access of the disadvantaged groups to higher education has been frequently articulated in the literature. Particularly, in developing countries the access of disadvantaged groups to higher education is a highly challenging task (Kondakci and Orucu 2016; Schendel and McCowan 2016). There are several problems in the access to higher education in developing countries among the disadvantaged groups. Firstly, the monetary limitations in these countries (especially in low-income ones) result in severe constraints in available public funding for the higher education system and possible cost-sharing with students and families. Atuahene and Owusu-Ansah (2013) stated that there are not enough universities in Ghana to provide education for all who are qualified for admission and this is another factor in the problem of access to higher education among disadvantaged groups in Ghana. Marginson (2016) stated that high participation in higher education systems is becoming universal around the globe. However, he added, it would not be adequate for low to middle income countries to just improve the quantitative participation to higher education institutions (HEIs) or just to ensure more egalitarian participation in terms of gender or underrepresented ethnic groups. He proposed that the difficult part is to regulate the relationship between educational inequality and socio-economic inequality and autonomous allocative social power for higher education and building egalitarian structures within it should be expanded to ensure educational services with adequate quality to disadvantaged groups.

The second problem in relation to access of disadvantaged groups is related to policies of HEIs. Several scholars argued that disadvantaged groups lack the social capital, which is necessary to gain access and successfully complete higher education study (Perna 2006; Perna and Titus 2004). As a result of this understanding, HEIs do not develop policies to attract the disadvantaged groups into their programs. They are concerned that participation of these groups, unless they are aided by additional support, will lower the quality of their provisions (Whiteford et al. 2013). According to this perspective, participation of the disadvantaged groups leads to expenditure of more resources because these groups potentially have lower performance and each repetition of class or grade level incurs more resources of the HEIs. Besides, this perspective argues that low capacity of the students will be reflected on the overall performance of the HEIs.

The third problem is related to the quality of the education disadvantaged students receive when they achieve access to higher education. Disadvantaged groups in developing countries are often left with the option of attending newly established HEIs (Shah et al. 2011). Schendel and McCowan (2016) indicated several dimensions of quality issues in the education of disadvantaged groups. Aside from budgetary issues, the inadequacy of qualified academic faculty poses another limitation to the expansion of high-quality HEIs. The lower levels of primary and secondary education in these countries plays a role in the high percentage of underprepared students entering tertiary education. Lastly, countries with fewer resources tend to be limited in their national autonomy because of the influence from external donors and supranational organizations. That being said, Schendel and McCowan (2016) proposed that neither equality nor quality without the other would effectively benefit society.

Limited access opportunities to quality programs negatively impacts the prospect of employability for the disadvantaged groups (Shah et al. 2011). In many countries, disadvantaged groups find access to newly established programs, which do not possess the necessary capacity for quality provision of higher education service (Shah et al. 2011). Since students coming from disadvantaged segments of society do not attend quality programs, the chances of finding a job after graduation are limited. For example, in Turkey, the teaching profession is commonly chosen by the low-income segment of society (Aksu et al. 2010); however, when they get their degrees they have very limited chances of being employed by state schools. According to the Ministry of Education in Turkey, there are approximately 350,000 teachers awaiting jobs while the total teacher needs in the country is approximately 67,000 (Hurriyet 2016).

Several different studies in different developing countries have validated the access, success, quality and employability issues of disadvantaged groups. Atuahene and Owusu-Ansah (2013) found gender, SES, spatial and program-based disparities as the key causes of inequalities in education in Ghana. The authors stated that the unemployment risk in Ghana arises as a problem for the students to repay the loans causing a fear of such financial aids. Chankseliani (2013) asserted that the rural participants perform lower in university entrance exams than the urban participants of the study in Georgia. Chin-Shan and Hui-Juan (2012) showed that family income, education and region significantly affect the higher education enrollments in Taiwan. Chin-Shan and Hui-Juan stated that in the education process, since the amount of government expenditure remains the same while the admission rates increase, the money spent per student decreases. The authors maintained that expansion in the number of graduates and the narrowing job market decreases the chances of the employability of graduates in Taiwan. Shamatov (2012) depicted how certain measures such as the National Scholarship Test and a centralized exam system bring additional challenges to promote equity in the higher education system of Kyrgyzstan. The standardized testing caused a rapid increase and perpetuated the disparities between high and low SES groups, and urban and rural segments of the society. Dias (2015) found that SES does not only affect student access to higher education but also the choice of program in Portugal. It appears that students with low income choose to study teacher training, management and nursing and health technologies while those with higher income mostly prefer law, fine arts, science and medicine. Such evidence is also found in the Turkish context. In their exploratory study of over 18,000 first year student teachers, Aksu et al. (2010) showed that Turkish student teachers are from middle–lower SES families in which mostly only the father works and that opportunity to find a job easily is one of the most stated reasons to choose teacher training programs. These results show that enrollment rates can be misleading when equity is concerned.

Remedies for the Challenges in Education of the Disadvantaged Groups

Disadvantaged students, if they find any access opportunity, start their higher education study in a deprived status and they do not possess equal opportunities for sustaining a successful study. Ensuring adequate higher education provisions with adequate quality has been a long discussion in the literature (Shah et al. 2011). Hence, there have been increasing calls to multiply the services provided for disadvantaged students (Perna and Titus 2004; Richardson 2012; Shiner and Modood 2002; Whiteford et al. 2013). Policies aiming at providing more support to students are necessary to eliminate any difference in their success which is based on their social background but not individual difference. As a result, eliminating any difference in success of the students which is caused by disadvantaged status originating from their ethnic, racial, social and cultural background, the geographical location and disability has been a big concern of governments. In many cases, countries employ multiple policies to serve disadvantaged groups. The belief that education can form socially just societies is not altogether true because higher education is a necessary factor for a more egalitarian society but not a sufficient one; therefore, policies should support higher education in its equalizing role with other programs (Marginson 2016). Therefore, governments develop and deliver solutions to deal with the disadvantaged status of these groups. These solutions largely focus on providing different forms of financial support to disadvantaged students, developing quantitative growth policies in higher education and advancing some quality oriented measures around academic practices; these are some of the most commonly articulated remedies towards higher education and employability of disadvantaged segments of society.

Financial Supports

Widening *financial and social supports* to students is a common social policy practice in many countries; particularly countries in which the social state or welfare state norm is still a strong state policy practice, providing support under different means is a common practice. Mainly in developing countries which follow quantity oriented growth policies in higher education these supports are necessary for students to make higher education affordable. Therefore, these countries need more comprehensive student support systems for sustaining higher education for disadvantaged groups of society. Scholarships and subsidized services (food, accommodation, travel, free health services etc.), exemption from tuition fees and other expenses are the most common forms of support provided to students. The high cost associated with higher education make these financial, material and social supports critical for sustaining the studies of disadvantaged groups at the higher education level.

Several scholars indicated the importance of financial supports for the students' academic and psychological well-being. Yavuzer et al. (2005) asserted that dependency on parents, grant/bursary opportunities and monthly income are some of the problems that students mostly suffer from and these problems may affect academic achievement and psychological/physiological health. Agasisti and Murtinu (2014) suggest that disadvantaged students who receive grants actually perform better compared to their peers who do not receive any grants. Melguizo et al.

(2016) depicted the effectiveness of a loan system in an increase of enrollment rates, decrease in dropout rates, and increase in academic outcomes among disadvantaged groups in Colombia.

Because of the positive impact of financial supports several scholars advocated extra financial supports and positive discrimination for disadvantaged students. Dias (2015) urged an increase in the grants and scholarships for disadvantaged students. As part of the financial support several countries adapted a positive discrimination towards financing the education of the disadvantaged. In the case of Taiwan, Chin-Shan and Hui-Juan (2012) advocated a balance between supply and demand in higher education, whereby the disadvantaged are supported, and other beneficiaries share the expenses in higher education. Marginson (2016) proposed a similar solution for financing disadvantaged students in higher education. According to Marginson (2016), if fees are charged, then there are loans that are adjusted accordingly with income and there is additional help for underrepresented groups. Bevc and Uršič (2008), in their analysis of funding, equity and efficiency of higher education, presented financial support to students as a complementary form of higher education funding. Financial supports to students have two forms; direct (fellowships, grants, families etc.) and indirect (meals, transport, reducing tuition fees etc.) forms. Their discussion explains that removing tuition fees as a form of funding higher education can be considered an efficient and equitable way of providing education only when states provide other sources of support, especially direct financial supports since tuition fees constitute only a small part of higher education costs for students. Melguizo et al. (2016) advocated a loan system for higher education of the socio-economically disadvantaged groups in Colombia, which, in their perspective, may have a significant role in helping countries with emerging economies.

Quantitative Growth Policy in Higher Education

The problems associated with disadvantaged groups' access to higher education (Keohane 2006) push the governments to develop policies aiming at widening the capacity of their higher education systems to ensure access of these groups into the higher education system (Whiteford et al. 2013). *Quantitative* growth policies in higher education are not specifically developed for the disadvantaged students. However, especially in developing and semi-developed countries (e.g., India, Brasil, Mexico, PRC and Turkey) there is a constantly growing demand for higher education among the disadvantaged segments of society. In many developing countries, disadvantaged groups suffer most from the limited number of HEIs and restricted capacity of these HEIs. With quantitative growth policies governments provide education for all who are qualified for admission. As a result, students with different social, cultural, economic and ethnic backgrounds find opportunity to access higher education. These quantitative measures are expected to be inclusive and a remedy for access of disadvantaged groups to higher education. Such measures are applied in Ghana (Atuahene and Owusu-Ansah 2013), and Turkey (Kondakci and Orucu 2016) and have resulted in growth in the number of HEIs and students at higher education level.

Quality Oriented Measures

Recently there have been increasing concerns about the quality of the higher education programs. The quality issue has been tackled as a measure for developing necessary skills during study experience, which may positively impact their chances of employability after graduation (Whiteford et al. 2013). Particularly in countries where aggressive quantitative growth policies were applied, higher education systems have been criticized for undermining quality and not ensuring employability of disadvantaged groups (Kondakci and Orucu 2016). According to McCowan (2016), quantitative oriented remedies may end up with increased stratification related to the prestige and quality of HEIs. Based on his analysis of Brazil, England and Kenya, the author proposed three principles to understand equity of access to higher education: availability, accessibility and horizontality. Availability is about "the overall number of places available, as well as the existence of adequate facilities, teaching staff and so forth." (McCowan 2016, p. 658). Accessibility is related to how accessible these available places are. Lastly, horizontality is about the egalitarian accessibility to HEIs. It is about preventing the hierarchy of prestige among universities with disadvantaged students confined to the less prestigious ones. Marginson (2016) raised the same concern and urged for policies supporting strong second-tier universities to ensure quality mass higher education. As a result, at a micro level, rigorous learning and autonomous institutions are valued, and assessment and selection are transparent and free from manipulations by strong groups or families to ensure the social mobility of low-SES students (Marginson 2016).

Other scholars advocated an inclusive curriculum, more academic support and guidance for disadvantaged groups as measures of ensuring equality. Scheurich and Skrla (2003) argued that education systems typically serve middle and upper classes and ignore disadvantaged groups. In particularl, students from high socio economic segments of society possess higher readiness for higher education. As a result, advantaged students develop more realistic and informed orientation during their studies. On the contrary, the case for disadvantaged students is more complicated as they lack such readiness. Therefore, realizing the potential of disadvantaged students largely depends on providing guidance and support for reinforcing their academic acquisitions (Trotter and Roberts 2006).

The Context: Turkey

Turkey is one of the country contexts which has been experiencing the stated problems and solutions in higher education in different forms. Although Turkey has been shifting its economic status from developing towards a semi-developed one, the issue of providing higher education opportunities to disadvantaged students and ensuring their transition to economy is still a challenging issue. Therefore, two goals have been guiding higher education in Turkey since the 1980s: firstly, building the capacity of its higher education system by pursuing an aggressive quantitative growth policy and secondly, investing in the quality of its HEIs. Since 1980, parallel to the trends and developments in other developing countries, Turkey has been following quantitative growth policies in higher education, which have resulted in an increased number of HEIs, academics and students (Gunay and Gunay 2011). The establishment of private universities (so-called foundation universities) is a part of the quantitative growth approach in Turkey. Despite these investments Turkey has accomplished 27.5% of schooling among 25–34-year olds, one of the lowest in OECD countries (OECD 2017). More importantly, the quantitative growth approaches in Turkey do not consider the challenges specific to the disadvantaged students. This mainly related to the transition system to higher education. Turkey employs a centralized exam system in recruiting students to higher education programs. Evidently students from a high socio-economic background and living in urban settings perform higher than the other students in getting access to high quality programs in the country. In Turkey, the centralized education and exam systems provide advantages to culturally and economically advantaged groups but constantly work against the disadvantaged ones.

Another issue in the quantitative growth of higher education in Turkey is related to access of disadvantaged students to quality programs and joining economic life after graduation (Kondakci and Orucu 2016). As discussed, in developing countries, the side issues associated with the quantitative policies in terms of granting access to quality programs and ensuring access to the job market after graduation for disadvantaged students is even more challenging. Like several other developing countries, in Turkey the quantitative approach is weak in ensuring social and economic inclusion of the disadvantaged groups. Although the number of HEIs and programs are multiplied, the number of quality programs remains limited. Access for disadvantaged groups to quality programs is even more limited (Kondakci and Orucu 2016). The well-known motto that equal policies do not ensure equality in higher education is still very valid in the Turkish higher education context.

Turkey has introduced financial supports in several forms to higher education students. The most common forms of these supports are limited amounts of scholarship, exemption from or reduced fees for certain services (e.g., accommodation, transportation) and a no-tuition fee policy. It is important to note that since the scholarships are reimbursed with certain levels of interest to the government after graduation, this financial support can be considered as a governmental loan rather than a true scholarship. Besides, in 2012 Turkish government stopped charging tuition fees to regular students both at graduate and undergraduate levels, though they continue to pay for some items related to their studies (e.g., books and materials, accommodation, meals, in some case fees for using sports facilities etc.). We argue that two considerations governing these financial supports weaken the impact of these policies for the disadvantaged students. First, governmental supports are delivered to almost all applicants without rating the students according to their needs and providing differentiated types and amounts of support. The scholarships, supports and subsidies are not delivered on the basis of need; rather on the basis of merit though it is argued that academic success does not show the potential of the students (Whiteford et al. 2013). Second, "small amount to every student" rather than "complete coverage of expenses of the disadvantaged ones" is another issue in the financial support of the Turkish government. Therefore, the amount of the scholarship is extremely limited compared to the total expenses of an individual student.

Issues in its quantitative policy, challenges in improving the quality of the system and limited financial support, make the Turkish higher education system a challenging one for disadvantaged groups. Therefore, additional policies towards ensuring access of these groups to quality programs, widening the services during their studies, and ensuring their employability after graduation is necessary.

Purpose Statement

As discussed, there have been increasing calls to enrich and multiply the support towards higher education students in Turkey. However, to what extent these financial and social supports serve their purposes has not been widely investigated with first hand data. Further, the direct and indirect role of these contributions in the careers of the students has not been studied. This study aims to reveal the perception of higher education level students on the effectiveness of financial supports provided by the government for their access to higher education, facilitating their study experience and contributing to their employability.

Method

This study was designed as a survey study. The sample of the study was purposively limited to the faculty of education students because of the background and status of these student groups in Turkey. Large scale studies conducted with pre-service teacher candidates suggest the students attending these faculties are coming from socio-economically disadvantaged segments of society. As stated earlier, in their exploratory study of over 18,000 first year student teachers, Aksu et al. (2010) showed that Turkish student teachers are from middle–lower SES families in which mostly only the father works and that opportunity to find a job easily is one of the most stated reasons to choose teacher training programs. The strong empirical evidence suggests that pre-service teacher candidates form an ideal group representing disadvantaged students in higher education in Turkey to investigate the perceived role of financial and social supports in their study and post-study experiences.

A self-developed survey with three different sections was prepared for data collection. The first part of the survey covers questions about the background of the students. The second section of the survey covers ten items on their perception of various supports (such as monetary support, accommodation, travel and academic material support) provided by the government. The final section includes three items on their perception about the role of these supports in their access to higher education and in their employability after graduation. Using a convenient sampling method, data from 773 students studying at ten different public universities in Turkey were collected.

Results

Of all the participants, 71.3% were female and 28.7% were male. The age of participants ranged from 17 to 38; however, most of the participants (90.5%) were in the range of 18–23. Almost all the participants were single (98.7%). Only 1.3% of the participants were married. The participants of the study were studying at faculties of education in 11 public universities in Turkey. Participants were studying in a wide range of areas. The distribution of the participants according to their study areas is provided in Table 15.1.

Further, the participants were mostly first-graders (48.1%) then fourth-graders (27.4%), third-graders (15.1%) and second-graders (9.2%), respectively.Most of the participants were graduates of public high schools (97.3%), the rest being graduates of private high schools (2.7%). When asked about their residence prior to their university experience, the majority of them were living in an urban area. Only 9.1% of the participants have a rural background. Among the participants, 70.4% stated that the university they study at is located in a different city to their hometown.

Table 15.1 The distribution of participants according to their study areas

Study areas	f	%
Primary school math teaching	138	17.9
English language teaching	124	16.0
Turkish language teaching	93	12.0
Secondary school sciences teaching	75	9.7
Guidance and psychological counselling teaching	68	8.8
Social studies teaching	66	8.5
Fine arts teaching	42	5.4
History teaching	31	4.0
Religious culture and moral knowledge teaching	19	2.5
Computer education and instructional technology	17	2.2
Classroom teacher	15	1.9
Special education	13	1.7
Preschool education	11	1.4
Geography teaching	7	0.9
Secondary school math teaching	7	0.9
Primary school sciences teaching	6	0.8
Chemistry teaching	4	0.5
Physics	2	0.3
Turkish language and literature	1	0.1
Other	28	3.6
Not specified	6	0.7
Total	773	100.0

When asked about their mothers' education levels, the group cumulate on primary school diploma (47.5%). The fathers' education levels were slightly higher; however, the primary school diploma is still the most frequent level of education (33%) among the participants' fathers. The data reveals that most of the participants' mothers are housewives (81.9%) while the fathers are either retired (28.7%) or civil servants (16.9%). The results on familial background indicate the disadvantaged status of these participants.

The students indicated that they had one or a combination of the following to finance their studies: familial support (73%), governmental scholarship (62%), part-time job (9.6%) and full-time job (6.2%). Evidently, significant numbers of the participants rely on governmental support in the form of scholarships to finance their expenses. When asked about the scholarship provider, the participants reported that they received governmental scholarships (51.1%) or scholarships from private organizations (6.2%) while 16.4% stated that they did not receive any scholarships at all. On the other hand, the participants are exempt from tuition fees, as all other students studying in public HEIs in Turkey. As the focus of this study, the governmental scholarships are also distinguished as scholarships provided by the university and other governmental institutions. The study showed that participants receive more scholarships from governmental institutions (71.4%) than their university (26.9%). Among governmental support, the most received scholarship is monetary (55.2%), which is followed by accommodation (dormitory) (11.5%) and meal support (4.7%). As for the scholarships provided by the university, the results show that 15.8% of the participants received monetary scholarships and 6.3% received accommodation scholarships while only 4.8% reported meal support.

In the second part of the survey data, analysis revealed the perception of the students about the role of financial supports they receive for their higher education study. Mean and standard deviation values of the 6-point Likert-type items in the second part of the survey are provided in Table 15.2 and frequency distribution of these items is provided in Table 15.3. The students found the role of supports extremely weak in their choices of the field for higher education study. The support is equally

Table 15.2 Mean and standard deviation regarding participant perceptions on the role of governmental supports in access to and quality life experience during higher education

	N	M	SD
It enables me to study in a city other than my hometown	773	3.75	2.28
It comforts my life as a student	773	3.75	1.98
It provides me with healthy nutrition	773	3.52	1.97
It ensures safe and healthy accommodation	773	3.85	2.03
It helps me to participate in cultural (movie, theater etc.) activities	773	3.57	2.06
It helps me to participate in personal growth activities	773	3.48	2.05
It helps me to participate in activities such as sports, hobbies and traveling	773	3.41	2.08
It motivated me to pursue higher education in the field of education/teaching	773	3.12	2.35
It helps me to actively participate in student clubs	773	3.29	2.17
It makes materials such as course books more affordable for me	773	3.82	2.08

weak when it comes to facilitate their academic and social lives during their study. In the open-ended section of the survey the participants advanced comments indicating the fact that governmental supports and scholarships are not significant in financing their studies. More importantly these supports are not instrumental in advancing their skills and contributing to their intellectual growth.

The final section of the survey assessed participants' perceptions on the role of supports in their access to higher education and their contribution to employability after graduation. Mean and standard deviation values of the 6-point Likert-type items in the last part of the survey are provided in Table 15.4 and frequency distribution of these items is provided in Table 15.5. The responses of the participants indicated the non-significant role of the governmental supports in their access to higher education. Of the participants, 29.1% stated that these supports did not play any role in their access to higher education. Likewise, the majority of the participants expressed their belief that these supports do not play any role in employability (41.8%) or building the skills contributing to their professional careers (32.2%).

Table 15.3 Frequency distribution of participant perceptions on the role of governmental support in access to and quality of life experience during higher education

	(1) f (%)	(2) f (%)	(3) f (%)	(4) f (%)	(5) f (%)	(6) f (%)	Not applicable f (%)
It enables me to study in a city other than my hometown	223 (28.8)	60 (7.8)	97 (12.5)	84 (10.9)	53 (6.9)	128 (16.6)	128 (16.6)
It comforts my life as a student	154 (19.9)	81 (10.5)	131 (16.9)	117 (15.1)	83 (10.7)	141 (18.2)	66 (8.5)
It provides me with healthy nutrition	162 (21.0)	114 (14.7)	145 (18.8)	111 (14.4)	73 (9.4)	92 (11.9)	76 (9.8)
It ensures safe and healthy accommodation	149 (19.3)	78 (10.1)	127 (16.4)	113 (14.6)	93 (12.0)	120 (15.5)	93 (12.0)
It helps me to participate in cultural (movie, theater etc.) activities	181 (23.4)	112 (14.5)	108 (14.0)	99 (12.8)	85 (11.0)	109 (14.1)	79 (10.2)
It helps me to participate in personal growth activities	192 (24.8)	105 (13.6)	121 (15.7)	102 (13.2)	83 (10.7)	86 (11.1)	84 (10.9)
It helps me to participate in activities such as sports, hobbies and traveling	205 (26.5)	117 (15.1)	112 (14.5)	91 (11.8)	74 (9.6)	94 (12.2)	80 (10.3)
It motivated me to pursue higher education in the field of education/teaching	346 (44.8)	67 (8.7)	59 (7.6)	64 (8.3)	40 (5.2)	81 (10.5)	116 (15.0)
It helps me to actively participate in student clubs	245 (31.7)	112 (14.5)	97 (12.5)	92 (11.9)	49 (6.3)	76 (9.8)	102 (13.2)
It makes materials such as course books more affordable for me	168 (21.7)	78 (10.1)	110 (14.2)	97 (12.5)	97 (12.5)	137 (17.7)	86 (11.1)

1 = completely disagree; *6* = completely agree

Table 15.4 Mean and standard deviation values regarding participant perceptions on the role of governmental supports in their access to higher education and their contribution for employability after graduation

	N	M	SD
What is the role of bursaries and supports that you receive in terms of access to higher education?	773	3.23	1.84
What is the role of bursaries and supports that you receive in terms of employment opportunities after graduation?	773	2.61	1.73
What is the role of bursaries and supports that you receive in terms of building the skills, knowledge and abilities contributing to your professional careers?	773	2.93	1.76

Table 15.5 Frequency distribution of participant perceptions on the role of governmental supports in their access to higher education and their contribution to employability after graduation

	(1) f (%)	(2) f (%)	(3) f (%)	(4) f (%)	(5) f (%)	(6) f (%)
What is the role of bursaries and supports that you receive in terms of access to higher education?	225 (29.1)	79 (10.2)	119 (15.4)	126 (16.3)	93 (12.0)	131 (16.9)
What is the role of bursaries and supports that you receive in terms of employment opportunities after graduation?	323 (41.8)	103 (13.3)	114 (14.7)	100 (12.9)	51 (6.6)	82 (10.6)
What is the role of bursaries and supports that you receive in terms of building the skills, knowledge and abilities contributing to your professional careers?	249 (32.2)	106 (13.7)	140 (18.1)	103 (13.3)	76 (9.8)	99 (12.8)

1 = completely disagree; *6* = completely agree

Discussion and Conclusions

The results of the study showed that the effectiveness of all forms of governmental supports remains limited in access to higher education, in survival during their studies and in transition to the work life among pre-service teacher candidates in Turkey. The results revealed that students find the role of supports weak in their choices of field for higher education study. The support was equally weak when it comes to facilitating their academic and social lives during their study. In the open-ended section of the survey the participants advanced comments indicating the fact that governmental supports and scholarships are needed but not effective enough in financing their studies. More importantly, in the opinion of the participants, these supports are not instrumental in advancing their skills and contributing to their intellectual growth and their employability.

These results show that there is a huge gap between what is aimed by the governmental support system and what is realized from the perspective of the beneficiaries. There are two possible reasons behind the perceived ineffectiveness of governmental supports for the students. As stated already, in Turkey, the scholarships, supports and subsidies are not delivered on the basis of need; rather on the basis of merit, which grant support to every student or partly on the basis of academic success. However, it is argued that academic success does not indicate the potential of the students (Whiteford et al. 2013). The second reason behind the perceived weakness of governmental supports is related to the amount of support. Compared to the total amount of their expenditures, governmental supports remain extremely limited. Ergen (2013) stated that grants and bursaries mees 72% of the needs among low income students in Turkey. However, this still does not seem to eliminate the differences between high income and low-income groups because the study also reveals that though grants and loans are mostly provided for low income students, high income groups also benefit from them.

These results are quite compatible with the findings in different country contexts (e.g., Callender 2010; Callender and Wilkinson 2013). Callender (2010) proposed that the government's intention to improve fair access through bursaries and scholarships may not always align with the actual allocation of them. While they sometimes helped improve fairness of access to HEIs, there have been occasions where bursaries and scholarships perpetuated or even exacerbated the inequities among HEIs. To the author, bursaries and scholarships may have an opposite effect on fairness of access when the government does not make an adjustment for differing regions in terms of living costs and when students with similar financial needs are provided with highly differing awards from the HEIs they are attending regardless of the similarities in living costs. Callender

(2010) concluded that bursaries and scholarships have been used more for the benefit of HEIs than for the needy students since they are used as a competitive means for shaping the student composition rather than supporting students in disadvantage.

The growing disparities in society suggest that disadvantaged groups will even be more adversely affected in access to higher education and building necessary personal and professional skills for ensuring employability. Therefore, social norms need to be put forward in governmental policies to ensure access to and benefit from higher education among disadvantaged groups of the society. Landry and Neubauer (2016) verified the need for a significant student support system even in developed countries. The authors stated that as a result of neoliberal policies in the US, there has been a decrease in grants available to students in need and in direct funding provided by governments to public universities, which ended up as a "student loan crisis". According to the authors, the failure in alignment of financial aid is not only a problem but also a result of a dilemma regarding the conflicting goals of higher education, which are "*"upward mobility"*, *"economic growth"* and *"incapability to sufficiently educate graduates"*. The growth rate of the economy is not able to follow up with the increase in the number of graduates while social and cultural needs that emerge as a result of neoliberalism and globalization require more than what higher education currently provides. Therefore, Landry and Neubauer (2016) conclude that unless such conflict is perceived, there is no way to entirely discern how higher education goals such as equality, access or equity can be best achieved. A similar call is advanced by Hillman (2011) as well. Hillman (ibid.) asserted that because of the hardships of using either a pure merit-based or a pure need-based strategy for designing aid programs, then a hybrid approach with four quadrants denoting four strategies was proposed. Along with the purely merit- and need-based strategies, the model proposed primarily need-based with a merit-based component and primarily merit-based with a need-based component. The author asserted that any aid provider can make use of this conceptual framework to design their aid program accordingly with their ethical and pragmatic concerns. The author also added that primarily need-based with a merit-based component could be the best option to enhance equal educational opportunity and at the same time to appease the pressure coming from neoliberal policies.

References

Agasisti, T., & Murtinu, S. (2014). Grants in Italian university: A look at the heterogeneity of their impact on students' performances. *Studies in Higher Education, 5079*(December), 1–27. https://doi.org/10.1080/03075079.2014.966670.

Aksu, M., Demir, C. E., Daloglu, A., Yildirim, S., & Kiraz, E. (2010). Who are the future teachers in Turkey? Characteristics of entering student teachers. *International Journal of Educational Development, 30*(1), 91–101. https://doi.org/10.1016/j.ijedudev.2009.06.005.

Atuahene, F., & Owusu-Ansah, A. (2013). A descriptive assessment of higher education access, participation, equity, and disparity in Ghana. *SAGE Open, 3*, 1–16. https://doi.org/10.1177/2158244013497725.

Bevc, M., & Uršič, S. (2008). Relations between funding, equity, and efficiency of higher education. *Education Economics, 16*(3), 229–244. https://doi.org/10.1080/09645290802338037.

Callender, C. (2010). Bursaries and institutional aid in higher education in England: Do they safeguard and promote fair access? *Oxford Review of Education, 36*(1), 45–62. https://doi.org/10.1080/03054980903518910.

Callender, C., & Wilkinson, D. (2013). Student perceptions of the impact of bursaries and institutional aid on their higher education choices and the implications for the national scholarship programme in England. *Journal of Social Policy, 42*(2), 281–308.

Chankseliani, M. (2013). Rural disadvantage in Georgian higher education admissions: A mixed-methods study. *Comparative Education Review, 57*(3), 424–456. https://doi.org/10.1086/670739.

Chin-Shan, L., & Hui-Juan, C. (2012). Education equity in the process of the massification of Taiwan's higher education. *Chinese Education & Society, 45*(5), 99–111. https://doi.org/10.2753/CED1061-1932450508.

Dias, D. (2015). Has massification of higher education led to more equity? Clues to a reflection on Portuguese education arena. *International Journal of Inclusive Education, 19*(2), 103–120. https://doi.org/10.1080/13603116.2013.788221.

Ergen, H. (2013). Uncertainties and risks determining individual demand for higher education: A sample from Mersin University. *Egitim ve Bilim, 38*(169), 433–446.

Gardner, K. S., & Holley, A. K. (2011). Those invisible barriers are real: The progression of first-generation students through doctoral education. *Equity and Excellence in Education, 44*(1), 77–92.

Grebennikov, L., & Skaines, I. (2008). University of Western Sydney students at risk: Profile and opportunities for change. *Journal of Institutional Research, 14*(10), 58–70.

Gunay, D., & Gunay, A. (2011). 1933'den günümüze Türk Yükseköğretiminde niceliksel gelişmeler. *Yükseköğretim ve Bilim Dergisi, 1*(1), 1–22. https://doi.org/10.5961/jhes.2011.001.

Hillman, N. (2011). The ethical dimensions of awarding financial aid. *Tertiary Education and Management, 17*(1), 1–16. https://doi.org/10.1080/13583883.2011.552629.

Hofman, A., & Van Den Berg, M. (2003). Ethnic-specific achievement in Dutch higher education. *Higher Education in Europe, 28*(3), 371–389.

Hurriyet. (2016). *Atanmayı bekleyen öğretmen sayısı 350 bine ulaştı* [Teachers awaiting appointment reaches 350 thousands]. http://www.hurriyet.com.tr/atanmayi-bekleyen-ogretmen-sayisi-350-bine-ulasti-40098572. Accessed on 22 Aug 2017.

Keohane, O. N. (2006). *Higher ground: Ethics and leadership in a modern university*. Durham: Duke University Press.

Kondakci, Y., & Orucu, D. (2016). Tertiary schooling patterns and disadvantaged groups in Turkey. In G. Whiteford & M. Shah (Eds.), *Bridges, pathways and transitions: International innovations in widening participation* (pp. 209–227). Sidney: Elsevier.

Landry, L., & Neubauer, D. (2016). The role of the government in providing access to higher education: The case of government-sponsored financial aid in the US. *Journal of Education and Work, 29*(1), 64–76. https://doi.org/10.1080/13639080.2015.1049027.

Marginson, S. (2016). The worldwide trend to high participation higher education: Dynamics of social stratification in inclusive systems. *Higher Education, 72*(4), 413–434. https://doi.org/10.1007/s10734-016-0016-x.

McCowan, T. (2016). Three dimensions of equity of access to higher education. *Compare: A Journal of Comparative and International Education, 46*(4), 645–665. https://doi.org/10.1080/03057925.2015.1043237.

Melguizo, T., Sanchez, F., & Velasco, T. (2016). Credit for low-income students and access to and academic performance in higher education in Colombia: A regression discontinuity approach. *World Development, 80*, 61–77. https://doi.org/10.1016/j.worlddev.2015.11.018.

OECD. (2017). *Population with tertiary education* (indicator). doi: https://doi.org/10.1787/0b8f90e9-en. Accessed on 18 Jan 2017.

Perna, L. W. (2006). Studying college access and choice: A proposed conceptual model. In İ. J. C. Smart (Ed.), *Higher education handbook of theory and research* (Vol. XXI, pp. 99–157). Amsterdam: Springer.

Perna, L. W., & Titus, M. A. (2004). Understanding differences in the choice of college attended. *The Review of Higher Education, 27*(4), 501–525.

Richardson, E. T. J. (2012). The attainment of White and ethnic minority students in distance education. *Assessment and Evaluation in Higher Education, 37*(4), 393–408.

Schendel, R., & McCowan, T. (2016). Expanding higher education systems in low- and middle-income countries: The challenges of equity and quality. *Higher Education, 72*(4), 407–411. https://doi.org/10.1007/s10734-016-0028-6.

Scheurich, J., & Skrla, L. (2003). *Leadership for equity and excellence: Creating high-achievement classroom, schools, and districts*. Thousand Oaks: Corwin Press.

Shah, M., & Widin, J. (2010). Indigenous students' voices: Monitoring indigenous student satisfaction and retention in a large Australian University. *Journal of Institutional Research, 15*(1), 28–41.

Shah, M., Lewis, I., & Fitzgerald, R. (2011). The renewal of quality assurance in Australian higher education: The challenge of balancing academic rigor, equity and quality outcomes. *Quality in Higher Education, 17*(3), 265–278.

Shamatov, D. (2012). The impact of standardized testing on university entrance issues in Kyrgyzstan. *European Education, 44*(1), 71–92. https://doi.org/10.2753/EUE1056-4934440104.

Shiner, M., & Modood, T. (2002). Help or hindrance? Higher education and the route to ethnic equality. *British Journal of Sociology of Education, 23*(2), 209–232.

Swail, W. S., Redd, K. E., & Perna, L. W. (2003). Retaining minority students in higher education. *ERIC Higher Education Report, 30*(2), 1–187.

Trotter, E., & Roberts, A. C. (2006). Enhancing the early student experience. *Higher Education Research and Development, 25*(4), 371–386.

Whiteford, G., Shah, M., & Nair, C. S. (2013). Equity and excellence are not mutually exclusive: A discussion of academic standards in an era of widening participation. *Quality Assurance in Education, 21*(3), 299–310.

Yavuzer, H., Meşeci, F., Demir, İ., & Sertelin, Ç. (2005). Günümüz üniversite gençliğinin sorunları [Current problems of university students]. *Hasan Ali Yücel Eğitim Fakültesi Dergisi, 1*(*1*), 79–91.

Index[1]

A

Academic identity, 53, 61–63
Academic rigour, ix
Academic standards, vii, ix, xi, xii, 99, 190
Academic support, 4, 10, 126, 182, 247, 252, 253, 255, 335
Access, xiii, xv, 2, 7, 8, 14–16, 18, 28, 54, 59, 63–65, 75, 86, 89, 97, 98, 104, 112, 114, 121, 125, 126, 136, 138, 146, 148, 149, 160, 174, 186, 188, 190, 205–207, 209, 219–233, 235, 236, 238–243, 247, 250–253, 266, 269, 273, 276, 288, 292, 294–296, 301, 314, 316, 318, 319, 329, 331, 333, 336–338, 341–344
access and equity trends, vii, ix–xi, 137, 182, 208, 289, 291, 293, 328, 330, 334, 345
Accessibility, 52, 90, 267, 334, 335
Active learning, 54
Admission, xii, xiv, 3, 32, 119, 123, 124, 127–131, 146, 151–154, 159, 179, 180, 186–189, 200, 202, 205, 207, 209–213, 221, 247–250, 253, 262, 270, 272, 276, 293, 294, 296–298, 308–310, 312, 316, 320, 322, 323, 329, 330, 334
  models of, 138, 158, 301
Affirmative action, xiii, 219–233, 296
Agency (student), 53, 176, 240, 262

---

[1] Note: Page numbers followed by 'n' refer to notes.

© The Author(s) 2018
M. Shah, J. McKay (eds.), *Achieving Equity and Quality in Higher Education*, Palgrave Studies in Excellence and Equity in Global Education, https://doi.org/10.1007/978-3-319-78316-1

American Educational Research Association (AERA), 235, 236, 256
Application rates, 146, 278–279
Aptitude tests, 145, 155, 156, 207, 209, 211
Aspirations, vii, xi, 30, 67, 68, 74, 146, 151, 153, 271, 277, 291, 297
  aspiration-raising, 60
Assessment
  accessible assessment practices, 52, 58, 86, 190, 335
  inclusive, xii, 54, 73, 84, 91
Australian higher education, vii, xii, 91, 289
Australian widening participation
  agenda, ix, x, xii, xiii, xv, 120
  equity, vii, ix–xi, xv, 74
  inclusive T&L, 92
  institutional approaches, ix, xi, xii, xv, 5–8
  non-traditional students, vii, ix, x, xii, xv, 2, 18
  regional students, xii, 18, 73–76, 202, 203, 209, 211
  students from low SES backgrounds, x, xii, 73–76, 211

B
Barriers, vii, 54, 59, 63, 78, 81, 90, 91, 109, 120, 135, 145–149, 152, 154, 294, 295, 297, 301, 314
Belonging, belongingness, 6, 9, 13, 19, 21, 33, 38, 52–54, 57–59, 61, 62, 68, 77, 133, 227

Bias, 130, 154, 155, 213, 291, 293, 294, 296, 301, 310
Bioecological System Theory, 55
Black and Minority Ethnic (BME), 4, 54, 60, 61, 200
Bourdieu, P., 53, 176, 295
Brazil
  affirmative action, xiii, 219–233
  quota policy, xiii, 231–233
  widening participation in, vii, xv
Bridging/foundation education, xii, 119, 123, 124, 127, 130–133, 138

C
Canada
  path on *Life's Way* project, xi, 31, 44–45
  systems of higher education, 26, 29
  vertically segregated higher education, 25–46
  widening participation in, vii, xi, 202, 297
Case study, viii, x–xii, xiv, xv, 7, 57, 61, 97–114, 174, 236, 240, 244, 247–256, 296–301
Challenges (in higher education), vi, vii, 244–246, 328–331
Chile
  income inequality, xiii, 174, 179
  types and causes of dropouts, xiii, 174
  widening participation in, vii, xiii
Class, 26, 30, 67, 78, 80, 144, 146, 159, 176, 177, 180, 182, 205, 219–222, 227, 230, 272, 275,

277, 293–296, 299–301, 315, 316, 319, 328, 329, 335
Communication, 15, 21, 63, 66, 206, 254, 294
open pathways of, 60
Community college, xii, 28, 29, 31, 34, 38–40, 97–103, 105–107, 114, 273
Community of practice, 53, 55, 56
Competitive programs, xii, 119
Completion rates, 3, 35, 113, 124, 175–177, 185, 189
Contextual admissions (CA), 155, 156, 210–211, 308, 310, 312–314, 317–323
Continuing Professional Development (CPD), 67, 68
Course design, xi, 4, 73–92
Cultural capital, 53, 58, 63, 67, 68, 76, 77, 79, 132, 176, 177
Cultural change, 144, 156, 158, 160
Cultural habitus, 53, 63, 67
Curriculum
inclusive, vi, xii, 15, 20, 73, 107, 131, 335

D

Deficit, 135, 154, 156, 157, 160, 245–246, 252, 254, 256, 291, 300
Developmental education, xii, 97–114
Disadvantage, 3, 7, 29, 137, 145, 146, 148, 153, 154, 200, 208, 210, 292, 295, 297, 301, 309, 312–316, 318, 320, 321, 323, 336, 345

Disadvantaged groups, 4, 30, 99, 144, 145, 153, 156, 328–337, 345
Discrimination, 220, 223–226, 237, 272, 308, 333
Diverse groups, vii, 1
Diversity, viii, xi, xiii, 1–22, 35, 56, 57, 79, 83, 84, 131, 136, 144, 148–153, 157, 160, 180, 189, 202, 213, 247, 288, 296, 299

E

Economic Commission for Latin America and Caribbean, The (CEPAL), 221
Educational achievement, 145
Educational inequities, 121–122, 137
Elite, elitism, xi, xii, xiv, xv, 25, 119–138, 146, 159, 289, 291, 293, 296–298, 300, 301
in higher education institutions, x, 29, 45, 151, 180, 288, 289, 294, 295
Employability, xv, 17, 20, 330, 332, 334, 337, 338, 341, 343–345
Engagement, 4, 6, 9, 12–15, 19–22, 53, 54, 58, 63, 65, 67, 85–86, 108, 109, 113, 114, 127, 203, 236, 253, 255
Enrolments, 26, 32, 33, 87, 238, 241–244, 250–252, 289–291
Entry requirements, 209–210
Equity, v–vii, ix–xvi, 8, 27, 29, 75, 91, 97–114, 123, 127–130, 137, 182, 186–189, 202, 221–227, 231–233, 256, 267, 287, 288, 298, 301, 330, 331, 333, 334, 345
groups, ix, xv, 74, 287, 289–291

Excellence, v–vii, ix–xvi, 3–5, 9, 27, 29, 144, 151, 152, 157, 159, 200–203, 205, 206, 209, 265, 267, 277
Exit examinations, 146, 248
Expectations, 20, 53, 62, 64–68, 78–80, 82, 84, 91, 104, 108, 112, 131, 134, 146, 147, 174, 185, 186, 189, 265, 277

F

Failure, 81, 154, 175–179, 253, 345
Fair access, ix, 2, 5, 6, 8, 155, 200, 201, 270, 308, 344
'Fair' selection procedures, 144, 152, 154, 158, 180
Familial expectations, 79, 147
Fees regimes, xiv, 261–283
Financial support, xv, 17, 126, 160, 252, 327–345
First-in-family, xiv, 287, 288, 296–301
Fitness for purpose, 236, 240, 256
Foundation programs, 127, 130, 149, 156, 207, 252, 253
Free tuition, 261, 262, 264, 266, 268–270, 274, 283
Funding models, regimes, vii, x, xiv, 226, 243, 261–283

G

Gender
  earnings by women, 46
  gender effect, 45
  representation of women, 200
Government
  pressures, 151, 279, 280
  support, xv, 253, 254, 256, 269, 327–345
Grades, 32, 106, 154, 176, 178–183, 187, 189, 202, 241, 248–250, 272, 275, 276, 292, 301, 308, 314, 315, 320, 323, 329

H

Heterogeneity, xiii, 34, 183
Higher Education Funding Council for England (HEFCE), 5, 7, 58, 315
Higher Education in British Columbia (report), 27
Higher Education Institutions (HEIs), ix–xi, xiv, 7, 11, 74, 83, 177, 185, 236, 238, 241–246, 250, 251, 256, 266, 277, 314, 315, 318, 319, 322, 329, 334–336, 340, 344, 345
  reputational risk, xi
High status degrees, xiv, 288, 289, 291, 296, 301

I

Inclusive assessment, xii, 54, 73, 84
Inclusive curriculum, xii, 15, 20, 73, 131, 335
Inclusive learning
  academic preparedness, ix
  curriculum design, 73, 107
  improving student outcomes, 4, 131, 132
Indigenous students, viii, xii, 125–130, 132, 133, 135–137, 229, 230, 289, 292, 293, 298, 299

Induction, 17, 54, 206, 252
Institutional capacity, 249–252, 256
Institutional change, xi, 1–22
Intellectualism, 236

L

Leadership, vi, xi, xv, 1–22, 108, 112, 126, 150
Learning, vii, ix, xii, xv, 1, 3–6, 8, 9, 11–15, 20, 21, 27, 28, 51–68, 79, 81, 83–87, 90, 91, 105, 111, 131–137, 149, 176–178, 183, 190, 199, 202, 246, 251–255, 273, 292, 293, 320, 335
Learning environments, 4, 8, 9, 14, 58, 62, 64, 65, 68, 79, 81, 131, 133, 135–137, 149, 251, 255, 293
  facilitative, 52, 56, 60, 61, 66–68

M

Marginalisation, 53, 54, 245, 292
Massification, 29, 238, 243, 287
Mentoring, 17, 63, 133, 153, 212, 254, 291
Minority students, 19, 134, 135, 315

N

Neoliberalism, x, 345
New Zealand, xii
  indigenous students, viii, xii, 120, 130, 134, 136
  Vision 20:20 and Indigenous Health Workforce Development, xii
  widening participation in, vii, 120

Non-elite institutions, 30
Non-traditional students, vii, ix, x, xiv, xv, 82, 84, 86, 87, 294, 296, 297, 301

O

Open access, 97, 99, 100, 241
Outcomes
  educational, xi, xv, xvi, 2, 5, 8, 11, 26, 27, 29, 30, 32, 36, 41, 42, 46, 100–102, 105, 106, 112, 125, 136, 137, 236, 240, 245, 256, 266, 267, 270, 271, 277, 282, 283, 315, 317, 322, 323
  employment, occupational, vii, xi, xv, 2, 4, 26, 27, 29, 30, 32, 37, 39–41, 44, 45
Outreach, 13, 17, 113, 153, 203–207, 210, 212, 213, 271, 282, 291, 308

P

Participation, vii–xiii, xv, xvi, 2–4, 6–8, 15–18, 25, 28, 30, 35, 39, 45, 46, 56, 73–76, 82, 91, 108, 110, 112, 113, 120, 122, 128, 131, 134, 137, 138, 143, 145, 151, 176, 178, 183, 184, 186, 189, 199–201, 208–209, 211, 230, 236–238, 242, 245, 248, 251, 257, 265–267, 271–273, 276, 277, 281–283, 289, 291, 297, 307–323, 329, 341, 342
Participation rates, 3, 74, 122, 242, 251, 277, 281, 282, 313

Pathways, xi, 27, 29, 32, 38, 39, 60, 68, 105, 107, 108, 113, 124, 125, 127–128, 130–131, 136–138, 157, 254, 288, 294, 297, 301
Pedagogy, vi, 52, 55, 56, 67, 111, 132, 135
Peer, x, 4, 56, 57, 61, 68, 80, 109, 110, 112, 133, 134, 147, 190, 203, 254, 255, 292, 295, 296, 313, 332
Policy
  policy interventions, xiv, 264, 272
  policy makers, v, viii, xv, 92, 143, 279, 293
Political directives, xiii
Positive learning experiences, xv
Postgraduate, 14, 122, 123, 298, 299
Psychosocial factors (of success), 62
Public funding, 51, 241, 328

Q

Quality
  compromising, 219, 236
  as a concept, x, 236, 240, 255, 295, 296, 301, 328
  conceptions of, 239–241, 247, 256, 301
  denaturalising notions of, xiv, 255, 288
  maintaining, xi–xiii, xv, 99, 144, 295, 301, 328
Quotas, xiii, 123, 136, 138, 187, 219–233, 247

R

Race, 29, 67, 68, 225, 225n9, 227, 237, 242, 243, 247, 251, 252, 328

Ranking, xi, 130, 249–251
Recruitment, xii, 3, 14, 17, 119, 123–128, 130, 131, 138, 201, 249–252, 274
Regional students, 74, 75, 85, 87, 88
Regional Universities Network (RUN), 75, 76
Relational success factors, 91
Remedial courses, 100
Resilience, 61, 149, 294
Resource, 16, 20, 150, 267
Respect, 52, 60, 61, 65, 87–88, 138, 224n7, 238, 309, 314, 315, 317
Retention, xii, 2, 4–6, 8, 9, 12, 15–19, 21, 22, 54, 58, 61, 74–76, 79, 91, 102, 113, 120, 122–124, 127, 130, 131, 133–136, 178, 181–183, 189, 309, 323
Risk, xi, 8, 11, 18–20, 33, 41, 42, 44, 147, 152, 160, 186n4, 187, 188, 202, 245, 246, 254, 255, 318, 330

S

Scholarships, 4, 74, 76, 177, 180, 185, 187, 187n5, 254, 263, 313, 332, 333, 336, 337, 340, 341, 344, 345
Scotland, vii
  no-fees system, xiv, 261–283
Selection criteria, 186, 208, 211, 248–250
Sense of belonging, 6, 53, 54, 57–59, 61, 62, 68, 133
Social capital, 76, 206, 329
Social engineering, xii, 143–161
Social inclusion, ix, x, xii, 137, 143–161

Social justice, vii, viii, x, xii, xvi, 120, 126, 137, 138, 202, 237, 238, 243, 266, 328
Social mobility, xiii, xv, 7, 147–149, 152, 153, 158, 160, 201, 202, 288, 289, 294–296, 335
Social support, xv, 327–345
Socioeconomic diversity, 144, 157
South Africa
  apartheid, 237, 239, 245
  Council on Higher Education (CHE), 235, 237–239, 242, 243, 246, 256
  curriculum reform, xiv
  infrastructural incapacity, xiv, 243
  institutional support, xiv, 253
  widening access in, ix, x, xiii–xiv, 236–239, 243, 245, 247, 250, 251, 256
Space, 57, 82, 133, 134, 222, 251, 253, 256
Staff development, 17, 90, 255–256
Staff–student relationships, viii, 89, 252–256
Standards, vii, ix–xii, xv, 18, 46, 97–114, 144, 151, 152, 156, 157, 190, 207, 209, 240, 294, 298, 308, 323, 340, 341, 343
  academic struggle, x
  "dumbing down" of, x
  low entrance scores, x
  lowered standards, x, 156
  maintaining, xi–xiii, xv, 99, 144, 152, 295
Strategic student selection, 247–249
Strategies, vii, x–xiii, xv, 6–8, 15, 19, 20, 29, 59, 73, 74, 81, 99, 101, 105, 106, 108, 114, 119–138, 173–190, 249, 253, 267, 270, 308, 345
Student-centred learning and teaching, vii, 3, 6, 13, 20, 85
Student equity, ix
Student-led assessment, 54
Student numbers, xiv, 3, 87, 131, 145, 150, 274, 279, 280, 282
Student performance, 189
Student preparedness, 79–81, 253
Students from low socioeconomic backgrounds, viii, xii, 73–92, 121, 122, 148, 153, 180, 272, 301
Student–teacher relationships, vii, xii, 51–68, 331, 338
Study habits, 176, 185
Success, vi–xv, 1–22, 46, 52–54, 58–60, 62, 65–68, 73–92, 99, 108, 113, 114, 120, 125, 128–135, 138, 144, 158, 160, 173–190, 208, 210, 235, 236, 238, 239, 241–246, 249, 250, 252, 253, 255, 264, 271, 289, 314, 321, 330, 331, 337, 344
Support schemes, vii, ix
Systemic change, 8, 144, 156, 160

T

Targets, 2, 7, 113, 125, 126, 130, 151, 159, 160, 200, 201, 208, 211, 213, 214, 221, 239, 241–244, 256, 266, 270, 314
Tertiary interventions, xii, 120
Theory of Opportunity, 53
Transformation, vii, 135, 221, 238–240, 243, 247, 252, 256

Transition, 28, 30, 31, 33, 34, 53, 54, 59, 67, 106, 122, 125, 229, 237, 322, 335, 336, 343
Tuition fees, 3, 18, 147, 201, 262, 266, 268–270, 277, 278, 280, 283, 332, 333, 337, 340
Turkey
  financial support, xv, 336, 337, 340
  governmental support, xv
  social support, xv, 327
  widening participation in, vii, xv, xvi
Turner, Ralph
  contest mobility, 25, 26

U
Undergraduate, xiv, 4, 10, 51, 56, 61, 122–124, 133, 150, 180, 181, 239, 244, 254, 262, 266–269, 274, 289–291, 297, 298, 307, 337
Underrepresented students, vii, x–xii, 97, 119–138, 152
United Kingdom (UK)
  Disparities in Student Attainment (DiSA), 52, 64, 65, 67
  increasing diversity, xiii
  National Strategy for Access and Student Success, xi, 7
  Selecting for Excellence project, xiii, 200, 201, 203, 205, 206, 209
  Social mobility, xiii, xv, 7, 147–149, 152, 153, 158, 160, 201, 202, 273, 288, 289, 294–296, 335
  Teaching Excellence Framework (TEF), xi, 3–5, 202, 265

What Works? project, 5–6, 8, 9, 16, 54, 59
widening participation in, ix–xiii, xv, 1, 2, 4–8, 13–15, 18, 199–214, 265–267, 271, 282, 291, 297, 308
United States (USA)
  developmental education programs, xii
  gateway courses, xii, 207, 209
  open-access, 97, 99, 100
  widening participation in, vii, xi, xii, 120

V
Vulnerable students, 176–179
Vygotsky, L. S.
  model of learning, 55

W
Wenger, E., 53, 55, 56, 63
  Communities of Practice, 55, 56
Widening access, vii, ix–xiv, 1–3, 18, 119, 130, 143–161, 208, 213, 220, 236–239, 243, 245, 247–252, 256, 261–283
Widening participation
  discourses of, xiii
  indicators, 15, 208–209, 308
  initiatives, xi, xii, xvi, 119–138, 208, 297
  practices, xi, 7, 120, 266
  program, xii, xiii, xv, 7, 15, 208, 291
Widening participation agenda, vii, ix, x, xiii, xv, 120

PGSTL 07/14/2018